**Legislative Intent
and Other Essays
on Law, Politics, and Morality**

Legislative Intent
and Other Essays
on Law, Politics, and Morality

Gerald C. MacCallum, Jr.

Edited by
Marcus G. Singer
and
Rex Martin

The University of Wisconsin Press

The University of Wisconsin Press
114 North Murray Street
Madison, Wisconsin 53715

3 Henrietta Street
London WC2E 8LU, England

5   4   3   2   1

Printed in the United States of America

Library of Congress Cataloging-in-Publication Data
MacCallum, Gerald C. (Gerald Cushing), 1925–1987.
    Legislative intent and other essays on law, politics, and morality /
Gerald C. MacCallum, Jr.; edited by Marcus G. Singer and
Rex Martin.
    310 p.   cm.
    Includes bibliographical references and index.
    ISBN 0-299-13860-7
    1. Law—Interpretation and construction.   2. Law and ethics.
3. Political ethics.   I. Singer, Marcus George, 1926–
II. Martin, Rex.   III. Title.
K290.M32   1993
340'.112—dc20   93-841

The editors dedicate this book to the memory of its author
Gerald C. MacCallum, Jr.
and to
Susan Feagin
who brought hope determination good cheer
invaluable help indomitable spirit love and care
into the last decade of his life
and without whom this book could not
have been brought into being

Contents

Notes on Contents

1 "Legislative Intent" is reprinted, with permission, from the *Yale Law Journal* 75 (1966): 754–87.
2 "Censorship in the Arts" is reprinted, with the permission of the editors, from *Arts in Society* 2.4 (1964): 3–23.
3 "On Applying Rules" is reprinted, with the permission of the editor, from *Theoria* 32 (1966): 196–210.
4 "Berlin on the Compatibility of Values, Ideals, and 'Ends'" is reprinted, with the permission of the editor, from *Ethics* 77 (1967): 139–45.
5 "Negative and Positive Freedom" is reprinted, with the permission of the editors, from *The Philosophical Review* 76 (1967): 312–34.
6 "Some Truths and Untruths about Civil Disobedience" is reprinted, with the permission of the publisher, from *Political and Legal Obligation: Nomos XII,* edited by J. Roland Pennock and John W. Chapman (New York: Atherton, 1970), pp. 370–400.
7 "Reform, Violence, and Personal Integrity" is reprinted, with the permission of the editor, from *Inquiry* 14 (1971): 301–12.
8 "Law, Conscience, and Integrity" was presented at the 1971 Oberlin Colloquium in Philosophy. It is reprinted, with the kind permission of the publisher, from the proceedings of that colloquium, *Issues in Law and Morality,* edited by Norman S. Care and Thomas K. Trelogan (Cleveland/London: Case Western Reserve University Press, 1973), pp. 141–59.
9 "The Extent to Which Legislators Should Serve Their Consciences or Their Constituents" was originally prepared for a conference on "Ethical Issues in Government" held at the University of Delaware, 8–9 November 1979, in a session entitled "Should Legislators Serve Constituents or Conscience?" It is reprinted here, with the permission of the publishers, from *Ethical Issues in Government,* edited by Norman E. Bowie (Philadelphia: Temple University Press, 1981), pp. 23–40.
10 "Dworkin on Judicial Discretion" was not previously published in this form. An abstract of it was published in *The Journal of Philosophy* 60.21 (1963): 638–41. "Afterthoughts" was previously unpublished.
11 "Violence and Appeals to Conscience." Previously unpublished.

12 "Competition and Moral Philosophy." Previously unpublished.
13 "Justice and Adversary Proceedings." Previously unpublished and left unfinished.
14 "What Is Wrong with Violence?" Previously unpublished and left unfinished. "Notes on 'What Is Wrong With Violence?'" was previously unpublished.

Preface

This book contains fourteen essays by the late Gerald MacCallum, along with Afterthoughts on one (ch. 10, "Dworkin on Judicial Discretion") and Addenda to another (ch. 14, "What is Wrong with Violence?"). Five of the essays have not been previously published, the other nine have been. Two of the published essays—"Legislative Intent" and "Negative and Positive Freedom"—are very well known indeed, widely cited and almost invariably regarded as permanent contributions of importance; the others are not nearly as well known, largely because of their being published for the most part in out of the way places—either in little known books containing conference proceedings, most of which, in accordance with the usual laws governing such matters, went out of print with great rapidity, or in journals that are little known and have little circulation. For these reasons, then, the vast majority of these papers have not been readily obtainable by or available to the public that could be expected to be interested in them. The lead essay, "Legislative Intent," appears here with author's revisions and some notes by the author indicating what further revisions are needed. The reader should perhaps also be informed in advance that MacCallum attached a short Appendix (further indication of its unfinished condition) to "Justice and Adversary Proceedings" (ch. 13).

The order of presentation is mainly chronological, with some exceptions. Previously published essays appear first, with the title essay taken out of chronological order and set in the premier position. These are followed by the previously unpublished essays, arranged chronologically with the exception of the final essay, which appears out of the standard chronological order because it is so largely unfinished and because the author's intentions with respect to it were so difficult to determine.

Except in overtly editorial matter, numbered footnotes are those of the author, though a number of them have been filled in with more detailed information about the works cited; such editorial additions are enclosed in brackets. By way of contrast, editorial footnotes are indicated by asterisks. MacCallum himself was given to using brackets for apparently varying purposes, especially in the unpublished pieces; in order to mark off clearly MacCallum's words from those of the editors, MacCallum's brackets have been replaced by parentheses. Thus, brackets always indicate editorial notes or interpolations. It should also be noted that MacCallum characteristically distinguished sharply between his use of single quotes and double quotes. As he put it in note 1 to chapter 8, he "use[s] double quotes around expressions that are being directly quoted or mentioned. Single quotes are used around expressions that are being used and not directly quoted but in need of having attention drawn to them because their use is, at least in the context, controversial or potentially at issue." MacCallum draws essentially the same distinction in note 5 to ch. 6, p. 104. However, this distinction is not always adhered to in the unpublished and especially the unfinished papers.

Following the table of contents are notes to the contents providing bibliographical information on the previously published essays. Editorial footnotes to the unpublished essays give information about their genesis. A bibliography at the end of the book provides other information and lists all of MacCallum's publications. MacCallum did not publish a great deal, and the bulk of what he did publish, with the exception of his book *Political Philosophy,* is contained in this book. MacCallum, in the tradition of Sidgwick, was a very careful thinker, who worked over his material very thoroughly, was always ready to learn from the comments of others and often revised in the light of these comments. He was typically undogmatic, conscientious, judicious, and considerate, and these personal traits carried over into his philosophical work.

These essays are in our judgment valuable contributions to philosophy, and there is special value in having them collected here. The fact that some of these essays are very well known adds value to those that are not, and having them in one volume enables one to see how MacCallum's mind worked on a set of problems with multiple overlapping strands, all in one place, in a way that one could not easily do if one relied on searching journals, etc. For the same reason, the essays here have a unity they might otherwise seem not to have, and they are readily available to a reader who either would not know about them or would not have ready access to them. Nothing more, of course, will come from MacCallum's pen. There exist masses of notes for books and lectures, as well as a few papers presented at conferences as comments on papers presented by others, but the notes are not sufficiently readable to be publishable, and the other completed papers and commentaries are not pieces that we can suppose MacCallum to have wanted published. It is anticipated that eventually these unpublished materials and the original manuscripts of the published writings will be deposited in a set of archives at the University of Wisconsin–Madison, probably in the Weinberg Memorial Library of the Department of Philosophy, in Helen C. White Hall, where they will be accessible to interested scholars.

We have a number of debts of gratitude it is a pleasure to acknowledge. Susan Feagin, Gerry MacCallum's widow, made available all of MacCallum's notes and papers, gave us carte blanche to proceed as our judgment dictated, and also facilitated the process of getting permission to reprint previously published pieces. The following acknowledged experts in legal, moral, value, social, or political philosophy were all consulted on the general idea and were generous with advice and encouragement, some going out of their way to offer help, observations, and advice beyond any we would have thought of troubling them with: Kurt Baier, Hugo Adam Bedau, Norman E. Bowie, Richard Brandt, David Braybrooke, Richard Bronaugh, Norman S. Care, Donald W. Crawford, Joel Feinberg, Tom Gerety, Martin Golding, James P. Griffin, H. L. A. Hart, Thomas Kearns, Robert Ladenson, David Lyons, Hans Oberdiek, Stanley L. Paulson, J. Roland Pennock, the late Edmund Pincoffs, John Rawls, Ian Shapiro, Robert S. Summers, and Carl Wellman. We are grateful to them for their advice, encouragement, and enthusiasm. We quote just a couple of the remarks we received:

> Gerald MacCallum's . . . work on concrete problems facing liberal democracies retains both its freshness and topicality—witness his paper entitled "Censorship in the Arts," for example. . .

> Two of his papers are classics that will be read and cited for many years. He was one of the first American analytic philosophers in the post-war period to discover (or rediscover) the philosophy of law, and I think he may well have become the dominant American figure in the field had his health not failed (classifying R. Dworkin for these purposes as British). . . .

David Lyons and Stanley L. Paulson reviewed the proposal and an unedited manuscript containing nearly all the papers for the University of Wisconsin Press and encouraged us and the Press to proceed with it; their careful reading and helpful and penetrating comments enabled us to put together a collection that is better than it would otherwise have been. We are grateful to them for this and also for allowing us to quote from their reports in the introduction.

We also received information that we needed on various matters from Professors Kenneth Cooley, Tom Gerety, Michael Pritchard, Richard Wasserstrom, and Vivian Weil, and we are pleased to thank them for their assistance.

We are furthermore happy to acknowledge the invaluable assistance of Michael F. McFall, a doctoral candidate at the University of Wisconsin and—by virtue of the generosity of former Chancellor Irving Shain of the University of Wisconsin–Madison and the Research Committee of the Graduate School of the University of Wisconsin—research assistant to one of the editors (MGS), for putting the manuscript in proper form and paginating it, a job that had to be undertaken more than once; for tracking down references and finding the books some of these papers had first appeared in; for putting references in proper form and checking them for accuracy, a particularly daunting task with "Legislative Intent," which, having been published in a law review, followed the typical and really inexcusable law review practice of listing authors only by last names and of providing very little information that would be of use to a reader wanting to check a source; for finding and copying materials that were needed or thought to be needed; and, in general, for providing such assistance as was necessary to keep this project from taking any longer than it actually did. We also want to thank David Reidy, a graduate student at the University of Kansas and research assistant to Rex Martin, for help in the reading of proofs.

Finally, MGS must acknowledge the continued research support provided by the Research Committee of the Graduate School of the University of Wisconsin, and in particular the advice and assistance received over many years from Graduate School Deans Eric Rude (retired as of June 30, 1992) and Carol Miller.

M.G.S. & R.M.

June 1992

Memoir

Gerald Cushing MacCallum, Jr., was born 16 June 1925 in Spokane, Washington, and received his early education in public schools in Spokane and in Watsonville, California. During World War II he served in the United States Army Infantry from 1943 to 1946, saw action in France and Germany, and at the end of the War was in the Philippines in preparation for the planned invasion of Japan. From 1946 to 1948 he attended the State College at Washington, and in 1948 he transferred to the University of California at Berkeley, where he received his A.B. in 1950 and was a graduate student from 1950 to 1958. He received an M.A. in political science in 1954, with a thesis on "The Administrative Theory of Mary Parker Follett," and received his Ph.D. in philosophy in 1961 with a dissertation entitled "Judicial Review by the United States Supreme Court: An Analysis of Some Controversies Concerning a Judicial Activity." In those days, Ph.D. candidates at Berkeley were required to take a master's degree in some other field and graduate students did not usually move through the program very quickly. MacCallum was especially delayed by a bout with polio, with which he struggled for about two years. In 1958–59, he was a Fulbright Predoctoral Fellow at Pembroke College of the University of Oxford, for the study of jurisprudence and English constitutional law.

MacCallum served as a teaching assistant at Berkeley 1952–56 and received his first academic appointment at Cornell, where he served as Instructor in Philosophy 1959–61. In 1961, he came to the University of Wisconsin as an assistant professor of philosophy, in 1966 was promoted to associate professor, and in 1969 to professor. In 1965–66 he was a visiting associate professor at the University of Washington in Seattle, and in 1969–70 was a fellow of the American Council of Learned Societies—his project title was "Conscience and Violence"—and some of the fruits of that year, spent in Europe, are contained in this book. In 1970–72, a particularly troublesome time at many universities, especially Madison, he served as chair of the Department of Philosophy and in 1972 or 1973 he began to experience the first symptoms of heart disease.

MacCallum was quite active for a number of years in the American Philosophical Association. He served as secretary-treasurer of the Western Division APA in 1967–69, during which time he served on the Association's National Board of Officers. He served again on the National Board when he chaired the Association's Committee on the Status and Future of the Profession from 1973 until he resigned for reasons of health in 1977; he also organized the Association's Conference of Philosophy Department Chairpersons in 1971 and served as chair of that group through 1972.

In April 1972 he took on an unusual assignment. Early in February he was invited by Rocky Pomerance, the Chief of Police of the City of Miami Beach Police Department, and Wayne B. Hanewicz, the Project Director, to lecture on "The Philosophy of Dissent in a Democratic Society" as part of a training program in preparation for the "effective and humane" policing of the Democratic National Convention scheduled for July 1972, with the object, obviously, of avoiding a repeat of the disastrous rioting that had occurred in Chicago in 1968. According to the original February letter, his topic was scheduled to be covered in three sessions: Saturday, 1 April 1972, 8 a.m. to 12 noon; 4 p.m. to 8 p.m. of the same day, and then again on 2 April 11 a.m. to 3 p.m. He accepted the invitation and forwarded an outline of his lecture soon thereafter. (No copy of the outline he sent was found amongst his papers; there is, however a thirteen-page handwritten outline that no doubt provides a reasonably accurate indication of the topics he covered. Nor is there a copy among his papers of the press release that was sent to the "media coordinator," or a copy of any clipping from a Miami newspaper, which was scheduled to be sent to him.) He had some interesting stories to tell about his reception and the means he used to try to get across his ideas. One thing he said afterward was that he had expected to meet at the outset with hostility, and he did meet with some. But he also met to some extent with the same apathetic lack of interest characteristic of so many beginning undergraduates who feel forced to take a course in philosophy—and that he was used to. So he also felt that after the initial hostility and indifference were defused he managed to be heard and to elicit some useful discussion with people who were not initially enamored of the idea of being lectured to by a professor, especially a professor of philosophy. One of the initial stereotypes he had to contend with was the idea, held apparently by at least some of the police to whom he lectured, that the riots that had been endemic on college campuses were actually being incited by professors of philosophy. It may be difficult now, some twenty years later, for many people to either remember or realize the apprehension generated by the upcoming convention. Shortly after

MacCallum's talk, the Republican National Convention was also scheduled to be held at Miami Beach, so whatever beneficial effects MacCallum's lecture and the whole training period had were enjoyed by both parties. A clipping from the *Los Angeles Times* of 23 June 1972 (preserved in the MacCallum file), under the by-line of Nicholas C. Chriss, brings out the fears and anxieties felt by citizens, officials, and the police of the city at the prospects facing them; it is headlined "Conventions Turn Miami Beach into an Uptight Island": " 'A hurricane we can handle, but not the politicians and the bearded ones,' one upset citizen said." [1]

MacCallum's adventure in Miami Beach was reported on in the Madison *Capital Times* in June of 1972, under the by-line of Pam Johnson, in an article that opened thus:

> If Miami Beach police manage to keep their cool during the Democratic convention in Miami this summer—a UW philosophy professor may get part of the credit. . . .

and continued (in part) this way:

> How did the Miami police react to being told in essence that the goading and confrontations they get from dissenters is a good thing?
>
> "At first they didn't understand me, and maybe they never did, but I tried to clarify it by giving them an example of the difference between

---

1. MacCallum, of course, was not the only academic invited to lecture to the police as part of the special training program in preparation for the conventions. There were a few others lecturing on other related topics, and other aspects to the training program. An article in *Time* (12 June 1972, pp. 16–17) entitled "Miami Battens Down," provides some interesting insights:

> Miami residents plan to flee town. Some storeowners are going to board up their windows. A battalion of National Guardsmen has canceled summer maneuvers to remain on stand-by call. . . . The scene is Miami Beach, and the preparations are not for a hurricane but for those grand old American blowouts, the Democratic and Republican national conventions. . . .
>
> . . . Fortunately, the coolest heads belong to those most directly involved in keeping the peace. The coolest of all is Police Chief Rocky Pomerance . . . who preaches that "the police do not have to be an abrasive force". . . .
>
> The professorial ring to Pomerance's utterances is no put-on. . . . he is preparing his 250-man force . . . by requiring that each officer take a special 96-hour training course at Florida International University. For the past five months the cops have been studying such heady subjects as the "history and contemporary modes of dissent" and "the philosophical foundations of the Bill of Rights, with emphasis on the First Amendment." Says Rocky . . . "I want my men to know why we must protect a citizen's right to protest. . . ."

We, of course, do not know what led Chief Pomerance to invite Professor Gerald C. MacCallum, Jr., to lecture as part of these preparations, but it seems clear that in doing so he acted on some very good advice.

dissent and disloyalty," MacCallum said. "It's not easy to say dissent is disloyalty because each of us is a member of several communities. For example, if a policeman knows of something crooked going on in his department and blows the whistle, he's being disloyal to the department. If he doesn't blow the whistle, he's being disloyal to the community". . . .

A few policemen did talk with him after his lectures. One asked MacCallum if he thought the guys who went to Canada to dodge the draft were loyal or disloyal. Before MacCallum could answer, the policeman told MacCallum he was responsible for the draft dodgers.

"How could that be?" asked MacCallum.

The policeman said "You are a professor and they are college kids."

MacCallum told the policeman: "I'm no more responsible for them than you are responsible for crime in Chicago."

"I am responsible for what happens in Chicago," the policeman said. "I'm responsible for what every policeman does."

No one knows just how much the police training will help. "I think I reached a few when I explained the difference between disloyalty and dissent, but some guys think the only form of dissent is at the polling booth," MacCallum said. . . .

"As soon as I was introduced and got up to speak, a hand went up," MacCallum said. "I thought, 'oh no, what's this going to be?' " The policeman asked MacCallum how old he was. "I was told that the kind of lighting they used for the lecture made me look much younger than I really am, so the policeman just wanted to establish my legitimacy." "I think my ties with the UW and Berkeley helped. It suggested that I had lived through something."

Did MacCallum help to cool things down in Miami? "I figured I reached some of them. I could tell by the looks on their faces and some of the questions they asked afterwards. But the rest of them were just bearing it." [2]

As MacCallum explained in a letter of 17 June 1972 to Mr. Hanewicz, enclosing a copy of the article, there were a number of mistakes in it. "I was not entirely pleased with the result . . . , e.g., the reporter made no mention of Chief Pomerance though I had; there were no catcalls nor had I claimed that there were; I was misquoted a couple of times." MacCallum also sent "a copy of [a letter and] some materials a local member of the rabid right sent me, these being copies in turn of materials he purports to have sent to the Miami Chief. A clear case of libel. . . . But my only concern at the moment

2. *The Capital Times* of Madison, 12 June 1972.

is that you be prepared for any flack that it might bring though my presumption is that it will readily be recognized as from a nut and thus dismissed."

The letter referred to was addressed to the Chief of the Miami Police Department, dated the day after the newspaper article appeared, and provides what may be the most amusing touch to the whole affair. It reads in part: "The enclosed article . . . describing the incursion into your bailiwick by professor Gerald MacCallum prompts me to send you two articles which may be of interest to you and your officers"—and then follow references to a publication of "the rabid right," to use MacCallum's language. The writer of the letter continued: "Agent provocateurs are a dime-a-dozen here in Madison as they are at Berkeley"; below the signature there appears the notation: "cc: Gerald MacCullum" [*sic*].

That anyone—even the local off-the-wall vigilante who sent this letter—could have regarded Gerald MacCallum as an "agent provocateur" has got to be wildly funny to anyone who in any way knew him. Both the fact that he took on such an assignment and his report of his experiences in Miami were thoroughly in character. MacCallum was one who constantly urged the essential role of discussion, discussion, and more discussion in clarifying issues and resolving disputes. He was a voice of sanity, good sense, and moderation in times of troubles—and he was at the University of Wisconsin in times of troubles, some of which erupted in unpredictable ways during his period as department chair. All who knew him during his teaching years and particularly after his illness were touched by his generosity, his gentleness, his courage, and his cheerfulness. He was never given to showboating or grandstanding—they were not in his nature. And he was the last person in the world to incite a riot—or to be an "agent provocateur."

In 1973 MacCallum took on another somewhat unusual assignment, one that unhappily did not come to fruition but that has special philosophical relevance. He was invited by the Harvard University Press to edit a collection of commissioned essays on the influence of John Rawls's *A Theory of Justice* on the essayists' varying fields of inquiry, such as moral philosophy, legal philosophy, political science, economics, sociology, education, etc.—that is to say, on new contributions to various fields provoked by Rawls's book. It is clear from the correspondence, Rawls's character, and our memory that this idea was not generated by Jack Rawls, but there is some reason to believe that he approved of the selection of MacCallum for the enterprise—if there was to be any such enterprise. MacCallum gave this a lot of thought, and though he drew up an initial plan for the book, he at first attempted to decline, on the ground that he was so busy with other projects he would not have enough time to do it justice and also that he was not really the right person for the task. This last demurrer was met by the following reply from the woman in charge of the project at the Press: "I hope you are not serious when you express doubt that you are the right editor for this book. I am convinced that you will build a distinguished collection of essays, in part because men of sound judgment have told me so, in part because your last letter was so judicious and astute. I would like to put an end to all such wonderings by sending you a contract." A contract was sent, MacCallum sent it back requesting various changes, the changes were made and another contract was sent and appears to have been signed on 4 January 1974. However, although MacCallum did send out letters of invitation to a number of very distinguished scholars (though without, incidentally, receiving a large number of acceptances), the project was delayed because, as MacCallum put it in a letter of 6 February 1974, "Jack Rawls approached me in Atlanta to tell me he was seriously contemplating a second edition of his book to be done, perhaps, during the 1974–75 academic year." Since no such second edition in fact appeared—at least in English and under one set of covers—the project, which had a delivery date of 1 January 1977, was abandoned.[3]

When MacCallum presented his paper on "Justice and Adversary Proceedings" to the philosophy department of the University of Wisconsin Center System in March 1977, Professor Kenneth Cooley of the University of Wisconsin Center at Waukesha was the official commentator. The meeting was in Madison, and MacCallum was that term on leave in Bowling Green, Ohio, so he was in the unusual situation of traveling back to his own home town to deliver a paper. A letter from Professor Cooley of December 1987 further delineates some of the features of MacCallum's character:

> When Gerry delivered this paper, he had to return to Madison from, as I recall, Indiana [actually, Ohio]. He and I roomed together for the night. . . . this was after his first or second major heart surgeries. He was not in the best of health, but maintained a personal regimen of exercise and mental discipline that was awesome. Our conversation in our room and his dedication to his craft and to his questions were deeply enriching for me. We sometimes love the ideals for which we aspire; we sometimes love persons. Although I knew him only briefly, I felt the ideal and the person were virtually one.[4]

3. MacCallum had earlier been involved in a somewhat similar (though, of course, also essentially different) project which also was abandoned, for somewhat similar reasons. He had, jointly with one of the editors of this volume, in April 1962 signed a contract with Prentice-Hall to edit a collection of commissioned essays to be entitled *Essays in Legal Philosophy*, with a flexible delivery date due to be specified by September 1964, which was made null and void largely because several of the people the prospective editors regarded as key contributors did not accept the invitation to contribute to it. At the time the contract was signed, MacCallum was the junior co-editor. Only a few years later it is clear he would have earned the status of senior co-editor.

4. Communication from Professor Kenneth Cooley of 2 September 1987. It was Professor Cooley who was able to provide us with a copy of the last version of this paper that, according

MacCallum was afflicted much of his life by ill health. His graduate student career was interrupted for two years by polio. His first wife, Paulette Griffith MacCallum, died of cancer in early 1975, at a time when he was suffering from heart disease, and he had coronary bypass surgery in May of that year. In the fall of 1977, on a trip to Kansas City (he was at that time commuting from Madison nearly every weekend to be with his second wife, Susan Feagin), he suffered a stroke which, though it left his mind untouched, effectively disabled his body, and he was from then on not able to do any further teaching. He continued on a course of physical therapy with the hope of recovering sufficiently to be able to return to teaching. That was not to be. In May of 1982 he suffered another massive stroke, which almost totally disabled him. The first stroke destroyed his hearing in one ear and partially paralyzed one side of his body, the second destroyed the hearing in his other ear, partially paralyzed the other side of his body, and made it very difficult for him to speak intelligibly.

Despite his disabilities, until near the end MacCallum continued work on a number of projects. Most importantly, he was able to complete his book on *Political Philosophy,* commissioned some years before for the Prentice-Hall Foundations of Philosophy Series. He was able to do this at first with the aid of dictating equipment sent him by the Department in Madison, with tapes sent for transcribing to the department office in Madison, typed for him by Janet Holt (now retired) of the department secretarial staff and sent back to him in the Kansas City area for further revision. His last published paper, "The Extent to Which Legislators Should Serve Their Consciences or Their Constituents," chapter 9 in this volume, was composed by tape recorder in this manner in 1979. After his second massive stroke in 1982, which took away his hearing completely, he could no longer use dictating equipment; he then tried to learn to write using a word processor, with which he had no prior familiarity, but that didn't work too well, so this procedure was abandoned fairly early. He then turned to dictating sentences to his wife, Professor Susan Feagin of the University of Missouri at Kansas City, who would insert them into the text. After about fifteen minutes of this kind of work, MacCallum would rest and then work would resume. It was a laborious process, lasting four years. Without this assistance, encouragement, and determination the book could not have been completed. In late 1986, just before his death, MacCallum was able to hold in his hand a copy of the published work, the result of much pain and determination and commitment. No doubt it would

---

to the evidence available to us, MacCallum was able to work on. He was working on it that spring; he had his first stroke that fall. The comments that Dr. Cooley delivered on the paper are quite interesting, just the sort of comments that would normally have led MacCallum to revise further, which he probably would have done if he had been in a position to do so.

be a better book if MacCallum had not been working under such handicaps and had been able to write in the way he had been able to write prior to his strokes. Under the circumstances it is remarkable that it came to be at all, and despite its defects, obvious in comparison with his earlier and best work, it has considerable merits. MacCallum had been planning this book for a long time, and there is no telling exactly what it would have been like if it had been prime MacCallum. What is certain is that we are better off with it, such as it is, than without it. After he finished the manuscript he was simply incapable of doing any more, of doing any further revising and rewriting, of learning from criticism and comments and rethinking and revising accordingly—as he had always done in the past when he had his health. He was not only suffering from exhaustion but his physical condition had declined so drastically that he tended no longer to trust his judgment on such matters. He would not because he could not, and he had done his best in the conditions in which he was placed. From a letter of February 1987 from his widow: "He definitely wanted it to be his and wrong [rather] than not to be his, wrong or right. He was quite adamant about the importance of accurately representing his views. . . ."

In the last years of his life he spent his days in a Day Care Center for handicapped adults, where he showed by example that the handicapped can do useful things; he served as an inspiration to others by the fact that he was writing a book that was to be published, and he found that he had a good deal to learn from observing the condition of others even more afflicted than he was. An article appeared about him in the *Kansas City Star* in March 1984, under the by-line of Brian Burnes, headlined "Strokes slow philosopher's pen, not his mind." Some passages from that article are instructive:

> He is an eminent political philosopher. One of his articles, "Negative and Positive Freedom," is a landmark essay in political philosophy. . . . His articles are discussed widely within the inner circles of a difficult and learned discipline. Now he has completed the manuscript for his first book.
>
> But to communicate with Gerald C. MacCallum, Jr., of Fairway, you must use a child's magic slate, the kind with a plastic pencil on a string. "Are you pleased with the book?" Mr. MacCallum reads on his slate. "Yes," says the 58-year-old Mr. MacCallum in the labored way of a victim of two debilitating strokes. "I think it's probably as good as the best thing I've done. It says what I currently believe, and that is very hard to do."
>
> Mr. MacCallum signed the book contract in 1973. . . . But in 1977 he suffered a stroke, and in 1982 a second. Although the strokes did not impair him mentally, Mr. MacCallum has impaired hearing and speech.

He does not have the balance or strength to walk for long distances or the dexterity to operate a typewriter keyboard for long. Still, he and his wife have completed a manuscript that he did not begin in earnest until after the first stroke.

"I was sitting around the house two years after my first stroke, feeling sorry for myself," Mr. MacCallum said in remarks that were read to his acquaintances at the adult day treatment center operated by Clinicare Family Health Services Inc. in Kansas City, Kan., where he spends most weekdays. . . . "My wife said, 'Why don't you think about what you can *do* instead of what you *cannot* do?'" He thought immediately of his book under contract. About a year after his stroke, Mr. MacCallum had written Prentice-Hall, offering to withdraw from the contract, but the publisher declined. . . .

The second stroke, which impaired his hearing, rendered the [transcribing] equipment useless. He had completed perhaps five chapters of his book. To finish the remaining eight chapters,[5] his wife acquired a computer word processor and began entering his rough outlines into it. He would write a sentence or two. Or sometimes he would dictate sentences to his wife, who would insert them into the text. Copies would then be printed for MacCallum to revise.

After about 15 minutes of this kind of work, Mr. MacCallum would have to rest. After another 15 minutes, the two would start again. It would be fair [his wife, Susan Feagin] says, to describe the process as tedious. Yet, more than four years after he and his wife began work in 1979, the manuscript is finished. . . .

"Seventeen years I've been writing philosophy," Mr. MacCallum says. "It's not a very long career. I started late and ended early". . . .

Cathie Poje, a social worker and assistant director of Clinicare, says that Mr. MacCallum is evidence that "just because you are handicapped, that doesn't mean your life ends."

"My experience," Mr. MacCallum said in his remarks read at the treatment center, "has convinced me that any disabled person who achieves anything has other people standing beside him or her. I suppose it is obvious by now that people stood beside me."

In Mr. MacCallum's case, that is his wife, who would not tolerate his discouragement. "I would be nowhere without her," he says. "She wouldn't stand for me being petulant."[6]

In the last half year or so of his life his condition deteriorated to the point where he could do no more work, and he was almost literally a prisoner in his

5. The published book has fourteen chapters.
6. *The Kansas City Star,* 13 March 1984, section B.

own body—able to feel and think and remember, but not able to hear and barely able to see or to communicate. Death, it may fairly be said, came as a relief and a release, on 14 January 1987.

In a letter he wrote (more accurately, dictated to his wife to type) dated 23 December 1986—just three weeks before he died—he said: "Thank you for acknowledging my book. I was glad to have been able to finish it. . . . I have been deaf for five years and feel like I have gotten out of touch with people. I am long overdue with my letters." It is signed with a scrawled "G." A communication from Susan Feagin of the same date says: "Gerry was very pleased to hear from you. . . . Completing [the book] was very important to him, and since then, I fear, his life has been without much meaning. He has become weaker and weaker over the last several months—something which hardly seems possible given how weak he was to begin with. However, he is not in pain. . . ."

Although he was not in pain, it is hard to believe that he was not suffering. But it is clear that Gerry MacCallum remained a philosopher until the end, and that he experienced, in this dark period of his life, at least some of the legendary consolations of philosophy.

Postscript by Susan Feagin

There were times when Gerry considered the possibility of making a collection of some of his published and unpublished writings. He indicated to me on more than one occasion that if such a collection were to be made by someone else, the two people he would trust for the task were Mark Singer and Rex Martin. It gave me great pleasure, as well as a feeling that it was more than serendipity, when Mark Singer proposed that he would like to collaborate with Rex Martin on such a project. Their care and perseverance in this project bears testimony to both their professional achievements and personal friendship, of which Gerry would have been very pleased and proud.

Susan L. Feagin
Fairway, Kansas
July, 1992

Gerald C. MacCallum, Jr.

Introduction

The philosophical themes running through and coordinating and unifying MacCallum's work and this collection include the following: legislative intent and the problems of judicial reasoning regarding "the intention" of the legislature and "the original meaning" of the statute (or the Constitution)[1] and the nature of legal reasoning in connection with other matters judges are called upon to deal with; the nature and correct analysis of freedom, one that would be truly useful in advancing the progress of thinking on important issues in social philosophy; the nature, scope, and force of conscience and the validity and meaning of "appeals to conscience"; the nature and justifiability of violence (an especially interesting topic for someone who had served three years in the infantry in World War II and who must therefore have engaged in some especially violent activity but who was characteristically a very unviolent person); competition, its role in moral philosophy, and its relation to the adversary system and justice, and, of course, the relations between adversary proceedings and justice. MacCallum had been planning a book on conscience and violence for some time, and also a book on competition, justice, and the adversary system; what little he was able to write coherently and in a way with which he was not too dissatisfied on these topics is contained in this book. He also thought and read a great deal on nationalism and the problems and possibilities it poses. There is material on that topic in his book *Political*

---

1. Considering the amount of loose talk that prevails among judges and lawyers, members of and nominees to the Supreme Court, members of the Senate Judiciary Committee and other legislative bodies, presidents and presidential candidates, other executive officials, certified pundits on television and in the press—and even Professors of Law—on "the original intent of the Founders," "the intent of the legislature," what "the drafters of the statute intended," and so forth and so on, a fairly strong argument can be made for the proposition that MacCallum's essay on "Legislative Intent" ought to be required reading for all who would hold forth on the matter. The same might said for some of the other contents of this volume.

Philosophy (see especially Chapter 4, "Nations and Nationalism: Ideological Foundations," as well as Chapter 11, "Subjects, Citizens, and Aliens"), but full-blown work on that project was in his thinking far off in the future, even in his most optimistic moods. Of course, nationalism links in fairly obvious though not easily stateable ways with competition and adversarial relationships, and an awareness of these relationships is one reason that led MacCallum to research the history and nature of nationalism and the history, law, and politics of international relations, war, and peace. (There is some other unfinished work on autonomy, freedom, and justice, and on different models of legal systems, none in shape to publish.)

MacCallum's usual method of working was to revise a piece three or four times before judging it ready for publication, and then of course he was prepared to revise again in light of editors' or readers' or colleagues' or auditors' comments. Naturally, not all of the pieces in this collection went through this thorough process, in particular the previously unpublished ones; however, some of the unpublished ones actually did. One of these is Chapter 10, "Dworkin on Judicial Discretion," which he revised after it was first presented and prepared for publication in an anthology; his permission to publish it, however, was conditional on Ronald Dworkin's paper "Judicial Discretion"—on which Chapter 10 is a commentary—appearing in the anthology essentially unchanged from its first appearance in print; unfortunately, the volume was never published.[2] Another unpublished paper that went through this process was Chapter 12, "Competition and Moral Philosophy," which he felt, shortly before his really damaging second stroke, about ready to publish in the condition in which it appears here. One paper (Chapter 11) stands intermediate between being finished for publication and being quite unfinished. It was originally presented at the "Buffalo Conference on the Justification of Violence," held in April 1974, and was one redraft away from being publishable in MacCallum's view. Two papers that did not get far in his process for revision are chapters 13 and 14, "Justice and Adversary Proceedings," which he was very close to finishing, and "What is Wrong with Violence?" which he was not close to finishing and certainly not ready to publish. But more on this last piece anon.

2. MacCallum's letter, of 13 February 1967, to the prospective editor of the volume said, rather characteristically: "I would be glad to appear in it provided that, in my judgment, my piece still has any relevance and forcefulness after Dworkin's own performance has reached the form in which it will appear in the book (on the assumption that you would want mine only if he approved of inclusion of his). Thus, I now give permission provisionally, and will give permission unconditionally only after seeing the final form of Dworkin's essay." The anthology being planned was never published because satisfactory arrangements to obtain permission to reprint certain other key pieces could not be arranged. MacCallum, nonetheless, had prepared his paper for publication, and it now appears in this volume some twenty-five years later (though some further editing of it was required to detach it further from the context to which it originally was so closely tied).

The title essay occupies (in the choice phrase of David Lyons) the premier place in the book, with good reason. These reasons have been so well expressed by Stanley L. Paulson, professor of law and philosophy at Washington University in St. Louis, that we are pleased to incorporate them here:

> The paper on "Legislative Intent" . . . is the locus classicus in the field. It continues to generate interest for two reasons. First, in place of the lawyer's "catch all" question—say, "what was the legislator's intent?"—MacCallum distinguishes a variety of different questions, among them: "Was his intent to enact a statute" (question of the nature of the act or performance); "was his intent to enact *this* statute?" (identity of the legal document, or, alternatively, a question of whether the words in the statute *mean* what he took them to mean when he enacted the statute); "what was his intent in enacting the statute?" (what did he hope to achieve legislatively, or, alternatively, what did he hope to achieve in terms of his own career?). MacCallum's point is that any one of these questions may, in the appropriate context, serve as the correct reading of the lawyer's "catch all" question. Here, as often in philosophy, carefully drawn distinctions are a first step toward clarity and understanding; MacCallum, in his ensuing discussion, draws on the distinctions he introduces early in the paper and succeeds in showing how complex and variegated the field is.
>
> A second front in MacCallum's paper is the examination of collective legislative intent—whether the legislature, as distinct from individual legislators, can be said to have an intent and, if so, how it is to be understood. Leading figures in jurisprudence—from Hans Kelsen, in his *Hauptprobleme der Staatsrechtslehre* (1911), to Ronald Dworkin, in *A Matter of Principle* (1985)—have confidently denied intent altogether where the notion is imputed collectively, that is, to the legislative body as a whole.
>
> MacCallum is more subtle. He looks to the sort of situations that would constitute a *prima facie* case for a legislature's having an intention and asks what sorts of conditions would have to obtain here. In a rich and suggestive argument, MacCallum answers with two different models, both of which lend support to the notion of (collective) legislative intent. In connection with the first, which he calls the "majority model," he writes:
>
> > [Where] a coincidence in behavior (voting affirmatively) by a majority of the legislators is sufficient for and equivalent to saying that the *legislature* has acted (i.e., has enacted a piece of legislation), then a coincidence in the intentions of the very same legislators vis-a-vis the bill and their affirmative votes for it should be sufficient in determining what the *legislature* intended (if anything) by the act . . . [p. 26]

But there is no wholesale acceptance, on MacCallum's part, of the
majority model. In fact, as he goes on to argue, the practice of judges
and administrators does not reflect the model. MacCallum responds with
a second model, the "agency model," and examines its strengths and
weaknesses too. The result of his painstaking development and examination of both models is an analysis true to the complexity of the institutional practice in question—an analysis that does not have, after a quar-
ter of a century, a serious rival.[3]

Paulson also observes that "the reader who considers MacCallum's theses
in 'Legislative Intent' alongside his arguments in . . . 'On Applying Rules'
[Chapter 3] and in '. . . Legislators Should Serve Their Consciences or Their
Constituents' [Chapter 9], will have a richer and more rounded picture of the
'Legislative Intent' paper. Ditto, *mutatis mutandis,* for the other truly cele-
brated paper in the collection, 'Negative and Positive Freedom'."

Here Professor Paulson strikes a note also struck by David Lyons, professor
of law and philosophy at Cornell, who observes that "the collection contains
some themes, the most obvious of which are (1) reflections on Isaiah Berlin's
famous inaugural address on 'two concepts of liberty' [chapters 4–5]; (2)
conscience and political action [chapters 6–9, 11, and also 14]; and (3) the
morality of competition [chapters 12–13]."[4] Lyons prefaces this remark with
a telling observation:

MacCallum seems a model analytic philosopher of his generation. He is
clear, sensitive, and nontechnical. His reasoning is careful and persuasive. He is evenhanded, undogmatic, dispassionate, and systematic. He
may initially give the impression of chopping a minor piece of logic;
before long, however, the reader discovers that MacCallum has cleared
the way and is now asking a fundamental question that never occurred to
anyone else.

Lyons adds that the essay on "Negative and Positive Freedom" is "far
more than a critique of Berlin on 'two concepts of liberty.' It is a constructive
analysis of the concept of freedom . . ."; the essay "Some Truths and Untruths About Civil Disobedience" [Chapter 6] "does for civil disobedience
what [Chapter 1] does for legislative intent. MacCallum never merely points
out error. Instead he offers an illuminating perspective . . ."; the essay "Law,
Conscience, and Personal Integrity" [Chapter 8] is "a . . . successful exploration of [the] idea that the law may threaten one's integrity and conscience . . . an intriguing essay, the very promising start of a major project

---

3. Stanley L. Paulson, in a communication to the University of Wisconsin Press 23 May 1991.
4. David Lyons, in a communication of February–March 1991 to the University of Wisconsin
Press.

(never completed)"; the "essay on competition [Chapter 12] soundly comments on a huge gap in the philosophical literature (which persists)"; and the "unfinished essay on adversary proceedings [Chapter 13] is another promising beginning."

Lyons goes on to say of the "essay on justifications of violence" ("Violence and Appeals to Conscience" [Chapter 11]) that it is "sensitive, and contains a very interesting discussion of conflicts of conscience. But it seems to use 'ordinary language' techniques mechanically; e.g., its claims about the limits of appeals to conscience should have been reviewed in relation to the connection, suggested in an earlier essay [presumably Chapter 8, "Law, Conscience, and Integrity"], between conscience and the exercise of moral judgment." It is probable that MacCallum would have agreed with him on this and, if time and health had permitted, gone on to rectify the difficulty and improve the paper, or else have gone on to write a more comprehensive treatment of the matter which would have included, in unpredictable ways, the material of Chapter 14, "What is Wrong with Violence?" Both chapters 11 and 14 can be regarded as unfinished as they stand, parts of a projected wider whole that would have included them and much else now not knowable.

This leads us to say something ourselves on this obviously unfinished and imperfect last chapter. It is in part inconclusive and tends to lose focus as it proceeds. At the outset it has a focus: injury (harm, destruction) to human beings, and injury here was something that one could "see." Then the paper starts to drift away from that focus: to human bodies (taken as integrated *physical* systems), then to human *persons* (distinct to a degree from their bodies), thence to issues of autonomy and even freedom. In the end the conclusion seems to be: violence is presumptively wrong when it harms or destroys a human being (but does this mean a human body or a human person?) in the way specified in three named conditions, though this presumption can be rebutted in a number of ways. It can be argued, however, that MacCallum does not succeed in tying the grounds of rebuttal into either the notion of injury to human beings or the three conditions, either to one or the other exclusively or to both.

On the other hand, MacCallum was aware that the paper has problems, which is presumably why he referred to it in a rather offhand way (in Chapter 11) as "unpublishable," and we have noted that it is "unfinished." It is plain that it is "unfinished" in more than one sense. And despite these drawbacks, taken together with "Violence and Appeals to Conscience" (Chapter 11) and "Reform, Violence, and Personal Integrity" (Chapter 7), we have an account of violence in progress—and which will now never be finished—that is distinctive and in our judgment of sufficient value to warrant publication here. It is clear that violence was done to Gerald MacCallum, and in the process to his book length project on violence and conscience, that fits at least one of the descriptions he gives of violence, and that has left us only with these unfinished yet not incoherent fragments. There is further discussion of this matter and the reasons why "What Is Wrong with Violence?" has been included in this volume in the editorial notes to chapters 11 and 14 (pp. 178 and 235–36).

Legislative Intent
and Other Essays
on Law, Politics, and Morality

I Legislative Intent*

Introduction

Appeals to legislative intent are a commonplace part of our judicial process. Nevertheless there are many unresolved disputes about the existence and discoverability of legislative intent. In 1930, Max Radin argued that the presence of genuine legislative intent in connection with a statute is at best a rare circumstance and that, in any event, the legislative intent could not be discovered from the records of the legislative proceedings.[1] This argument drew an immediate response from James Landis. Landis distinguished between two senses of "intent"—"intent" as "intended meaning" and "intent" as "pur-

---

1. Max Radin, "Statutory Interpretation," *Harvard Law Review* 43 (1929–30): 863–85. Radin also denied the relevance of appeals to legislative intent. This article, however, is only concerned with the prior questions of the existence and discoverability of legislative intent. For earlier criticisms of the notion of legislative intent, see Theodore Sedgwick, *The Interpretation and Construction of Statutory and Constitutional Law,* 2d ed. (New York: Baker, Voorhis & Co., 1874), pp. 327–28; Ernest Bruncken, "Interpretation of Written Law," *Yale Law Journal* 25 (1915–16): 129–40; Albert Kocourek, *An Introduction to the Science of Law,* (Boston: Little, Brown, 1930), p. 201.

*This paper was first published in the *Yale Law Journal* 75.5 (1966): 754–87. It was reprinted with some corrections, included here, in *Essays in Legal Philosophy* (Oxford: Basil Blackwell, 1968) edited by R. S. Summers, and, somewhat abridged and without these corrections, in Philip Shuchman's revision, or second edition, of Morris R. and Felix S. Cohen's *Readings in Jurisprudence and Legal Philosophy* (Boston: Little, Brown and Co., 1979). In his "personal copy," MacCallum had made a number of corrections and some notes for revision, which have been incorporated here. These revisions were not incorporated in the Shuchman reprint. At the time of his correspondence with Shuchman, MacCallum had already suffered his first stroke, and he may have forgotten these notes to himself; in any case, at that time he had no ready access to his personal copy. He had told one of us (MGS) some time ago that the editors of the *Yale Law Journal* had in their editing transformed a valid argument into an invalid one. We think this has now been rectified in virtue of MacCallum's notes in his personal copy. Not all changes made on the basis of MacCallum's marginal notes are specifically marked. Eds.

pose." He maintained that legislative intent in the first sense (and apparently in the second also) is an ordinary although not invariable feature of legislative processes. Furthermore, he contended that this feature, when present, is clearly discoverable in the records of the legislative proceedings.[2]

The Radin-Landis dispute has had a curious history. Since 1930, treatises and articles on statutory interpretation have often mentioned the dispute and have sometimes taken sides. But commentators siding with Radin, although abandoning talk about legislative intent, proceed to talk freely about the "legislative purposes," "policies," and "objectives" of statutes. Because it is not obvious that these expressions refer to anything different from legislative intent,[3] one would expect careful discussion of where the differences lie. In particular, one would expect to find a showing that arguments leading to the rejection of talk about legislative intent have no force against these new expressions. But no such showing is to be found in the leading discussions of the matter—including those by Willis,[4] Frankfurter,[5] Corry[6] and Radin himself.[7]

On the other hand, commentators siding with Landis have done so on the basis of inadequate arguments. For example, we find Radin falsely accused of assuming "that the legislative intent is the sum of the total intents of the individual members of the legislature."[8] This is accompanied by the mysterious assertion that the intention of the legislature is "not a collection of subjective wishes, hopes and prejudices of individuals, but rather the objective footprints left on the trail of legislative enactment."[9] Such a statement is mysterious because it appears to mistake what could at most be *evidence* of intent for intent itself. It is surely in need of further elucidation and support if it is to show Radin wrong.

Again, we find unsupported assumptions that statutes would be wholly

2. James M. Landis, "A note on 'Statutory Interpretation,'" *Harvard Law Review* 43 (1929–30): 886–93.

3. As Johnstone remarks, "purpose" often seems simply another name for intent. Quintin Johnstone, "An Evaluation of the Rules of Statutory Interpretation," *Kansas Law Review* 3 (1954–55): 1–25, at p. 15. See also Bruncken, "Interpretation of Written Law," p. 134.

4. John Willis, "Statute Interpretation in a Nutshell," *Canadian Bar Review* 16 (1938): 1–27.

5. Felix Frankfurter, "Some Reflections on the Reading of Statutes," *Columbia Law Review* 47 (1947): 527–48.

6. J. A. Corry, "Administrative Law and the Interpretation of Statutes," *University of Toronto Law Journal* 1 (1935–36): 286–312. See also J. A. Corry, "The Use of Legislative History in the Interpretation of Statutes," *Canadian Bar Review* 32 (1954): 624–37.

7. Max Radin, "A Short way With Statutes," *Harvard Law Review* 56 (1942–43): 388–424.

8. See Jabez Gridley Sutherland, *Statutes and Statutory Construction,* 3d ed., edited by Frank E. Horack, Jr. (Chicago: Callaghan and Co., 1943), vol. 2, p. 322. For what Radin actually says see Radin, "Statutory Interpretation," p. 870.

9. Sutherland, *Statutes.*

meaningless in the absence of anything identifiable as legislative intent,[10] and that the meaning assigned to them "must be one intended by the law-makers or the law-makers do not legislate." [11] Such remarks raise interesting issues, but, as will be seen below, the arguments supporting them cannot stand.

These claims and counterclaims are fully representative of the curious career of the Radin-Landis dispute. Writers siding with Radin apparently find it impossible to reject every trace of what he rejected. Writers siding with Landis have done so on the basis of inadequate (although sometimes interesting) arguments. Clearly the issues raised by the dispute have not yet been satisfactorily resolved, and are still in need of careful discussion.

I

The most obvious difficulty with the notion of legislative intent concerns the relationship between the intent of a collegiate legislature and the intentions of the several legislators. Many difficulties would remain, however, if a legislature had only one authoritative member. We would profit, therefore, by asking what it could mean to speak of the legislative intent of a single legislator.

The fundamental question "what was the legislator's intent" subsumes a number of more specific questions:

> 1. Was his intent to enact a statute—i.e., was the "enacting" performance not, perchance, done accidentally, inadvertently or by mistake?
> 2. Was his intent to enact *this* statute—i.e., was this the *document* (the draft) he thought he was endorsing?
> 3. Was his intent to enact *this* statute—i.e., are the *words* in this document precisely those he supposed to be there when he enacted it as a statute?
> 4. Was his intent to enact *this* statute—i.e., do these words *mean* precisely what he supposed them to mean when he endorsed their use in the statute?
> 5. How did *he* intend these words to be understood?
> 6. What was his intent in enacting the statute—i.e., what did he intend the enactment of the statute to achieve?
> 7. What was his intent in enacting the statute—i.e., what did he intend the enactment of the statute to achieve *in terms of his own career?* [12]

10. Cf. Earl T. Crawford, *The Construction of Statutes* (St. Louis: Thomas Law Book Company, 1940), p. 255.

11. Crawford, *The Construction of Statutes* p. 256.

12. Joseph P. Witherspoon, "Administration Discretion to Determine Statutory Meaning: 'The Middle Road'," part 1, *Texas Law Review* 40 (1961–62): 751–848, at pp. 796–800,

Failure to distinguish between these more specific questions is responsible for much of the confusion in debates about the existence, discoverability and relevance of legislative intent. It is therefore important to examine closely the relationships between the more troublesome of these questions.

A. The aims of the legislator: the distinction between

6. What did he intend enactment of the statute to achieve? and
7. What did he intend enactment to achieve in terms of his own career?

These questions distinguish between two kinds of reasons the legislator may have for enacting a statute—reasons looking to the effects of enactment upon the legal system, and reasons looking to the effects of enactment on his own career.[13] This distinction is crucial to any discussion of the relevance of legislative intent, since judges and administrators are unlikely to regard as significant the legislator's concern with his own career. The distinction is also important when one is discussing the existence and discoverability of legislative intent. To say there was no intent at all, for example, might mean that the enactment was motiveless, e.g., inadvertent or accidental. On the other hand, it might mean that no intent of the relevant sort was present, that the legislator had only his personal career in mind when enacting the statute. Furthermore, depending on the records available, one kind of intent might be discoverable while the other is not. Thus the two must be kept distinct.

B. Intent as intended meaning and intent as purpose: the distinction between

6. What did he intend the enactment of the statute to achieve? and
5. How did *he* intend these words to be understood?

Landis notes the way the distinction between intent as (intended) meaning and intent as purpose becomes obscured when he says:

---

distinguishes twenty-two "forms or configurations of legislative purpose that may be discovered at work in any particular legislative process productive of a statute." He does not attempt to order his list as I have, but I believe that it all lies somewhere within the range of my numbers 3–6. Some of the entries are further specifications of what I have distinguished; but some of them also appear to conflate matters I wish to keep distinct, e.g., each of his numbers 5–8 could cover what I wish to distinguish above in (4) and (5).

13. Cf. Radin, *Statutory Interpretation,* p. 873. See Frederick J. de Sloovère, "Preliminary Questions in Statutory Interpretation," *New York University Law Review* 9 (1931–32): 407–28, at p. 415, where his remark about "individual and combined motives" encourages, if it does not actually constitute, a conflation of the questions.

> Purpose and meaning commonly react upon each other. Their exact dif-
> ferentiation would require an extended philosophical essay. . . . [T]he
> Distinction . . . is a nice one.[14]

Even though the distinction may be a "nice one," no lengthy essay is needed
to underscore the importance of distinguishing questions about the purposes
of specific legislators from general questions about the meanings of statutory
words. The major source of confusion has been the belief that we must always
guide our understanding of statutory words by an understanding of legislative
purposes, as though we could not understand the words without prior knowledge of the purposes.[15] This belief is most readily countered with the reminder
that our primary source of "evidence" of specific legislative purposes in connection with a statute generally lies in the words of the statute itself, and that
these words could not provide such evidence if their meanings were not determined independently of consideration of the purposes in question.[16]

Confusion about the interplay between purpose and meaning has become
so embedded in discussions of statutory interpretation that a more extended
argument may be desirable. In particular, it may be helpful to show that the
distinction between purpose and meaning exists even when the considerable
concessions suggested by question 5 are made in the direction of establishing
a connection between the purpose of a legislator and the meaning of what he
says in a statute. Suppose we stipulate (i) that a legislator's words always
mean precisely what he thinks they mean, and (ii) that the purposes in question concern the career of the statute rather than the career of the legislator.
The first stipulation seems to go as far as possible in the direction of a tight
connection between statutory meaning and the intentions or purposes of the
legislator. The second stipulation restricts the purposes in question to those
most generally thought to enter legitimately into issues of statutory interpretation. Even with these stipulations, however, one may show that persons
normally need not be aware of legislative purposes in order to understand
legislative words.

Although the problem is an "interpreter's" problem, it will be helpful to
consider the matter first from the point of view of the legislator, and on the

14. See James M. Landis, "A Note on 'Statutory Interpretation'," *Harvard Law Review* 43
(1929–30): 886–93, at p. 888.

15. Cf. Crawford, *The Construction of Statutes,* pp. 255–56; Karl N. Llewellyn, "Remarks
on the Theory of Appellate Decision and the Rules or Canons About How Statutes are to be
Construed," *Vanderbilt Law Review* 3 (1949–50): 395–406, at p. 400; Witherspoon, "Administrative Discretion to Determine Statutory Meaning," p. 765.

16. Cf. Elmer A. Dreidger, *The Composition of Legislation* (Ottawa: E. Cloutier, Queen's
Printer and Controller of Stationery, 1957), p. 159. It is true that we sometimes allow our understanding of legislative purposes to shed light on puzzling passages in a statute. But we could not
even attempt this if we did not believe we already understood most of the words in the statute.

simplifying assumption that he is the author of the statutes he enacts.[17] He is typically interested in enacting a piece of legislation because he wants to effect certain changes in the society. The words he uses are the instruments by means of which he expects or hopes to effect these changes. What gives him this expectation or this [hope is his belief that he can anticipate how others (e.g., judges and administrators) will understand these words. The words would be useless to him if he could not anticipate how they would be understood by these other persons].* Insofar as this concern for how his words will be understood is a concern about the "meaning" of his words, this "meaning" must thus generally be determinable independently of consideration of his purposes; for, until he forms opinions about the "meaning" of the words, he cannot consider whether they will serve his purpose.

The legislator can attempt to assure that his words will be correctly understood in various ways, e.g., by stipulation. But if he stipulates he must use other words about which he will have the same general concern. Ultimately, he must recognize that with the bulk of his words he cannot create but only can utilize the conventions in the light of which his words will be understood.[18] The legislator will be interested primarily in the conventions of statutory interpretation—that is, in the current conventional approaches by judges, administrators, lawyers and citizens to the understanding of statutes. Although these conventions will not guarantee specific results, they are all that he has to work with.

Consider the matter now from the point of view of the interpreters of statutes. Maintaining a perspective favorable to the association of legislative purpose with statutory meaning, suppose that the interpreters declare themselves bound

17. Complications introduced by the presence of draftsmen who are not themselves legislators will be considered later in connection with the intentions of collegiate bodies such as modern legislatures.

18. Of course, one convention of statutory interpretation might permit or require that one's understanding of statutory language be guided by consideration of the legislator's purpose. Cf. Sutherland, *Statutes and Statutory Construction,* p. 315. Such a convention would invite the legislator to attempt to lay down a trail of his "purposes" for others to follow; hence the use, in jurisdictions where legislators believe that interpreters of statutes will seek and heed such "evidence," of statutory preambles, carefully manufactured "legislative histories," etc. The only feature of note about this convention is that it offers the legislator an opportunity to influence rather than merely to anticipate how his statutory words will be understood. In this respect, it is analogous to conventions for stipulation and for formal definition. Nevertheless, the "trail" he is able to lay down, both within and outside of the statute, will be primarily if not exclusively a verbal one. As with stipulations, if the legislator believes he can influence the understanding of his statutory words, it is only because he has certain expectations about how certain other words will be understood. These expectations also must be formed independently of consideration of his purposes, because until he has the expectations he can have no notion of whether these other words will serve his purposes.

*In MacCallum's personal copy, the lines bracketed here were marked "needs rewrite." Eds.

by what the legislator wanted at the time the statute was enacted. Suppose, in particular, that, rather than raising any questions about how the legislator *ought* to have expected his words to be understood, the interpreters assume that their only legitimate task is the discovery of the legislator's actual expectations.

Difficulties arise immediately. There may be a lack of fit between how the legislator expected the words of the statute to be understood, and what he hoped to achieve by means of the statute. That is, the statute itself, or some constituent parts of it, may have been poorly chosen instruments for the achievement of his goals—not in the sense that the words were not understood as he expected them to be, but rather in the sense that, even when the words *were* understood as he expected, behavior in accordance with this understanding did not produce the results he thought it would produce. There are, in short, at least *two* distinct ways in which things could go wrong from the legislator's point of view: (1) people might not understand the words of the statute in the way he thought they would, or (2) the behavior of people who understand the words as he thought they would and who act truly in accordance with this understanding, might not produce the results that the legislator anticipated. In the first case, the legislator would have made a mistake in predicting how his words would be understood; in the second case, he would have made a mistake in predicting what would happen if people behaved in certain ways.[19] The difference between the two kinds of mistakes is obscured for the "interpreter," and his view of statutory interpretation is consequently muddied, if he supposes that an understanding of the legislator's "purposes" is either a sufficient or normally necessary guide to how the legislator expected the words of the statute to be understood.

As the legislator may simply have misjudged the effectiveness of the statutory scheme in achieving the purported purpose, a resolve to interpret the words of the statute so that the statute *will be* an effective instrument for the achievement of the purpose would be simply a refusal to consider the possibility of this kind of legislative misjudgment. The importance of this observation lies in the fact that, where such legislative misjudgment has actually occurred, the method of interpretation under consideration may not produce an understanding of the words of the statute corresponding to that which the legislator expected—the very understanding that figured in his deliberate choice of those words. In the end, there may be nothing *wrong* with this; the legislator may be delighted with a method of interpretation which hides his own mis-

19. The distinction between the two is clear enough even though there may be a large shadowy area between them where the legislator's expectations were not well-formed, and where even he might not be able to say whether, on the one hand, his words had not been understood as he expected, or rather, on the other hand, that he had proposed in the statute an ineffective way of achieving what he wished to achieve. See Axel Hägerström, *Inquiries into the Nature of Law and Morals,* trans. by C. D. Broad (Stockholm: Almqvist & Wiksell, 1953), pp. 79–81.

judgment. But are the interpreters really being faithful to the "intentions" of the legislator when they interpret his words differently from what he had expected?[20] At the very least, this problem should be brought into the open and faced squarely—something that has not been done and is not likely to be done so long as intent as "meaning" and intent as purpose are conflated.

One may wonder how intended legislative meaning could possibly be discovered *without* appeal to knowledge of legislative purpose. The answer is that discovery depends primarily upon our awareness of the linguistic conventions the legislator looked to in forming his expectations about how his words would be understood. Awareness of these conventions will provide us with good (although not infallible) grounds for believing we know what his expectations were. Moreover, there is no great problem in attaining this awareness. We know perfectly well how to tell whether a man speaks the same language we do, and how to tell whether we can speak his language. Our capacity to do this provides us with a generally adequate basis for determining when the legislator and we are both familiar with the linguistic conventions in the light of which various understandings of his words will be formed, and for determining whether we can understand these conventions in the same ways. Further, if we are the specific audience to whom his remarks are directed, we are merely asking ourselves what our own linguistic conventions are, and how well he might have understood them. The fact that statutory language ordinarily serves us quite well in this respect indicates that we are able to use the same linguistic conventions as the legislator and to know that we are doing so.

In sum, for us as well as for the legislator, practical understanding of his language is ordinarily founded on a grasp of the linguistic conventions utilized, rather than a grasp of his specific purposes in enacting the statute. This explains both how his words can serve us as evidence of his purposes, and why there is ordinarily no need to search for his purposes in order to understand what he meant.

C. Can the legislator misunderstand his own words? the distinction between

4. Do these words *mean* precisely what he supposed them to mean when he endorsed their use in the statute? and

5. How did *he* intend these words to be understood?

---

20. Hägerström apparently thinks that the whole "intention" theory founders on just this issue. See Hägerström, *Nature of Law and Morals*, pp. 99–101. And, for people who come down on different sides of the question, see John Austin, *Lectures on Jurisprudence*, 5th ed., edited by Robert Campbell (London: J. Murray, 1885), vol. 2, pp. 628–30; and J. P. Witherspoon, *Administrative Discretion to Determine Statutory Meaning*, pp. 831–32.

Question (4) pinpoints, as question (5) does not, the possibility that the *legislator* has misunderstood the words he used in a statutory document. Reading some discussions on statutory interpretation, one would think it impossible for a legislator to misunderstand what he has written or endorsed.[21] In these discussions, the entire burden of understanding or misunderstanding the statute seemingly is placed upon others—the judge, the lawyer, the citizen. The effective slogan of these discussions might well be that the words of the statute mean what their author-endorser (the legislator) intended them to mean. But, as we have seen, words in statutes are of use both to legislators and to others because they have acquired significance through the growth or stipulation of conventions regarding their use. Indeed, we could not recognize something *as* a word, rather than as merely a contour (or range of contours) of sounds or a certain form (or range of forms) of scribblings if we were not aware that sounds and scribblings with such contours and forms have a significance, function, or value resulting from the growth or stipulation of such conventions. *Our* belief that we can understand what a man says, and *his* belief that he will be understood, mutually depend upon the recognition, acceptance, and utilization of such conventions. Furthermore, as we have also noted, even when such conventions are stipulated by a speaker, the stipulations ultimately rely upon words whose meanings are not stipulated but are assumed to be already understood in the light of existing conventions. It follows that if a speaker is not understood as he expected to be, this may be because *he* misunderstood or because some member of his audience misunderstood linguistic conventions of which they should have been aware.

Of course, having recognized that a legislator might possibly misunderstand the conventions determining the commonly accepted significance of the words he uses, we might for some reason wish to give more importance to his (mistaken) beliefs about the significance of his words than to their actual significance—that is, we might feel bound more by what he *meant* to say than by what, on any ordinary view, he *did* say. We could remind ourselves of this with the slogan that the words in statutory documents mean what the legislators intended them to mean, and could regard as always authoritative, even when mistaken, the beliefs of legislators as to how their words would be understood, and, in particular, their beliefs as to the commonly accepted significance of their words.

The adoption of such a policy, however, would lead to practical and conceptual problems. The legislator's audience (judges, lawyers, administrators, citizens) would have to ignore what the legislator said (the commonly ac-

---

21. Cf. Crawford, *The Construction of Statutes*, p. 245, and Sutherland, *Statutes and Statutory Construction*, vol. 2, pp. 315–16.

cepted significance of his words) and take upon itself the responsibility of seeking out what the legislator meant (what he expected them to understand). A serious attempt to fulfill this responsibility would, to say the least, require complex and tedious investigation.[22] Furthermore, if we insist that the audience is responsible for what the legislator meant reather than for what he said, we must concede that either (a) the statute consists of the string of words actually on the rolls, in which case that statute (i.e., that string of words) may not be binding, or (b) the statute is binding but may consist of a different string of words from that on the rolls.*

Perhaps this analysis merely reveals that we are in a quandary when it comes to interpreting statutes. With statutes, some peculiar authority attaches to what the legislator *says* (for that is virtually all that most persons may have to go by), and some authority may attach also to what the legislator is *trying* to say (after all, under the separation-of-powers doctrine we have in some way obligated ourselves to submit to his wishes on certain matters).[23] But at least we need a formulation of the issues that allows us to see the quandary for what it is. Wholehearted acceptance of the slogan that statutory words mean what the legislator intended them to mean would make this insight impossible.

We have seen that appeals to the legislative intent of even a single legislator are attended by numerous difficulties and sources of confusion. But we have not yet approached the major problem about legislative intent. Judges and administrators appeal to the intent of entire *collegiate* legislatures. Many commentators believe that such appeals are futile—that it is senseless to speak of the intent of a collegiate legislature. Our examination of the intent of the single legislator is a prologue to this central controversy.

22. Judges and commentators, in protesting the seemingly overwhelming importance given to "legislative intent" in statutory interpretation, have sometimes been in part protecting against the placement of this responsibility on the interpreters of statutes. See e.g., *Schwegmann Bros.* v. *Calvert Distillers Corp.*, 341 U.S. 384, 395–96 (1951) (concurring opinion of Jackson, J.); *McBoyle* v. *United States*, 283 U.S. 25, 27 (1931); James C. Quarles, "Some Statutory Construction Problems and Approaches in Criminal Law," *Vanderbilt Law Review* 3 (1950): 531–43.

23. Crawford approaches the problem when he says "And the meaning must be one intended by the law-makers or the law-makers do not legislate." Crawford, *The Construction of Statutes,* p. 256. See also Felix Frankfurter, "Foreword to a Symposium on Statutory Construction," *Vanderbilt Law Review* 3 (1950): 365–68, at p. 366; Robert H. Jackson, "The Meaning of Statutes: What Congress Says or What the Court Says," *American Bar Association Journal* 34 (1948): 535–58, at pp. 537–38.

*In its initial outing in the *Yale Law Journal* this phrase appeared (top of p. 763) as: ". . . string of words) is not binding, or (b) the statute is binding but consists of a different string. . . ." This is the passage MacCallum modified and marked "editor's misprint" and is in all probability the argument he later said had been modified by the editors from a valid argument into an invalid one. Eds.

II

A. *Introduction to the skeptical arguments*

Does it make any sense at all to talk about the intentions of a collegiate legislature? Radin says:

> A legislature certainly has no intention whatever in connection with words which some two or three men drafted, which a considerable number rejected, and in regard to which many of the approving majority might have had, and often demonstrably did have, different ideas and beliefs.[24]

Stronger views have been taken. Kocourek's argument to the effect that such intentions "never existed" is based upon an unsupported assertion that: "Legislation is a group activity and it is impossible to conceive a group mind or cerebration."[25] Willis says flatly and without argument: "A composite body can hardly have a single intent."[26] More recently D. J. Payne also appears to dismiss the possibility when he says: "[T]he legislature, being a composite body, cannot have a single state of mind and so cannot have a single intention."[27]

Concerning at least the latter three views, there are two issues to be sorted out: (a) the extent to which they are based on the notion that two or more men cannot have the same intention, and (b) the extent to which they are based on the notion that a group of men is incapable of having an intention. Kocourek's remark appears to raise the second of these issues; Payne's, despite appearances, raises the first.

Although we shall deal with Payne's arguments more fully below, consider for a moment the supposition in (a). *Is* it possible for two or more men to "have a single intention"? Anyone wishing to deny the possibility must tell us why we cannot truthfully say in the simple case of two men rolling a log toward the river bank with the purpose of floating it down the river that there is at least one intention both these men have—viz., to get the log to the river so that they can float it down the river. It would be unhelpful to reply that one man's intention cannot be identical with another man's because each is his

24. Radin, "Statutory Interpretation," p. 870.
25. Kocourek, *Introduction to the Science of Law,* p. 201.
26. Willis, *Statutory Interpretation in a Nutshell,* p. 3.
27. D. J. Payne, "The Intention of the Legislature in the Interpretation of Statutes," *Current Legal Problems* 9 (1956): 96–112, at pp. 97–98. I say "appears to" because despite the above statement and several others equally strong, Payne also seems to endorse Gray's view that the intention of the legislature, far from being always non-existent, is often perfectly obvious (pp. 101–2). It also turns out, as we shall see below, that Payne's arguments don't support a conclusion as strong as that quoted in the text above.

own and not the other's. There is no reason to confine ourselves to counting intentions *only* in this way. Further, if we did so confine ourselves, the central claim that two men cannot have the same intention would turn out to be merely a disguised tautology.

B. The deeper roots of skepticism

The claim in (b) raises much more difficult issues. Should we agree that legislatures, being *groups* of men, cannot have intentions? One possible argument here might be: legislatures are not men; only men can have intentions; therefore, legislatures cannot have intentions.[28]

Kocourek makes a more specific claim that there are necessary conditions for having intentions—conditions absent in the case of legislatures. His candidates are mind and "cerebration."[29] But it is clear that the temptation to name these as necessary conditions lies only in thinking of them as preconditions for purposive behavior and for deliberation—two more immediate preconditions for having intentions. When one moves directly to a consideration of whether legislatures are capable of purposive behavior and deliberation, the reply that they are seems neither false nor (without further argument) only figurative. We do, after all, speak quite freely and precisely about legislatures deliberating, and this, aside from our talk about their debating, investigating, etc., implies a capacity for purposive behavior. Of course, if someone tried to elucidate such talk without any reference whatever to the deliberating, investigating, debating, etc., of officers, members, agents, or employees of the legislature, we might find this mysterious or unacceptable. But no one has proposed eliminating these references, and the point remains that we have clear notions of what it means to say that a *legislature* is doing these things and we know that legislatures sometimes do them. Thus, a protest that legislatures do not ever do them, or, perhaps, do not "literally" do them, is not prima facie intelligible.

But the skeptic may argue that when he claims that a capacity to deliberate is a necessary condition for having intentions, he is not thinking of the deliberating in which legislatures are conventionally said to engage; rather, he is

28. But of course this argument will founder on the shoals of debate about whether things other than men, e.g., animals, have intentions.

Perhaps, however, the arguer means to say that talk about the intentions of legislatures involves a category mistake or a "fallacy of composition." Men have intentions, but legislatures are *associations* of men, etc. As it stands, the principle of the argument would have to be this: from the fact that X is a collection of Y's, it follows that predicates applicable to Y's (taken distributively) are *therefore* inapplicable to X. There are apparent counter examples to the principle—e.g., Jones, the left tackle, is heavier this year than last; the team of which he is a member is also heavier this year than last. Responses to such counter examples will hardly avoid raising the complex issues discussed below.

29. See text accompanying note 25, above.

thinking of the deliberating engaged in by individual men. Though the former normally requires at least some cases of the latter, the two are not sufficiently alike for him.

The skeptic may feel that the notion of intention and the allied notions of deliberation, etc. are stretched "too far" when applied to legislatures. Although no one can say precisely how far is "too far," the line of reply to the skeptic is clear. Legislatures are not men, and if only men clearly have intentions, then one's arguments must cultivate analogies between legislatures and men—the point being to argue that legislatures are enough like men in important respects to be counted as having intentions. Such arguments cannot lead to a *discovery* that legislatures might, after all, have intentions. Rather, the arguments can at most persuade us that it would not, under certain circumstances, be unreasonable to attribute intentions to legislatures—because the expression "intention of the legislature" could still have practicable and reasonable applications without moving from what many people now understand it to mean, and *also* without moving too far from what they understand such an expression as "intention of Jones" to mean. This is a long road, requiring travel through considerable detail about legislative procedures and the practices of judges, administrators, etc. Furthermore, it is a road that does not lead to neat and decisive results. Perhaps, however, this road can be avoided, and the skeptics challenged in another manner.

C. The importance of legal and linguistic conventions

There have long been arguments about the extent to which any organization or association (e.g., a company, corporation, club, union, team, etc., as well as a legislature) can, not being a man, nevertheless behave like or be treated as a man. The view that some can is buttressed by modern law, which treats certain types of organizations and associations in ways that could be variously described as (i) treating them *for certain purposes* as (or as though they were) men, and (ii) treating them *in certain respects* as (or as though they were) men. Furthermore, in everyday speech we sometimes speak of them in ways suggesting the appropriateness of such treatment, and suggesting furthermore the appropriateness of ascribing intentions to them—e.g., we speak of them as *competing* with each other, *attempting* this, *succeeding* in that. The prevailing tendency in most of these cases has been to accept the talk,[30] but, when

30. The acceptance with respect to corporations has sometimes been justified by an appeal notably absent in discussions of legislative intent—viz. by arguing that the extent to which corporations may reasonably be treated in this way is simply a matter of public policy. Thus, for example, against the claim that corporations, *unlike* men, are solely creatures of law and hence incapable of illegal intent, one might argue that *as a matter of public policy* it would be better to treat corporation[s] as *like* men in this respect; this would bring corporate assets and perhaps even corporate officers within easier reach of sanctions against behavior contrary to the public

pressed, to attempt to "translate" it into talk about the intentions or behavior of various members, employees, officers, agents, or trustees of the organization or association in question. The claim is then common (at least in the Fiction, Bracket, and Purpose Theories of the nature of corporate personality)[31] that the "translation" provides the truth behind claims about the organizations which, if taken literally, would simply be fictions.*

The skeptic thinks that statements of the form—"The intention of the legislature is X"—are "fictional" or at best "figurative," and that they cannot be true if taken "literally." But he would be careless to assert this in the absence of any clear understanding of the "literal" significance of the statements. Since these statements have been made for several centuries without special stipulation as to their meaning, what plausible account of their present "literal" significance would show them to be fictional or figurative? The considerations involved can perhaps be made clearer by an examination of talk about the *activities* of legislatures. Why should we agree that claims such as—"the legislature enacted a sales tax bill in 1961"—must, when taken literally, be fictions or only "figurative" even though there are perfectly well-established legal criteria for determining what can count as an act of the legislature? It is true that in order for a legislature to have acted, it is necessary that certain men have acted. But (i) it would be a mistake to say that the legislature's having acted was nothing more than these men having acted.[32] And (ii) there is nothing fictional about the legal significance of the criteria for determining whether the legislature acted.

In view of well-established legal criteria for telling when legislatures have acted, and in view of the obvious truth that these criteria are often satisfied, it seems futilely dogmatic to insist without special excuse that statements about legislatures having acted can never be *literally* true. Such statements may sometimes be false, but their *sense* when taken "literally" is surely a matter of which conventions are well-established in, or have been stipulated for, the relevant linguistic community. The question now is whether there are

---

interest. In contrast to this approach, the dispute concerning legislative intent has almost universally been treated as though it were a factual and not a policy issue. The leading question has not been, "what is to be gained by treating legislatures as capable of intent?" Rather it has been "Are legislatures capable of intent?"

31. Cf. George Whitecross Paton, *A Textbook of Jurisprudence,* 3d ed., ed. by David P. Durham (Oxford: Clarendon, 1964), pp. 365–76.

32. It would miss the role of rules in determining which of the activities of these men could count as activities of the legislature. See H. L. A. Hart's discussion of this point with respect to corporations in H. L. A. Hart, *Definition and Theory in Jurisprudence* (Oxford: Clarendon, 1953), pp. 21–24 [reprinted in Hart's *Essays in Jurisprudence and Philosophy* (Oxford: Clarendon, 1983), pp. 40–43. *Eds.*]

*MacCallum's note: "poor transition." Eds.

any such conventions with respect to legislative intentions, and if so, how well-established are they?

It is important to be clear about what is being asked. We are not asking whether legislatures are conventionally supposed to have intentions; nor are we asking whether there is "evidence" that is conventionally supposed to be good evidence of the presence of such intentions. Rather, we are asking whether there are any generally accepted conventions concerning *what it would be like for a legislature to have an intention*—i.e., concerning the conditions that actually would constitute a case of a legislature's having an intention.

The importance of keeping these questions distinct is shown by the recent, and otherwise highly rewarding, discussion of similar problems by Witherspoon.[33] Witherspoon seems to consider the matter of legislative purpose from a standpoint much like the above. But he does not focus the issue sharply enough; as a result he moves too far too fast. He points to the undeniable fact that courts, administrative agencies, legislators, scholars and practitioners talk in terms of legislative purpose; he concludes that, given such firmly established practices, there are such things as legislative purposes.[34] This is an error; one could, if allowed to select the appropriate linguistic communities, use the same kind of argument to prove the existence of Santa Claus, Zeus, and dragons. The fact that people talk about certain things as though they existed does not warrant the conclusion that these things exist. Nor does the fact that people conventionally appeal to certain kinds of data as good evidence for the existence of something, warrant the conclusion that these data are indeed good evidence for the existence of that thing. The crucial task is to discover generally accepted conventions concerning *what it would be like* for a legislature to have an intention or a purpose. Only then (barring objections of the types sketched in Section B above) can one go on in an intelligent way to discuss whether there ever are such things, and to discuss what should be accepted as good evidence of them.

What are the facts, then? It is obvious that there is considerable disagreement within the legal community as to whether legislatures ever have intentions. There is also disagreement as to what would be adequate evidence of the presence of such intentions. But is there any appreciable disagreement on *what it would be like* for a legislature to have an intention? The answer to this question appears initially to be "no." With the exception of Kocourek and Bruncken,[35] we have found no author reluctant to agree that a legislature

---

33. Witherspoon, "Administrative Discretion," cited above, note 12, pp. 756–58, 790–91.

34. Witherspoon, "Administrative Discretion," pp. 789–91.

35. Bruncken's acceptance of the unanimity and majority models of legislative intent is clearly a concession he makes for the sake of further argument. See Bruncken, "Interpretation of Written Law," p. 130.

should be admitted to have an intention vis-a-vis a statute if each and every member of the legislature had that intention.[36] Furthermore, we have found very few authors showing any unwillingness to accept an even weaker condition—namely, that a legislature should be acknowledged to have an intention vis-a-vis a statute in case each of the majority who voted for the statute had that intention.[37] Virtually all the persons who have discussed the issue of legislative intent seem to *assume* that the fulfillment of this last condition is sufficient to support claims about the intention of a legislature. No one, as far as we have been able to discover, thinks it necessary even to *argue* the point. All the hullaballoo has been about whether that many legislators ever do share any significant intentions vis-a-vis a statute, and whether, if they do, we can ever know of it.

This apparent agreement should be approached cautiously. Perhaps it is only a product of the confidence of many skeptics that they need not go so far as to question it because they can show that the majority of legislators never share intentions. It is therefore desirable initially to see whether such confidence is misplaced, or whether it is indeed unnecessary to investigate the (provisional?) agreement. We shall consider this by way of a detailed examination of the arguments used by Payne to support his skeptical position. His arguments are not only the most substantial yet to be offered on the subject, but they also share crucial claims with the bulk of commentators, both pro and con, on this problem. One caveat: Payne thinks of legislative intent more or less in terms of our question number 5—i.e., in terms of how the legislature intended the (general) words of a statute to be understood. Perhaps he would extend the argument to include other items on our list, but this is uncertain.

D. The futility of the common skeptical arguments

Payne accepts without question the common view that the intentions of a legislature relative to a statute must be identified with the intentions of those

36. There may be difficulties with this if it is taken straightforwardly, but these difficulties have not troubled the skeptics. For example, a legislature can enact a bill into law; a legislator (that is, a member of a legislative assembly) cannot. He can only vote for the bill in the hope that it will be enacted into law. Thus, for example, a legislator can at most intend by his vote to help enact the legislation with a view to what it would, if enacted, achieve. The achievement of the latter is what the legislature might be said to intend; a contribution to the achievement of the latter might be what the legislator intends. In what follows, I shall suppose such shifts to be understood.

37. Of course, Kocourek would be unwilling. Bruncken considers it a concession. Bruncken, "Interpretation of Written Law," p. 130. Radin did not come down decisively either way. Radin, "Statutory Interpretation," p. 870. Corry shows a decided reluctance to accept it. J. A. Corry, "The Use of Legislative History in the Interpretation of Statutes," *Canadian Bar Review* 32 (1954): 624–37, at 625–36. However, he did not show the reluctance earlier. J. A. Corry, "Administrative Law and the Interpretation of Statutes," *University of Toronto Law Journal* 1 (1935–36): 286–312, at p. 290.

legislators who voted for the bill, and further that the intentions of the legislature are the intentions those legislators share. But he claims that the legislature cannot have a single state of mind.

> Context does much to fix the extension of a general word, but even the fullest consideration of context generally leaves an uncertain fringe of meaning, and it is this uncertain fringe of meaning which gives rise to so many problems of statutory interpretation. For example, is linoleum "furniture"? . . . It is impossible to decide such questions by reference to the intention of the legislature since the mental images of the various members of the legislature who vote for a bill containing such a general word will exhibit the same imprecision and lack of agreement as found in the common usage of the word. This would be true even if every member of the legislature voting for the bill reflected at length on the extension of the particular general word, *for reflection would not necessarily entail agreement.*[38]

What Payne says here seems quite sensible, but the italicized portion shows his error. He has tried to move from saying that reflection does not entail agreement to saying that, even with reflection, agreement is impossible. This move is illegitimate, and consequently he has not shown that there *cannot* be a single state of mind (agreement).

Notice next that his claim about the unlikelihood or impossibility of a single state of mind is indeterminate. This is revealed by his concentration in the above passage upon borderline or "fringe areas" of the extensions of general words. The question which should be asked about his claim is—a single state of mind pertaining to what? The whole extension of the word? Or only some part of that extension? It is surely not necessary for persons to agree in *all* cases in order for them to agree in *some* cases. What Payne has done here (and does elsewhere in his essay)[39] is to claim that there cannot *ever* be agreement, although he demonstrates only that there cannot *always* be agreement. But surely, if agreement among the legislators is a prerequisite of legislative intent, a person who wishes to claim that there is legislative intent in this or that specific case is not bound to claim that there is always intent in every case. It is true that some persons may have committed themselves to the view that there is *always* intent of the sort Payne is discussing;[40] his argument might shake them. But he is very far from having shown that there cannot sometimes be such intent, or even that there cannot often be such intent.

Consider next his supposition, shared without argument by Radin, Jones,

---

38. Payne, "The Intention of the Legislature in the Interpretation of Statutes," (cited above, note 27), p. 38 (emphasis added).

39. Payne, "The Intention of the Legislature," 101–2.

40. Perhaps such a view is implied by Crawford and Llewellyn. See note 15, above.

de Sloovère, and perhaps Landis, that in order for several legislators to have the same intention relative to the understanding of a general word in a statute, it is necessary for them to have had the same "mental images," at least relative to the instant case.[41] Payne argues:

> How can it be said that [the legislator] has any intention in respect of a particular covered by the general word which did not occur to his mind . . . ? [I]t would, I suggest, be a strange use of language to say that the user of such a general word "intends" it to apply to a particular that never occurred to his mind.[42]

Payne has only the vestige of a good point here. The behavior of a man who took Payne seriously could be extraordinary. Suppose that, needing a large number of ashtrays for an impending meeting in a building unfamiliar to me, I ask my assistant to scout around and bring back all the ashtrays he can find in the building. He comes back emptyhanded, saying the following: "I found a good many ashtrays, but naturally wanted to bring back only those you intended me to bring back. So, as I picked up each one, I asked myself—did he intend me to bring this ashtray back? Upon doing this, I realized in each case that it would certainly be a strange use of language to say that you 'intended' me to bring back that ashtray, as it was virtually certain that the thought of that ashtray had never occurred to you—after all, you had never even been in this building before. In the end, therefore, I found it most sensible to return without any."

Clearly, such behavior would be idiotic. But it is also true that my assistant could have erred at the opposite extreme. Suppose he had ripped built-in ashtrays off the walls of the building, snatched ashtrays from persons using

41. See Radin, "Statutory Interpretation," pp. 869–70. Landis is chary of this kind of talk, but his discussion of "determinates" implies a similar view. James M. Landis, "A Note on 'Statutory Interpretation'," *Harvard Law Review* 43 (1929–30): 886–93, at p. 889. For other examples of the view in question, see Harry Wilmer Jones, "Statutory Doubts and Legislative Intention," *Columbia Law Review* 40 (1940): 957–74, at p. 967; and Frederick J. de Sloovère, "Extrinsic Aids in the Interpretation of Statutes," *University of Pennsylvania Law Review* 88 (1939–40): 527–55, at pp. 533–38. Perhaps Frankfurter would also be sympathetic to this view; see Frankfurter, "Some Reflections on the Reading of Statutes."

42. Payne, "The Intention of the Legislature in the Interpretation of Statutes," p. 101. But he also says later:

> A statute is a formal document intended to warrant the conduct of judges and officials, and if any intention can be fairly ascribed to the legislature, it is that the statute should be applied to situations not present to the mind of its members (105)

The whole challenge lies, if one is to make sense of Payne's arguments, in understanding how the claims in these two sets of remarks are related to each other; but he does not enlighten us here. Perhaps he is moving toward the agency theory discussed below.

them and removed a hundred thousand ashtrays from a storage room. In each of these situations I might protest that I had not intended him to do that, and that he should have known better than to think I did. The ground for the latter claim, however, would not be that he should have realized that the thought of those particular ashtrays had never occurred to me; after all, he was already virtually certain of this. Rather, the ground would be that, given the circumstances, he should have understood that I did not need a hundred thousand ashtrays and that my interest in having ashtrays was not so pressing as to require him to rip them off walls, etc. It is true that I might say that the thought never occurred to me that there were any built-in ashtrays in the building; or, the thought never occurred to me that he would snatch ashtrays out of people's hands. Thus, I might react against the claim that I had intended x by making statements roughly in the form: "the thought of such a thing as x never occurred to me." But the point of this remark is not merely that the thought of such a thing as x had not occurred to me; there is also a clear suggestion that *if* such a thought had occurred to me I would have *excepted* such things as x.[43] Without this further suggestion, my remark would surely seem pointless.

The mere fact that the thought of such a thing as x hadn't occurred to me does not imply anything about what I did or did not intend. It follows that in our ashtray case the thought of this or that kind of ashtray, or the thought of getting ashtrays in this or that kind of circumstance, need not have occurred to me in order for me to have intended that my assistant get such ashtrays or get ashtrays under such circumstances. Payne, Radin and any others who have discussed legislative intent in terms of "mental images," "mental pictures," and "the contents of the mind of the legislator" have been fundamentally wrong in certain important respects. If, as the above discussion shows, a legislator voting for a bill need not actually have thought of each and every particular that he can reasonably be said to have intended the words of the bill to cover, nor thought of each and every *type* of particular, then the mere fact that two legislators have not thought of the same particulars or of particulars of the same types in connection with some general word in a bill shows neither

43. Note also that the key phrase is not that which Payne's remarks suggest: for, "such a thing as X" refers to a *type* of a particular rather than to a particular. (Furthermore, some of the types referred to were types of circumstances rather than types of ashtrays.)

Radin, and by implication Landis, may have had this in mind when discussing the "determinate" as the issue in litigation. They may, that is, have been referring to issue-types. More likely, they may have been counting issues in such a way that one and the same issue could appear in many cases. But if they were doing either, then Radin's talk about "mental images" and "pictures" becomes inappropriate, as Payne rightly recognizes and argues. See Payne, "The Intention of the Legislature in the Interpretation of Statutes," p. 99; see also Radin, "Statutory Interpretation," p. 887; Landis, "A Note on 'Statutory Interpretation'," p. 887.

that they disagreed nor that they agreed in their intention to have those particulars or particulars of those types covered by the bill. Of course, what a legislator did think of does make a difference. But what he did not think of does not make a difference *unless* he would have excepted it had he thought of it.

But how are we to *know* whether he would have excepted it? Supposing that we cannot interview him (or that, if we did, he and we might find it difficult to distinguish between his intention *then* and his decision *now*), would we not always be uncertain? Hägerström, in the course of arguing against certain appeals to the intention of the legislator, thinks so.[44] In an interesting discussion of the "unprovided for case," he concludes that in reality the decisive factor is only the degree to which the *interpreter's feelings of value* are shocked. If, for example, my assistant, while out gathering ashtrays for me, were to be shocked by the idea of snatching ashtrays from people currently using them, he will impute to me an intention not to have him do that, even though I had made no mention of such a case but had merely said "bring back all the ashtrays you can find."

But such results are not inevitable. My assistant may react differently. He may be a very crude fellow, or one who places a much greater importance on having ashtrays for the meeting than I do. In either case, *he* might not be disturbed at all by the thought of snatching ashtrays from people; but, knowing me, he might think: "That silly old fool *would* be shocked by this, so I'd better not do it." We can also imagine the reverse—that is, a case where the assistant *is* shocked, but, realizing that I would not be, steels himself to the task.

Imputing intentions may require a fair degree of intimacy with the person whose intentions are being considered. Even then, there may be circumstances in which the imputations would be highly uncertain. These two considerations are important—especially in dealing with the intentions of legislators vis-a-vis circumstances that, so far as we can tell, they did not contemplate or foresee. The interpreter of a statute may be remote in time, place, social stratum or background from many or all of the legislators who had a hand in enacting the statute. There may only be a small range of cases in which he can reasonably impute to them approval or disapproval* of various outcomes. But there will surely be such a range, provided that the inter-

---

44. Hägerström, *Inquiries into the Nature of Law and Morals*, pp. 82–83. For other discussion of this point see Harry Melvin Hart, Jr., and Albert M. Sacks, *The Legal Process: Basic Problems in the Making and Application of Law* (Tentative ed.), (Cambridge, Mass.: Harvard University Press, 1957), pp. 97–98, and Witherspoon, "Administrative Discretion to Determine Statutory Meaning: 'the Middle Road'," pp. 776–82.

*MacCallum's note: "wrong words." Eds.

preter is not completely ignorant of the beliefs and attitudes of these men. The *frequency* with which such imputations may be made depends upon the cases that arise; there may be many or few cases within the range of reasonable imputation.[45]

What, however, of cases where the uncontemplated and unforeseen things, circumstances, or types thereof are such that the legislator would not unhesitatingly have designated them by the general words he used? To return to the ashtray example, suppose that when I asked my assistant to bring back all the ashtrays he could find, it never occurred to me that he might run across some items that were for me not clearly ashtrays, but were enough like ashtrays to have made me hesitate over them.[46] If he ran across such items, neither he nor I might be clear about whether I had intended him to bring them back. Insofar as I was not certain whether they *were* ashtrays, I could not be certain that I had intended him to bring them back; insofar as I was not certain they *were not* ashtrays, I could not be certain that I had not intended him to bring them back. Thus, the question of whether I would have excepted them if I had thought of them may have no decisive answer.

A common move at this point is to claim that I had no intentions whatever in connection with such cases.[47] This is misleading. The occurrence of such a case may be an occasion for abandoning reliance upon what was intended; but the abandonment should not be justified by denying that one had any intentions at all in connection with the case; it should be justified simply by pointing out that the applicability of one's intentions to the instant case is not clear, and that appeal to intentions therefore does not afford guidance in the case. The undecidability is not due to limitations on our tools of investigation (e.g., that we do not have total recall); rather it is due both to the fact that there are limitations on the preciseness of the intentions a person can have, and to the fact that new experience can challenge the rationale of old classifications. But it is misleading in such circumstances to claim that we had no intentions whatsoever. This claim suggests something quite false—that there is no connection between the circumstances and our intentions—whereas, the whole

45. Perhaps it is worth pointing out that the imputation spoken of here is not what Cohen calls "legisputation." Julius Cohen, "Judicial 'Legisputation' and the Dimensions of Legislative Meaning," *Indiana Law Journal* 36 (1960–61): 414–23, at p. 418. While it agrees with "legisputation" in referring to probable legislative meaning, it concerns meaning at the time of enactment and not what the legislature would have thought if it had "the awareness of the problems that hindsight now permits." See also Bruncken, "Interpretation of Written Law," p. 135, and Charles P. Curtis, "A Better Theory of Legal Interpretations," *Vanderbilt Law Review* 3 (1949–50): 407–37, at p. 412.

46. As most everyone recognizes, this is the type of circumstance faced by the Court in *McBoyle* v. *United States,* 283 U.S. 25 (1930).

47. Cf. John Chipman Gray's oft-quoted remark in *The Nature and Sources of the Law,* 2d ed. (New York: The Macmillan Co., 1921), p. 173.

problem lies in the fact that there is a connection but one which is not clear enough to afford us guidance when we appeal to the intentions.

It is now timely to reconsider the crucial assumption on which all the arguments and counterarguments were based—the agreement that an intention vis-a-vis a bill shared by all the legislators in the majority voting for the bill would count as an intention of the legislature. As previously noted, one might argue that this agreement has only been provisional. One might claim that Radin, Payne and other skeptics stop here only because they believe they can, even on this assumption, show the impossibility of such a thing as an intention of a legislature.[48] But the examination of Payne's arguments shows the skeptical arguments to be insufficient. Thus, we are forced to confront the agreement in question, and consider its status. Is it only provisional? *Would* most or all of the skeptics retreat to some position behind it? What would this position be?

E. The path of further argument

The skeptic might argue that the widespread agreement about the conditions under which a legislature can have an intention was *unreasonable*. His grounds could be any or all of the following:

> 1. That not even the majority condition is taken seriously by a significant section of the legal community (viz., judges and administrators)—that even though legislative intent is possible and its occurrence not in every respect infrequent, conventional appeals to it are clearly fictional in the sense of being based upon wholly inadequate evidence of its presence.
> 2. That no other models of legislative intent could find serious support in legislative, judicial and administrative practices.
> 3. That all models in the end make the obviously unsound move of treating legislatures as human beings.
> 4. That, in view of the difficulty of using any of the models proffered to arrive at plausible accounts of what "legislative intent" could mean, there are no policy considerations sufficient to support continued use of the expression.

The first argument should be approached cautiously. Commentators using it generally exhibit a fatal tendency to assume that the majority condition discussed above is not merely a sufficient but also a necessary condition for legislative intent. They have failed to recognize that acceptance of weaker and perhaps even quite different conditions might be reasonable, and that, there-

---

48. The clearest case of this attitude is in Bruncken, "Interpretation of Written Law," p. 130.

fore, the common run of claims about legislative intent may not be so strikingly irresponsible or "fictional" after all.

But this defense merely calls in the second argument: *are* there any other such conditions? This is a difficult question. Support for the "literal truth" of claims that legislatures have *acted* comes from the citation of explicit legal rules (for example, constitutional ones) setting out the circumstances under which the behavior of legislators will count as an act by a legislature. It is true that even the rules for determining when a legislature has acted (such as rules determining the circumstances under which an "enacting" vote can be taken on a bill, the ways of casting and tallying votes, the proportion of affirmative votes needed for enactment) are sometimes difficult to interpret and apply; but legislators clearly go to great lengths to establish explicitly and precisely the conditions under which the legislature will be regarded as having enacted a statute. They have not, however, given any such formal and extended consideration to the conditions under which the legislature will be regarded as having an intention, except perhaps the intention to enact the statute itself and to use the words appearing in the statute. The acceptance by the legislators of a majority of affirmative votes as constituting (under certain conditions) the enactment of a statute, sheds no light whatever on what they would accept as constituting a legislative intent outside of an intent to enact the statute itself. There is no evidence, indeed, that any legislature has, for its own use, attempted to establish *formal* criteria for the determination of legislative intent vis-a-vis statutes other than the use of statements of intent somewhere within the statutes themselves.[49]

Although legislatures have not provided criteria for the determination of legislative intent, there are relevant judicial and administrative practices. Not only do judges and administrators regularly refer to "the intentions of the legislature," but, in various jurisdictions at various times, more or less regular use is made of "presumptions" as to the intentions of the legislature—e.g., that there is no intent to interfere with the common law unless explicitly stated. Use is also made of appeals to records of legislative proceedings as "evidence" of the intentions of the legislature.*

The third argument was that all models of legislative intent will in the end make the unsound move of treating legislatures as human beings. As shown earlier, the roots of this argument are very deep. We shall not pursue the matter further, except to suggest below some relevant analogies and disanal-

---

49. This is not surprising. One can imagine that authoritative expressions about legislative intent outside the individual statutes would fare no better before judges, administrators and the public than statutory preambles. They too would require "interpretation" if we were to take them seriously.

*MacCallum's note: "sum. sentence needed here." Eds.

ogies to legal treatments of persons and to suggest in closing some possible variations in our attitudes toward the issue.

The fourth argument was that, in view of the difficulties in arriving at plausible accounts of what "legislative intent" could amount to on any of the models put forward, there are no policy considerations sufficient to support continued use of the expression. Although considerations bearing on this argument will also be mentioned briefly at various stages of the discussion below, it will be raised again directly only at the end of the paper.

F. Models of legislative intent

The following discussion of models of legislative intent attempts to discover what support each can muster against the above arguments.

1. *The Majority Model.* Consider initially the following straightforward argument for the sufficiency of the majority model of legislative intent. On the supposition that judges and administrators believe themselves to have a legitimate interest in the intentions of the legislature, if there were any such intentions, they might argue as follows:

"The idea of a legislature intending *x* without *any* of its members, officers or agents intending *x* would hardly give us even a beginning for an acceptable account of the intentions of the legislature. But, if at least some member(s), officer(s) or agent(s) of the legislature must intend *x,* then which and how many? Given that our interest is in the intentions of the legislature concerning a statute enacted by it, we may start by considering the conditions under which the statement 'The legislature enacted the statute' is true. What, in short, counts as a legislature's enacting a statute?

"The important thing is to see what, in accordance with constitutional and legislative rules, results in and amounts to the enactment of a statute. Ordinarily this has to do with majorities of affirmative votes by the legislators, taken and tallied under specified conditions.[50] But, if such a coincidence in behavior (voting affirmatively) by a majority of the legislators is sufficient for and equivalent to saying that the *legislature* has acted (i.e., has enacted a piece of legislation), then a coincidence in the intentions of those very same legislators vis-a-vis the bill and their affirmative votes for it should be sufficient in determining what the *legislature* intended (if anything) by the act or relative to the act.

"The main principle behind our argument is as follows: When there is a group, organization or association recognized by a legal system as a unit for

---

50. Excluding executive endorsement or acquiescence (the expression "intention of the legislature" does not require us to consider them), and leaving open whether we would allow something to count as a statute if it were not subsequently enrolled or promulgated. Accounting for bicameral legislatures would, of course, complicate but not vitiate the argument.

the assignment of rights, powers, duties, etc. (e.g., the *legislature* has the legal capacity to legislate, and the legislators do not, either separately or collectively, *except* when acting in such a way that they constitute a legislature), certain activities on the part of officers, agents or employees of the organization will in certain circumstances be recognized at law as resulting in and amounting to acts of the organization. In such cases, it is reasonable to identify as the intention of the organization in so acting at least whatever intentions are shared by those of its officers, agents, etc., who have discretionary powers in determining or contributing to the determination of what the group does. This is a conventional approach to the intentions of corporations.[51] It should apply to legislatures as well."

From the viewpoint of judges and administrators, this hypothesized argument might seem reasonable. But do the actual practices of these officials support the majority model argued for? Anyone taking a close look at current judicial and administrative practices must conclude that these practices have only the slightest relationship to that model. While judges and administrators obviously utilize evidence of the intentions of various individual legislators, they make no serious attempts to discover the actual intentions of the voting majorities; further, our records of legislative proceedings are still not sufficient to support such an enterprise. There are presumptions galore about what, in the light of our records, the legislators must have been aware of and agreed with, but the realities of legislative processes are such that few of these presumptions are thought to be reliable *enough*.

This may persuade some commentators that courts and administrators generally have not been genuinely interested in the intentions of legislatures. But the behavior of judges and administrators vis-a-vis legislative intent would clearly be capricious and irresponsible only if they believed that the majority model set out necessary as well as sufficient conditions for the existence of legislative intent. There is no reason to suppose the judges and administrators believe this, nor did "their" argument above suppose it. Thus there is no good reason to believe that their behavior is either capricious or irresponsible until it is seen to be so in the light of a model plausibly supposed to be their model of the *minimal* conditions for the existence of legislative intent.

Of course, it may not be necessary to move immediately to searching for such a weaker model. Instead we may attempt to uphold the majority model, but restrict the scope of its legitimate application. The conventional move by commentators is to reject appeals to legislative intentions in favor of appeals to legislative purposes.[52] For these commentators, appeals to the former are appeals to the aims of the *details* of statutes, whereas appeals to the latter

51. See Gray, *The Nature and Sources of the Law,* p. 55.
52. This is characteristic of the writers cited in notes 4–7 above.

are appeals to the much more highly generalized purposes behind the statutes, taken as wholes.[53]

The motive behind such a move is obvious. It is an attempt to show that judicial and administrative practices do support the majority model of legislative intent if the applicability of the model is restricted to the more highly general intentions of the legislators.[54] The argument is that, in view of modern legislative processes, coincident purposes among the legislators regarding the highly general aims of a statute are more likely than coincident purposes regarding the specific aims of portions of the statute. Thus, special investigations of each legislator in the majority relative to such more "general" purposes are not needed.[55]

Is it a valid presumption that consensus among the legislators on various purposes of a statute is more likely in proportion to the generality of the purposes? A distinction must be drawn between a purpose that a legislator actually has, and a purpose that he is aware of as one he is supposed to have or is presumed to have. For, as one considers purposes of greater and greater generality, it becomes more and more likely—not so much that the legislators share those purposes—but rather that they are aware of them as purposes that others have, or as purposes that they themselves are presumed to have. One of Witherspoon's examples of such a general "purpose" is:

53. See, e.g., J. A. Corry, "Administrative Law and the Interpretation of Statutes," *University of Toronto Law Journal* 1 (1935–36): 286–312, at pp. 290–92:

> Even the majority who vote for complex legislation do not have any common intention *as to its detailed provisions.* Though the intention of the legislature is a fiction, the purpose or object of the legislation is very real. *No enactment is ever passed for the sake of its details; it is passed in an attempt to realize a social purpose.* It is what is variously called the aim and object of the enactment, the spirit of the legislation, the mischief and the remedy. (Emphasis added.)

It is not always clear when a commentator is in fact making this move. Talk about the (general) purposes of the statute sometimes seems to refer to what the statute was designed to achieve and sometimes to the purposes interpreters can find for the statute. See Radin, "A Short Way with Statutes," pp. 422–23, and pp. 406, 408, 411, and 419.

54. Witherspoon in fact extends this generality to consideration, not merely of specific aims vis-a-vis a particular statute, but also to whole programs of statute-making, and even to the aims of the legislative process itself, as seen in the light of the traditional functions of legislatures. See Witherspoon, "Administrative Discretion to Determine Statutory Meaning," pp. 758, 795–805, 831–32.

55. Another argument sometimes made in support of the restriction is that highly general aims are more important to the legislators themselves than specific aims. Cf. Witherspoon, "Administrative Discretion to Determine Statutory Meaning," pp. 790, 812, 827. See also Hart & Sacks, *The Legal Process,* p. 1285, where the authors say that "the probative force of materials from the internal legislative history of a statute varies in proportion to the *generality* of its bearing upon the purpose of the statute or provision in question" (emphasis added). They are here seemingly appealing to both of the above considerations.

> To have the statutory formula so administered as to avoid specific procedural or substantive evils collateral to the main purposes of the statute: e.g., undue federal intrusion into matters normally committed to resolution by state authority.[56]

It is easy to imagine a legislator knowing that he is supposed or presumed to have this purpose or that others have it, but it is also easy to imagine him not having it—even though he votes for the legislation in question. Some commentators, realizing that more legislators are likely to be *aware* of such purposes than are aware of the specific purposes of the details of the legislation in question, have either (i) too facilely assumed that being aware of the purpose is equivalent to having it, or (ii) too facilely assumed that silence in the face of knowledge that one may possibly be presumed to share a certain purpose is a good sign that one actually does share the purpose. In fact, there seems little reason to believe that the generality of the purpose alone much increases the confidence with which we can say that the voting majority has it.

It is not much easier to learn about the general purposes of legislators than to learn about the specific intentions of legislators. Thus, even if we look only at general purposes, current judicial and administrative practices are insufficient to support the majority model. We must search for another model of legislative intent which comports more closely with judicial and administrative behavior.

2. *The Agency Model.* It is possible that judges and administrators use an agency model of legislative intent. This model recognizes that legislatures delegate certain responsibilities (such as filling in the statutory details) to various persons (legislative draftsmen, committee chairmen, judges, administrators), and that this may justify appealing to the intentions of these persons as the intentions of the legislature regarding the aims of statutes or the details thereof.

Few commentators have explicitly appealed to the agency model, but several have touched on it. Driedger appears to identify the intention of the legislature with the intentions of the draftsmen. The competent draftsman

> has in his mind a complete legislative scheme and he attempts to give expression to that scheme in a logical and orderly manner; every provision in the statute must fit into that scheme, and the scheme is as complete as he can conceive it.
>
> It is this legislative scheme that should be regarded as the purpose, object, intent, spirit, of the Act.[57]

56. Witherspoon, "Administrative Discretion to Determine Statutory Meaning," pp. 799–800.

57. Driedger, *The Composition of Legislation*, p. 161. See also Bruncken, *Interpretation of Written Law*, p. 130.

The following remark by Judge Learned Hand suggests identifying the intentions of the legislature with the intentions of legislative committees. He says:

> [Courts] recognize that while members deliberately express their personal position upon the general purposes of the legislation, as to the details of its articulation they accept the work of the committees; so much they delegate because legislation could not go on in any other way.[58]

A remark by de Sloovère, taken in isolation, suggests turning in quite a different direction—viz., to the interpreter, or at least to a class of interpreters. He says:

> The only legislative intention, whenever the statute is not plain and explicit, is to authorize the courts to attribute a meaning to a statute within the limitations prescribed by the text and by the context. . . . In other words, a single meaning which the text will reasonably bear must, if genuine, be considered not as the conclusion which the legislature would have arrived at, *but one which the legislature by the text has authorized the courts to find.*[59]

These remarks suggest that the legislature delegates certain responsibilities to other persons in connection with statutes, and in doing so, the legislature exhibits its intention to rely on the judgment and discretion of these persons concerning how to achieve what the legislature wants the statute to achieve. Consequently, the judgment of these persons, having been authorized by the legislature, may stand for the judgment of the legislature. These persons now have somewhat, if not actually, the status of agents of the legislature.[60] Thus, our discovery of what these persons intended in attempting to carry out the assignment of the legislature (e.g., to draft a bill that would, in their judgment, achieve what the legislature wanted to achieve; to interpret the language

58. *SEC* v. *Collier,* 76 F.2d 939, 941 (2d Cir. 1935). At least one commentator agrees that Judge Hand's statement here implies agency. See Johnstone, "An Evaluation of the Rules of Statutory Interpretation," p. 14.

59. Fredrick J. de Sloovère, "Preliminary Questions in Statutory Interpretation," *New York University Law Quarterly Review* 9 (1932): 407–28, at p. 415. (Emphasis added.) See also Curtis, "A Better Theory of Legal Interpretations," p. 425; and, in comment on Curtis' view, Charles E. Clark, "Special Problems in Drafting and Interpreting Procedural Codes and Rules," *Vanderbilt Law Review* 3, (1949–50): pp. 494–95, 503, 506. But Sloovère clearly disclaims that the result of such authorization accords with any supposed legislative intention.

60. "An agent . . . is one who acts as a conduit pipe through which legal relations flow from his principal to another. Agency is created by a juristic act by which one person (the principal) gives to another (the agent) the power to do something for *and in the name of* the principal so as to bind the latter directly." Paton, *A Textbook of Jurisprudence,* p. 285 (emphasis added).

of the bill so as, in their judgment, to achieve what the legislature wanted to achieve) is a discovery of intentions that the legislature stood behind, wished us to attend to, wished us to regard as authoritative as their own—indeed, wished us to regard *as* their own. These intentions may therefore be taken as, and in fact are, the intentions of the legislature.

The agency model *would* render rational the present "investigations" of judges and administrators into legislative intent, and it would do this without reliance on so many presumptions about the significance of the silence of individual legislators. Investigations of the intentions of "agents" would be sufficient to establish (because they would be equivalent to) the intentions of the legislature. However, the agency model is extremely perilous. It not only requires us to consider whether any of its variations are persuasively similar to typical agency situations, but it confronts us with difficult problems concerning agency itself and in particular concerning the reasonableness of identifying the will of the agent with the will of his principal. Consider the following:

(a) If the legislature is to be thought of as the principal, we presumably would need to know how to identify the actions and intentions of this principal. But, what model of the *latter* are we to use? We would need to feel at home with some *other* model of legislative intention and purpose before we could get on with establishing the plausibility of this new model. Presumably, this earlier model would be the majority model. But the adequacy of this model has not yet been decisively established.

(b) Even within the traditions of agency the proposal that the actions and judgment of an agent be taken for the actions and judgment of his principal is open to charges of fictionalizing every bit as severe as the initial charges concerning the intentions of legislatures (and by way of them, concerning the nature of corporate personalities).[61] For example, as with the initial controversy, there would be difficulties about whether analogies sufficiently strong to support a claim of identity could be found between the relationship of a principal to his own acts and his relationship to the acts of his agent.[62] Also there will be a worry similar to our earlier worry about the *explicitness* of the legal rules supporting the claims made—that is, a worry about the character of the "juristic act" by which a person designates someone as his agent, and about the degree of explicitness needed in such a "bestowal" of power.[63]

61. Cf. Oliver Wendell Holmes, *Collected Legal Papers* (New York: Harcourt, Brace and Company, 1921), p. 49.

62. Cf. Holmes, *Collected Legal Papers,* pp. 52–53, where Holmes is patently exploring precisely this.

63. Cf. Paton, *A Textbook of Jurisprudence,* p. 287.

(c) Finally, and closely connected with this last point, each variation of the agency-model—delegation to committee, to courts, etc.—would have to be examined separately in order to discover the justifiability of saying that such a specific "bestowal" of power had actually been made by the legislature.

The strongest case for the bestowal of such power could surely be made in the case of legislative reliance upon draftsmen and committee chairmen. In view of the realities of legislative proceedings, it is certainly plausible to say that legislatures go very far in relying on the judgment and discretion of such persons.[64] When it comes to the interpreters of statutes such as judges and administrators, the claim that legislatures have bestowed such power seems highly dubious. Hägerström, for example, gives such a claim short shrift. He says:

> Such a general authorization cannot usually be shown to exist. It is a mere fiction motivated by desire to defend the will-theory, and it may be compared with similarly motived fictions concerning customary law as the general will.[65]

It should be noted, too, that Hägerström is here talking about a well-hedged and limited authorization.

One might counter, however, by claiming that the authorization need not be explicit. In the law of agency, after all, the authorization is not always explicit either—as in instances of so-called "agency of necessity." [66] It would surely be a matter of "necessity" that the best judgment of judges and administrators be relied upon by legislatures. But this argument appears to go too far. We would not want in any wholesale way to hold legislatures responsible for what judges and administrators make out of statutes.

So much, then, for various models of legislative intent and for the justifiability of *de novo* introduction of the use of such models. We have seen that one strongly justified model of such intentions (the majority model) finds little serious support in current judicial and administrative investigations of the intentions of legislatures. We have also seen that the model fitting these investigations best (the agency model) is also the most difficult to justify. But, while the arguments on behalf of either model cannot be decisive, neither are they negligible. In the end our use of either or both of the models may depend simply upon how many ragged edges we are willing to tolerate in the conceptual framework we use to approach legal problems; or, alternatively, our use

---

64. Cf. Joseph P. Witherspoon, "Administrative Discretion to Determine Statutory Meaning: 'The Low Road'," *Texas Law Review* 38 (1959–60): 392–438, at p. 430. It should be noted, however, that the work of draftsmen and committee chairmen has no legal effect until endorsed by the legislature. This is a striking *dis*analogy with the customary situation in agency.

65. Hägerström, *Inquiries into the Nature of Law and Morals,* p. 93.

66. See Paton, *A Textbook of Jurisprudence,* p. 287.

may depend, as will be suggested below, on how far we are willing to go in developing our legal institutions in such a way as to eliminate these ragged edges.

G. The significance of model-entrenchment

Our exploration of the justifiability of talk about legislative intentions cannot stop here. The "realism" of such talk must be examined not only from the standpoint of the reasonableness of *introducing* such talk in light of our present institutions and practices; it must also be examined from the standpoint of how the reasonableness of such talk is supported by the fact that it is already a well-established part of the legal environment. That is, one should consider whether the established use of *references* to legislative intent does not itself produce conditions under which the references become more reasonable as the practice of making them becomes entrenched.

Quite apart from any consideration of whether starting the practice was a good idea in the first place, once it *has* been started it provides part of the institutional background against which legislators recognize themselves to be acting when proposing, investigating, discussing, and voting for bills. For example, all legislators now understand that views of the intentions of the legislature may well be formed in the light of certain standard presumptions (e.g., that there is no intent to interfere with the common law unless explicitly stated) and "investigations" (e.g., of debates and committee reports on the bill). If the legislators have a capacity to contribute to the materials and to rebut the presumptions they know will be used by judges and administrators as indicia of the intentions of the legislature, their behavior will influence what the intentions of the legislature can reasonably be said to be.

At present, judicial and administrative uses of materials and presumptions are not always clear or predictable enough to provide a guide for the legislators. But one *can* describe circumstances in which the picture would be much clearer. Courts and administrators could establish much greater regularity in their use of preparatory materials and of "presumptions" concerning legislative intent—a regularity sufficient to enable trained persons to predict with reasonable accuracy what the outcomes of these uses would be in specific cases.[67] Furthermore, legislatures could control the issuing of preparatory materials with a view to their use in just such ways by judges and administrators. In such circumstances, judicial and administrative investigations of the "in-

---

67. Cf. Frank E. Horack, "Cooperative Action for Improved Statutory Interpretation," *Vanderbilt Law Review* (1949–50): 382–94, at p. 387; Herbert Mayo, "The Interpretation of Statutes," *Australian Law Journal* 29 (1955–56): 204–23; Jackson, "The Meaning of Statutes: What Congress Says or What the Court Says," pp. 537–38. And, for an extreme view, see Helen Silving, "A Plea for a Law of Interpretation," *University of Pennsylvania Law Review* 98 (1949–50): pp. 499–529, at p. 512.

tentions of the legislature" would surely look more realistic and reasonable than they do today. Even today, however, circumstances provide *some* reason, although perhaps not *enough* reason, to say that realistic references to legislative intent can be made. Even now these references are made in an institutional environment which to some extent sustains their reasonableness.[68]

Conclusions

We have proposed several models of legislative intent and have examined (1) whether judges and administrators actually could be regarded as taking any of them seriously, and (2) whether they would be justified in taking any of them seriously. As predicted, the results of this examination are not conclusive. No one model of legislative intent is either so strongly or so weakly supported as to make its use either unproblematic or absurd. This is not surprising, given that the controversy about the intentions of legislatures has gone on for so long. But it is an important result to reach and to substantiate. We too often continue to demand clear-cut and decisive answers in the face of facts that simply will not support such answers, thus perpetuating controversy (because there always *is* something to be said for the other side) and rendering ourselves ineffective in dealing with the matters at hand. Our detailed discussion of the controversy over the existence and discoverability of legislative intent enables us to understand, for example, the inappropriateness of treating it only as a straight-forward controversy over facts.* Instead of continuing to ask only—*Are* legislatures capable of intent?—we should also shift to such questions as the following:

(a) Are there any policy considerations sufficient to justify continuance of

---

68. Notice in particular how present practices strengthen the temptation of all participants to treat legislatures as persons. When attempting to discover the intentions of a person vis-a-vis an action of his, we would think it helpful to be privy to his deliberations (if any) on whether to engage in that action. On analogy, when attempting to discover the intentions of a legislature vis-a-vis a statute, we obviously think it helpful to be privy to *its* deliberations on whether to enact the statute. Clearly, insofar as judges and administrators appeal to proceedings on the floor of the house, they are appealing to the deliberations of the legislature (as well as to the deliberations of the legislators). This is just what one would do, if he could, when attempting to learn more about the intentions of any creature. Furthermore, insofar as the investigator thinks that being privy to such deliberations would be helpful, it is not because he supposes that the picture gained will be clear, unequivocal, and decisive. Deliberations of individuals on important acts may well be rehearsals of pros and cons quite as indefinite in character as the proceedings of many legislative deliberations.

*MacCallum's marginal note to these last few words: "Much more discussion needed here, e.g., 'The question is not really whether something is the case. The question is rather largely about what is to *count* as that thing's being the case. It is typical of such questions as this that they do not have open and shut answers short of stipulation. The danger to be avoided is that such stipulation will be high-handed and arbitrary. Thus, . . . '." Eds.

references to legislative intent in view of the difficulties exposed? What, after all, *hangs* on whether the references are continued? This is essentially an inquiry into the *relevance* of appeals to legislative intent—an inquiry that has not been embarked upon here. But it is an inquiry given a new twist by what we have shown. The question is no longer simply: (i) Supposing that there is a legislative intent, what hangs on appealing to it? It is rather: (ii) Does enough hang on such appeals to make their continuance worthwhile even in the face of the difficulties exposed?

But, we may also ask: (b) Is it worth our while in terms of the ideological and practical importance of such appeals, to seek institutional changes strengthening the analogies between these appeals and appeals to intentions elsewhere in law and in life generally (this being the same for us as increasing the rationality of the appeals)? It is important to notice that the difficulties exposed above are not unavoidable facts of life; legislatures and the institutional environments in which they operate are, in a sense, our creatures and can be altered. Depending upon the model of legislative intent one has in mind (and I should emphasize that only the most obvious ones have been examined here), one may seek to bring the appeals closer to the conditions under which we attribute intentions to corporations, to principals via the intentions of their agents, or, above all, to individual men. The institutional changes accomplishing this could amount to such diverse measures as the fixing of formal limits on what may count as good evidence of legislative intent on the one hand, and alterations in the operating procedures of legislatures on the other.*

---

*Filed with MacCallum's "personal copy" were two carefully annotated documents: (1) a copy of the opinion in *Key Buick Company, Petitioner* v. *Commissioner of Internal Revenue, Respondent* (68 United States Tax Court Reports 1977), 178–84, referring to PL 94-559, 90 Stat. 2641, 19 October 1976, which amended 42 U.S.C. sec. 1988; and (2) a portion of *The Congressional Record,* 95th Congress (1977–78), containing a statement by Senator Allen introducing S. 1610, May 10, 1977, "Taxpayer's Attorney Fee Award Act of 1977," intended (i.e., intended by its sponsors, Senators Allen and Cranston) to reverse the holding by the Tax Court on May 16, 1977 in (1). S. 1610 was not passed by the 95th Congress and was not reintroduced in the 96th Congress. Nonetheless, the points that intrigued MacCallum relating to legislative intent are plain in the opinion and in the remarks of Senator Allen, and the finding of this carefully annotated material shows that a dozen or so years after this paper was published—at least until his stroke in the fall of 1977—MacCallum was still thinking about the matter of legislative intent. Eds.

2 Censorship in the Arts

Governments can interfere in many ways with the circulation of art. Speaking narrowly, "censorship" labels only the most notorious of the ways, but there are others. As private citizens have been clever enough to discover, there are also informal and non-governmental ways of interfering; these, insofar as governments must either tolerate or forbid them, also raise issues of governmental policy.

Differences among these ways are important. If the government is going to interfere directly, criminal prosecution *after* initial distribution or exhibition of the works is preferable to a flat prohibition on distribution or production ("prior restraint," or "censorship" in the narrow sense) because only in the former case will the crucial decisions necessarily be made in an open and public forum (a court) and in accordance with well-established standards of evidence and procedure. The disadvantages of prior restraint, on the other hand, have been notorious at least since the time Milton argued them in the *Areopagitica,* when he attacked the English licensing laws of 1643. These laws continued in force royal and Star Chamber decrees forbidding unlicensed printing, and established a committee of twenty licensers. Milton saw this, and we now see it, as one of the more obnoxious and uncontrolled forms of public regulation.

On the other hand, we are sometimes urged to abandon public regulation altogether in favor of such informal sanctions as ostracism or the loss of public reputation. This advice is usually offered on the ground that it is better for people to manage their own affairs than to cry for government intervention at every hint of an injured sensibility. When people *do* attempt to manage the matter in this way, however, they turn very readily to proliferating "citizen's committees" who visit and perhaps picket distributors and exhibitors of the offending works, expressing their displeasure and occasionally threatening some kind of organized, although still non-governmental, coercive action.

36

Thus we have letters to the editor protesting the booking policies of a local theater. But we also have pickets patrolling in protest against a performance of "Showboat" or a performance by Kirsten Flagstad, and committees of mothers visiting the neighborhood druggist to examine his stock of paperback novels and perhaps to threaten some kind of retaliation "if these racks aren't cleaned up." The latter actions raise disputes about how far governments should tolerate such private coercive measures.

Aside from these important disputes about *what form* control should take, there is fundamental disagreement about whether there should be *any control at all*. This, too, raises an issue of governmental policy, viz., whether the only task of government in this area should be to "protect" the circulation of any and all works of art. Because we will make no headway in discussing desirable *forms* of control until we at least agree that there ought to be *some* control, I shall discuss especially this latter issue. It is complex enough to occupy us for some time.

We have come to expect discussions of this matter to be conducted in an atmosphere of inflammatory charges and counter-charges. This is unfortunate, and we might at least do what we can to promote a calm and judicial atmosphere. My thesis, however, is that our difficulties run much more deeply than those we experience in remaining dispassionate in debate; they run also to dimly perceived but unresolved disagreements and indecisiveness about what the problems at bottom really are, about what ought to count when we discuss these problems, and about what the answers are to some admittedly subsidiary questions.

It is not surprising to find these difficulties latent and unrecognized in some of the more superficial popular discussions, but it is disturbing to find them latent and at least seemingly unrecognized in even the most sober and exhaustive public discussions. Consider, for example, the 1956 Kefauver Interim Report entitled "Obscene and Pornographic Literature and Juvenile Delinquency." [1] Here is a summing up of the results of a lengthy investigation by a Senate subcommittee into one aspect of the censorship problem, an aspect which might be thought clear if anything is clear, viz., the injurious effects of viewing "hard-core" pornography. The investigation was conducted by responsible and intelligent public officials, and although any such investigation is subject to political pressures which may warp its outcome, it is reasonable to suppose that these officials did their best to provide the public with a straightforward account of what they found. Yet the Report offers prime examples of equivocation and confusion about the scope of the problems at hand. Such equivocation and confusion can only obscure public vision when we come to ask even the limited but practical question, "What shall we do

1. Senate Report number 2381, 84th Congress, 2nd Session 1956.

about 'hard-core' pornography?" That this feature of the Report has not been widely observed is especially disturbing, for it may indicate that we already had our minds made up about "hard-core" pornography, and that no one looked at the Report very carefully because the investigation was only shadow-play. But if we do not take the trouble to get matters clear even where most people agree that some sort of interference is needed, we will be ill-equipped to deal clear-sightedly with other areas where the value of interference is more disputed.

Consider the Report. On page 4 we read:

> Once again we think it is important to reiterate that the type of material with which the subcommittee concerned itself is not as many persons might mistakenly believe, a hetrogeneous collection of off-color jokes. The quantity and quality of the material beggars description; it is wanton, depraved, nauseating, despicable, demoralizing, destructive *and capable of poisoning any mind at any age.* (Italics mine.)

The italicized claim makes the scope of the problem appear enormous. But *none* of the expert testimony quoted in the Report supports that claim,[2] and it is directly contradicted on page 63, where it is said:

> There would be few deleterious psychological effects of pornographic literature if this were exposed to people who are normally developed and have been able to develop normal inhibitions, repressions, and controls.[3]

As the Report eventually makes clear (and as its title suggested in the first place), it is concerned primarily with the effects of viewing such materials on persons "of adolescent age, which from our point of view is a very unstable period of life." But even here the Report is not clear enough. This is perhaps best illustrated by Senator Kefauver's own summary of its findings in *Federal Probation,* a periodical published by the Administrative Office of the United States Courts.[4] On page 7 of this summary, Senator Kefauver, in a master-piece of equivocation, states clearly only that the findings of the investigation show that viewing pornography leads to anti-social behavior *in adolescents who are already emotionally disturbed.* (My italics) He does declare also that "large numbers of relatively emotionally normal children can develop harmful attitudes because of the pornographers;" but he makes no straightforward claim about any relationships between "harmful attitudes" and anti-social behavior.

2. See especially pp. 11 and 13 of the Report for the strongest of the genuinely expert testimony.

3. If this is so, then what *is* pornography? See below.

4. *Federal Probation* 24.4 (December 1960): 3.

The production of "harmful attitudes" alone may, of course, be important. Nevertheless, the relevance of this effect is strikingly different from the relevance of the production of anti-social behavior, as I hope to show below. Further, the fact that viewing pornography often leads to anti-social behavior in adolescents who are already emotionally disturbed is important. If this is the only effect, however, the scope of the problem takes on a different look, and different avenues of solution may come into view. It is all the more important, therefore, to notice that in an equivocating way the Kefauver Report claims, hints at, and implies much more.

This fuzziness, appearing in public documents produced by respected public officials, is not only a symptom of existing difficulty; it is likely to produce a greater difficulty in future discussions. It both manifests and encourages blindness to crucially important considerations. When one notes that it concerns only the effects of viewing "hard-core" pornography, the challenge may appear staggering; surely the issues will be more complex and the confusion greater when dealing with works more clearly having serious aesthetic intention or worth, or with works less generally thought offensive.

I

As the Kefauver Interim Report shows, we are often insufficiently clear about the *scope* of the problems at hand. This is dangerous in part because it affects our search for, and our choice of, remedial measures. Protecting emotionally disturbed children is one thing; protecting all children is another; protecting both children and adults is yet another. Indeed, our carelessness in answering the question, "Who needs protection?" is closely related to the fruitlessness of many debates about censorship. Too many people have approached the problem with the assumption that if anybody needs protection from certain materials, then everyone must be denied access to the materials. This, of course, is false, although the importance of its being false may be difficult to make clear to people who are thinking only of "hard-core" pornography. There are significant differences between blanket restrictions placed on all members of the public, and restrictions which operate selectively against only certain classes of persons, e.g., children (as in movies "for adults only"), members of a laity (as in permission from a church hierarchy to read heretical works), or persons not professionally concerned with the materials in question (as in restrictions on the use of archives of pornography in government and university libraries). The more narrowly our restrictions are placed, the easier they may sometimes be to justify. It follows that if we make our restrictions needlessly broad in these cases we involve ourselves in fruitless and unrewarding debates. Obviously, such needless debates have occurred and still occur too often.

The situation is not simple, however. Depending upon whom we wish to protect, strikingly different techniques of control may be possible or required if one is to be effective. Consider dealing with such diverse materials as books sold on the open market, exhibitions viewable only at theaters and art galleries, and television and radio shows beamed into an indefinite number of private homes. If we are to protect even a small class of persons in some of these cases, we may find it necessary to make certain materials inaccessible to a vast number of other persons as well. When we are convinced that this is the case, we may believe it simply scholastic to strive for precise answers to the question "Whom are we protecting?" Further, we may suppose (as we do most often with pornography) that if anyone needs protection from certain materials, then no one can really have a moral right to access to those materials, because the materials must be such that no legitimate purpose could be served by distributing and viewing them.

Both these conclusions seem to me to be mistaken. Concerning the first, notice that the "necessity" of rendering certain materials inaccessible to many in order to protect a few is most often solely a function of our ingenuity and imaginativeness. Even where overprotection seems necessary, we should constantly remind ourselves that it *is* overprotection, and that we might be able to avoid it if we were clever enough.

This, however, raises the second issue: why should we *want* to avoid it if the materials in question must be such that no legitimate purpose could be served by making them accessible to anyone, even to persons not in need of protection from them?

We must recognize at the start that the very characterization by the Kefauver Subcommittee of the materials they were investigating as "hard-core" pornography was an attempt to suggest that no legitimate purpose could be served by the distribution and viewing of such items. Since we are concerned with censorship in the arts, I think we may correctly assume that "hard-core pornography" is a label intended at least to relegate what is so labelled to the class of works without either aesthetic worth or aesthetic intention. We would be wise in this case always to ask whether what is so labelled actually deserves such treatment. But we would be wise also to recognize that there may be some public confusion about whether the label refers primarily to the *intention* and *content* of the work, or rather to its *effect*. In the former case, "hard-core" pornography would presumably not be intended as a work of art; in the latter case, it might very well have aesthetic intention, and indeed aesthetic merit as well. Most important, in the latter case one could claim a legitimate interest in the distribution of the work even while admitting that the effect of the work might be "pornographic" for some persons, i.e., arouse prurient interests in them.

This consideration serves to show that censorship issues may in the end be immensely complex. We may in fact find that in most cases where the issues arise there are both reasons *for* and reasons *against* interfering with the works in question. We should not allow emotively laden labels such as "hard-core pornography" to obscure our awareness of this. Nor should we allow them to obscure our awareness of something else at once more subtle and profound: not only are there most often both reasons for and reasons against interference, but even when we find that the reasons on one side *outweigh* the reasons on the other, we should not thereby suppose that the latter reasons can safely be put out of sight and out of mind. To do this would be to put controversies about censorship on a level with games of tug-of-war; it would be as though we had, in the end, to declare the side with stronger arguments to be the "winner," and as though once this were done, the game would be over and the losers would have to pack up and go home. Such a view might be reasonable and even necessary in making short run decisions about censorship, but in the long run it would be poison. It would blind us to the fact that our decisions on such matters most often involve sacrifices as well as gains. We would thus be blocked off from any realistic understanding of what we have done in making decisions—that we may have lost something as well as gained something. We would lose appreciation of the full effect of our decisions upon the character of our communities.

This latter point is of immense importance. One reason treatments of censorship so often seem both confused and confusing is that in our partisanship we have failed to admit the full effects, negative as well as positive, of the solutions we advocate. Why not face fully the fact that our solutions most often involve sacrifices as well as gains? This would lead us to take a more appropriate attitude toward what we are doing; namely, influencing the development in our communities of ideals of social and personal life by making choices from among already existing ideals found in conflict. If we are unwilling to admit that censorship poses problems resulting from a conflict among ideals of social and personal life, all of which we may cherish, we will remain blind. The task is to get clear what ideals are involved and how they get involved. If we complete this task, we will at least be in a position to act responsibly, because we will know more fully what hangs on our decisions.

II

Some ideals are common to many communities, and some are characteristic of only one community; alternatively, one might say instead that some ideals are those of a larger community (e.g., "the western nations"), and others are characteristic of subcommunities within the larger one. They are commonly expressed in highly general terms such as those appearing below, and, for example, those appearing in certain passages of the United States Constitution (e.g., "due process of law"). The terms acquire strong emotive force, and under cover of this emotive force, changes in their descriptive content are often made and conflicts resolved. The histories of the terms "moral" and "religious" afford prime examples of this.

In attempts to specify and clarify the descriptive content of the ideals, further concepts—sometimes called "satellite concepts"—are developed and occasionally later discarded. In censorship discussions, two prominent satellite concepts are "obscenity" and "subversion." One could even, when thinking of the United States as part of the Anglo-American community, regard "due process of law" as a satellite concept relative to the ideals of that larger community. Naturally, the satellite concepts sometimes develop their own satellites; for example, "prurient interest" and "patent offensiveness" are satellite concepts of criminal obscenity.

There are thus available various levels of appeal to community values. One could deal with censorship entirely in terms of such obviously satellite concepts as "obscenity" and "due process of law."[5] Alternatively, one could move directly to the more general ideals of which the satellites are attempted specifications and clarifications. I have adopted the latter course, both in order to give my remarks more general application, and to free myself to evaluate and criticize certain satellite concepts. There is, of course, danger in talking on a level where the emotive rather than the descriptive force of one's words plays a large role—a danger not so much of polemics as of vacuity. But, for the reasons just stated, the venture must sometimes be made.

The involvement of such general ideals in censorship issues may be revealed by assessing the relevance of various claims about the benefits and dangers of such restrictive practices.

To discover the relevant possible *benefits* of interfering with the circulation of works of art, one should ask: How can the unhindered circulation of movies, books, paintings, etc.,[6] injure the members of a community? Answers to this question, however, need to be sorted out by the following more specific questions:

5. Relative to the United States, this has recently been done with great clarity and persuasiveness by Louis Henkin in "Morals and the Constitution: The Sin of Obscenity," *Columbia Law Review* 63 (1963): 391–414.

6. Not all of which may merit the partly honorific title "work of art," or even the partly honorific title "art," but all of which must be considered at the start. These are clearly the general types of materials with which we should be concerned. Distinctions based on aesthetic merit or on meritorious intention will be noted in the appropriate places. I do not discuss how such distinctions should be made, however, nor am I especially qualified to do so. They are undeniably important, but I think it unwise to permit any account of censorship in the arts to rest solely upon partly honorific distinctions no matter how well founded.

1. Can the circulation of these materials lead to anti-social behavior?

2. Can it lead to morally or religiously blameworthy thoughts, or
to behavior which is blameworthy even though not clearly anti-
social?

3. Can it lead to yet other harmful effects, such as emotional
disturbances or the loss of chances for personal happiness or
fulfillment?

4. Are there any significant differences among answers to questions 1, 2, and 3 regarding works having aesthetic worth, those
having only aesthetic intention, and those having neither?

First, the relevance of these questions; then some problems connected with
attempts to answer them:

Question 1. This question focusses on anti-social behavior, i.e., behavior
which violates the rights or interests of persons other than the actor. There is
no real problem about the relevance of such behavior. If unhindered circulation of certain books, movies, etc. raises the incidence of behavior violating
human rights or interests—if, for example, it raises the incidence of unpro-
voked violence, theft, or wanton recklessness—this is surely a good reason
for interfering with that circulation. Only two general cautions are needed.
First, we should notice that the reasons for interference thus provided may be
insufficiently strong to countervail other considerations. One should at least
ask in each specific case what must be done in order to interfere with the
materials, and what may be lost by the interference. The importance of either
of these may outweigh the importance of the anti-social behavior led to by the
circulation of the materials.

Secondly, one should recognize that because our notions of human rights
and interests have changed from time to time and may continue to change,
our view of what behavior violates those rights and interests also has changed
and may continue to do so. This is important because as these changes are
encouraged or resisted within a community, divergent opinions on the subject
will be reflected in disagreements about which books, movies, paintings, etc.,
could possibly have directly injurious effects upon the community if their free
circulation were permitted. For example, if one person disagrees with another
on whether warfare should be condoned or homosexuality tolerated, he may
differ with the other in his identifications of offending works, i.e., works
whose circulation "leads to" or raises the incidence of offending behavior.

Disagreements of this latter sort are undoubtedly at the bottom of much
controversy over censorship. There is no easy way of resolving the disagreements, but one should remain sensitive to the role they play. One should also
notice that if he is himself confused or indecisive about what human rights or

interests are or ought to be, he will be confused or indecisive about what does or ought to count as anti-social behavior.

The very occurrence of divergent opinions on human rights and interests raises yet another issue: the possibility of a kind of anti-social behavior which assuredly may be produced by the circulation of various works, but which may not seem relevant in determining governmental policy toward that circulation.

It is the third of three ways the circulation of various works might lead to anti-social behavior. The first is by direct viewing, which may intensify the impulses leading to such behavior. This possible effect figured importantly in the Kefauver investigation although, unfortunately, the anti-social behavior in question was not sufficiently distinguished from behavior which was simply degenerate, immoral, or "naughty" (the importance of such distinctions will emerge in the discussions of questions 2 and 3). Nevertheless, the Subcommittee did hear testimony concerning the connection between the commission of certain brutal crimes and the prior viewing by the criminal (generally a juvenile) of various pornographic materials. We are all familiar with such reports, and with reports of how criminally violent behavior depicted in comic books or on the television screen has "led to" juvenile crimes.

The Kefauver Subcommittee also heard testimony involving a second way in which the circulation of various materials may lead to anti-social behavior, viz., in the effects of unhindered distribution upon persons in search of standards of behavior (e.g., children). Unhindered distribution was thought by some witnesses to serve as a sign to those in search of standards of behavior that whatever is implicitly or explicitly endorsed in the works is at least tolerated by the community. If what is so "endorsed" includes anti-social behavior, (the story went) this will encourage indulgence in such behavior. Again, one is faced with the problem of verifying these claims; and again it is important to distinguish claims about anti-social behavior from claims about behavior which may simply be immoral, degenerate, or "naughty." Concerning the general production of offensive behavior, some of which may be anti-social, such claims are generally thought to have some plausibility. Surely the protests by the N.A.A.C.P. against "Uncle Tom" characterizations of Negroes and the protests of some groups in the past against the characterization of Shylock in the *Merchant of Venice* have been based not only on the belief that these characterizations were offensive to Negroes and Jews, but also on the belief that toleration of the characterizations would encourage impressionable people to regard misbehavior toward Negroes and Jews as tolerable and tolerated.

But, although unmentioned in any testimony before the subcommittee, there is yet a third way in which the circulation of various works may lead to anti-social behavior. It stands spectrally behind every public investigation of censorship issues and concerns the effects of unhindered circulation upon persons who believe strongly that some viewers of the works will be affected deleteriously, and who are willing themselves to disrupt the public peace in order to prevent such viewing.[7] The peculiarity of this third way is that while it obviously provides impetus to many public investigations, some persons argue that it is an irrelevant consideration; that is, that it *ought not* to be considered. I think they are mistaken.

Persons whose behavior falls in this third and questionably relevant category need not have viewed the works under consideration at all (true also of the second category), and in most instances probably have not viewed them; indeed, persons may behave in this way quite irrespective of what the actual effects of viewing the works are. Nevertheless, the occurrence or threat of their behavior must be counted as relevant in determining whether to interfere with the circulation of the works. If, for example, sentiment in a community is such that police protection of a theater will be required if a certain film is shown, then this is a reason for not showing the film (although not a decisive reason). Counting this as a reason has nothing to do with condoning the behavior of the persons threatening the public peace, nor has it anything to do with the value, in the abstract, of the work under fire; it has only to do with

7. Such behavior may likewise be produced by the desire simply to eliminate something that is thought offensive. The argument in the text need not treat these cases differently. But when one comes to consider the relevance of reasons for such behavior, an important difference may be seen. Persons who protest that a movie is offensive may be told: "If it offends you, walk out, or don't see it in the first place. You are not forced to see it." Fortunately, such an argument is available with respect to most aesthetic works; one can easily escape seeing them if one wants. One difficulty, however, lies in the fact that persons who are offended by a work (or think they will be) are notoriously unable to distinguish between the pain and discomfort the work produces in *them,* and the threat the work constitutes to the welfare of the community. Another difficulty lies in the fact that persons who find a work offensive are likely also to find offensive the *showing* or *sale* of the work in their community. The issue is then whether merely the showing or sale of the work invades an interest these people have in a community free from what is offensive to them. The issue is important because it is the key to understanding the driving force behind many censorious-minded persons: we urgently need to ask what consideration we owe persons with these feelings. Governments are ordinarily conceded to have some power to prohibit and remove what is offensive to the bulk of the members of the community; such things are "public nuisances." But they are usually things with which direct contact cannot be avoided because practically inescapable (such as pervasive and obnoxious odors), or things which cannot reliably be avoided because they cannot be anticipated (such as exhibitionism). It does not seem to me, however, that the presence in a community of works being shown to those who wish to see them, and shown in such a way that others may easily and reliably avoid seeing them if they wish, is the kind of nuisance against which people ought to be protected. Indeed, I don't see how anyone with the slightest interest in a free society could hold it to be that kind of nuisance; if we allow it to be, we will not have a free society. Nevertheless, it is important to see that this is a comment solely on the relevance of the *offensiveness* of the showing or sale of the work, and not a comment on the relevance of the other ways mentioned in which the showing or sale may appear to constitute a threat to the welfare of the community; concern about the latter is perfectly legitimate.

the distribution of human and other resources in a world where conditions are not always as favorable as we would like them to be.[8]

The threat to public peace, whether we approve it or not, is by hypothesis present and must be taken into account. It is a danger to the rights and interests of innocent persons. How is it to be met? A calculation of the community's resources and of the losses and gains involved in various alternative courses of action is called for; the answer is by no means automatic unless one imagines only cases where the size of the threat is negligible relative to the resources the community has to meet it. To say, then, that the presence of the threat is a reason for not showing the film is to say simply that it legitimately enters into the calculation of whether or not to show the film, and its presence weighs against showing the film. In a free society, the presence of the threat may generally be outweighed by the importance attached to freedom of communication and freedom of choice, although even this may depend upon how grave the threat is. But the fact that the importance of the threat is generally outweighed does not imply that the threat has no importance. To suppose that it did would be to adopt the tug-of-war approach already rejected above.

In sum, then, there are three ways in which the circulation of art or pseudo-art might lead to anti-social behavior, and all three are relevant in determining whether to allow circulation of the works. They are relevant because the minimization of anti-social behavior is one of the ideals of our communal life; this, in turn, is an ideal because our view of what counts as anti-social behavior involves our views on when and where men ought to be protected from each other.

Question 2. Can the unhindered circulation of books, movies, paintings, etc. lead to morally or religiously blameworthy thoughts, or to behavior which is blameworthy even though not clearly anti-social?

Opinion is bound to be divided in the relevance of moral and religious considerations in dealing with the circulation of works of art or pseudo-art; that is precisely why this question needs to be distinguished from the others. The failure of the Kefauver Report to distinguish these issues sharply and clearly from each other is, in my view, one of its more significant failures.

It is easy, of course, to confuse issues here. Many persons seem to believe

---

8. It might be helpful here to remember a distinction suggested by Aristotle in the *Politics* (1288b 10ff.) between:

> (a) what we would regard as best if we could imagine circumstances as favorable as possible, and
>
> (b) what we would regard as best given the present circumstances (which are not wholly favorable).

Plato also suggests the importance of this distinction in the *Laws* (Bk. 4, 709ff.).

that such immoral or irreligious thoughts and behavior are important because they tend to lead to anti-social behavior. But if this is true, then any circulation of books, movies, etc., leading to the former leads also to the latter and thus falls squarely within the scope of Question 1. The question at hand, however, asks us to consider the possible corrupting influences of circulation quite apart from the social effects of this corruption.

The confusion is introduced whenever one is asked to eliminate a purported corrupting influence, and yet not asked at the same time to consider what value to the community can lie in eliminating that influence. The answer is supposed to be obvious. It *is* obvious if one is considering the elimination of anti-social behavior resulting from the influence, but not otherwise. For it is not obvious that avoidance of morally or religiously blameworthy thoughts and behavior by means of external controls (by restricting the circulation of materials contributing to such thoughts and behavior) is of great moral or religious importance. Unfortunately, this issue is not even raised in most public discussions of censorship issues. The prurient-interest test now used in the United States as one of the criteria of criminal obscenity is infected with confusion on this matter. No one is quite sure whether we are worried about prurient interests because they tend to lead to anti-social behavior, or simply because they are immoral or "naughty." [9]

The question raised concerns the importance in religion and morals of *character* as well as of *action* vis-a-vis other persons. In discussing this, one need not take the extreme stand that *only* character and strength of character are important. The importance of effects of one's actions upon other persons can be admitted. But that consideration has now been left behind in our discussion, and one should be careful to ask what else remains to be achieved.

The issue concerning character is surely in the minds of persons who oppose censorship on the grounds that "we cannot legislate morality." These persons need not go so far as to say that laws against murder and theft are of no moral or religious importance. They need merely ask in our present context, "Can a person really be counted a good person, or can he ever really achieve religious salvation if his avoidance of blameworthy thoughts and behavior is achieved by means of external controls protecting him from temptation?"

One might claim that only in the fire of temptation can anyone prove or, even, make himself worthy. This need not be pushed to the extreme of holding that temptation should be *invited;* one need only hold that the use of external controls in order to protect persons from temptation does not achieve anything lastingly worthwhile either in religion or in morals. Strength of character is

9. For an example of how this confusion has become embedded in the law, see the recent discussion in *Manual Enterprises* v. *Day* 370 US 478 (1961). For a helpful treatment of constitutional traditions in this area, see Henkin, "Morals and the Constitution."

what makes a person worthy, and strength of character is not achieved by such means. This view of religion and morals is important, even if it is not universal. At least it cannot be ignored in assessing the relevance to censorship and allied problems of the question at hand.

Nevertheless, one might hold that this view, while possibly applicable to adults, is clearly not applicable to children. In the latter case, varying degrees of protection might be thought entirely justifiable paternalism (i.e., benevolent interference). But if so, this in turn could at most be protection with a view to eventual independence, and in order to make this claim convincing, some reasonable measures for the achievement of intelligent and stable independence would have to accompany the program. For, after all, if children don't choose wisely, we can give them immediate protection by narrowing their range of choice to what we believe harmless. But no one believes that this trains them to choose wisely.

The protection of children would, in any case, not justify the withdrawal of offending materials from adults unless the latter withdrawal were, for practical reasons, inseparable from the former (as is sometimes claimed about television and radio shows, and even about books for sale); this claim in turn would have to be examined carefully in order to determine whether some ingenuity on the matter wouldn't enable us to avoid the difficulty. The challenge here has become increasingly severe because modern living conditions (large-scale communities and tremendous physical mobility) have made less effective than ever suppressive control over children by their parents (a kind of control which at least has the advantage of not denying adults access to the works in question). Reliance on parents for the moral and religious training of their children is deep in our tradition; but at least insofar as that reliance is based on the presumption that parents can effectively "censor" the materials viewed by the children, the need for abandoning it is becoming increasingly obvious. This raises more than ever the spectre of community-wide programs involving denials to adults as consequences of denials to children.[10]

10. The course of public discussion in the United States of some of the issues raised by this difficulty is fascinating. For example, compare the declaration of the U.S. Supreme Court in *Butler* v. *Michigan* (352 US 380, 383 [1957]) that Michigan could not reduce its adult population to reading only what is fit for children, with the declaration of the Chicago police sergeant once in charge of that city's censorship unit, who said, "Children should be allowed to see any movie that plays in Chicago. If a picture is objectionable for a child, it is objectionable period." Chicago *Tribune,* 24 May 1959, p. 8. Quoted by Chief Justice Warren in his dissent in *Times Film Corp.* v. *Chicago* (365 US 43, 72 [1960]).

The statement of the police sergeant deserves comment. It is certainly plausible, although debatable, to say that something objectionable *for* children is objectionable to adults (or perhaps, ought to be). But it is not even plausible to assert that what is objectionable for children is also objectionable *for* adults: this would imply that everything which must be kept from children must also be kept from adults. Does anyone really believe this? It certainly seems to be what the sergeant is suggesting.

In dealing with the general issues raised by Question 2, there is the problem of further distinguishing between the moral and the religious grounds for judging behavior or thoughts to be blameworthy.[11] This is a problem because we are considering what is relevant to *governmental* policy concerning the circulation of art, and because, while we believe it suitable for governments to reinforce morality in some areas, we are becoming increasingly cautious about letting governments reinforce religion in any area. The core of the problem is this: insofar as we now *distinguish* between what is a matter of morals and what is a matter of religion, we regard the latter as a sectarian concern. Thus, for behavior or thoughts to be blameworthy on religious grounds is for them to be blameworthy within a religious sect, and in the light only of the tenets of that sect. It is believed to be of moral importance for one to maintain the tenets of the sect to which he is committed, but it is likewise thought that the government has no legitimate concern with a person's commitment to any given sect. The watchwords, "freedom of religious choice," imply not only that a person should be free to make whatever religious commitments he likes, but also that he should be free to lift or alter his commitments as he likes. Insofar as this view is acceptable, it follows that the government has no legitimate concern with enforcing the standards of any sect; the blameworthiness of thoughts or behavior on sectarian grounds would thus be irrelevant in determining governmental policy.

Enough has been said, perhaps, to indicate why the relevance of the various issues raised by Question 2 is disputable, to suggest where the difficulties lie, and to show how our community ideals are involved. The discussion has indicated also why one should be sensitive to possibly important differences between the status of children and that of adults in these matters. It is unfortunate that neither the Kefauver Report nor most other public discussions of censorship have seen fit to separate these issues sharply from the issues raised by Question 1.

Question 3. Can the free circulation of books, movies, etc., lead to yet other harmful effects such as emotional disturbances, or the loss of chances for personal happiness or fulfillment?

As before, the relevance of answers to this question should be discussed only after the question itself has been clearly distinguished from the others, something which the Kefauver Committee failed to do. It is true that harmful effects such as emotional disturbances may themselves lead to anti-social behavior, or simply to blameworthy thoughts or behavior. But insofar as they do so, consideration of them would fall squarely under one of the questions already asked. The present question, on the other hand, intends to get at the relevance of the production of such phenomena as emotional disturbances quite apart from any possible further effects of the sorts already discussed.

11. I owe this point to Professor George Dickie.

Once this issue is clearly seen the relevance of the question appears to depend solely upon admission that paternalism is a legitimate means of reducing human misery and enhancing chances for human happiness. In the light of such an admission, censorship in the narrow sense could be seen to protect persons absolutely from their susceptibility to harm occasioned by viewing the materials in question. Restrictive devices less absolute than such censorship could be seen to protect only certain classes of persons, or perhaps to warn them of potential dangers. It would be as if the government were to build or to tolerate the building of a fence around a dangerous bog or precipice (to use Locke's imagery about law generally); the object in this case, too, would be to protect persons from danger that lay ahead, or at least to warn them of it.

Locke's imagery suggests something that hasn't yet been established; viz., that free viewing of certain works may be as dangerous to the welfare of individuals as bogs and precipices. This may or may not be convincing to one who thinks of the issue in terms of the desirability of avoiding nightmares "produced" in some children by horror movies. Or the parallel may or may not be convincing to one who considers the possible persuasive effects of various works "leading" people to do or advocate something unwise (politically? Consider the "Hollywood Ten.") or imprudent (neurotically? Consider protests against a film purportedly making Lesbianism seem attractive). The difficulties special to these latter cases are two: (1) there is the question of the *efficacy* of the works in producing the purported injurious effects, to be discussed later in this paper and (2) the prior question of whether the action or advocacy produced is actually unwise or imprudent. The controversy in some cases may not be very great, but the presence of any controversy at all is enough to make these cases strikingly different from discussions of the consequences of falling into bogs or over precipices. We must take care not to let Locke's imagery mislead us.

Further, even if the dangers of these metaphorical bogs and precipices are admitted, one need not suppose that this alone settles any censorship issues. For, even if we were to take this talk quite literally, we would understand that while travel through bogs and over or down precipices is ordinarily thought to be avoided if possible, these might be precisely the places where experiences of value in themselves are to be found, possibly in their most desirable form. Careful consideration of the conditions of aesthetic experience may lead us to believe that in such "dangerous" works are to be found values not available elsewhere. This is a highly speculative hypothesis, but surely not one to be rejected out of hand.

Alternatively, one might see travel through such "dangerous" territory as a necessary means to getting where one is going. Here, at least, we have a clear story, and one which is now deeply embedded in our cultural tradition.

It is this: If "fences" were built around certain works, perhaps some threats to human happiness of the sort under discussion could be avoided; but people would be denied free opportunity to learn from experience and exploration. If the development of human character is important, and if the presence of free opportunity to learn from experience and exploration is essential for that development, as John Stuart Mill argues in his essay *On Liberty,* then there may be a considerable cost incurred by the restriction. Of course, Mill might wish, and we might wish, to make *some* distinctions between adults and children in this matter (but, if so, issues raised in the discussions of Question 2 as well as some issues to be raised later in this paper will have to be faced). Nevertheless, the point remains that the danger against which censorship in these cases might protect us, while relevant, might not in the end be decisive. Other considerations may countervail them.

None of this, however, requires us to deny that paternalistic protection of its citizens from harm is a legitimate governmental enterprise. The only question concerns the importance of the sacrifice likely to be incurred when such protection is provided; this must be weighed against the relative seriousness of the harm from which persons are to be protected. As the former is a function of the methods of protection proposed, ingenuity in devising such methods is obviously again to be prized. One need not suppose that the only alternatives are absolute prohibition on the one hand and absolutely unqualified freedom on the other.

Question 4. Are there any significant differences among answers to the above questions regarding works having aesthetic worth, those having only aesthetic intention, and those having neither?

If our only reason for interfering with the circulation of aesthetic and pseudo-aesthetic materials is that their circulation would somehow be socially injurious, and if at the same time we wish to maximize the development and availability of aesthetic values, we should consider carefully the claim that the injurious effects of viewing works having aesthetic worth, if indeed such effects exist at all, are appreciably fewer than the injurious effects of viewing works having neither aesthetic worth nor aesthetic intention. Such a claim seems to have been made by Eberhard and Phyllis Kronhausen in their book *Pornography and the Law.*[12] The authors attempt to distinguish between "erotic realism" and "pornography" on this account. Such claims may very well be true, and the public-at-large should not close its eyes to that possibility; ignorance here would blind them to important distinctions. Nor should

---

12. Eberhard and Phyllis Kronhausen, *Pornography and the Law: The Psychology of Erotic Realism and Pornography* (New York: Ballantine Books, 1959). I say the claim "seems to have been made," because I am not sure of the extent to which the Kronhausens regard "erotic realism" as an aesthetic concept, or "pornography" as a non-aesthetic one.

the artist close his eyes to the possibility that such claims may be false; igno-rance here would deceive him as to the true nature and extent of his social responsibilities. The Kefauver Report did not touch on this matter because the Subcommittee considered itself to be dealing with materials notoriously hav-ing neither aesthetic worth nor aesthetic intention.

The discussion of the above four questions has so far attempted merely to consider their relevance, and, in so doing, to reveal the ways in which our social and personal values may be involved in calculations of the possible *benefits* of censorship. (The ways such values are involved in estimates of the possible *losses* incurred by censorship is yet to be discussed.) But besides the relevance of the questions just discussed, the various difficulties which have been met in attempting to *answer* the questions in any reliable way merit some attention. Why have we not been able to find and agree upon straight-forward answers to these questions? Our failure must surely be one of the ultimate embarrassments to anyone inclined to think that censorship might sometimes be desirable; it should as well be an embarrassment to all of us since the answers to these questions are important for all citizens no matter what they are inclined to believe about censorship.

In the first instance, difficulty has undoubtedly been produced by our gen-eral unwillingness to confront and examine carefully two plausible hypothe-ses. These hypotheses, if true, would enormously complicate the task of for-mulating intelligent censorship policies; but they also, if true, would reveal opportunities which ought to be seized. They are: (a) that susceptibility to the possibly injurious influences of viewing various works may not be along lines easily recognized by law or other forms of social regulation; that susceptibility in any given way may not be uniform among children, nor among adults and children of any particular class, race, or easily identifiable situation; nor might it be the case that persons susceptible in certain ways to materials of some kinds are so susceptible to materials of all kinds; and (b) that the viewing of books, movies, paintings, etc., may never be more than a contributing influ-ence in the production of the injurious effects in question; that the victim's unfavorable reaction may also be dependent upon many other alterable fea-tures of his environment and character.

We have not been sufficiently willing to face up to the possibility that these hypotheses are true, nor to their implications if they are true. This charge can be supported in detail by a look at attempts to answer Question 1: Can unhindered circulation of movies, books, paintings, etc., lead to anti-social behavior?

I have mentioned three ways in which the circulation of such materials could lead to anti-social behavior. The first is by direct viewing of the mate-rials, which may intensify the impulses leading to the behavior. The second is by the effects of free circulation of the works upon persons in search of standards of behavior. The third is by the effects of free circulation upon persons who believe that viewers of the works will be injured, and are willing to threaten the public peace in order to prevent such viewing. Not much difficulty is met in determining that threats of the last sort have occurred; the only question has been the extent to which governments ought to cater to them. Great difficulty seems to have been met, however, in determining the extent to which effects of the first two sorts have occurred.

The matter is the focus of considerable controversy. Some social scientists and legal scholars claim that studies of it are in a state of confusion.[13] In our examination of the Kefauver Report we have already seen some evidence as to the sources of that confusion, e.g., failure to distinguish sharply enough from each other the various questions guiding the investigation, and failure to delineate precisely enough the scope of the problems faced by the policymakers who hope to make use of the investigation. But, what else is involved?

We are not, after all, entirely ignorant. As Senator Kefauver rightly points out in his summary of Subcommittee findings in *Federal Probation,* we have at least the intuitive impressions of persons with expert knowledge in the field. Many clinical psychiatrists, youth counselors, and law enforcement officials concur in their impressions that the deleterious effects, at least of viewing pornography, are socially significant; such informed impressions cannot be discounted (although they certainly ought to be tested). In addition, one can, as Senator Kefauver does, argue against those who would deny the injurious effects of viewing certain materials by pointing out that such denial is inconsistent with assumptions made elsewhere about the relationship between constant viewing and overt expressions. Advertising, propaganda, and many forms of education all presume this relationship. (Here, however, Senator Kefauver should have distinguished between *constant*—regular and persistent—viewing and casual, irregular viewing. Which of these pertains most to the problem of pornography?)

It is probably trivial but true to say that our trouble is produced at least in part by the simple tendency of censorious-minded persons to inflate grossly the modest amount of information we have. The temptation is great. In the United States, for example, punishment of distributors and exhibitors of books, paintings, etc., is clearly thought justifiable if continued circulation of the materials in question can be shown a clear and present danger to the community of evils that government has power to prevent; this, at least, is the now classic test used in dealing with subversion and revolution, and incitement to riot. Although the test has hardly been more than latent in other areas,

---

13. For a recent review of the studies, see Bernard Green, "Obscenity, Censorship, and Juvenile Delinquency," *University of Toronto Law Journal* 14 (1962): 229–52.

as for example in cases dealing with obscenity, and although there has been a good deal of equivocation and confusion in that area about what evils the government *has* power to prevent (see again note 8 of the present paper) it is still the test which most clearly legitimizes governmental interference with the circulation of *any* materials of communication.[14] The continuing temptation on the part of the censorious-minded has therefore been to show the injurious effects of the materials in question in such a light as to indicate they pass this test (whatever the "evils" in question may be). We find evidence of this in the overstatements of the Kefauver Report. The simple fact, however, is that we lack the knowledge sufficient to demonstrate this in accordance with legally acceptable standards of evidence. Hence equivocation, conflict, and confusion.

But the difficulties run deeper. They are also due in part to our failure to face up fully enough to the fact that viewing various materials at most can be a contributing influence in the production of anti-social behavior, or for that matter in the production of any deleterious effects whatever. Turning again to the *Interim Report,* one discovers the following curious juxtaposition of sentences suggesting precisely this point:

> The impulses which spur people to sex crimes unquestionably are intensified by reading and seeing pornographic materials. The sharp increase in crimes of this type is largely the result of social and family upheavals which occurred during and immediately after the Second World War.[15]

Senator Kefauver, in *Federal Probation,* is clearer. He says:

> The almost complete lack of sex education in the established institutions, such as the home, the school, and the church on the one hand, coupled with the excessive stimulation received in this area from repeated presentations in all forms of mass media, plus his own biological urges, predisposes the youngster to seek sources of knowledge and information. We find the pornographer ever present to provide this information at a price.[16]

This, of course, deals with only one kind of material, and perhaps only pseudo-aesthetic material at best. But a similarly complete picture of the background against which the viewing of certain movies, books, etc., is capable of producing anti-social behavior must always be filled in if one is to have any reasonable understanding of the role of viewing these materials in

14. Some persons believe it should be the only test. Cf. the remarks of Patrick Murphy Malin before the Kefauver Committee, cited in *Federal Probation* 24.4 (December 1960): 12.

15. Ibid., p. 62.

16. Ibid., p. 5.

producing such behavior, and of the feasible and practicable *alternatives* to restricting or prohibiting the circulation of the materials. Insofar as we are interested in reducing anti-social behavior, we should be aware that censorship is not the only way of doing this, and may not even be needed at all. This lesson obviously applies as well to all the other injurious effects about which we have been speculating.

Failure to admit fully the other contributing influences, coupled with more or less vague awareness of their presence, renders us susceptible to further confusion on this important issue. Our astigmatism is undoubtedly due in part simply to our failure to accept responsibility for what we ourselves have contributed to the unfortunate situation. But it is also undoubtedly due in part to our awareness that some of the contributing influences are built deeply into our society; it often seems difficult if not impossible to imagine politically and socially feasible ways of correcting them. For example, one reason for our horror at art and pseudo-art calling attention to adolescent sexuality or threatening to enlarge it is that our institutions are simply not equipped to cope with it. Contrast our attitudes toward these works with our attitudes towards works calling attention to or threatening to enlarge the scale of violence in our society. The latter do not arouse the public to such a degree because the public believes, whether mistakenly or not, that its institutions can cope with this problem. Restriction of the works in question is thus not thought urgent because other avenues of correction seem readily available. This goes some way toward explaining why the public is more censorious toward erotic works than toward sadistic works.

Discussions of attempts to answer questions 2 and 3 would reveal similar difficulties. But on the restricted issue of blameworthy thoughts, aside from the questions already raised about their relevance, there is a further problem. Our "evidence" on the production of such thoughts is still almost exclusively introspective, and has been collected and published in a most arbitrary fashion. We have highly impressionistic observations from many persons about the causal connection between viewing certain works and the occurrence of blameworthy thoughts. Very often, they support the claim that censorship or some related restriction is needed. But this support is challenged by persons who say that the observations are by those who are themselves unusually susceptible to the kinds of influence in question, and who are thus not reliable informants on the general and widespread effects of viewing the works under consideration. There is no special reason to believe that this is true, but we are surely not yet in any position to demonstrate that it is false. We must, therefore, if we conclude that the occurrence of blameworthy thoughts is relevant, recognize the need to devise less arbitrary means of assuring ourselves what role viewing aesthetic and pseudo-aesthetic works can play in producing them.

III

What are relevant *losses* which might be suffered as a result of interfering with the circulation of aesthetic and pseudo-aesthetic works? The following questions are intended to mark out systematically the range of such losses, and thus to reveal clearly what social and personal ideals may be destroyed or damaged by censorship in the arts.

Question 1. What are the possible losses to the community of aesthetic and related values? Members of the Kefauver Subcommittee, for reasons we have already considered, did not believe that their investigation raised this question. But readers of this journal will surely suppose that this question is raised by the censorship issues of most concern to them, the issues involving estimable or at least serious art works. What these readers may overlook, however, is that arguments to establish the *relevance* of this question are not, as perhaps too many persons suppose, supernumerary. The need for argument must be taken seriously if those who wish to fight censorship are to be in anything like as strong a position as that which they require of their opponents.

Further, the need to be in a position of strength cannot be taken lightly. Not only is the requirement rational and equitable, but dismal failures to win the day against restrictions may be due partly to failure to meet it straightforwardly and explicitly.

The nature of the challenge may be specified by the following questions (which are not simply rhetorical but are meant to be taken seriously):

(a) Do works of aesthetic worth or intention aid either directly or indirectly in the education of sensitivities appropriate to human beings? This question is intended to touch on the common assumption that aesthetic sensitivity is one of the central dignifying features of human life, one of the features distinguishing humans from other creatures. If this is so, its loss or the loss of opportunities for developing it would not be trivial to any community.

(b) Do such works either directly or indirectly contribute to satisfaction of sensitivities already present? This, of course, is important because the works would then be direct contributions to human happiness and contentment.

(c) Do they either directly or indirectly increase the potentialities for enrichment of human experience in ways not directly associated with the aesthetic? It is often said that works of art can on occasion bring persons to an awareness of features of human experience which they had not heretofore noticed or appreciated. If true, this is important.[17]

17. This hypothesis borders closely on the matters discussed in connection with Question 3 below.

To the extent that these questions can be answered affirmatively, the loss of aesthetic values to a community can be shown as important.

As these questions suggest, the loss may be direct or indirect. Interference with the circulation of various materials obviously results in direct loss when it renders items of aesthetic worth inaccessible to persons who could profit from them in any of the above ways. Interference with works having only aesthetic intention, on the other hand, may result in indirect loss. One might argue, for example, that artists and observers must learn from failures as well as successes, and, indeed, that circulation of failures as well as successes ought to be protected as an essential condition of creativity and appreciation in the arts.

There is, however, a further possibility of loss worth considering. Commentators on the conditions of aesthetic creativity have noted quite regularly that the *mere presence* of a censor saying, "Here is a line you must not cross," sharply inhibits creative imagination and hence creative production; this may be so even when the line is one which the artists themselves don't care to cross. This suggestion seems plausible and surely worth investigation when one considers the frequency of remarks about the "flatness" of artistic production in communities where censors are active and effective, e.g., recent Russia.[18]

Given that we wish to maximize opportunities for gaining aesthetic values, the intelligent formulation and administration of *any* restrictive policy whatever is a formidable task. Any attempt whatever may result in some loss of these values to the community, if only by influencing the quality of artistic production. Even if restrictions on some materials were found desirable in the end, however, we should still wish to minimize the unnecessary loss of aesthetic values resulting from the exercise of restrictive powers in unenlightened, prejudiced, or self-interested ways. The dangers here, as most people recognize, are immense. Anyone desiring a reasonably horrifying catalogue of a *modern* chamber of administrative horrors on censorship matters in the United States can turn (to cite merely one place) to the dissenting opinion of Chief Justice Warren in *Times Film Corporation* v. *Chicago* 368 US 43, 69ff (1960).

In such matters, we need to identify our problems carefully. Differing precautions will be needed depending upon whether the problem lies in the *formulation* or in the *administration* of the standards of restriction used, and depending upon whether the greatest lack appears to be lack of enlightened judgment or lack of curbs on prejudice and self-interest.

18. Cf. Green, "Obscenity, Censorship, and Juvenile Delinquency," pp. 251–52. And see Sir Herbert Read's account of the reaction of D. H. Lawrence to the censoring of one of his (Lawrence's) works; Sir Herbert Read, *To Hell With Culture* (London: Routledge and Kegan Paul, 1962).

Question 2. To what extent does censorship arouse socially harmful interests in the works so treated? This question suggests that restrictive devices may lead to harm of the very type which they are designed to forestall. The Kefauver Subcommittee considered this possibility, but turned away without much exploration of it. Awareness that something is "forbidden fruit," even if not forbidden to oneself, may raise socially harmful attitudes toward it, and may actually increase its harmfulness in any of three ways:

> (a) It may alert persons who would have viewed the work anyway to certain aspects of the work, and lead these persons to give undue attention and emphasis to these aspects.
>
> (b) It may serve to call the work to the attention of persons who would be harmed by it but who would not otherwise have been aware of or interested in the work. (Remember that "banned in Boston" used to be the best advertisement a book or movie could get.)
>
> (c) It may encourage profitable or simply perverse subversion of the restrictions by arrangements for viewers among those whom the restrictions were designed to protect. (Pornography, for example, is a big business as the Kefauver Subcommittee investigation made plain).

Insofar as these claims are true (and their general correctness has been recognized at least since the time of Ovid, see *Amores,* III, iv, 17), a person who restricts circulation of a work actually throws a spotlight on what he wishes to hide, not, perhaps, on the specific thing he wishes to hide, but at least on that *type* of thing. Hardly a negligible result.

Question 3. To what extent can censorship lead to emotional or other disturbances in those whom the restrictions seek to protect? Claims have been made that restrictions can lead to emotional or other disturbances and deprivations simply by cutting persons off from the feelings, behaviors, and ideas dealt with in the suppressed works. In *Pornography and the Law,* Eberhard and Phyllis Kronhausen suggest that suppression of what they call "erotic realism" leads to ignorance about fundamental matters in human life, and that this in turn raises the incidence of deprived and emotionally disturbed persons. (This issue was seemingly not raised by the materials investigated by the Kefauver Subcommittee. I do not know, of course, whether the Kronhausens would be inclined to challenge the Subcommittee's judgment on any of the materials the Subcommittee examined.) The Kronhausens' claim operates in the interests of psychological growth and enrichment against restriction. But this and similar claims could reasonably be made only about some types of work. Further, arguments that a type of work is of the appropriate sort are bound to be sticky because there is probably as much myth on one side of the fence as on the other about what the conditions of psychological or political or economic (etc.) growth and enrichment are. This is not to say that argument will be hopeless, but only that allegations and counter-allegations will most likely be controversial and will bear close scrutiny.

More importantly, one should remember at this point the earlier discussion about "contributing influences." Clearly, the very fact that "injurious" restrictions of this sort are imposed in a community on the production or circulation of certain works shows that general conditions are not favorable for the relevant kinds of growth and enrichment. The presence of the restrictions is undoubtedly a symptom of more fundamentally unfavorable conditions in the ideological, institutional, and emotional life of the community. This is not to deny that the restrictions may themselves play a role in worsening the situation; they may very well do so. But one needs to maintain a sense of proportion as to the importance of that role.

Question 4. To what extent will restrictions produce dangerously authoritarian or elitist results in what is supposed to be a free society? The extent to which such results will be produced depends in part upon how the restrictive standards are established and applied. In this connection, one must deal separately with the issues raised by restrictions on adults, and those raised by restrictions on children. The Kefauver Subcommittee did not consider this question at all, probably because it saw itself as concerned primarily with children. But as we shall see, the issue ought to be raised even there.

Concerning adults, there is a simple, and for our society, decisive argument against any restrictions designed to protect persons with the voting franchise from the injurious effects of voluntary viewing of any works. In a democracy, the extension of the voting franchise assumes, in an iron-clad and totally committed way, that *all* adults with the vote (excluding, that is, persons in prisons, mental institutions, etc.) have both the character and intelligence needed to avoid the bad effects alleged to follow from the voluntary viewing of any work, whether the work in question is alleged politically subversive, immoral, obscene, or whatever. This assumption may be false, but if we abandon it or fail to act on it, we abandon democracy by inevitably introducing paternalistic protection of adult and franchised citizens *from themselves*. The democratic commitment requires us to believe that the individual voter is not in need of protection from himself. This is decisive for anyone intending to preserve democracy. It requires also that we not inquire into what legitimate interest could be served by adult viewing of materials we find questionable; such judgments must be left to each adult to determine for himself.

This argument, however, does not cover two important classes of restrictions. It does not cover denials to adults when these are necessary accompaniments of denials to children, nor does it cover at least temporary denials to adults when these are needed to avert serious and imminent threats to the public peace. The argument, of course remains relevant and, indeed, very important in these cases; but it is not decisive because the denials in question are not designed to protect franchised adults from themselves; they are, rather, only incidental to the achievement of other and perfectly legitimate goals. The argument does not, in any case, reach children or adults without the franchise. Attempts to protect these persons from themselves are not obviously inconsistent with the democratic commitment.

Concerning children at least, there are other arguments against restriction, although not decisive ones. In the first place, as already mentioned, effective denial to children sometimes involves denial to adults. Where this genuinely is the case, it is surely a reason against restriction.

Secondly, if we propose to restrict the fare of children and not that of adults, we will find ourselves using somewhat arbitrary criteria for singling out the "children," arbitrary, that is, in determining which persons are actually able to benefit from the works in question and yet not likely to be damaged significantly by them. Capacity for benefit and immunity from harm are, after all, the only reasonable considerations here; but these capacities and immunities may not be neatly distributed chronologically, or along any other lines readily usable in a large-scale program of control. It is therefore at least probable that in the light of the needs of community administration some injustices will occur no matter what program is adopted; some "children" who could profit from the works and would not be injured by them will not be allowed to view them, and, of course, some "adults" who will perhaps be harmed by the works will be permitted to view them.

Thirdly, the denial to children of free opportunity for exploration and discovery in the world of books, movies, paintings, etc. may bring some benefits, but it undeniably risks losses as well in both the character and the subsequent performance of the children. We cannot safely "protect" our children from some areas of life, and then suddenly, when they reach a certain age, thrust them into adult life, and reasonably expect them to function in a stable and socially useful way regarding the matters previously closed to them. Protection at some stages may be desirable or even essential; but protection merely postpones the day of reckoning—the day when the child must learn to manage for himself whatever it is that has been closed to him. There is always as least the danger of postponing the day of reckoning too long out of sheer laziness and under the pleasant illusion that "innocence" is being preserved.[19]

___

19. It is true, however, that what the child finds when he is eventually allowed to explore freely will be somewhat up to us. For the child will be exploring our communities and the characters in them, and we must accept some responsibility for what these are like. Nevertheless, we must recognize the limits of our power, and distinguish carefully between genuinely elimi-

IV. Summary and Conclusions

After this examination of relevant issues and evocation of relevant ideals, where do we now stand? Concerning restrictions on the fare of children, no decisive considerations have emerged. We obviously need to consider much more carefully than we have, what we want here and how to get it. We especially need to be much more certain than we are of the actual deleterious effects upon children (and upon adults, for that matter) of viewing various kinds of materials. We must also remain alert to the possibility that these effects, whatever they may be, might be avoided by policies other than restrictions of the sort in question, namely, by eliminating other influences contributing to the production of the deleterious effects. Consider, for example, the multiple influences mentioned by Senator Kefauver in connection with the problem of pornography, e.g., the vacuum created by the lack of sex education in the home, and the excessive stimulation of sexual impulses by all forms of mass media. To what extent would elimination or even mitigation of these influences dissolve the problem of pornography? Such alternatives, even though sometimes superficially more difficult, might in the long run be much less costly in terms of our most permanent goals and ideals.

Further, while we must, because of the democratic commitment, treat every voter as an adult for purposes of policy in this area, it does not follow that all non-voters must be treated as children. The "child-adult" distinction is often—one might say virtually always—drawn ineptly by communities insofar as it is intended to reflect who is immune from harm or capable of benefiting from the various materials in question. We should search constantly for improved yet practicable means of drawing the line so that it makes sense in the light of what we are trying to do. For example, we sometimes allow the age of a child to create a *presumption* against his being permitted to view certain works, but allow the presumption to be defeated by clear evidence of parental permission to view. This policy may be limited both in its effectiveness and its rationality, but it at least represents an attempt to introduce flexibility based on relevant considerations.

If, when considering children alone (however we identify them), we decide that it would sometimes be best to restrict their fare, we will certainly find that this sometimes seems to involve denials to adults as well. We should always keep in mind that a bit of ingenuity may show us how to avoid or mitigate this difficulty. One step in this direction is to transmit "objectionable" radio or television shows at a later hour than usual, rather than taking

nating evils, and simply ignoring them or sweeping them under the rug. The censorious-minded are often too facile in supposing that they have done the former when, in fact, they have done only the latter.

them off the air entirely. This was done a year or so back, for example, with the *Defenders* television show on abortion. It doesn't produce "perfect" results (assuming that the show would have damaged any children), but we must, after all, balance the supposed gains with respect to children against the losses to adults. If we are inclined to demand perfect protection of children, we should at least be fully aware of how this demand will in the end influence the character of our adult community. The above mentioned show on abortion was a serious effort to raise a helpful discussion of an important social problem. Are we to deny television absolutely the right to perform such a service?

Concerning adults alone, one *decisive* consideration against restriction seems to have emerged. Restrictions of any sort imposed on adults with the right to vote, and aimed at protecting the adults from their own susceptibilities, are inconsistent with a central tenet of democracy. Restrictions of this sort might, to be sure, reduce human misery and social disorder, and perhaps even lower the incidence of immoral behavior; but these benefits would be purchased at too great a price—the price of compromising a fundamental article of democratic faith.

We have noted that this consideration, while it continues to be relevant, is not decisive against denials to adults which are incidental either to restrictions upon children or to the maintenance of public order. In these cases at least, we are still faced with the difficulties of "weighing" gains and losses of the many different kinds surveyed in this paper. Furthermore, even in cases where the democratic commitment *is* decisive, it is important for us to recognize the cost of that commitment. As far as it concerned the susceptibility of franchised adults, the discussion above was an exploration of what the cost of maintaining our democratic faith might be in this area of life.

On the other hand, we have also explored what the rewards, aside from simply keeping the faith, might be. We are in no position to act sensibly and resourcefully until we are aware of both. Nor are we even in a position to understand fully the true import of our faith. The democratic commitment in the area of the arts, as well as in every other area, brings with it liabilities as well as benefits for our community life. If we don't know this, we simply don't know what democracy is all about, nor are we in a position to evaluate its genuine worth.

We cannot, in any case, avoid the need to investigate the full range of possible gains and losses surveyed in this paper. The ultimate problem which then follows is this: When called upon to do so, how are we to weigh against each other considerations of so many different types, e.g., the preservation of aesthetic values against the occurrence of emotional disturbances, or the importance of the democratic commitment against the occurrence of anti-social behavior?

Conflicts among these categories of appeal often do not emerge very clearly. Because of the emotive force of the terms used in making the appeals (e.g., "anti-social" and "aesthetic value"), the resolution of conflict is often attempted *within* the categories. For example, it is likely that persons threatening the public peace in order to prevent the showing of a movie will protest that their behavior is *not* anti-social. And consider the claim that failure to preserve aesthetic value is itself anti-social.

Conflicts among appeals of different types will undoubtedly sometimes appear and be recognized. In such cases, one may itch for a formula of weights and measures and a neat ledger to tote up the results. But it would be futile to offer a formula. Apart from dealing with the specific cases in which the issues are raised, no one is in a position to judge the sharpness or the extent of the conflicts in question. As the relevant considerations, pro and con, are embodiments of community and personal ideals, and as we wish, of course, to maximize the attainment of them all, we cannot judge apart from specific cases which policies will achieve this aim.

More fundamentally, no formula can reasonably be provided because the conflicts *are* conflicts of ideals, and a society which is sufficiently open to permit the *development* of its ideals will not have a fixed and static hierarchy of them.[20] Resolutions of conflicts among ideals in such societies will not be calculations made only in the light of already developed hierarchies of values, but will at the same time be influences upon their development. We not only discover in such cases what we *do* value, but we also make up our minds about what we *shall* value. Full recognition of this reveals not only our freedom to develop, but also our responsibility for reasoned choices of the character we wish our communities to attain.[21]

20. Nor, of course, will even the *kinds* of ideals be fixed in such a society. Consider in this connection the disputed relevance in our society of the various moral and religious considerations discussed earlier in this paper; we are clearly moving away from an interest in "sectarian" ideals. But changes in kinds of ideals are made for the most part by attaching new significance to old labels. The terms I have used in this paper when appealing to community values are the old labels, as became clear, for example, in my discussion in Section III of rights and interests.

21. Of those who have helped me along the way with criticisms and suggestions, I should like especially to thank Professor Donald Arnstine and Dr. Peter Weiss. I don't suppose for a minute, however, that they will approve of everything I have said.

3   On Applying Rules

What is it to apply a rule? Some people seem to think that it is using the rule to find out something. They seem furthermore to suppose that a person who has not used a rule to find out something has not applied the rule. This paper argues that the latter supposition is a mistake, and that applying a rule may sometimes be nothing more than invoking the authority of the rule in support of a course of action already determined.

I

Applying rules is, of course, only one of many things men do with respect to rules; men also comply with, act on, cite, violate rules, and—in certain more restricted contexts—establish, revoke, modify rules, etc. Many such activities are currently of interest to philosophers working on problems in language, logic and ethics as well as in jurisprudence, but it is often in connection with the law that the activities appear most clearly. A person with any of these interests would therefore do well to look carefully at the law, at least for initial insights into what he might find elsewhere.

Within the law, the question—what is it to apply a rule?—has not been asked in straightforward fashion, but an answer to it has come to have importance because of a controversy about whether judges apply rules in deciding cases. Until roughly thirty or thirty-five years ago, it was commonly although not universally said that judges characteristically applied rules, and, indeed, that they had a duty to do so; but many commentators, especially in America but also elsewhere, now believe that at least the former is not true or not often true—at any rate of judges sitting on highest courts of appeal. The claim that these judges do not often or characteristically apply rules does not reflect a change in the judicial practice of appealing to rules in justifying judgments or decrees. The practice continues. The claim is made in the face of this continuance, sometimes being used to support a contention that judges are not doing what they are supposed to be doing, and sometimes to support a contention that we have misconceived what these judges are supposed to do. In either case, the claim has introduced (or at least supported) the notion that the judges, in formulating their opinions and appealing therein to rules, are most often engaged in some kind of empty show or pretence. Judicial opinions[1] have thus been regarded as relatively unimportant indicia of the law, and worries have been created about what judges really *are* doing behind that screen of pious pretension. This, in turn, has abetted concern about the role of relatively 'independent' (non-representative?) judiciaries in democratic societies. For, if judges are not in fact applying the rules which, according to their opinions, they seem to be applying, then perhaps they are engaged in the exercise of relatively uncontrolled or 'free' discretion in making decisions of obvious social and political importance.

Although the question—what is it for a judge to apply a rule?—has not been explicitly asked or answered by persons discussing these matters, presumptions concerning its answer naturally have figured importantly. The leading presumption, as we shall see, has been that for a judge to apply rules is for him to use the rules in discovering the proper resolutions of cases and controversies. It is this presumption that has led to the arguing of the issues in terms of contentions about the psychology of judicial decision-making—i.e., about how judges make up their minds in cases. I shall argue that this view of applying rules is mistaken, insofar as it presumes that a judge who did not use a rule in this way could not have applied the rule.

The importance of noting such a mistake is as follows: (1) One is thereby invited to reassess the *relevance* in legal and political philosophy of reports on how judges make up their minds in cases, and in particular the relevance of these reports to worries about the role of the judiciary in democracies. In feeding skepticism about whether judges apply rules, the reports also feed worries about the judicial use of 'free' discretion. To show them indecisive on the former issue is to call for reconsideration of their relevance and importance vis-a-vis the latter. (2) One is also encouraged to reflect, with respect to contexts somewhat broader than concern for judicial uses of rules, on the way applying rules may or may not be related to decisionmaking. The point to be noticed is that the possible relationships may be more diverse than expected. Recognition of this may decrease the urge to be dogmatic about what it is to apply a rule, and may lead to reconsideration of the importance to be attached to occasions on which rules are applied.

II

Consider the claim that is central to the controversy—the claim that a judge has not applied the rules he says or implies in his opinion that he has applied.

---

1. Not judgments. The latter have been considered by members of this school to be the *most* important indicia.

In dealing with such a claim, one might begin by distinguishing it from quite another—viz., that *saying* of a judge that he has applied these rules is not a helpful or revealing characterization of what he has done. Failure to distinguish between these two claims may lead some commentators to suppose that they are supporting the former when in fact they are supporting only the latter. Thus, to show that there is (a) another rule to which the judge could reasonably have appealed (in the light of the circumstances of the case), or (b) another reasonable interpretation of the rule to which he did appeal, or to show that (c) the argument supporting his appeal to the rule "could have gone either way," is not alone enough to show that he didn't apply the rule he said he did. It is only enough to show that it might be worth asking *why* he applied the rule as he did, and to suggest that all the answers to this question are not laid out in his opinion. Notice, for example, that there is no distortion resulting from describing the above circumstances as follows: (a) there is another rule which the judge could have *applied,* (b) there is another reasonable interpretation of the rule he *applied,* and (c) the argument supporting his *application* of the rule "could have gone either way." Nevertheless, such information *could* be made relevant to claims about whether judges have applied rules; this will be shown below, and it is this circumstance that produces the confusion. What is not noticed is that without the support of controversial claims about what it is to apply a rule, the above information is simply irrelevant.

Those who wish to deny that a judge has applied those rules he claims in his opinion to have applied, depend upon distinguishing between how a judge makes up his mind, and how he justifies his conclusions. This has manifested itself in their belief that what a judge says in his opinion (his justification of his judgment) is not highly relevant to whether he has applied the rules he cites in his opinion. It is supposed that if a judge has applied rules at all, he has applied them in making up his mind on the case, and it is clear to everyone that his opinion may be, and probably is, something other than a report of how he made up his mind. Thus, although it is admitted that judges *invoke* and *appeal* to rules, it is denied that they always or even often *apply* them.

Two supporting arguments are offered. They are: (1) that the judge has not arrived at his judgment in the case *by way of reflection on* whether the circumstances of the case fall within the scope of these rules, or (2) that he has not arrived at his judgment *out of conviction that* they do. Each argument supposes that something having to do with *how the judge made up his mind* may be presented as a necessary condition for his having applied a rule.

We have evidence appearing to show that in some judicial decisions one or the other of the above conditions is not fulfilled.

Evidence that judges sometimes arrive at judgments without first reflecting on whether the circumstances of the case fall within the scope of those rules later invoked in judicial opinions comes from reports by judges that they sometimes arrive at their judgments without any *need* for reflection, or by means of 'intuitions' or 'flashes.'

Evidence that judgments are sometimes arrived at before judges are *convinced* that the circumstances fall within the scope of the rules they later cite in their opinions appears to lie in the lack of persuasiveness of some judicial arguments. Here, as will be seen, is the source of the confusion between the two questions distinguished above—the question concerning whether a judge *has* applied rules and the question concerning whether *saying* that he has is interesting or revealing. It sometimes appears that there was another rule that the judge could equally reasonably have applied to the circumstances of the case but did not mention, or another reasonable interpretation of the rule he did 'apply,' or that the argument supporting his 'application' of the rule "could have gone either way." Supposing that the judge is a reasonable and well-informed man, and an able practitioner of his craft, we find it hard to believe, when his supporting argument is weak, that he could have concluded the way he did solely because of, or due to his conviction that the circumstances of the case fell within the scope of the rule he invoked. It is unlikely in such cases that he was so convinced, although, of course, there are defenses against such a claim.

It is wrong, however, to take either of these kinds of information— information gained from reports by judges as to how they sometimes reach their conclusions, or information showing certain weaknesses of judicial arguments—as evidence that judges have not applied rules. Neither reflection on the rules just before making up one's mind, nor making up one's mind the way one has solely out of conviction that the circumstances fall within the scope of the rules, are necessary conditions for applying rules.

Consider the claim that the judge must have reflected on whether the circumstances of the case fell within the scope of the rules before making up his mind. Even on the assumption that applying rules *must* be using them somehow in making up one's mind, such reflection is not clearly needed in order to apply a rule. This may be shown by comparing judges to umpires in games. It would be perilous to describe the interval, sometimes so small, between an umpire's observation of a player's action and the declaration of an infraction or whatever as a time during which the umpire was considering whether the circumstances fell within the scope of a relevant rule. Why say, e.g., that the umpire observes the action, considers whether it is an infraction of the rule, and then decides that it is? Why not say that in seeing the action he immediately *recognizes it as* an infraction of the rule? The interval between the action and the umpire's announcement can be explained simply as the time needed for him to declare what he has recognized, not as the time needed for him to decide what to say about what he has seen or the time needed for him to determine whether the circumstances fit the rule. Early in one's career as an umpire, there may be something like the latter; but as experience accumulates this seems to disappear. It *may* be true that on some occasions the interval between the action and the umpire's declaration is due to a need to reflect on whether the circumstances fit the rule; but this doesn't seem invariably or even character-istically the case with experienced umpires who are doing their duty—i.e., applying and enforcing the rules of the game.

The nearest analogies in judicial practice to umpires are found when judges, for example, recognize instances of inadmissible testimony. The judges need not ordinarily reflect on the fit of the circumstances to the relevant rules in 'applying' the latter. The interval between their observation of the event and their declaration may be very like the interval between an umpire's observing the batter taking a cut at the ball, and the umpire's cry of "strike!"

Aside from such cases, it seems reasonable to say that the chances of immediate recognition that a set of circumstances fall within the scope of a legal rule—as contrasted with an interval needed for reflection on the matter—lessen as one moves from, e.g., traffic courts to courts dealing with a wider range of legal matters, and as one moves from trial courts to appellate courts. In a court dealing with a wide range of legal matters, the judge is less likely to be drilled or highly practiced in using the rules he may be called upon to apply. He is, for example, more likely to need to remind himself or be re-minded by counsel of the rules. Thus, it is at least more likely that he will actually be attending to the rules before deciding what his judgment shall be, even though he may not need to *reflect* on the fit of the circumstances to the rules. In litigation on appeal—which is simply litigation in which a court is asked to pass judgment on a decision by another court or by the same court on an earlier occasion—it is reasonably certain that the judges will, before deciding what their judgments shall be, attend to and consider carefully the fit of the circumstances to at least most of the relevant rules.

One may see in consequence that if it is necessary in order to apply a rule that a person clearly reflect on the fit of the circumstances to the rule before making up his mind, then umpires and perhaps traffic judges do not often apply rules, whereas appellate judges are more likely to do so. This result suggests that such reflection is *not* a necessary condition of applying rules; further, it is precisely *not* the result anticipated by the rule skeptics. These skeptics have had no desire to impugn claims that umpires and traffic judges apply rules; rather, they have wished especially to impugn claims that appel-late courts and judges apply rules.

Nevertheless, one can suggest what may concern those people who treat reflection as a necessary condition for applying rules. We purport to want judges not simply to end controversies, but to end them fairly—not simply to apply legal rules, but to apply these rules correctly—i.e., at least to apply all or only applicable rules.[2] There is some reason to regard this as a duty of judges, but the question—were these rules applied?—might be asked either primarily in the interests of the parties to a case, or primarily out of an interest in whether the judge was acting responsibly.[3] In the former instance, one might be interested principally in the outcome of the case; he is given what he needs in order to find out its correctness when he is given information on what the judgment was, what the rules were, and what were the circumstances of the case. This may be an oversimplification, but these are the types of information he needs.[4]

On the other hand, one interested in whether the judge did his duty to apply all or only the applicable rules may not be satisfied with solely the above information. He may feel that he should know how the judgment was reached. His claim could be that the correct judgment may have been reached, but not by way of the judge's acting dutifully; perhaps it was reached by chance (the tossing of dice—cf. Rabelais' Judge Bridlegoose), or by reasoning not involving the rules. In these cases (the claim would be), the judge was not doing his duty.

What seems wanted here is that the judge intend to apply the rules and that his reason for applying them be that they are applicable. But since this is all that's wanted, there is no difficulty created by the absence in any particular case of obvious reflection on the part of the judge. A person who is well-drilled in applying certain rules, and who is presented with a case that is not unusual, can apply a rule intentionally and out of conviction that it is applicable without any need for obvious reflection on the matter. And it is not inconceivable that even in difficult cases on appeal a rule might suddenly be *recognized* as applicable. What, after all, *would* be evidence that a judge had not intended to apply the rule? It would presumably have to be evidence that

2. When is a rule applicable? For the present, suffice it to say roughly that a rule is applicable when it is constitutive or regulative of the circumstances being considered and these circumstances fall within the scope of the rule. In order to better this explication, one must struggle with how it is that we identify the circumstances of cases and the regulative force of rules, and one must translate the metaphor out of the expression "fall within the scope of."

3. The supposition that judges have a duty to apply all applicable rules leads to difficulties in any reasonably complex legal system. Briefly, the difficulties concern conflicts of rules. It may appear that of the various rules applicable to a set of circumstances, the application of some will lead to end results in the case different from the results led to by application of the other(s). The question then arises as to how we would describe the duty of judges in such cases. We could, for example, launch immediately into talk about the use of judicial discretion; or we could search for higher order rules governing the application of the rules at hand; or we could consider the possibility that the rules at hand were actually more complex than initially imagined, and that they embody in themselves certain qualifications as to the conditions that fall within their scope. One meets problems like this in ethics (conflicts of duties), in the philosophy of language (in treatments of loose and open-textured terms), and very likely elsewhere.

4. It of course might not be enough to find out the advisability or desirability of the judgment.

he had applied it inadvertently.[5] But simply to suggest this is to reveal how foolish it is to suppose that a person could not have applied a rule unless he somehow had meditated beforehand on the matter. We often do what we intend to do without anything recognizable as reflecting on it. There is still, however, a difficulty produced by distinguishing between the occasion on which the judge makes up his mind on the case and the occasion on which he writes his opinion. The notion at work is that on the latter occasion he is occupied with justifying what went on on the former occasion. It is then thought that the judge did not apply the rule unless he applied it on the former occasion.

But *contra* this, suppose that the Supreme Court of the U.S., after hearing a case, votes on the outcome, and a justice is assigned the task of writing the majority opinion. He writes the opinion, circulates it among the members of the court, as is the custom, and the manuscript is returned with a notation on it by the last justice to see it. This justice points out a rule of law which, if used, would simplify the argument presented in the opinion. The justice writing the opinion *accepts* this suggestion and rewrites the opinion accordingly. The revised opinion is accepted as the opinion of the court.

Now, has the justice who rewrote the opinion *applied* the rule suggested by his comrade? What would be the point in saying that he had not? The justices made up their minds on how to dispose of the case without the thought having occurred to anyone of applying the rule in question. Yet the rule was invoked in the opinion, and the case now looks to have been decided under the authority of that rule (among others, probably).

If there is any difficulty about this being an instance of applying the rule, then it may be a difficulty over what constitutes the decision in the case. One could say the following about this: Since what counts in law is the *declaration* by a judge *in* court of the judgment *of* the court, and that is called *delivering* the judgment or decision of the court, *that,* while perhaps not the occasion on which the court makes up its mind on the case, is both the culmination and the principal point of the judicial process. To make this plain, consider what would happen if the justices were to make up their minds on the case, and then wander off without delivering their decision. Given this circumstance, it may be of some interest to speak of the intentions of the justices when making up their minds on the case, but it is much more to the point to speak of their intentions when delivering the judgment. In considering the duty of justices, it is the *declaration* that counts. It is clear here that if the justices, after *delivering* the judgment, think of a rule that could have been applied, it is too

---

5. Or that he had not *planned* to apply it—something which, however, would be irrelevant in determining whether, in the end, he did his duty.

late. It is simply a rule that *could* have been applied, not a rule that *was* applied.

Consider now what is at work in the tendency to resist this account. This can be done by referring back to the second of the conditions mentioned above as candidates for being necessary conditions of applying rules. It was that a person has not applied a rule unless his reason for making up his mind the way he did was that the rule was applicable; that is, that the outcome of the case must be explainable as due to his conviction that the circumstances of the case fell within the scope of the rule. If this were correct, then the hypothetical Supreme Court case pictured above would *not* be a case where the rule in question was applied. It would be a case where the rule was appealed to in justifying the judgment, but not a case where the rule was applied—because the judgment would not be explainable as due to a conviction that the rule applied.

What is at work here is a notion of applying a rule to a case as we might apply a yardstick to a wall. A yardstick might be used, for example, to find out whether a wall is more than twelve feet wide. But we haven't applied the yardstick in this case, i.e., made practical use of it as a yardstick, unless we have used it as a help in finding out whether the wall is or is not more than twelve feet wide. Likewise, it is thought, with rules. We haven't applied a rule unless we have used it as a help in finding out something. One may think here of Wittgenstein's mention of rules as guides or signposts.

This notion of applying rules might be supported by looking at judicial oaths in a certain way. A judge typically swears to perform his duties agreeably to, or in accordance with, the laws. This suggests that he must look to the laws in deciding what to do, and that he must not do anything inconsistent with the laws. It suggests that he uses the laws to this extent in finding out what to do. It is not difficult to see *this* as applying the laws. If this is so, then if he appeals to a legal rule in justifying his judgment in a case but hasn't arrived at the judgment by finding out that the rule applied, then he hasn't applied the rule. The parallel circumstance would be that of a man who has found out, but not by using a yardstick, that a particular wall is more than twelve feet wide, and who tells us that by using a yardstick we will find out that the wall is more than twelve feet wide. He hasn't applied the yardstick to the wall.

But there is also at work especially clearly in the law a notion that applying a rule is like applying coercion. Not a yardstick, but a club. Applying coercion and applying a rule are both actions done to produce an effect. This view of rules finds support in statutory descriptions of the duties of courts. Judges assigned to these courts are to carry out the duties of the courts—viz., to hear and determine or to hear and decide cases and controversies arising under the laws of the government from which they receive their authority. This *is* the duty which judges swear in their oath to perform agreeably to the law.

It is beyond question that the terms "determine" and "decide," as they occur in these official descriptions, are not describing a duty to determine *whether* or decide *whether* something is the case. The duty to determine or decide a case or controversy is a duty to *put an end to* the case or controversy, to conclude it, terminate it. A judge applies rules in the course of doing this as a person might apply coercion to the same end. He settles the controversy in a certain manner or style by applying a rule.

Applying rules, while not exactly like applying a yardstick *or* like applying coercion, is more like the latter than is commonly recognized. That is, there is a focus in both cases on producing a resolution of a controversy. It is true that some controversies can be settled by applying a yardstick to a wall, and that applying the yardstick settles the controversy. But, while it makes sense to ask whether to apply the yardstick, it doesn't make sense prima facie to ask whether the yardstick applies; that is there isn't a *practice* of applying yardsticks in certain situations. It *does* make sense right off, however, to ask whether a rule applies. In judicial practice, it is very often true that to ask whether the rule applies is to ask whether to apply the rule. (Not surprisingly, applying a rule is like applying a word; considering whether a word applies is very often considering whether to apply the word.) But consider the distinction between the questions (a) Does the rule apply? and (b) Shall I apply the rule? Asking whether the rule applies is asking whether the circumstances of the case fall within the scope of the rule; a judge may know this and yet ask—shall I apply the rule? This shows that he does not apply the rule in order to find out something; he applies it in order to bring a controversy to an end of a certain sort. To ask—shall I apply the rule?—is for a judge to ask either (a) shall I bring the controversy to *this* end? or (b) shall I support the (predetermined) resolution of the controversy in *this* way?

The point is that the rules applied *count* for something in the practice in which the judge is engaged. Even the judicial oath helps one to understand this. The judge swears to do his duty conformably to the laws; this, it is likely, means that he swears to comply with the laws where compliance by him is called for, and to apply them where they are applicable. Consideration of this oath suggests that when a judge applies a rule he is invoking that rule as authority for deciding the case the way he has. He claims that the authority of the rule supports his resolution of the case. Perhaps he has *not* fulfilled this duty. He may have misapplied the rule, or he may have applied the wrong rule. That is, respectively, he may have mistaken the results in fact dictated by the rule, or he may have applied a rule to circumstances which did not fall within the scope of the rule. Nevertheless he has applied the rule if he invokes the authority of the rule in justification of the results he has reached. For him to apply the rule is for him to present his judgment as in accordance with the results dictated by the rule. It makes no difference whether he is convinced or not convinced that the rule applies; for him, applying a rule may amount to nothing more than a manner or style of presenting his decision. Therefore, if he says or implies in his opinion that a rule has been applied, then it has been applied.[6]

III

The conclusions to be drawn from the above discussion seem as follows:

1. Skepticism about whether judges apply rules has been based upon too limited a view of what it can be to apply a rule. Contrary to what the skeptics seem to have thought, (a) reflection on whether a rule applies is neither a necessary condition for applying the rule nor a necessary condition for being convinced that it applies; (b) being convinced that a rule applies is not a necessary condition for applying it—it is at most a condition of dutiful or responsible application of the rule; (c) a judge may have applied a rule in a case even though he did not use the rule at all in making up his mind on what his judgment in the case would be—hence, applying a rule need not be something a judge does on the way to discovering the proper resolution of a case. (Whether it is ever this, I leave open.)

2. Admittedly, someone interested in the motives, skill, or even craft of judges will need to go beyond or behind judicial opinions for relevant information. But he will never need to do so in order to determine whether a judge has applied the rules he says or implies in his opinion that he has applied. In this last matter, at least, studies of the psychology of judicial decision-making are irrelevant and cannot provide any legitimate grounds for skepticism about whether judges ever or even very often apply rules.

3. Insofar as reports on the psychology of judicial decision-making have provided grounds for worries about the extent to which judges have 'free discretion' in deciding on cases and for discounting the importance of studying judicial opinions, one may say the following: As has been seen, applying rules is an activity of use to judges at least in part because it can amount to invoking the authority of the rules in support of judgments. The mere facts (i) that judges bother to do this, and (ii) that such invoking will misfire if the rules are too obviously misapplied or inapplicable, show what is in the claim that judges find rather than make the law, and thus what is in the claim that the discretion of judges is limited. No one, at least, can afford to overlook the *usefulness* of these invokings to judges and the limits (however broad they may sometimes seem to be) placed on judicial judgments by the general de-

6. Note that the issue as to whether a judge may have applied a rule not invoked is left entirely open by this discussion. The claims have been about what is sufficient, not what is necessary.

sirability for judges of avoiding obvious misapplications of rules and applications of obviously inapplicable rules.

4. Because applying a rule can, on analogy with applying coercion, be something done to produce a certain effect, it can work to produce that effect only when the rule applied has a relatively firm authority—i.e., when it is such that there is some sense in the circumstances to talk about invoking the authority of the rule. In this respect, judicial decision-making may be a somewhat special setting; the special responsibilities and authority of judges, and the especially firm authority of the rules themselves, combine to give the account of applying rules offered here a firmness it might not otherwise have. Thus it might have only a shadowy application elsewhere, depending upon where one seeks to use it. Nonetheless, it may help one to see even elsewhere the extent to which applying rules may be something other than a means of *discovering* what is legitimate or authoritatively dictated. It may, that is, help one to see the extent to which applying rules may be a means of *sanctioning* a decision or action *as* legitimate or authoritatively dictated—i.e., the extent to which rules may be used as bludgeons as well as guides.

4 Berlin on the Compatibility of Values, Ideals, and "Ends"

> One belief, more than any other, is responsible for the slaughter of individuals on the altars of the great historical ideals—justice or progress or the happiness of future generations, or the sacred mission or emancipation of a nation or race or class, or even liberty itself, which demands the sacrifice of individuals for the freedom of society. This is the belief that somewhere, in the past, or in the future, in divine revelation, or in the mind of an individual thinker, in the pronouncements of history or science, or in the simple heart of an uncorrupted good man, there is a final solution. This ancient faith rests on the conviction that all the positive values in which men have believed must, in the end, be compatible, and perhaps even entail one another.
>
> Isaiah Berlin.[1]

The above passage in Berlin's inaugural lecture launches an attack on what might be called the "compatibility conviction," one version of which is provided in the last sentence quoted. Berlin has attacked this conviction or something like it elsewhere also.[2] He charges that it[3] is both demonstrably false (p. 54) and malignant in its effects. Concerning the latter, he claims that holding the conviction leads to (i) devaluation of the permanent importance of freedom of choice (pp. 53–54), (ii) support of ruthless tyranny (p. 54), and (iii) obscuration of the multiplicity and diversity of human values and ideals (pp. 56–57 and passim).[4]

Given this bill of particulars by such a distinguished historian of social and political theory, we might think ourselves well advised to reject the conviction in question and to fight it where we find it. This would be a mistake. Not only

1. Isaiah Berlin, *Two Concepts of Liberty* (New York: Oxford University Press, 1958), p. 52; hereafter [in this chapter] page numbers from this book will be given in parentheses.

2. See Isaiah Berlin, "Equality," *Proceedings of the Aristotelian Society*, N.S. 56 (1955–56), 319; reprinted in Frederick Olafson, ed., *Justice and Social Policy* (Englewood Cliffs, N.J.: Prentice-Hall, 1961).

3. Or perhaps only something near to it; see Section I, below.

4. As these effects commonly are connected both with views about what authoritarianism involves and with views about what would constitute a "libertarian" chamber of horrors, it is not surprising to find Berlin also suggesting that acceptance or rejection of the conviction in question is a significant point of division between, on the one hand, some advocates of "the great, disciplined authoritarian (social and political) structures" and, on the other, individualistic libertarians (pp. 54, 56, and passim).

do Berlin's charges fail to succeed, but they reveal a misunderstanding of what is being attacked. This misunderstanding is no doubt encouraged by the fact that his target shifts as he argues; "the" conviction in question is not a single thing, but rather, in his hands, several significantly different things. But, within the rather broad area sketched out by his varying formulations of the conviction or cluster of convictions, one finds for the most part views which are not only utterly harmless with respect to the malignancies he claims to result from them but also, so far as he shows, not false, let alone demonstrably false. More important, some of them are such that the charge of falseness reveals a misunderstanding of their character. Of these latter, indeed, some express guiding principles so basic to an understanding of what it is to choose and adopt ideals and goals that rejection of these principles would render incomprehensible any claims that people *have* ideals and goals. Berlin's discussion should not be allowed to obscure the roles of views such as these.

I

In his discussion, at least the following formulations of the conviction or convictions under attack are expressed or implied:

> 1. that all the positive values in which men have believed must, in the end, be compatible, and perhaps even entail one another (p. 52);
> 2. that all the ideals of mankind are compatible (p. 53);
> 3. that all the diverse ends of men can be harmoniously realized (p. 54);
> 4. that all the ends of men are in principle compatible with each other (p. 54);
> 5. that in some perfect state, realizable by men on earth, no ends pursued by them will ever be in conflict (pp. 53–54);
> 6. that we can have everything (p. 55);
> 7. that all good things are compatible or reconcilable with each other (p. 53);
> 8. that a total harmony of true values is somewhere to be found—perhaps in some ideal realm the characteristics of which we can, in our finite state, not so much as conceive (p. 53);
> 9. that it is false that the fulfilment of some of our ideals may in principle make the fulfilment of others impossible (p. 53).

Examination of this list will reveal that there are striking differences among the formulations. Not only is the character of the compatibility condition variously estimated but also the identity of what is said to be compatible changes.

These changes need to be sorted out. Rather than discuss them at the moment, however, I shall refer back to items on the list at various stages during the subsequent discussion. Berlin himself gives little sign of wishing to treat these formulations differently for purposes of his arguments. But, as will be seen, they cannot reasonably be regarded as merely alternative ways of converging on one and the same "conviction"; their effects on the persuasiveness and even the appropriateness of his arguments are too profound for that.

II

Within the broad area sketched out by these formulations, one distinction of central importance is as follows: A person may hold (*a*) that the *actual* values, ideals, or "ends" of some man or group of men at a given moment are such that they would be fully compatible (i.e., such that no sacrifice of one would ever be necessary for the sake of another) in some world realizable by men on earth, or at least in some logically possible world.[5] Alternatively, he may hold (*b*) that, relative to relationships among a man's own values, ideals, or "ends," or among the collective ones of members of a community, or among those of members of a community or set of communities considered distributively, *all acceptable, indorsable, or, in some sense, correctly chosen and identified* values, ideals, or "ends" would be compatible in some realizable or logically possible world.

Between them, (*a*) and (*b*) are designed to accommodate *most* of the divergences in Berlin's formulations of the compatibility conviction.[6] They are, of course, still quite complex and dangerously indefinite in many ways (see below). But even as they stand they are clearly distinguishable from each other. Berlin's discussion seems to be sometimes about one or more of the constituent disjuncts of the first, and sometimes about one or more of those of the second. At one extreme is his talk in number 3 (above) about "all the diverse ends of men"; it is clear from the context at this point that he is thinking of ends that a historian or social scientist might discover by making an empirical investigation into what men *in fact* strive for. At the other extreme is the mention in number 8 of "true values." Most of the other formulations are more equivocal on the matter than these and, depending upon how one wishes

5. One might easily press for further elucidation of this notion of compatibility. But nothing further is needed for the points I wish to make in this paper.

6. Most notably, they do not accommodate number 6, above. But they also do not accommodate the possibility, left open by some of the formulations, that the compatibility envisioned is in the world *here and now* and not merely in some realizable or logically possible world. This is a difficult point; as will be seen, some of Berlin's arguments would be more effective if this were the compatibility in question. Nevertheless, he never stipulates this and *does* stipulate otherwise; furthermore, many of the details of his discussion reveal that he is not thinking of compatibility here and now.

to push them, shade off into something roughly like one or the other of these perspectives.

The difference, however, is utterly crucial to Berlin's charge that the compatibility conviction is false. Insofar as the charge is understood to be about some application of one or more constituent disjuncts of (a), one at least knows how to *start* evaluating it. He should conduct an empirical investigation to determine what are the values, ideals, or "ends" (goals?) of the man or men being studied. Having completed this, the investigator could then go on to consider whether, if the values, ideals, or ends discovered are well enough defined to make the project feasible, there are any good reasons to believe or disbelieve that their mutual and complete attainment would be possible in some realizable future or some logically possible world. This might or might not be a large order, depending upon what the values, etc., turned out to be. And one might or might not be able to show the compatibility claim to be demonstrably false.[7]

If, however, Berlin's charge is understood to be about one or more of the constituent disjuncts of (b), then reliance on initial investigations such as those just suggested would be inappropriate. This is not because consideration of the actual values, etc., of men would be of no importance but merely because those to be identified would not necessarily be ones men *do* have but, rather, ones men *ought* in some sense to have or might *unobjectionably* have. To be sure, it is not immediately clear what sorts of investigation or reflection would lead to correct identification of these. More important, it is not clear that any investigations whatever would be appropriate.

The disjuncts of (b) need not, after all, be viewed as synthetic claims about independently identifiable values, etc. Whether they *can* be so viewed depends upon whether we can see the compatibility specified as being in no way a prerequisite of the acceptability, indorsability, or "correctness" of values, ideals, or ends.[8] Otherwise, the compatibility will appear, more or less clearly, as a qualifying condition for membership in the sets of values, etc.,

7. One must do more, of course, than merely point out that men's values, etc., *have* conflicted or *are* conflicting—which is all that Berlin does. The conflicts must be shown to be, in some sense, unavoidable—a sense that is shifting, no doubt, with shifts in one's understanding of whether the alleged compatibility is in some realizable future or in some logically possible world. Perhaps Berlin does not argue this because he thinks the point too plain to need arguing. This depends, however, upon who the men in question are and, if argument is not to be offered, upon whether their values, etc., obviously would be incompatible in *every* logically possible world. In such cases, of course, one *never* would be able to achieve one of the values, etc., without sacrificing the others. But which among the actual values, ideals, and "ends" of men are so related? This is not clear. Berlin thus appears to have some distance to go before he will have shown any applications of the disjuncts of (a) to be false.

8. Berlin's quotes from Condorcet (p. 52), for example, seem to me to leave this issue quite open.

under consideration, and the disjuncts will emerge, not as falsifiable statements of fact, but rather as, roughly, expressions of guiding principles or policies or rules of procedure to be used in the *selection* of values, etc.[9] The clear and relevant question then would not be "Is the disjunct true?" but, rather, "Why adopt only values (ideals, ends) compatible in the way specified therein?"

Pursuing this matter further, one can see in most cases the primary relevance of what are clearly policy considerations. For example, relative to whether one should tolerate or find acceptable selections of values, etc., resulting in irremediable conflicts among the values, ideals, or ends of one person and those of another, or those of one group and those of another, appeal clearly would be appropriate to the advantages or disadvantages of the resulting interpersonal conflict and of the measures required to avoid it.[10] Concerning the former, for example, appeals *against* toleration of irremediable conflict might range anywhere from reference to a desire to act in accordance with the presumed wish of God that we at least eventually live together noncompetitively (thus explaining the use of "true" in connection with values, etc., so compatible; cf. number 8, above) to reference to a desire to reap "fully" the fruits of a universe presumed to be melioristic[11] (thus explaining

9. The notion that we *select* our values, rather than simply *have* them (or even find ourselves the helpless victims of them), may appear overly rationalistic, but it fits in well with our practices of advising and attempting to persuade one another about what to find worthwhile. Berlin's position on this is not clear and indeed may be the source of many of his difficulties. See his remarks about "fundamental" and "absolute moral categories" (pp. 54, 56, 57).

10. Concerning the latter, of course, some of Berlin's arguments *would* be appropriate, namely, those concerned with the malignant effects of the "conviction" he is attacking (the effects cited above in the first paragraph of this paper). But it should be clear that there is no disjunct either of (*a*) or (*b*) whose acceptance would lead to such effects unless supplemented by one or more of the following: (i) a shift throughout from "compatibility in some realizable (or logically possible) world" to "compatibility here and now" (see note 6, above); (ii) a view that the compatibility in question is a *sufficient* condition for values, etc., to have been "correctly" or wisely or reasonably chosen; (iii) dogmatic views about how to proceed toward a world in which compatibility would be realized. The disjuncts of (*a*) and (*b*) thus in themselves are utterly harmless with respect to having the malignant consequences alleged. Furthermore, insofar as acceptance of any disjuncts of (*b*) would make any detectable difference at all in one's behavior, why not argue that it would increase one's commitment to exercising ingenuity in reconciling apparent conflicts among values, etc., using foresight in avoiding such conflicts, and being willing to reconsider whether one is valuing what one ought to value? The plausibility of claims that these *are* effects to be expected may go some way toward explaining support of the principles or policies in question.

11. Berlin does not believe the universe to *be* wholly melioristic, and, indeed, this sometimes seems to be his main point against the "conviction" in question. Perhaps this would be a ground for believing that acceptance of any of the above disjuncts of (*b*) would be in some way *self-frustrating;* but one would be quite mistaken to suppose it a ground for believing the disjuncts themselves to be *false*. These points would be relevant also in connection with disjuncts concern-

the use of "positive"; cf. number 1, above). On the other hand, appeals *for* toleration of such conflict might aim toward pointing out that interpersonal conflict is not always disadvantageous and that, for example, it may bring rewards in both personal satisfaction and the advancement of societies.[12]

It should be obvious, however, that arguing in these clearly appropriate ways involves adopting a view of the relevant disjuncts of (*b*) utterly remote from treating them as statements having truth values. The view of them is, rather, as expressions of policies or rules of procedure concerning what is to be sought or allowed. To treat them as false or falsifiable, let alone as demonstrably false, thus would be to misunderstand their role.

Furthermore, there are yet other cases where such treatment of disjuncts of (*b*) might be said to involve an even more radical misunderstanding. These are cases where the disjuncts concern relationships among the ideals or ends of a single person or among the collective ideals or ends of the members of a community, group, or culture (cf. number 9, above). Showing this, however, requires a somewhat more extended argument.

III

Consider the question initially with respect to intrapersonal and collective *ideals*. The first thing to notice is that our ideals are principles in accordance with which we aspire to regulate our behavior.[13] When, following Berlin, we declare that some of "the great historical ideals" are justice, progress, the happiness of future generations, liberty, and political equality, presumably we are thinking of these in the form of principles and saying that action in accordance with them is something to which men have persistently (if not universally and continuously) aspired. Some care is needed here, however, because justice, etc., can also be considered as "ends" or goals, that is, as something that men can set out to achieve. And they can be considered values, that is, something that men value or find in some sense "worthwhile" trying to achieve. Nevertheless, there is a distinction to be made between finding something in some sense "worthwhile" and setting out to achieve it. Likewise,

---

ing relationships among intrapersonal or among collectively held values, where the question would be, e.g., "Why should a person adopt for himself only values mutually compatible in the way specified?"

12. Cf. Karl Aschenbrenner, "The Roots of Conflict and Action," *Inquiry* 7 (1964): 248; also P. F. Strawson, "Social Morality and Individual Ideal," *Philosophy* 35 (1961): 1–3, 17.

13. This has something to do with the adjectival use of "ideal" and thus with our view of the world "as it should be," or perhaps even with some view of "what would be ideal" (cf. note 6, above); but it surely is distinguishable from these. Being principles in accordance with which we aspire to act, our ideals may be such that *if* we succeed in acting in accordance with them, and *if* conditions generally are propitious, we may achieve what we would regard as "ideal" in the adjectival sense. The latter thus may guide our choices of ideals but is not identical with them.

there is a difference between setting out to achieve something and *aspiring* to regulate one's behavior in accordance with a principle designed to achieve it or even logically implying its achievement. Thus, while "justice," "progress," etc., have sometimes been considered labels of ideals, sometimes of ends or goals, and sometimes of values, this has only been by a kind of systematic equivocation or, less pejoratively, by a kind of systematic analogy.

For the sake of convenience (and I believe it is only that), one could speak of "justice," "progress," etc., as ends or goals and identify the corresponding ideals by such expressions as "to strive for justice." A way of asking whether some principle was one of the great historical ideals would therefore be as follows: picking out the relevant end, one could ask, "Is striving for that end something to which men have persistently (if not universally and continuously) aspired?"

The question could then be raised intelligibly whether men have, for example, aspired in this way to strive for justice regardless of sacrifice and progress regardless of sacrifice.[14] A straightforward affirmative answer at the least would seem to be a dangerous oversimplification. It is true that men very often speak as though striving for justice *simpliciter* and progress *simpliciter* both were their ideals; but, to consider only one possibility, perhaps they have not been speaking precisely. Such imprecision is common enough in talk about ethical, social, and political ideals and may even have its uses. But one also may press reasonably for more precise characterizations of these ideals. Do men, for example, aspire to strive for unlimited and unqualified justice here and now? Or for such justice eventually—perhaps even after their lifetimes? Or do they perhaps aspire merely to approximate one of these as closely as they are able, but with due attention to the demands of freedom, progress, etc., and to the attendant possibilities of qualification of their pursuit of justice here and now?

Getting down to specifics, what, for example, about striving for justice-even-at-the-expense-of-progress and for progress-even-at-the-expensive-of-justice?[15] Have men generally aspired to either of these? Perhaps the thought never occurred to them; or perhaps it did but was rejected as unworthy of serious consideration because of a conviction that the stipulated sacrifices always would be avoidable. If the choice were ever to be given serious consideration, however, one thing would be clear; no one could seriously, consciously aspire simultaneously to both (nor could members of a community do so collectively).

To say that no one could do this is simply to say that we could not even

14. A question obviously relevant to assessments of certain disjuncts of (*a*).

15. Cf. Kenneth Boulding's essay in Richard Brandt, ed., *Social Justice* (Englewood Cliffs, N.J.: Prentice-Hall, 1962).

make sense out of a man who claimed to be doing it (barring unexpected or special construals of his claim), nor could we make sense of the supposition that we ourselves might consciously do it, that is, aspire to strive *both* for justice-even-at-the-expense-of-progress and progress-even-at-the-expense-of-justice. The reason for this is that, in order for a person to be said to *have* ideals in any clear way, he must be said to have serious interest in whether he *could* achieve that to which he claims to aspire and believe that this achievement is not utterly out of the question. A person making the claim cited above could not be said plausibly to have such an interest and belief. This is what is behind what I take to be the fact that serious contemplation of genuine conflicts, actual or foreseen, among one's own ideals or the collective ideals of one's community is always an occasion for reidentification or respecification *of* those ideals with respect to the contemplated areas of conflict; it is incoherent to suppose that one could aspire simultaneously to them all in precisely the respect in which, and for precisely the occasion on which, he believes them in conflict. This is true, of course, not only for conflicts between areas of ideals grossly identified as "striving for freedom," "striving for progress," etc., but also for conflicts of ideals within each of these areas, as is revealed by the common practical force of such a question as "*Whose* freedom?" and by the efforts this question can trigger to specify "the ideal" more precisely.

This point is enough to show how closely connected the relevant disjuncts of (*b*) are to our capacity to recognize something as an ideal of ours or of anybody else's. The compatibility specified therein is after all, despite its indefiniteness, of a minimal sort in at least the sense that, if members of a set of ideals are not compatible in any "realizable" or "logically possible" world, they are not compatible in "our" world. A person not concerned to have ideals compatible in at least *some* realizable or logically possible world thus could not be said to *have* ideals in any clear way because, as already suggested, he could not be said to be concerned with whether he *could* achieve that to which he claims to aspire.[16] Likewise, such concern must characterize attempts to co-ordinate our social and political affairs by any honest appeals to a collection of collective ideals; the appeals would make little sense if this were not so.

Because similar considerations obviously apply to those disjuncts of (*b*) concerned with intrapersonal and collective ends or goals also, one can now understand the source of difficulties concerning any claims that members of *these* two sets of disjuncts are false. An explanation is also suggested as to why Berlin might find it difficult to focus separately on these disjuncts of (*b*),

---

16. The question will still remain whether he could achieve it *here and now* and not merely in some "realizable" or "logically possible" world. Attempts to meet this issue will create pressure for further specification of the ideals (of the sort already suggested above).

on the one hand, and parallel disjuncts of (*a*), on the other. The *sense* of belief in the latter relative to one's own ideals and goals, and of belief or disbelief in them relative to someone else's ideals and goals, depends at least in part upon the supposition that the person whose ideals and goals they are believes himself to have chosen them without clear violation of the principles expressed in the former. If this were not so, we would not find intelligible the claims that the ideals and goals in question were actually his. But, of course, this belief just *is* his belief that the relevant disjuncts of (*a*) are or may be true of his ideals and goals. There seems nothing wrong, however, with treating these last as falsifiable propositions at least "in principle," whereas the relevant disjuncts of (*b*) are, as can be seen now, so deeply imbedded in our understanding of what can qualify as *having* ideals and goals that attempts to treat them as falsifiable propositions are bound to raise confusion. They express methodological assumptions or guiding principles so characteristic of our adoption of ideals and goals as to render what we are doing quite unintelligible if we were to discard them. Whether the disjuncts ought, on this ground, to be called necessary truths, I leave open. But it is clearly inappropriate to declare that they are false, let alone that they are demonstrably false. To do so would be to reveal a serious misunderstanding of their role.[17]

IV

In sum, Berlin's charge of demonstrable falsity, insofar as it is understood to be about one or more disjuncts of (*a*), is perhaps correct in the case of some applications of these disjuncts; but nothing Berlin says shows it to be correct. His remarks on the issue are all about present and past worlds, not about "realizable" or "logically possible" worlds.

Insofar as it is understood to be about one or more disjuncts of (*b*), however, his claim would reveal more or less serious misunderstandings of the roles these can and do play in our attempts to think about and cope with actual or foreseeable conflicts among values, ideals, and goals. In the case of relationships among intrapersonal or collective ideals or goals, the conscious effort to avoid *at least* the conflicts in question is a necessary condition for the

---

17. It is important to recognize that the above argument is limited in scope. It does not apply to disjuncts of (*b*) concerned with the ideals or goals of members of groups or groups considered distributively; nor does it apply to any disjuncts of (*b*) concerned with values alone. The intelligibility of a man's claim to have certain ideals or goals, e.g., is not in the least impugned by his consciousness that they are incompatible with the ideals or goals of some other person. Nor is the intelligibility of his claim to have certain values impugned in the slightest by his consciousness that the attainment of these would result in the sacrifice of his chances for attaining yet other values he claims to have; it is perfectly intelligible, e.g., that a man might find both justice and progress in some sense "worthwhile" even though he recognized that he could not pursue or obtain one without sacrificing some portion of the other. But in all these cases the arguments offered in the last half of Section II, above, would apply.

intelligibility of our claims to *have* ideals and goals. Advice to "reject" these disjuncts of (*b*) thus would seem to amount to advice to give up meaning what we now mean when saying that people have two or more ideals or goals and, apparently, to give up also what we now recognize as having two or more ideals or goals. In the case of other disjuncts of (*b*), the conscious effort to avoid conflicts does not play so fundamental a role; but these are most readily seen as expressions of policies or rules of procedure concerning which the charge of falsity also would be inappropriate, although in another way. What is needed here, rather, is a discussion of quite a different sort and, further- more, a discussion far more careful than that which Berlin provides.[18]

18. See notes 10 and 11, above, and the text at [that] point.

5 Negative and Positive Freedom

This paper challenges the view that we may usefully distinguish between two kinds or concepts of political and social freedom—negative and positive. The argument is not that one of these is the only, the "truest," or the "most worthwhile" freedom, but rather that the distinction between them has never been made sufficiently clear, is based in part upon a serious confusion, and has drawn attention away from precisely what needs examining if the differences separating philosophers, ideologies, and social movements concerned with freedom are to be understood. The corrective advised is to regard freedom as always one and the same triadic relation, but recognize that various contending parties disagree with each other in what they understand to be the ranges of the term variables. To view the matter in this way is to release oneself from a prevalent but unrewarding concentration on "kinds" of freedom, and to turn attention toward the truly important issues in this area of social and political philosophy.

I

Controversies generated by appeals to the presence or absence of freedom in societies have been roughly of four closely related kinds—namely (1) about the nature of freedom itself, (2) about the relationships holding between the attainment of freedom and the attainment of other possible social benefits, (3) about the ranking of freedom among such benefits, and (4) about the consequences of this or that policy with respect to realizing or attaining freedom. Disputes of one kind have turned readily into disputes of the other kinds.

Of those who agree that freedom is a benefit, most would also agree that it is not the *only* benefit a society may secure its members. Other benefits might include, for example, economic and military security, technological efficiency, and exemplifications of various aesthetic and spiritual values. Once this is admitted, however, disputes of types (2) and (3) are possible. Questions can be raised as to the logical and causal relationships holding between the attainment of freedom and the attainment of these other benefits, and as to whether one could on some occasions reasonably prefer to cultivate or emphasize certain of the latter at the expense of the former. Thus, one may be led to ask: *can* anyone cultivate and emphasize freedom at the cost of realizing these other goals and values (or vice versa) and, secondly, *should* anyone ever do this? In practice, these issues are often masked by or confused with disputes about the consequences of this or that action with respect to realizing the various goals or values.

Further, any of the above disputes may stem from or turn into a dispute about what freedom *is*. The borderlines have never been easy to keep clear. But a reason for this especially worth noting at the start is that disputes about the nature of freedom are certainly historically best understood as a series of attempts by parties opposing each other on very many issues to capture for their own side the favorable attitudes attaching to the notion of freedom. It has commonly been advantageous for partisans to link the presence or absence of freedom as closely as possible to the presence or absence of those other social benefits believed to be secured or denied by the forms of social organization advocated or condemned. Each social benefit is, accordingly, treated as either a result of or a contribution to freedom, and each liability is connected somehow to the absence of freedom. This history of the matter goes far to explain how freedom came to be identified with so many different kinds of social and individual benefits, and why the status of freedom as simply one among a number of social benefits has remained unclear. The resulting flexibility of the notion of freedom, and the resulting enhancement of the value of freedom, have suited the purposes of the polemicist.

It is against this background that one should first see the issues surrounding the distinction between positive and negative freedom as two fundamentally different kinds of freedom. Nevertheless, the difficulties surrounding the distinction should not be attributed solely to the interplay of Machiavellian motives. The disputes, and indeed the distinction itself, have also been influenced by a genuine confusion concerning the concept of freedom. The confusion results from failure to understand fully the conditions under which use of the concept of freedom is intelligible.

II

Whenever the freedom of some agent or agents is in question, it is always freedom from some constraint or restriction on, interference with, or barrier to doing, not doing, becoming, or not becoming something.[1] Such freedom is

1. The need to elaborate in this unwieldy way arises from the absence in this paper of any discussion of the verification conditions for claims about freedom. The elaboration is designed to leave open the issues one would want to raise in such a discussion.

thus always *of* something (an agent or agents), *from* something, *to* do, not do, become, or not become something; it is a triadic relation. Taking the format "*x* is (is not) free from *y* to do (not do, become, not become) *z*," *x* ranges over agents, *y* ranges over such "preventing conditions" as constraints, restrictions, interferences, and barriers, and *z* ranges over actions or conditions of character or circumstance. When reference to one of these three terms is missing in such a discussion of freedom, it should be only because the reference is thought to be understood from the context of the discussion.[2]

Admittedly, the idioms of freedom are such that this is sometimes not obvious. The claim, however, is not about what we say, but rather about the conditions under which what we say is intelligible. And, of course, it is important to notice that the claim is only about what makes talk concerning the freedom of agents intelligible. This restriction excludes from consideration, for example, some uses of "free of" and "free from"—namely, those not concerned with the freedom of agents, and where, consequently, what is meant may be only "rid of" or "without." Thus, consideration of "The sky is now free of clouds" is excluded because this expression does not deal with agents at all; but consideration of "His record is free of blemish" and "She is free from any vice" is most probably also excluded. Doubt about these latter two hinges on whether these expressions might be thought claims about the freedom of agents; if so, then they are not excluded, but neither are they intelligible *as* claims about the freedom of agents until one is in a position to fill in the elements of the format offered above; if not, then although probably parasitic upon talk about the freedom of agents and thus perhaps viewable as figurative anyway, they fall outside the scope of this investigation.

The claim that freedom, subject to the restriction noted above, is a triadic relation can hardly be substantiated here by exhaustive examination of the idioms of freedom. But the most obviously troublesome cases—namely, those in which one's understanding of the context must in a relevant way carry past the limits of what is explicit in the idiom—may be classified roughly and illustrated as follows:

(*a*) *Cases where agents are not mentioned:* for example, consider any of the wide range of expressions having the form "free *x*" in which (*i*) the place of *x* is taken by an expression not clearly referring to an agent—as in "free society" or "free will"— or (*ii*) the place of *x* is taken by an expression clearly not referring to an agent—as in "free beer." All such cases can be understood to be concerned with the freedom of agents and, indeed, their

<hr/>

2. Of writers on political and social freedom who have approached this view, the clearest case is Felix Oppenheim in *Dimensions of Freedom* (New York: St. Martin's, 1961); but, while viewing social freedom as a triadic relation, he limits the ranges of the term variables so sharply as to cut one off from many issues I wish to reach. Cf. also T. D. Weldon, *The Vocabulary of Politics* (Harmondsworth: Penguin, 1953), esp. pp. 157 ff.; but see also pp. 70–72.

intelligibility rests upon their being so understood; they are thus subject to the claims made above. This is fairly obvious in the cases of "free will" and "free society." The intelligibility of the free-will problem is generally and correctly thought to rest at least upon the problem's being concerned with the freedom of persons, even though the criteria for identification of the persons or "selves" whose freedom is in question have not often been made sufficiently clear.[3] And it is beyond question that the expression "free society," although of course subject to various conflicting analyses with respect to the identity of the agent(s) whose freedom is involved, is thought intelligible only because it is thought to concern the freedom of agents of some sort or other. The expression "free beer," on the other hand (to take only one of a rich class of cases some of which would have to be managed differently), is ordinarily thought intelligible because thought to refer to beer that *people* are free *from* the ordinary restrictions of the market place to drink without paying for it.

For an expression of another grammatical form, consider "The property is free of (or from) encumbrance." Although this involves a loose use of "property," suppose that the term refers to something like a piece of land; the claim then clearly means that *owners* of that land are free *from* certain well-known restrictions (for example, certain types of charges or liabilities consequent upon their ownership of the land) *to* use, enjoy, dispose of the land as they wish.

(*b*) *Cases where it is not clear what corresponds to the second term:* for example, "freedom of choice," "freedom to choose as I please." Here, the range of constraints, restrictions, and so forth, is generally clear from the context of the discussion. In political matters, legal constraints or restrictions are most often thought of; but one also sometimes finds, as in Mill's *On Liberty,* concern for constraints and interferences constituted by social pressures. It is sometimes difficult for persons to see social pressures as constraints or interferences; this will be discussed below. It is also notoriously difficult to see causal nexuses as implying constraints or restrictions on the "will" (the person?) in connection with the free-will problem. But the very fact that such difficulties are the focus of so much attention is witness to the importance of getting clear about this term of the relation before such discussions of freedom can be said to be intelligible.

One might think that references to a second term of this sort could always be eliminated by a device such as the following. Instead of saying, for example, (*i*) "Smith is free *from* legal restrictions on travel *to* leave the country," one could say (*ii*) "Smith is free *to* leave the country *because* there are no legal restrictions on his leaving." The latter would make freedom appear

---

3. Indeed, lack of clarity on just this point is probably one of the major sources of confusion in discussions of free will.

to be a dyadic, rather than a triadic, relation. But we would be best advised to regard the appearance illusory, and this may be seen if one thinks a bit about the suggestion or implication of the sentence that nothing hinders or prevents Smith from leaving the country. Difficulties about this might be settled by attaching a qualifier to "free"—namely, "*legally* free." Alternatively, one could consider which, of all the things that might still hinder or prevent Smith from leaving the country (for example, has he promised someone to remain? will the responsibilities of his job keep him here? has he enough money to buy passage and, if not, why not?), could count as limitations on his freedom to leave the country; one would then be in a position to determine whether the claim had been misleading or false. In either case, however, the devices adopted would reveal that our understanding of what has been said hinged upon our understanding of the range of obstacles or constraints from which Smith had been claimed to be free.

(*c*) *Cases where it is not clear what corresponds to the third term:* for example, "freedom from hunger" ("want," "fear," "disease," and so forth). One quick but not very satisfactory way of dealing with such expressions is to regard them as figurative, or at least not really concerned with anybody's freedom; thus, being free from hunger would be simply being rid of, or without, hunger—as a sky may be free of clouds (compare the discussion of this above). Alternatively, one might incline toward regarding hunger as a barrier of some sort, and claim that a person free *from* hunger is free *to* be well fed or to do or do well the various things he could not do or do well if hungry. Yet again, and more satisfactorily, one could turn to the context of the initial bit of Rooseveltian rhetoric and there find reason to treat the expression as follows. Suppose that hunger is a feeling and that someone *seeks* hunger; he is on a diet and the hunger feeling reassures him that he is losing weight.[4] Alternatively, suppose that hunger is a bodily condition and that someone seeks it; he is on a Gandhi-style hunger strike. In either case, Roosevelt or his fellow orators might have wanted a world in which these people are free from hunger; but this surely does not mean that they wanted a world in which people were not hungry despite a wish to be so. They wanted, rather, a world in which people were not victims of hunger they did not seek; that is, they wanted a world without barriers keeping people hungry despite efforts to avoid hunger—a world in which people would be free *from* barriers constituted by various specifiable agricultural, economic, and political conditions *to* get enough food to prevent hunger. This view of "freedom from hunger" not only makes perfectly good and historically accurate sense out of the expression, but also conforms to the view that freedom is a triadic relation.

In other politically important idioms the *range* of the third term is not

4. I owe this example to [the late] James Pratt.

always utterly clear. For example, does freedom of religion include freedom *not* to worship? Does freedom of speech include *all* speech no matter what its content, manner of delivery, or the circumstances of its delivery? Such matters, however, raise largely historical questions or questions to be settled by political decision; they do not throw doubt on the need for a third term.

That the intelligibility of talk concerned with the freedom of agents rests in the end upon an understanding of freedom as a triadic relation is what many persons distinguishing between positive and negative freedom apparently fail to see or see clearly enough. Evidence of such failure or, alternatively, invitation to it is found in the simple but conventional characterization of the difference between the two kinds of freedom as the difference between "freedom from" and "freedom to"—a characterization suggesting that freedom could be either of two dyadic relations. This characterization, however, cannot distinguish two genuinely different kinds of freedom; it can serve only to emphasize one or the other of two features of *every* case of the freedom of agents. Consequently, anyone who argues that freedom *from* is the "only" freedom, or that freedom *to* is the "truest" freedom, or that one is "more important than" the other, cannot be taken as having said anything both straightforward and sensible about two distinct kinds of freedom. He can, at most, be said to be attending to, or emphasizing the importance of only one part of what is always present in any case of freedom.

Unfortunately, even if this basis of distinction between positive and negative freedom as two distinct kinds or concepts of freedom is shown to collapse, one has not gone very far in understanding the issues separating those philosophers or ideologies commonly said to utilize one or the other of them. One has, however, dissipated one of the main confusions blocking understanding of these issues. In recognizing that freedom is always *both* freedom from something and freedom to do or become something, one is provided with a means of making sense out of interminable and poorly defined controversies concerning, for example, when a person really is free, why freedom is important, and on what its importance depends. As these, in turn, are matters on which the distinction between positive and negative freedom has turned, one is given also a means of managing sensibly the writings appearing to accept or to be based upon that distinction.

III

The key to understanding lies in recognition of precisely how differing styles of answer to the question "When are persons free?" could survive agreement that freedom is a triadic relation. The differences would be rooted in differing views on the ranges of the term variables—that is, on the ("true") identities of the agents whose freedom is in question, on what counts as an obstacle to or interference with the freedom of such agents, or on the range of what such agents might or might not be free to do or become.[5] Although perhaps not always obvious or dramatic, such differences could lead to vastly different accounts of when persons are free. Furthermore, differences on one of these matters might or might not be accompanied by differences on either of the others. There is thus a rich stock of ways in which such accounts might diverge, and a rich stock of possible foci of argument.

It is therefore crucial, when dealing with accounts of when persons are free, to insist on getting *quite* clear on what each writer considers to be the ranges of these term variables. Such insistence will reveal where the differences between writers are, and will provide a starting point for rewarding consideration of what might justify these differences.

The distinction between positive and negative freedom has, however, stood in the way of this approach. It has encouraged us to see differences in accounts of freedom as resulting from differences in concepts of freedom. This in turn has encouraged the wrong sorts of questions. We have been tempted to ask such questions as "Well, who *is* right? Whose concept of freedom *is* the correct one?" or "Which *kind* of freedom do we really want after all?" Such questions will not help reveal the fundamental issues separating major writers on freedom from each other, no matter *how* the writers are arranged into "camps." It would be far better to insist that the same concept of freedom is operating throughout, and that the differences, rather than being about what *freedom* is, are for example about what persons are, and about what can count as an obstacle to or interference with the freedom of persons so conceived.

The appropriateness of this insistence is easily seen when one examines prevailing characterizations of the differences between "positive" and "negative" freedom. Once the alleged difference between "freedom from" and "freedom to" has been disallowed (as it must be; see above), the most persuasive of the remaining characterizations appear to be as follows:[6]

> 1. Writers adhering to the concept of "negative" freedom hold that only the *presence* of something can render a person unfree; writers adhering to the concept of "positive" freedom hold that the *absence* of something may also render a person unfree.

5. They might also be rooted in differing views on the verification conditions for claims about freedom. This issue would be important to discuss in a full-scale treatment of freedom but, as already mentioned, it is not discussed in this paper. It plays, at most, an easily eliminable role in the distinction between positive and negative freedom.

6. Yet other attempts at characterization have been offered—most recently and notably by Sir Isaiah Berlin in *Two Concepts of Liberty* (Oxford: Clarendon, 1958). Berlin also offers the second and (more or less) the third of the characterizations cited here.

2. The former hold that a person is free to do x just in case *nothing due to arrangements made by other persons* stops him from doing x; the latter adopt no such restriction.
3. The former hold that the agents whose freedom is in question (for example, "persons," "men") are, in effect, identifiable as Anglo-American law would identify "natural" (as opposed to "artificial") persons; the latter sometimes hold quite different views as to how these agents are to be identified (see below).

The most obvious thing to be said about these characterizations, of course, is that appeal to them provides at best an excessively crude justification of the conventional classification of writers into opposing camps.[7] When one presses on the alleged points of difference, they have a tendency to break down, or at least to become less dramatic than they at first seemed.[8] As should not be surprising, the patterns of agreement and disagreement on these several points

7. A fair picture of that classification is provided by Berlin who [in *Two Concepts of Liberty*] cites and quotes from various writers in such a way as to suggest that they are in one camp or the other. Identified in this manner as adherents of "negative" freedom, one finds Occam, Erasmus, Hobbes, Locke, Bentham, Constant, J. S. Mill, Tocqueville, Jefferson, Burke, Paine. Among adherents of "positive" freedom one finds Plato, Epictetus, St. Ambrose, Montesquieu, Spinoza, Kant, Herder, Rousseau, Hegel, Fichte, Marx, Bukharin, Comte, Carlyle, T. H. Green, Bradley, Bosanquet.

8. For example, consider number 1. Perhaps there is something to it, but the following cautionary remarks should be made: (a) the so-called adherents of "negative" freedom might very well accept the *absence* of something as an obstacle to freedom. Consider a man who is not free because, although unguarded, he has been locked in chains. Is he unfree because of the *presence* of the locked chains, or is he unfree because he *lacks* a key? Are adherents of "negative" freedom prohibited from giving the latter answer? and (b) even purported adherents of "positive" freedom are not always straightforward in their acceptance of the lack of something as an obstacle to freedom. They sometimes swing toward attributing the absence of freedom to the presence of certain conditions causally connected with the lack, absence, or deprivation mentioned initially. For example, it may be said that a person who was unable to qualify for a position owing to lack of training (and thus not free to accept or "have" it) was prevented from accepting the position by a social, political, economic, or educational "system," the workings of which resulted in his being bereft of training.

Also, in so far as this swing is made, our view of the difference mentioned in number 2 may become fuzzy, for adherents of "positive" freedom might be thought at bottom to regard those "preventing conditions" counting as infringements of freedom as [being] most often if not always circumstances due to human arrangements. This might be true even when, as we shall see is sometimes the case, the focus is on the role of "irrational passions and appetites." The presence or undisciplined character of these may be treated as resulting from the operation of certain specifiable social, educational, or moral institutions or arrangements. (Berlin, e.g., seems to acknowledge this with respect to the Marxists. See Berlin, *Two Concepts of Liberty*, p. 8, n. 1, and the text at this point.) Thus one might in the end be able to say no more than this: that the adherents of "negative" freedom are on the whole more inclined to require that the *intention* of the arrangements in question has been to coerce, compel, or deprive persons of this or that. The difference here, however, is not very striking.

are in fact either too diverse or too indistinct to support any clearly justifiable arrangement of major writers into two camps. The trouble is not merely that some writers do not fit too well where they have been placed; it is rather that writers who are purportedly the very models of membership in one camp or the other (for example, Locke, the Marxists) do not fit very well where they have been placed[9]—thus suggesting that the whole system of dichotomous classification is futile and, even worse, conducive to distortion of important views on freedom.

But, even supposing that there were something to the classification and to the justification for it in terms of the above three points of difference, what then? The differences are of two kinds. They concern (*a*) the ("true") identities of the agents whose freedom is in question, and (*b*) what is to count as an "obstacle" or "barrier" to, "restriction" on, or "interference" with the freedom of such agents. They are thus clearly about the ranges of two of the three term variables mentioned earlier. It would be a mistake to see them in any other way. We are likely to make this mistake, however, and obscure the path of rewarding argument, if we present them as differences concerning what "freedom" means.

Consider the following. Suppose that we have been raised in the so-called "libertarian" tradition (roughly characterized as that of "negative" freedom). There would be nothing unusual to us, and perhaps even nothing troubling, in conventional accounts of what the adherent of negative freedom treats as the ranges of these variables.

1. He is purported to count persons just as we do—to point to living human bodies and say of each (and only of each), "There's a person." Precisely what we ordinarily call persons. (And if he is troubled by nonviable fetuses, and so forth, so are we.)

2. He is purported to mean much what we mean by "obstacle," and so forth, though this changes with changes in our views of what can be attributed to arrangements made by human beings, and also with variations in the importance we attach to consenting to rules, practices, and so forth.[10]

9. Locke said: "liberty . . . is the power a man has to do or forbear doing any particular action according . . . as he himself wills it" (*Essay Concerning Human Understanding* [1690], bk. 2, ch. 21, sec. 15). He also said, of law, "that ill deserves the name of confinement which hedges us in only from bogs and precipices," and "the end of law is, not to abolish or restrain, but to preserve and enlarge freedom" (Second *Treatise of Government* [1690], sec. 57). He also sometimes spoke of a man's consent as though it were the same as the consent of the majority.

Why doesn't all this put him in the camp of "positive" freedom vis-a-vis at least points (2) and (3) above? Concerning the Marxists, see note 8, above.

10. The point of "consent theories" of political obligation sometimes seems to be to hide from ourselves the fact that a rule of unanimity is an unworkable basis for a system of government and that government does involve coercion. We seem, however, not really to have made up our minds about this.

3. He is purported to have quite "ordinary" views on what a person may or may not be free to do or become. The actions are sometimes suggested in fairly specific terms—for example, free to have a home, raise a family, "rise to the top." But, on the whole, he is purported to talk of persons being free or not free "to do what they want" or (perhaps) "to express themselves."[11] Furthermore, the criteria for determining what a person wants to do are those we customarily use, or perhaps even the most naïve and unsophisticated of them—for example, what a person wants to do is determined by what he *says* he wants to do, or by what he manifestly *tries* to do, or even *does* do.[12]

In contrast, much might trouble us in the accounts of the so-called adherents of "positive" freedom.

1. They sometimes do not count, as the agent whose freedom is being considered, what inheritors of our tradition would unhesitatingly consider to be a "person." Instead, they occasionally engage in what has been revealingly but pejoratively called "the retreat to the inner citadel";[13] the agent in whose freedom they are interested is identified as the "real" or the "rational" or the "moral" person who is somehow sometimes hidden within, or has his seed contained within, the living human body. Sometimes, however, rather than a retreat to such an "inner citadel," or sometimes in addition to such a retreat, there is an expansion of the limits of "person" such that the institutions and members, the histories and futures of the communities in which the living human body is found are considered to be inextricable parts of the "person."

These expansions or contractions of the criteria for identification of persons may seem unwarranted to us. Whether they are so, however, depends upon the strength of the arguments offered in support of the helpfulness of regarding persons in these ways while discussing freedom. For example, the retreat to the "inner citadel" may be initiated simply by worries about which, of all the things we want, will give us lasting satisfaction—a view of our interests making it possible to see the surge of impulse or passion as an obstacle to the attainment of what we "really want." And the expansion of the limits of the "self" to include our families, cultures, nations, or races may be launched by awareness that our "self" is to some extent the product of these associations; by awareness that our identification of our interests may be influenced by our

11. These last ways of putting it are appreciably different. When a person who would otherwise count as a libertarian speaks of persons as free or not free to express themselves, his position as a libertarian may muddy a bit. One may feel invited to wonder which of the multitudinous wants of a given individual *are* expressive of his nature—that is, which are such that their fulfillment is conducive to the expression of his "self."

12. The possibility of conflicts among these criteria has not been much considered by so-called libertarians.

13. See Berlin, *Two Concepts of Liberty,* pp. 17ff. (though Berlin significantly admits also that this move can be made by adherents of negative freedom; see p. 19).

beliefs concerning ways in which our destinies are tied to the destinies of our families, nations, and so forth; by the way we see tugs and stresses upon those associations as tugs and stresses upon us; and by the ways we see ourselves and *identify* ourselves as officeholders in such associations with the rights and obligations of such offices. This expansion, in turn, makes it possible for us to see the infringement of the autonomy of our associations as infringement on our freedom.

Assessing the strengths of the various positions taken on these matters requires a painstaking investigation and evaluation of the arguments offered—something that can hardly be launched within the confines of this paper. But what should be observed is that this set of seemingly radical departures by adherents of positive freedom from the ways "we" ordinarily identify persons does not provide us with any reason whatever to claim that a different concept of *freedom* is involved (one might as well say that the shift from "The apple is to the left of the orange" to "The seeds of the apple are to the left of the seeds of the orange" changes what "to the left of" means). Furthermore, that claim would draw attention away from precisely what we should focus on; it would lead us to focus on the wrong concept—namely, "freedom" instead of "person." Only by insisting at least provisionally that all the writers have the same concept of freedom can one see clearly and keep sharply focused the obvious and extremely important differences among them concerning the concept of "person."

2. Similarly, adherents of so-called "positive" freedom purportedly differ from "us" on what counts as an obstacle. Will *this* difference be revealed adequately if we focus on supposed differences in the concept of "freedom"? Not likely. Given differences on what a person is, differences in what counts as an obstacle or interference are not surprising, of course, since what could count as an obstacle to the activity of a person identified in one way might not possibly count as an obstacle to persons identified in other ways. But the differences concerning "obstacle" and so forth are probably not due solely to differences concerning "person." If, for example, we so-called adherents of negative freedom, in order to count something as a preventing condition, ordinarily require that it can be shown a result of arrangements made by human beings, and our "opponents" do not require this, why not? On the whole, perhaps, the latter are saying this: if one is concerned with social, political, and economic policies, and with how these policies can remove or increase human misery, it is quite irrelevant whether difficulties in the way of the policies are or are not *due to* arrangements made by human beings. The only question is whether the difficulties can be removed by human arrangements, and at what cost. This view, seen as an attack upon the "artificiality" of a borderline for distinguishing human freedom from other human values, does not seem inherently unreasonable; a close look at the positions and arguments

seems called for.[14] But again, the issues and arguments will be misfocused if we fail to see them as about the range of a term variable of a single triadic relation (freedom). Admittedly, we *could* see some aspects of the matter (those where the differences do not follow merely from differences in what is thought to be the agent whose freedom is in question) as amounting to disagreements about what is meant by "freedom." But there is no decisive reason for doing so, and this move surely threatens to obscure the socially and politically significant issues raised by the argument suggested above.

3. Concerning treatment of the third term by purported adherents of positive freedom, perhaps enough has already been said to suggest that they tend to emphasize conditions of character rather than actions, and to suggest that, as with "us" too, the range of character conditions and actions focused on may influence or be influenced by what is thought to count as agent and by what is thought to count as preventing condition. Thus, though something more definite would have to be said about the matter eventually, at least some contact with the issues previously raised might be expected in arguments about the range of this variable.

It is important to observe here and throughout, however, that close agreement between two writers in their understanding of the range of one of the variables does not make *inevitable* like agreement on the ranges of the others. Indeed, we have gone far enough to see that the kinds of issues arising in determination of the ranges are sufficiently diverse to make such simple correlations unlikely. Precisely this renders attempts to arrange writers on freedom into two opposing camps so distorted and ultimately futile. There is too rich a stock of ways in which accounts of freedom diverge.

---

14. The libertarian position concerning the borderline is well expressed by Berlin in the following passage on the struggle of colonial peoples: "Is the struggle for higher status, the wish to escape from an inferior position, to be called a struggle for liberty? Is it mere pedantry to confine this word to the main ('negative') senses discussed above, or are we, as I suspect, in danger of calling any adjustment of his social situation favored by a human being an increase of his liberty, and will this not render this term so vague and distended as to make it virtually useless?" (*Two Concepts of Liberty,* 44) One may surely agree with Berlin that there may be something of a threat here; but one may also agree with him when, in the passage immediately following, he inclines to give back what he has just taken away: "And yet we cannot simply dismiss this case as a mere confusion of the notion of freedom with those of status, or solidarity, or fraternity, or equality, or some combination of these. For the craving for status is, in certain respects, very close to the desire to be an independent agent." What first needs explaining, of course, is why colonial peoples might believe themselves freer under the rule of local tyrants than under the rule of (possibly) benevolent colonial administration. Berlin tends to dismiss this as a simple confusion of a desire for freedom with a hankering after status and recognition. What need more careful evaluation than he gives them are (*a*) the strength of reasons for regarding rule by one's racial and religious peers as self-rule and (*b*) the strength of claims about freedom based on the consequences of consent or authorization for one's capacity to speak of "self-rule" (cf. Hobbes's famous chapter 16 in *Leviathan* [1651], "Of Persons and Things Personated"). Cf. note 10, above.

If we are to manage these divergences sensibly, we must focus our attention on each of these variables and on differences in views as to their ranges. Until we do this, we will not see clearly the issues which have in fact been raised, and thus will not see clearly what needs arguing. In view of this need, it is both clumsy and misleading to try to sort out writers as adherents of this or that "kind" or "concept" of freedom. We would be far better off to insist that they all have the same concept of freedom (as a triadic relation)—thus putting ourselves in a position to notice how, and inquire fruitfully into why, they identify differently what can serve as agent, preventing condition, and action or state of character vis-a-vis issues of freedom.

IV

If the importance of this approach to discussion of freedom has been generally overlooked, it is because social and political philosophers have, with dreary regularity, made the mistake of trying to answer the unadorned question, "When are men free?" or, alternatively, "When are men *really* free?" These questions *invite* confusion and misunderstanding, largely because of their tacit presumption that persons can be free or not free *simpliciter*.

One might suppose that, strictly speaking, a person could be free *simpliciter* only if there were no interference from which he was not free, and nothing that he was not free to do or become. On this view, however, and on acceptance of common views as to what counts as a person, what counts as interference, and what actions or conditions of character may meaningfully be said to be free or not free, all disputes concerning whether or not men in societies are ever free would be inane. Concerning such settings, where the use and threat of coercion are distinctively present, there would *always* be an air of fraud or hocus-pocus about claims that men are free—just like that.

Yet one might hold that men can be free (*simpliciter*) even in society because certain things which ordinarily are counted as interferences or barriers are not actually so, or because certain kinds of behavior ordinarily thought to be either free or unfree do not, for some reason, "count." Thus one might argue that at least in certain (conceivable) societies there is no activity in which men in that society are not free to engage, and no possible restriction or barrier from which they are not free.

The burden of such an argument should now be clear. Everything *from* which a person in that society might ordinarily be considered unfree must be shown not actually an interference or barrier (or not a relevant one), and everything which a person in that society might ordinarily be considered not free to *do* or *become* must be shown irrelevant to the issue of freedom. (Part of the argument in either or both cases might be that the "true" identity of the person in question is not what it has been thought to be.)

Pitfalls may remain for attempts to evaluate such arguments. For example, one may uncover tendencies to telescope questions concerning the *legitimacy* of interference into questions concerning genuineness *as* interference.[15] One may also find telescoping of questions concerning the *desirability* of certain modes of behavior or character states into questions concerning the *possibility* of being either free or not free to engage in those modes of behavior or become that kind of person.[16] Nevertheless, a demand for specification of the term variables helps pinpoint such problems, as well as forestalling the confusions obviously encouraged by failure to make the specifications.

Perhaps, however, the claim that certain men are free *simpliciter* is merely elliptical for the claim that they are free in every important respect, or in most important respects, or "on the whole." Nevertheless, the point still remains that when this ellipsis is filled in, the reasonableness of asking both "What are they free from?" and "What are they free to do or become?" becomes apparent. Only when one gets straightforward answers to these questions is he in any position to judge whether the men *are* free as claimed. Likewise, only then will he be in a position to judge the *value* or *importance* of the freedom(s) in question. It is important to know, for example, whether a man is free from legal restrictions to raise a family. But of course social or economic "arrangements" may be such that he still could not raise a family if he wanted to. Thus, merely to say that he is free to raise a family, when what is meant is only that he is free from legal restrictions to raise a family, is to invite misunderstanding. Further, the *range* of activities he may or may not be free from this or that to engage in, or the range of character states he may or may not be free to develop, should make a difference in our evaluations of his situation and of his society; but this too is not called for strongly enough when one asks simply, "Is the man free?" Only when we determine what the men in question are free from, and what they are free to do or become, will we be in a position to estimate the value for human happiness and fulfilment of being free from *that* (whatever *it* is), to do *the other thing* (whatever *it* is). Only then will we be in a position to make rational evaluations of the relative merits of societies with regard to freedom.

V

The above remarks can be tied again to the controversy concerning negative and positive freedom by considering the following argument by friends of "negative" freedom. Freedom is always and necessarily *from* restraint; thus, in so far as the adherents of positive freedom speak of persons being made free *by means of* restraint, they cannot be talking about freedom.

The issues raised by this argument (which is seldom stated more fully than here) can be revealed by investigating what might be done to make good sense

15. Cf. notes 10 and 14, above.

16. E.g., is it logically possible for a person to be free to do something immoral? Cf. Berlin, *Two Concepts of Liberty*, p. 10n.

out of the claim that, for example, Smith is (or can be) made free by restraining (constraining, coercing) him.[17] Use of the format of specifications recommended above reveals two major possibilities:

1. Restraining Smith by means *a* from doing *b* produces a situation in which he is now able to do *c* because restraint *d* is lifted. He is thereby, by means of restraint *a,* made free from *d* to do *c,* although he can no longer do *b.* For example, suppose that Smith, who always walks to where he needs to go, lives in a tiny town where there have been no pedestrian crosswalks and where automobiles have had right of way over pedestrians. Suppose further that a series of pedestrian crosswalks is instituted along with the regulation that pedestrians must use only these walks when crossing, but that while in these walks pedestrians have right of way over automobiles. The regulation restrains Smith (he can no longer legally cross streets where he pleases) but it also frees him (while in crosswalks he no longer has a duty to defer to automobile traffic). Using the schema above, the regulation (*a*) restrains Smith from crossing streets wherever he likes (*b*), but at the same time is such as to (make it practicable to) give him restricted right of way (*c*) over automobile traffic. The regulation (*a*) thus gives him restricted right of way (*c*) because it lifts the rule (*d*) giving automobiles general right of way over pedestrians.

This interpretation of the assertion that Smith can be made free by restraining him is straightforward enough. It raises problems only if one supposes that persons must be either free or not free *simpliciter,* and that the claim in question is that Smith is made free *simpliciter.* But there is no obvious justification for either of these suppositions.

If these suppositions *are* made, however, then the following interpretation may be appropriate:

2. Smith is being "restrained" only in the ordinary acceptance of that term; actually, he is not being restrained at all. He is being helped to do what he really wants to do, or what he *would* want to do if he were reasonable (moral, prudent, or such like); compare Locke's words: "that ill deserves the name of confinement which hedges us in only from bogs and precipices."[18] Because of the "constraint" put upon him, a *genuine* constraint that *was* upon him (for example, ignorance, passion, the intrusions of others) is lifted, and he is free from the latter to do what he really wishes (or would wish if . . .).

This interpretation is hardly straightforward, but the claim that it embodies is nevertheless arguable; Plato argues it in the *Republic* and implies such a claim in the *Gorgias.* Furthermore, insistence upon the format of specifica-

17. This presumes that the prospect of freeing Smith by restraining *someone else* would be unproblematic even for the friends of negative freedom.

18. *The Second Treatise of Government,* sec. 57. As is remarked below, however, the proper interpretation of this passage is not at all clear.

tions recommended above can lead one to see clearly the kind of arguments needed to support the claim. For example, if a person is to be made free, whether by means of restraint or otherwise, there must be something *from* which he is made free. This must be singled out. Its character may not always be clear; for example, in Locke's discussion the confinement from which one is liberated by law is perhaps the constraint produced by the arbitrary uncontrolled actions of one's neighbors, or perhaps it is the "constraint" arising from one's own ignorance or passion, or perhaps it is both of these. If only the former, then the specification is unexceptionable enough; that kind of constraint is well within the range of what is ordinarily thought to be constraint. If the latter, however, then some further argument is needed; one's own ignorance and passion are at least not unquestionably within the range of what can restrain him and limit his freedom. The required argument may attempt to show that ignorance and passion prevent persons from doing what they want to do, or what they "really" want to do, or what they *would* want to do if. . . . The idea would be to promote seeing the removal of ignorance and passion, or at least the control of their effects, as the removal or control of something preventing a person from doing as he wishes, really wishes, or would wish, and so forth, and thus, plausibly, an increase of that person's freedom.

Arguments concerning the "true" identity of the person in question and what *can* restrict such a person's freedom are of course important here and should be pushed further than the above discussion suggests. For the present, however, one need observe only that they are met again when one presses for specification of the full range of what, on interpretation (2), Smith is made free to *do*. Apparently, he is made free to do as he wishes, really wishes, or *would* wish if. . . . But, quite obviously, there is also something that he is prima facie *not* free to do; otherwise, there would be no point in declaring that he was being made free *by means of* restraint. One may discover how this difficulty is met by looking again to the arguments by which the claimer seeks to establish that something which at first appears to be a restraint is not actually a restraint at all. Two main lines may be found here: (*a*) that the activities being "restrained" are so unimportant or minor (relative, perhaps, to what is gained) that they are not worth counting, or (*b*) that the activities are such that no one could ever want (or really want, and so forth) to engage in them. If the activities in question are so unimportant as to be negligible, the restraints that prevent one from engaging in them may be also "not worthy of consideration"; if, on the other hand, the activities are ones that no one would conceivably freely choose to engage in, then it might indeed be thought "idle" to consider our inability to do them as a restriction upon our freedom.

Admittedly, the persons actually making the principal claim under consideration may have been confused, may not have seen all these alternatives of interpretation, and so forth. The intention here is not to say what such persons did mean when uttering the claims, but only more or less plausibly what they might have meant. The interpretations provide the main lines for the latter. They also provide a clear picture of what needs to be done in order to assess the worth of the claims in each case; for, of course, no pretense is being made here that such arguments are always or even very often ultimately convincing.

Interpretation (2) clearly provides the most difficult and interesting problems. One may analyze and discuss these problems by considering them to be raised by attempts to answer the following four questions:

(a) What is to count as an interference with the freedom of persons?

(b) What is to count as an action that persons might reasonably be said to be either free or not free to perform?

(c) What is to count as a legitimate interference with the freedom of persons?

(d) What actions are persons best left free to do?

As was mentioned above, there is a tendency to telescope (c) into (a), and to telescope (d) into (b). It was also noted that (c) and (d) are not distinct questions: they are logically related in so far as criteria of legitimacy are connected to beliefs about what is best or most desirable. (a) and (b) are also closely related in that an answer to one will affect what can reasonably be considered an answer to the other. The use of these questions as guides in the analysis and understanding of discussions of freedom should not, therefore, be expected to produce always a neat ordering of the discussions. But it *will* help further to delimit the alternatives of reasonable interpretation.

VI

In the end, then, discussions of the freedom of agents can be fully intelligible and rationally assessed only after the specification of each term of this triadic relation has been made or at least understood. The principal claim made here has been that insistence upon this single "concept" of freedom puts us in a position to see the interesting and important ranges of issues separating the philosophers who write about freedom in such different ways, and the ideologies that treat freedom so differently. These issues are obscured, if not hidden, when we suppose that the important thing is that the fascists, communists, and socialists on the one side, for example, have a different concept of freedom from that of the "libertarians" on the other. These issues are also hidden, of course, by the facile assumption that the adherents on one side or the other are never sincere.

6 Some Truths and Untruths about Civil Disobedience

Feelings about civil disobedience run high during times of public stress, and high feelings, in turn, lead to crude perceptions of the phenomena one is hastening to defend as acceptable or praiseworthy or hastening to condemn as outrageous and dangerous. One may find parallel deficiencies in the work of scholars and other serious writers who, seeking to be helpful by laying certain issues to rest or by providing a unified perspective of the phenomena, hasten in their own, sometimes indirect, way to various defenses or condemnations.

Take the matter of what civil disobedients are up to. Though lip service is occasionally paid to significant diversity in the aims, intentions, hopes, and expectations of civil disobedients, and though one sometimes finds at least implied recognition of the occasional multiplicity of these aims, and so on, the prevalence of over-simple and artificially constrictive accounts of them has bedevilled our thinking about the character, limits, effectiveness, and justifiability of civil disobedience. That, at least, is the thesis of this paper.[1]

The thesis will be developed through an examination of each of a small set of claims currently playing important roles in discussions of civil disobedience. The claims are alike in having acquired in extensive quarters, and even in some of the most serious discussions of the topic, the status of unquestioned truths—or at least of truths not seriously questioned. They are also alike, as will be shown, in that each is either flatly false or badly in need of an analysis sorting out what is true and what is false in it. They are alike

1. The key question here is, What are civil disobedients up to? One can sometimes answer satisfactorily questions about what a person is up to by speaking of the person's aims, sometimes by speaking of his intentions, sometimes by speaking of his hopes, his expectations, or even his attitudes. I have spoken impartially in this variety of ways in this paper—recognizing that there are important differences, for example, between intentions, on the one hand, and hopes, on the other, but being careful always to speak of each only insofar as it focuses answers to the question: What is he up to?

furthermore, as will also be shown, in that each rests in part upon over-facile assumptions concerning what civil disobedients are up to.

Showing these things is not a purely negative task. It provides a basis also for seeing questions we ought to be asking ourselves about civil disobedience. Some of the questions emerging will not be surprising. They will seem old and familiar. Others will be recognizably fresher, if only in the sharpness of their focus. We should ask them too if we wish to get straight about civil disobedience.

I

Consider the claim that civil disobedience is nonviolent.

Since the time of Gandhi, claims about the nonviolence of civil disobedience have gained increasing prominence, though their precise strength and import have not always been clear.[2] Most centrally, these claims have played a role in exhortations (as by Gandhi) concerning the spirit and method of this kind of disobedience. But they have also figured in attempts to reassure publics confused and distraught by the phenomenon, and even in attempts to support radical cynicism concerning the disarmed docility and consequent ineffectiveness of ordinary or traditional civil disobedience.

All this attention to the nonviolence of civil disobedience has encouraged some persons (to judge by debates I have heard) to see nonviolence as the principal if not sole significant limitation on the demeanor of civil disobedients. These persons have, furthermore, found it easy to suppose that demeanor is always either violent or nonviolent and not both. This supposition in turn has put a variety of strains on the credibility of assertions about whether the behavior of purported civil disobedients has or has not been nonviolent. Those persons starting with common notions of violent behavior as behavior likely to produce destruction of property or physical injury to persons see all other behavior as nonviolent and thus of a piece; they thus suppress our perfectly legitimate interests in whether force has been used, whether the behavior has been resistant or nonresistant, considerate or inconsiderate, restrained or unrestrained, polite or impolite, active or passive, and so forth. They even suppress our interests in what are clearly the ramifications or expectable consequences of the behavior in question—e.g., our interests in whether the behavior has been obstructive or nonobstructive, disruptive or

2. That is, it has not always been clear whether the nonviolence of the disobedience is being considered a necessary, a 'characteristic,' or (when combined with openness) a sufficient condition, or all three, of civil disobedience or of that civil disobedience deserving of toleration, or of both. The use of the expression "authentic civil disobedience" in many discussions points up one portion of the problem: it so nicely echoes the common equivocation between claims about what civil disobedience is, and claims about when civil disobedience is justifiable or at least deserving of toleration.

nondisruptive of the activities of other persons (or, to cite a special case, of the routine operations of governmental agencies or other institutions).

If, on the other hand, they start from the super-rich but extensionally narrow notions of nonviolence encouraged by Gandhi (who thought of humility, self-restraint, considerateness, politeness, and truth-telling as important features of nonviolent behavior), they will see violence where others do not ordinarily see it (e.g., as with Gandhi, they will see it in lying, hatred, insults, economic and social boycotts, fasting against a tyrant, and even in impatience).[3]

Clearly, we need to correct this situation either by rejecting the assumption that all behavior is either violent or nonviolent or by allowing the notions of violence and nonviolence to shrink back to plausible size and making open and independent use of a richer stock of contrasts.[4] But, supposing that we do return to a more reasonable understanding of the richness and multiplicity of our interests here, can we also come to an understanding of the temptation to name nonviolence and perhaps other kindred limitations on demeanor as, in some way, defining conditions of civil disobedience?

The rationale most readily offered cites the word "civil" in the expression "civil disobedience."[5] This qualifier is often cited also, of course, in explanation of other alleged features of civil disobedience—e.g., its political, public, or noncriminal character. These matters will be discussed below. But in the present context, the qualifier is seen as operating straightforwardly to delimit a range of eligible demeanors. The suggestion drawn from it is that demeanor must somehow qualify as polite, restrained, mannerly, decent—i.e., 'civil.'

One may ask, however, why such a restriction on what is to count as civil disobedience is reasonable or fitting. Here one treads on shaky ground though this is not often realized. A short reply to the question is to say that disobedients whose demeanor did not fall within these limits simply would not be *civil* disobedients; but, though even Gandhi gave it at times, this reply is hardly better than a pun.[6] It merely leads to the question of why a notion of disobedience so limited should ever become so prominent.

3. See M. K. Gandhi, *Non-Violent Resistance* (New York: Schocken, 1961), pp. 41–42, 73, 77, 79, 145, 148, 161–62, 182.

4. These matters seem hinted at in Professor [James Luther] Adams' discussion (ch. 13) [*Political and Legal Obligation: Nomos XII,* edited by J. Roland Pennock and John W. Chapman (New York: Atherton, 1970)] of the applicability to civil disobedience of the fifth criterion of just war. That paragraph of his [p. 308] could be used happily as a springboard, at least, for reaching the above points.

5. In this paper, double quotes are used around expressions that are mentioned but not used and around expressions quoted from other writers or speakers (actual or hypothetical). Single quotes are used as scare-quotes around expressions that are being used and to which special attention is being called.

6. See Gandhi, *Non-Violent Resistance,* p. 173, and also pp. 4, 60, 172.

A deeper rationale may be thought provided by pointing out connections between the limitations, on the one hand, and the presumed point or aim of civil disobedience, on the other hand. The argument would be that the limitations are reasonable in the light of the aim. Materials for such an argument could be found in the work of Gandhi and of Martin Luther King.

Both Gandhi and King saw civil disobedience as a form of nonviolent resistance, and they justified their interest in the latter by way of characterizing it as a certain very special kind of effort to change societies. The nonviolence of the resistance, and hence also of that form of it called "civil disobedience," was seen for the most part to follow from the nature of the effort involved.

King, for example, asserted that violence "destroys community and makes brotherhood impossible. It leaves society in monologue rather than dialogue."[7] He thus focused a view of civil disobedience as part of an effort and as itself constituting an effort to achieve social and political change through creation of a dialogue that would awaken in members of the society a sense of community and brotherhood with the victims of injustice in their midst. This view of the aim or point of civil disobedience makes available a seemingly profound rationale for the "civil" of "civil disobedience," viz., that the disobedience in question is "civil" because it embodies an effort to change societies by building, strengthening, and utilizing communal ties between the victims of injustice and other members of the society. In this, the rationale obviously closely parallels those mentioned above pointing to the alleged public, political, or noncriminal character of civil disobedience, but it affords much firmer guidance in the further task of exposing the appropriateness of the "nonviolent" constellation of limitations on the demeanor of civil disobedients. The limitations are more easily and plausibly seen to be reasonable in the light of this expanded understanding of the aim.

Gandhi, whose work had inspired King, had earlier characterized civil disobedience (and other forms of nonviolent resistance) as resistance to the acts but not the persons of those in power. He did so on an explicit understanding of nonviolent resistance as an effort to achieve change through soul force—i.e., through personal suffering designed to convert through love, "touching the heart and appealing to reason rather than fear."[8] This was the understanding of the aim of civil disobedience that made his disallowance of resistance to the persons rather than merely the acts of those in power seem so reasonable. It was also an understanding that afforded a rationale for stress on the nonviolence of the resistance; the limitation, again, served to rule out

7. M. L. King, *Stride Toward Freedom* (New York: Harper & Row, 1958), p. 213.

8. Gandhi, *Non-Violent Resistance,* esp. pp. 17, 32, 64, 87, 169, 172. See also p. 69. For emphasis on the ramifications of the appeal of reason and thus to the importance here of truth, see pp. 6, 29, 34, 40–42.

behavior that would be counterproductive to achievement of the aim, the aim being to touch the heart of those in power and to appeal to their reason, not their fear.

Such accounts as these of the roots of stress on the nonviolence of civil disobedience, rationalizing the nonviolence by connecting it with the aim, are surely attractive.[9] But their acceptability rests in the end not only on (i) the correctness of various empirical and conceptual claims about how nonviolence is connected with effective achievement of the supposed end or aim of civil disobedience (e.g., *does* violence always leave society in monologue rather than dialogue?) but also on (ii) the correctness of the proffered identifications of this end or aim. The discussion in the next section is intended to expose the dubiousness of the latter. What is shown is that such over-simple accounts of the end or aim of civil disobedience are implausible, and that there is thus a need to rethink the whole question of the importance of nonviolence in connection with civil disobedience. If the appropriateness of nonviolence is contingent upon the end or aim of civil disobedience, then we had better be careful that we have correctly identified this end or aim. The argument below, however, is that claims that civil disobedience per se has any such central aim or point are so far from the truth that no general account of the importance of nonviolence is possible. This does not in itself, of course, mean an end to reasoned stress on the importance of nonviolence. It means merely that the reasoning will have to be richer (to suit the multiplicity of aims that may be involved) and will have to vary to suit the cases (as the aims vary).

II

Consider the claim that civil disobedience has one central aim or point.

One who looks carefully at the relevant literature will soon recognize that a wide variety of aims has been imputed to persons engaged in civil disobe-

---

9. If one were pressed to sum up their definitional point, perhaps the argument would run as follows: Just as an object may lend itself so little to the uses for which hammers are designed that it cannot reasonably be considered a hammer at all, so certain demeanors are so out of line with or counterproductive to the aim or point of civil disobedience as to disqualify what so happens as an act of civil disobedience.

Such an argument would at best be convincing, however, only in the most gross cases of lack of fit between aim and demeanor. There doubtless are such cases, but attempts to apply the argument to specific instances of disobedience will be plagued by the controversiality of many of the empirical claims needed to underlie the assertion that there is a lack of fit (see text below). This difficulty, furthermore, when combined with the common lack of extremely well-defined aims on the part of persons who violate the law in circumstances roughly approaching these (again, see text below), shows how unsafe it is for us to do here what men commonly do in a wide variety of other circumstances, viz., make imputations about a person's aims on the basis of observations of his demeanor.

dience. Civil disobedience has variously been seen as an effort to maintain or achieve or "witness to" moral integrity or a morally sound position on some issue, or to communicate something to law enforcement officials or to a government or members of a community, or to change or nullify or test or produce some law or policy. From this plentiful array, sometimes one, sometimes another of the imputations occupies the center or even the whole of the stage. Occasionally the result amounts only to a difference of emphasis. Sometimes it amounts to a sharply etched disagreement.

For example, the view of Gandhi and King that civil disobedience is to be understood at least as part of an effort to achieve social change must surely be questioned by persons who believe that open and unevasive noncooperation with contemporary selective service regulations should count as a form of civil disobedience and have noticed that many such noncooperators seem interested only in establishing or maintaining a certain personal style of life, and declare themselves (and appear to be) totally uninterested in the reactions of other people to what they are doing.[10] Again, consider a recent difference of opinion between Judges Wyzanski and Fortas. Wyzanski holds that civil disobedience does not involve an aim of testing the constitutionality of the law or policy being protested; Fortas holds that when it is endorsable it involves precisely that—at least in the United States.[11]

The importance of such disagreements and of the wide spread in the range of aims normally cited goes, of course, far beyond an interest merely in finding a secure rationale for the common stress on the nonviolence of civil disobedience. As has already been suggested, for example, it goes to definitional issues or at least to issues that threaten to be definitional ones. The differences in the aims cited, especially when accompanied by the working (though perhaps not the theoretical or acknowledged) assumption that civil disobedience has a single characteristic aim or point, raise the question of what is going to count as civil disobedience. Insofar as our notion of what a person is up to does count in our determination of whether he is engaged in civil disobedience (as it surely does), disagreements such as the above suggest that various persons purportedly engaged in dialogue about civil disobedience may not be

10. The appearance of disagreement on the matter could of course be dissipated if Gandhi and King were understood to have meant only that civil disobedience is an instrument of social change; for that in turn might mean only that civil disobedience can function so as to promote social change regardless of the intentions of the participants. This, however, appears to alter drastically what Gandhi and King intended to say.

11. Charles Wyzanski, "On Civil Disobedience," *Atlantic Monthly,* February 1968 (see also Joseph Sax, "Conscience and Anarchy," *Yale Review* 57 (1968), 481, 485); Abe Fortas, *Concerning Dissent and Civil Disobedience* (New York: Signet, 1968), esp. pp. 16, 32–34, 63. They do, however, agree that civil disobedience is an act of protest and an effort to communicate protest. This, as we have just seen, is at least equally controversial.

talking about the same thing at all, or, at least, that they see what they are talking about under such different aspects as to make further disagreements among them not only understandable but inevitable.

In coping with this situation, we must justify our eventual inclusion or exclusion of various aims or intentions as eligible ones. Presumably, we will be guided by an interest in preserving distinctions between civil disobedience and certain competing concepts (e.g., lawful dissent?) or contrasting concepts (e.g., nullification?).[12] But it is clear that our arguments will not be knock-down ones. Aside from the likelihood that the role of references to aims and intentions in characterizing the relevant and most clearly viable candidates for competing or contrasting concepts (e.g., lawful dissent, nullification, 'common criminality,' revolution)—a role that must be worked out very carefully—will not in the end be clear, none of these candidates is unarguably a competing rather than merely a contrasting concept to civil disobedience. Thus, knock-down arguments will not be available because such arguments on these matters are at best possible only in the case of clearly competing concepts (e.g., this thing *can't* be a tiger, because it clearly *is* a lion). Concerning, for example, the status even of 'lawful dissent' relative to this issue, there are sound reasons exposed elsewhere in this chapter for uncertainty about whether it is a competing rather than merely a contrasting concept.[13]

If, consequently, a permissive attitude toward these definitional issues relative to the aims of civil disobedients seems advisable, the wide spread in the range of aims normally cited has also a considerable further importance. Depending upon the circumstances of actual or contemplated civil disobedience, there may very well be an appreciable lack of congruence in the patterns of reasonable and unreasonable, productive and counterproductive behavior relative to various different but, by hypothesis, equally eligible aims.

For an example that is difficult but centrally located, the behavior required in order truly to 'witness' what one might wish to witness may, under the circumstances, be counterproductive to the success of efforts to communicate to law enforcement officials the grounds for one's witnessing or of one's beliefs about the need for change in law enforcement policies. This divergence is possible, perhaps, only because the 'witnessing' is often to oneself or to God, and not (necessarily) to other persons such as governmental officials. Its possibility has been obscured, however, because people have not noticed the importance of the shift from an interest in witnessing to oneself or to God, to

12. The use of competing and contrasting concepts in arriving at reasoned determinations of whether a given thing 'is an x' is worked out by Thomas R. Kearns in "On Vagueness" (unpublished Ph.D. dissertation, University of Wisconsin, 1968). Kearns offers, among other examples, 'lion' and 'tiger' as competing concepts; 'game' and 'gang-war' as contrasting concepts.

13. See note 16 and Section IV below; and compare carefully the discussions cited in note 11 above.

an interest in communicating something successfully to, e.g., governmental officials, and because there have been too many facile assumptions about the latter.[14] Given that it exists, we must surely understand which of the two aims is present before we can think clearly about whether the piece of actual or contemplated civil disobedience is (or will be) either effective of justifiable.[15]

14. What will succeed in efforts to communicate to officials depends on what the officials are like and what the circumstances are. The assumption that nonviolence, considerateness, and so on will always be reasonable or productive, for example, seems grounded either on dubiously generalizable empirical claims or on further restrictions on the 'communicative' efforts in question—e.g., that they be efforts to communicate through Gandhian soul force. But, in the first place, the generalizability of the empirical claims is not certain, the issues being not merely, for example, whether nonviolence might not occasionally be less productive than violence, but also whether it might not on occasion be downright counterproductive. Gandhi of course understood this, and was careful to argue these points in upholding his claim that communication through soul force would always be maximally effective. But many persons find his claims dubiously generalizable, and the claims certainly merit continuing investigation (though part of the dispute here is doubtless due to lack of clarity and agreement on what is going to count as 'communication' or a 'communicative effort'—an important matter, considered in Section III).

Restricting the communicative effort to efforts to communicate through soul force might eliminate the possible noncongruence of productive behavior, and so forth affirmed above. But even if such restricted efforts were always maximally effective, the restriction of civil disobedience on definitional grounds to the use only of such efforts would hardly seem plausible. That is, it would hardly seem clear that efforts to communicate in any other way would reasonably *thereby* be disqualified as acts of civil disobedience. Thus it hardly seems clear that the possibility of noncongruence cited in the text would be eliminated. [Note: the text here reads "would reasonable." We have construed this as "would reasonably," but it could also be construed as "reasonable would." Eds.]

Perhaps, nevertheless, one might hold that there are other (somewhat broader) plausible restrictions on eligible communicative efforts—and, indeed, on any or all of the loosely characterized aims mentioned at the beginning of this section—and that, given these restrictions, congruence in the patterns of reasonable and unreasonable, productive and counterproductive behavior for the achievement of each would be guaranteed. But this prospect seems highly speculative, and I do not see how one could establish (so securely as to dissipate concern for the problems discussed here) the necessary presence of one or more of these restricted aims in every case of genuine civil disobedience (cf. note 22 below and the text at that point).

15. Normally our interest in the effectiveness of what a man is doing is an interest in whether his activities will contribute to the achievement of aims we assume him to have. Thus there should be no question about the claim just made insofar as it concerns effectiveness. But the role of assumptions about a man's aims is equally important to consideration of the justifiability of what he is doing, though this may not seem so clear. The importance is obvious where the justifiability question is (as it often is) about whether the man is reasonable to do what he is doing, given his aims and beliefs. But even where the question veers more clearly in the direction of concern for the moral acceptability of what he does, we can hardly reach the full range of this concern if we eliminate consideration of his aims, intentions, hopes, and expectations in doing it. Even if one is something of a utilitarian, for example, and assesses the rightness or wrongness of what a man does solely in terms of an estimate of 'its' probable consequences, 'it' is most often not identifiable independently of consideration of the man's aims, intentions, and so forth in behaving as he is behaving (e.g., as in the case of lying), and, even where it is so identifiable (e.g., grabbing

And if both aims are present, we must understand this also if we are to perceive the depths of the problems into which both civil disobedients themselves and those called upon to respond to them may be plunged.

As a prolegomenon to closer pursuit of these issues, one could consider some such general taxonomy as the following of the intentions/aims/hopes/expectations commonly attributed to law violators: [16]

> 1. 'Secretive' violations, where we impute an aim to avoid both detection and arrest, and
>   a. a primacy of interest in personal advantage, as in so-called ordinary crime.
>   b. a political aim, as in some assassinations of public figures.
>   c. an aim of helping others, as in some so-called crimes of compassion (e.g., the beneficent abortionist).
>   d. an intention of following the dictates of one's conscience, as in crimes connected with the operation of the Underground Railway in the nineteenth-century United States. [17]

---

food out of someone's hand?), estimates of its consequences could seldom exclude consideration of the consequences of the fact that his aims in doing it were imputed by others to be thus and so, or even that they were thus and so (the former because the influence of his act on other persons may be in part *via* their impression of what he is up to, and the latter because the effects of the act on the development of his character and thus on his future actions may depend importantly on his view of what he is doing).

16. Putting the matter concerning law violation awkwardly but accurately, civil disobedience is generally conceded to be a kind of manner of violating, or a violating in certain circumstances, of an actually or purportedly valid law or an actually or purportedly lawful and authoritative order or command. These distinctions between what is actual and what is purported do not become of especial importance until Part IV, and are consequently ignored until then though, of course, they bear upon the issue already raised concerning whether 'lawful dissent' is a competing rather than merely a contrasting concept to 'civil disobedience.' The distinction between laws and orders and commands is ignored here entirely because it is not of especial importance to anything discussed here, though it would be important if we were, for example, to discuss the ways in which various persons in a society (e.g., persons who happen to be policemen, prosecutors, judges, jurors, legislators, ordinary citizens) should or might acceptably but diversely respond to civil disobedience. Further, though we commonly speak of orders and commands being disobeyed and of laws being violated, this distinction is also ignored here for the sake of simplifying discourse and because nothing said hangs on it, though something might sometime hang on it because the practice among scholars of speaking also of laws being disobeyed—and thus of civil disobedience in connection with some (purported) violations of these laws—may persist only as a survival of the mistaken view that laws are orders or commands.

17. Clearly, the borderlines between the above classes are not always crisp, and the classes are not always mutually exclusive (which is to say that sometimes one and the same act may correctly be described in several of the ways listed). This is true also of the items listed under 2 below, and its importance there is considerable.

The listings above may seem superfluous because agreement appears unanimous that civil disobedience is nonsecretive. Nevertheless, both here and elsewhere where the taxonomy may

2. Nonsecretive violations, where we impute little or no aim to avoid detection, and
   a. no sober thought of arrest, either because the case involves assignment of criminal liability for the consequences of irresponsible or negligent behavior or because the act is seen as 'insane' or a 'crime of passion.' [18]
   b. an expectation of avoiding arrest
      i. through timely payment and forfeiture of bail, or timely payment of fines, as in cases of deliberate and open traffic offenses by railroad companies whose operations block crossings beyond the legal limits, or through the normal exercise of police discretion in failing to make arrests for certain kinds of 'minor' violations.
      ii. through influence of personal prestige or bribery, and so on in leading enforcement officers to look the other way.
      iii. through (possibly coordinated) audacity in committing the violation, as in smash-and-grab raids, daylight bank robberies, massive looting, or even coups d'état.
   c. a hope or expectation of contributing to overthrow of the administrative apparatus presently giving the concept of arrest clear application in the society in question, as in the storming of the Bastille, putsches, and most guerrilla warfare.
   d. a hope or expectation of nullifying the law or order in question, at least with respect to its applicability to oneself or some class of violators, by violating it in a way or under circumstances making arrest of any, or perhaps only of most, violators impracticable, as in the behavior of some Bostonians in connection with the Fugitive Slave Law of 1850.
   e. a hope or at least an expectation of being arrested, and an intention not to resist arrest. Relevantly distinguishable cases here of what the violators may be up to are suggested by the seeming appropriateness or inappropriateness of imagining the following remarks in their mouths:

---

appear excessively extensive, its extensiveness is not idle. The taxonomy exhibits, and its extensiveness suggests, some of the rich variety of law violations with which, as one may find, civil disobedience may usefully be contrasted. Endless confusion in discussions of civil disobedience seems to me to have been produced by failure to see and discriminate sufficiently these contrasting cases.

18. Including in the latter, of course, such crimes as homicide occurring during the course of a drunken brawl.

   i. "Please put me away for my good (or for yours)," as with the town drunk who wants a night's shelter, or a person who believes that he is dangerous to himself or to others

  ii. "I want to get this into the courts and am using a 'standard' way of doing so," as with an inductee's refusal to step forward for induction when he thinks that, under the existing law, he has been wrongly classified.[19]

 iii. "I want to confront you with the need to arrest me, in order to get you or those on whose authority you are acting to reconsider what you or they have done (or have failed to do)";[20] and, further,

    . "Do you really, now that you are confronted with the issue, intend to enforce this law—e.g., against persons such as myself?"

    .. "Shouldn't you, in view of this manifestation of the strength of my feelings, rethink the whole matter?"

 iv. "I cannot, in conscience, accept or conform to the law, and seek, in my present violation,

    . to avoid an evil worse than the violation itself."

    .. to bear witness to my stand and thus 'be right' with myself by this positive affirmation of what I believe."

    ... to disassociate myself from complicity in, and thus answerability (to whom?) for, the law or policy."[21]

  v. "I will not obey 'laws' such as these; they have no legitimate claim to my obedience because

    . they are instruments of my oppression, not my welfare."

    .. they are immoral."

    ... the government administering them lacks legitimacy because:

      it is not a power establishing justice" (cf. Thoreau).

      its charter is deficient."

---

19. Cf. *Dickinson* v. *U.S.* 346 US 389 (1965); *Estep* v. *U.S.* 327 US 114 (1946).

20. The aim here may not be to focus attention on the very law violated or even to focus attention on any law at all. It may instead be to focus attention on the absence of a law (e.g., of an open housing law) or on the way (some) laws are administered—e.g., as in inequitable issuing of parade permits. (Whether such variations can count either as genuine or as justifiable civil disobedience is controversial. Cf. Fortas, *Concerning Dissent and Civil Disobedience.*)

21. The differences between entries iii and iv respectively correspond very roughly to the differences between Gandhi's 'aggressive civil disobedience' and his 'defensive civil disobedience.' Cf. Gandhi, *Non-Violent Resistance*, p. 175.

its form is not acceptable—e.g., not democratic, not
rule by a super-race, not theocratic:
. though it purports to be."
.. and it doesn't even purport to be."
no government whatever is legitimate."

This taxonomy is at best suggestive of what might eventually be needed in
order to deal with the issues raised earlier. Its sketchiness is perhaps indicated
most dramatically by the fact that one cannot, even on the assumption that
every question but the question concerning what the person thinks himself up
to has been settled favorably to an act's being a case of civil disobedience,
point to any one spot on the format and say noncontroversially, "Here, at
least, is a clear case of civil disobedience." One cannot do so because the
intentions and so on mentioned are not yet fully enough delineated. Reference
back to the discussion of Gandhi and King would show this, as would reference to the views of yet other persons who believe that civil disobedience
must embody an effort to achieve or contribute to the achievement of justice,
equality, or freedom of association, and so forth.[22] As can readily be seen,
even the sections of the taxonomy most congenial to these suggestions do not
reach this far.

Nevertheless, the sketch can be used as it stands to pinpoint and sharpen
the definitional and other issues raised earlier.

Note that, while certain positions on the format can be excluded noncontroversially from the ambit of civil disobedience (e.g., 1; 2a; 2b, all three
subsections; 2e, i), and others might reasonably or justifiably be excluded
(e.g., 2c; 2d; and all those under 2e, v)—though not by knock-down arguments—there is clearly no hope of reasonably or justifiably reducing the ambit of civil disobedience to only one or even two or three of the positions.
This result, furthermore, is not merely an appearance resulting from peculiari-
ties of the taxonomy offered here. It would emerge even if alternative plausible taxonomies were used—taxonomies whose basic divisions might fall
along lines quite different from those used here and involve aims, etc., not
even mentioned in the present one (though it is difficult to imagine any less
controversial basis for the major divisions than attitudes toward detection and
arrest). For, though these alternatives might put immediately to one side some
of the positions on the presently offered format (e.g., those listed first in this
paragraph), and might considerably narrow the scope of others, none could
eventually avoid inclusion of the others, however narrowed or segmented.

22. Cf. The essay by Professor [James Luther] Adams, "Civil Disobedience: Its Occasions
and Limits," in *Political and Legal Obligation, Nomos XII,* edited by J. Roland Pennock and
John W. Chapman (New York: Atherton, 1970), pp. 293–331. For another dimension of possible
further specifications, see note 20 above.

Thus, unless one is going to argue that all of the remaining entries (e.g., 2e, iii, all subsections; 2e; iv, all subsections), perhaps narrowed or segmented in some way, must apply in every genuine case of civil disobedience (and why should they?), the need for some definitional permissiveness with respect to the aims of civil disobedients will be inescapable.

Much of the importance of the multiplicity of the remaining aims to the other issues mentioned earlier, however, would survive even if one were to accept the claim that these (perhaps narrowed) aims must all be present in every genuine case of civil disobedience. It is true of course that the aims—at least those under 2e, iii, and 2e, iv—could all be present simultaneously. Furthermore, situations where some several of them, and others on the format as well, are so present seem more common than not among persons generally thought to be engaging in civil disobedience. Consider, for example, the S.N.C.C. workers sitting-in in the South ten years ago (reference: 2e, iii, both subsections; 2e, iv, at least the second subsection; 2e, v, the first subsection; and [at least marginally?] 2e, ii). And consider the more politically oriented of today's draft resisters (reference: 2e, iii, at least the second subsection; and 2 iv, at least the first and third subsections). Often persons so situated, and others in allied movements, do not seem to have fully marked and discriminated their multiple aims. For example, within the span of three pages of *Stride Toward Freedom*, King offers, as characterizations of the message of the movement he is summing up, several of the variations appearing in our format; but he does not mark the differences between them, nor does he mark his shifts from one to another.[23] If these are to stand also as characterizations of the aims or points of the civil disobedience associated with the movement, then we must ask whether participants contemplating or engaging in civil disobedience and inspired by such words fully recognize the multiplicity and diversity of the aims cited. If they do not, they will not understand that in some circumstances action productive or justifiable relative to some (one of) the aims might be counterproductive or unjustifiable relative to another. They will not even be in a position to think clearly about whether this is so.[24]

If, for example (to echo a case offered earlier), circumstances were such that their attempts to 'be right' with themselves (2e, iv, second subsection) would involve them in behavior more likely to provoke escalation of the evil in question than to encourage reflection on its possible abandonment

---

23. King, *Stride Toward Freedom*, pp. 216–18.

24. Thus, something would seem amiss even if productive behaviors, and so on, were in the end congruent.

One might say of these people that their definiteness of intention would not be sufficient for these tasks. (The expression "definiteness of intention" is taken from Arne Naess, "Toward a Theory of Interpretation and Preciseness," in Leonard Linsky, *Semantics and the Philosophy of Language* [Urbana: University of Illinois Press, 1952], p. 248. See especially pp. 256–57.)

(2e, iii)—as where tensions were high and those persons securely in power were becoming increasingly vindictive about dissent—these actual or potential civil disobedients would not be fully equipped to recognize and understand this. Nor would they be equipped to explain their situation to others, or guide others to appropriate responses when, as would not be surprising, others were not responding appropriately. They would not fully see or understand that persons responding to them or even (perhaps only temporarily) they themselves might be seeing or emphasizing one of these aims but not the other, and consequently mistakenly assessing the reasonableness (or unreasonableness) of estimates that either or both of the aims might be achieved by the civil disobedience in question, or mistakenly assessing the justifiability of seeking to achieve the aims by such means.

In confronting such difficulties, of course, the actual or potential civil disobedient is in a position no different from that of many men in many situations. What men do very often expresses a multiplicity of aims, hopes, and expectations, sometimes only dimly recognized, and things don't always work out smoothly nor can they always even be planned smoothly without the confrontation of dilemmas. The commonness of this fact, however, is all the more reason why we should stop approaching civil disobedience as though it were all of a piece, internally a smoothly coherent act with a single unifying theme, and so on. Such a view only prevents us from recognizing fully the importance of the possible variations in aims just discussed and keeps us from systematic and orderly investigations of their ramifications. It is not surprising that, insofar as such an over-simple view has expressed our expectations concerning the subject matter, some of us have seen some segments of the truth and others have seen other segments of the truth and we have all been sent off in different intellectual and emotional directions. Nor, of course, is it surprising that, in the face of the actual richness of the phenomena, we should be subject to bouts of doubt about the rational basis of the common emphasis on the nonviolence of civil disobedience.

III

Consider the claims that civil disobedience is a political act, an act of protest, an act of communication.

The applicability of the remarks made in Section II to these claims is not immediately obvious. To say, for example, that civil disobedience is a political act may be only to say that it is politically significant—either because it has ramifications that are or may be politically relevant or important, or because it marks a person's attempt to establish or alter his personal, moral, or even legal relationships to certain political events or circumstances (e.g., by disassociating himself from further responsibility for them—though, of course, questions remain about whether he *can* do this and about what it

would mean to do this). The first interpretation makes the claim unobjectionable though it hardly differentiates civil disobedience from any other purportedly illegal act nor from any of an enormous range of purportedly legal acts.
The second (because it has to do with what the person is up to) is, at least
as a perfectly general claim, readily questionable on grounds exposed in
Section II.

More commonly, however, the claim that civil disobedience is a political
act amounts to a claim that the act is done for the sake of expected or hoped-
for political consequences, that it is (part of) an engagement in or continua-
tion of politics, an exercise of a technique for influencing the political life of
the community.

Because this view too is grounded on claims about what the disobedient is
up to, it also is readily questionable on the grounds exposed earlier. But its
popularity and the popularity of the related views cited at the beginning of
this section excuse giving them special attention. Furthermore, further careful
thinking in these restricted cases about what civil disobedients are or might
be up to will be helpful in exposing roots of further serious confusions about
civil disobedience.

Most broadly, of course, the views in question slight the inward-looking
concern for one's own moral integrity and identity that occupies the center of
attention for some civil disobedients (e.g., the noncooperators with selective
service regulations mentioned in Section I), and may on occasion do so even
for the more politically oriented disobeyers. The view, for example, that civil
disobedience is the exercise of a technique for influencing the political life of
a community carries the suggestion that civil disobedience can comfortably
be arraigned alongside such activities as electioneering, to be judged and
criticized in much the same terms—with only perhaps the special and especially interesting disadvantage that it is illegal. The wrongheadedness of this
approach as a perfectly general one is indicated by the occasional but predictable inappropriateness of remarking to a man (e.g., a Jehovah's Witness) who
has just been confronted with a need to choose obedience or disobedience
now and has chosen to disobey, "That is not a legitimate way of trying to get
the law changed." [25]

25. One might of course criticize the man for not having tried earlier to get the law changed
so that he would not now have been confronted with a need to make the present dreadful decision.
But if he had tried and (obviously) failed, we hardly evidence full understanding of his situation
if we say only "Be a good loser," or, more solemnly, "Having tried to use the mechanisms of
change, you implied acceptance of their use and thus of their outcome, and it is dishonorable for
you now not to submit to their outcome." The point is that the man may be trying to save
himself—not so much his life (for there might be dishonorable ways of trying to do that) but his
integrity, his moral identity or even his soul (what would be dishonorable ways of trying to do
these things?)—and his earlier efforts might best be compared to the efforts of a man trying to

But even where an outward-looking aspect dominates, and an act of civil disobedience is appropriately seen principally as part of an effort to bring about political or social change, one should not suppose that it can thereby be characterized quite comfortably in any or all of the above ways—viz., as a political act, an act of protest, or an act of communication. The issue hangs on important differences in how the actor sees his law violation as contributing to political or social change.

He may see it as a means (hopefully) of initiating a court test of some law or policy.[26] Alternatively, he may see it principally as a means of notifying authorities or the public generally of the presence of his dissent (and perhaps of the dissent of others of whose dissent his is representative). He may think that this latter is all that can reasonably or appropriately be expected of civil disobedience in contributing to change, and that such notification itself must be depended upon to initiate further processes leading to change or to provide an entering wedge for further activities by himself and others leading to change.[27]

Or he may see his act not only as notificatory but also as persuasive with respect to the merits of his dissent. One of Gandhi's reasons, for example, for thinking of civil disobedience as something for the very few—to be engaged in only by persons of great moral purity—was that he depended upon the capacity of the act to persuade in this way; only if the authorities were confronted with persons of recognizable and steadfast moral purity would they be led to think again about and doubt the merits of a policy that would have to be enforced against such persons.[28]

Lastly (for our present purposes) the civil disobedient may instead see his act as embodying a threat to the authorities and to the public generally, a threat of impending administrative difficulties if they do not accept his position. (Even some of Gandhi's remarks suggest this view.)[29]

---

talk a gangster out of killing him, i.e., not as efforts that somehow bind him to acceptance of defeat if they don't work.

26. Though if he sees it only as this, with none of the further visions detailed below, we would run afoul of Judge Wyzanski's position—though not that of Fortas—in regarding the violation in question as a genuine case of civil disobedience. Cf. note 11 above and the text at that point.

27. As, for example, if he were hoping to initiate a court test of a law or policy by 'notifying' the public prosecutor of his willingness to be prosecuted, but fixing his eye past the prosecutor and the court and on the legislature or the public, thinking to utilize the probable negative outcome of the court test as an instrument in further efforts to influence the legislature or the public. Concerning why he might think such a dramatic means of notification needed in cases where he does not have his eye at all on the outcome of a court test, see below.

28. Gandhi, *Non-Violent Resistance,* especially pp. 35, 77, 178.

29. Ibid., pp. 14, 131. See also Harry Prosch, "The Limits to the Moral Claim in Civil Disobedience," *Ethics* 75 (1965): 103–4. Thus, as some commentators might say, we approach the border between civil disobedience and nullification or even revolution.

In conflations of these last three views, and in confusions about borderlines between them we obviously find a source of much unease about civil disobedience. An effort to notify is not, at least in isolation, comfortably describable as a political act. Neither is an effort to persuade comfortably describable as an act of protest. Nor is a threat comfortably describable as an act of communication. The popularity of reliance on such descriptions, and careless readiness to interchange them, thus quite naturally put a strain on the credibility of assertions about civil disobedience—even in cases where that disobedience is clearly outwardlooking and part of an effort to achieve social or political change. The descriptions too often seem awkward and somehow unfitting. The unease thus produced is further compounded by general realization that neither disobedients nor their respondents are always so clear as they might be about when the borderlines between the above three efforts have been crossed.

There are, it seems (to go a bit deeper into the matter), two major sources of this unclarity. The first is a failure to examine carefully enough at the start what can reasonably be expected of civil disobedience as an instrument of social or political change. Much talk about the effectiveness of civil disobedience deals only with whether it succeeds in producing the changes ultimately desired. But, while perhaps fitting into a program designed to bring about change, civil disobedience need not be thought of as the quintessence of such a program any more than a feint by a basketball player need be thought the quintessence of an effort to sink a basket. Just as the feint might be entirely successful (its aim being to pull an opponent off guard) though the basket is not sunk, so the aim or point of civil disobedience might be fully achieved even though the hoped-for change does not occur. There is at least nothing decisive to exclude such a view of the role of civil disobedience in contributing to social change, and there is much to be said in its favor.

Insofar as this is the case, one would be reasonable to ask again whether the aim is to notify or to persuade or to threaten, and so ask precisely what—if the civil disobedience in question is indeed to be seen as only *part* of a series or sequence of efforts to achieve social or political change—precisely what is supposed to come after it, and precisely how it is supposed to prepare the way for what comes after and thus fit into a sustained effort to achieve change. These questions have not been sufficiently considered, and thus we have remained confused about the appropriateness of viewing civil disobedience (even in the outward-looking cases) in the various ways suggested by the cluster of claims collection in Section III above.[30]

30. This in turn has, among other things, left us unclear about issues that must be dealt with in debates about whether civil disobedience does (or is intended to) put a society on a slippery slope toward anarchy, or, perhaps, toward tyranny. Cf. also the discussion by Stuart M. Brown, Jr., of whether acts of civil disobedience may be implicitly treasonous. Brown, "Civil Disobedience," *Journal of Philosophy* 58 (1961): 669, 677–78.

Confusion here has been exacerbated, however, by another peculiarly modern conceptual difficulty, viz., the difficulty in settling on acceptable and, in modern social and political conditions, helpful criteria for determining when one has been successful in notifying others of his dissent.

Under the simplest conditions one may, for example, post a letter to another man, and, for certain purposes, this may count at law as notifying the other man. But surely, unless one is certain of thereby triggering certain legal responses and is counting on these responses as further steps in another 'notifying' process (cf. note 27 above), *this* 'notifying' is not all that is wanted by persons who see civil disobedience as a step in the achievement of social or political change. What is wanted is more like eventually telling a man something to his face.

But even in this latter case the man's attention may have been momentarily distracted; he may not have heard. Or, perhaps though no markable distraction has occurred, what has been said doesn't seem to have sunk in. Has the man heard or hasn't he? Such problems are compounded in mass, and at least somewhat democratically run, societies. In such societies, depending upon the law, policy, or condition from which one is dissenting, the number of people who have to be 'reached' or notified may possibly be very large and their specific identities may not be clear. In such societies, furthermore, something sharp, shocking, or dramatic may be thought needed, especially by those who are not fortunate enough to be generally considered men of light and learning, to penetrate or even to gain opportunity to penetrate (by gaining notice in the mass media) the consciousness of those who must be reached. The spiraling escalation in the forcefulness of tactical devices and ever higher thresholds of public sensitivity to which such considerations have led are already familiar. They have led from techniques of clearly lawful dissent to civil disobedience and beyond, and from isolated to massed as well as massive acts—acts which may serve only to 'notify' members of the larger community consisting of the nation, but which are threatening and coercive-seeming to the smaller communities in which they sometimes occur.

In the midst of such circumstances, perfectly legitimate concerns for when dissent has been heard, supplemented perhaps by firm conviction of the rightness of the cause and faith in the vindication of one's judgment by a public actually made aware of it and of its grounds, have sometimes swelled to such proportions as to be satisfied only by policy changes dramatically in the direction of the dissent. Dissent not markedly agreed with has increasingly been thought in some circles to be dissent not heard. This conviction has led to harder pushes to 'be heard.' And efforts of the most forceful and even coercive nature thus travel under the title of efforts to be heard.

In such circumstances, important distinctions between notification, persuasion, and threat fade away. But the process of escalation has not originated solely out of bad faith or even outrageously bad judgment on anybody's part.

Rather, though exacerbated by current general anxieties about personal political impotence, it has had a source in the presence of the serious and peculiarly modern problems just suggested—problems concerning the assessment of the effectiveness of a person's efforts to communicate in and to a mass society.

The bearing of this upon the thesis of the present paper is as follows: Recognition of such a small but important source of confusion about civil disobedience depends in the end upon our capacity and willingness to distinguish and isolate for special and careful attention the segments of even such a close cluster of accounts as those considered here of the aim or point of civil disobedience—e.g., those suggested in the remarks that civil disobedience is a political act, an act of protest, an act of communication. Thus, even where civil disobedience does have the outward-looking aspect indicated by such characterizations, both actual and potential civil disobedients themselves and persons called upon to respond to them will have further careful and discriminating thinking to do about the aims of civil disobedience. Even then, as should now be clear, such persons will be ill-equipped to talk sensibly about either the effectiveness or the justifiability of civil disobedience until they pay closer attention to precisely how it does or might fit into an ongoing and possibly sustained effort to achieve social and political change, and thus closer attention to how civil disobedients do or might see what they are up to.

IV

The importance of another dimension of concern for what civil disobedients are up to emerges from consideration of the following claim—a claim which, though it hasn't received acceptance so wide as that received by the earlier claims, has nevertheless been influential in some significant quarters:

IV. That civil disobedience is an act of respect rather than of disrespect for law.

Most justifications for the claim cite the characteristically public and open nature of civil disobedience, the subsequent nonresistance to arrest, and the 'acceptance' of normal penalties. They thus perhaps slightly confuse what is the case with what, in the view of the commentators in question, ought to be the case about civil disobedience.[31] But a more fundamental criticism may be launched by noting the rather limited view of respect and disrespect embodied in the position. The position encourages us to see the contrast between respect and disrespect as clearly revealed in a contrast between behavior that is open

31. The issue depends, for example, on what 'acceptance' of normal penalties amounts to. Though purported civil disobedients do not ordinarily attempt to escape penalties once imposed, they do often enough hire lawyers who plead that imposition of normal penalties for the offense would be either unnecessary or unjust, and, whether or not they have such lawyers, they often enough appear to believe that the penalties imposed (or even impositions of any penalties whatever) are inappropriate or unjust.

and nonresistant and behavior that is neither. But this is a mistake. The sneaky, furtive, evasive, and resistant behavior of a 'common criminal,' instead of clearly revealing disrespect for the law, reveals an important aspect of respect, and one furthermore that is prima facie absent in the case of civil disobedience; it is that aspect of respect linked up with heeding, giving serious attention to, believing that one has good reason not to run afoul of, and even fearing the thing respected. Compare the boxer who respects his opponent's left jab. The civil disobedient who so deliberately and openly steps into the path of the full weight of the law may be thought to show prima facie the same 'disrespect' for the law that a boxer might show for his opponent by stepping deliberately into the path of the opponent's most earnest blows.

Yet another aspect of respect is even more decisively (i.e., not merely prima facie) absent in the case of civil disobedience, at least in part; it is deference to what is respected. It is true that, insofar as the civil disobedient 'accepts' arrest, conviction, and normal punishment, he defers to *these* operations of the legal system. But there is obviously also something important to which he does not defer. He does not defer to 'accept,' or 'honor' the guidance or requirements of the very law he deliberately violates.

His failure to defer in this way may not, of course, be inconsistent with his having or showing respect for that very law or for the law generally.[32] But admitting this is a long way from admitting that the violator's failure to defer is itself an act of respect for the law violated or even for the law generally, and the latter claim is the one here being examined. That claim, insofar as it rests only on citation of the openness, and so forth of civil disobedience, remains absurd because it cannot explain how one can at the same time both defer to and violate the law. It is not surprising, therefore, that the claim that civil disobedience is an act of respect rather than of disrespect for the law is suspect and ultimately unconvincing so long as it rests only on these grounds.

Further attempts to explain how violating a law can count as an act of respect for, and even of deference to, law have of course been made by some commentators. The lines of argument are easily sketched. They all involve the claim that violation of *this* (perhaps only purported?) law is an act of deference to *that* law, and the claim that the latter is superior to or more genuine than, and thus overrides or even invalidates (*ab initio?*), the former.

32. Consider the unexceptionableness of saying: "With all respect, I decline . . . ;" "Though I respect . . . , nevertheless . . . ;" or "I respect . . . , but. . . ." The pattern of argument offered in support of such remarks normally is: 'Though I respect x, something more important is at stake here, viz., y' (where y may be the truth, my integrity, my self-development). If such protestations are to be fully convincing, however, there should be grounds for believing that they are not merely ceremonial and intended only to mollify, placate, and so on. Perhaps that is why a civil disobedient's previous history of obedience or disobedience to the law has come to have the relevance it has.

These claims are sometimes fancied by the use of distinctions between the letter or 'color' of the law and its spirit or essence, but the claims remain pretty much as they have just been stated.

The prospects for success of these arguments may be ultimately dim. The most basic difficulty is that of preserving a basis for recognizing the prevailing view that civil disobedience does most certainly involve a violation of a law. The distinction threatened is that between civil disobedience and lawful dissent. If, of course, one has no interest in preserving that distinction, then little stands in the way of the argument. But the distinction has played, at least in modern times, a fundamental role in identifying what civil disobedience is. To give it up is to run the risk of changing the topic so radically as to dissipate the relevance of what one says to persons now attracted to, repelled from, or thoughtful about civil disobedience precisely because they see it as involving a deliberate and solemn violation of a law.

Nevertheless, the issues raised by these arguments are very deep. They extend back into the indecisive treatment within the natural law tradition of commands of civil authorities contrary to natural law. They extend forward to, for example, present controversies about the relationship of national law to the United Nations Charter and to the so-called law of Nuremburg. Under one aspect, the issues center around the relationships of subordinate to superordinate laws, how to tell definitively when and precisely where one set of laws is subordinate to another, whether there can be genuine or only apparent conflicts between the former and the latter, and how and where to draw the line between appeals to superordinate laws and appeals to mere overriding considerations in justifications of departures from conduct required by some specific (purported) law. Under another aspect, the issues center on the situations of persons living within the ambit of laws and on how to describe fairly the act of a person who, though deliberately violating a (purported) law, sees himself nevertheless acting on maxims that should be (or, he believes, are) acceptable to all persons or in the best interests of all persons to accept as their own.

Consider the range of imputations perhaps most congenial to the claim at hand: The civil disobedient, engaged, let us suppose, in a solemn act of conscience, presumably believes that he would be vindicated if judged (correctly) in the appropriate forum. He believes not only that he, though engaging in civil disobedience, would be found guiltless of acting contrary to any of the considerations guiding judgments in that forum, but also that he could not have remained guiltless except by engaging in civil disobedience. He believes, in short, that civil disobedience in his case was required by the—let us say—'law' of the forum. All this can perhaps be admitted about him. It would provide a basis for saying that his act showed deference to and respect for the 'law' of that forum.

But can we accept without complaint the claim that his act showed deference to and respect for law *simpliciter?* It depends upon the forum, and upon how the 'law' of that forum is or is not related to what we commonly and unhesitatingly consider to be law. And it depends also upon the details concerning how the 'law' of that forum overrides or fails to override, invalidates or fails to invalidate, the 'law' whose violation made his act genuinely an act of civil disobedience. In the end, we may, for example, be willing to say only that he thought that his was an act of deference to law, but that he was mistaken because he was mistaken in how he resolved one or more of these issues.[33]

Behind the concern leading us into such issues may lie an assumption that should be gotten into the open—viz., the assumption that if we are to show the civil disobedient worthy of respect, we must show that he is, at least in intention, steadfastly law-abiding. This assumption may seem peculiar, especially to persons who think of being law-abiding as conforming to various and sundry laws and think of laws as the sort of things inscribed on legislative rolls and brought into force by executive signatures. It will seem less peculiar to persons who think of being law-abiding as conforming to something 'higher' and more permanent than merely such enactments of 'King-in-Parliament.' But even in the latter case, there are significant divergences in possible interpretations of the position. Fidelity to law may mean fidelity to a constitution, to some allegedly deeper requirements of a way of social or political life, or to requirements for maintaining or developing a national, or narrower or broader, cultural or political heritage or character, or to some version of the permanent interests of mankind either as simply a collection of secular beings or as creatures of God.

When carried so far, the assumption may in the end amount only to a demand that the civil disobedient, if he is to be worthy of respect, be acting in conformity to, or at least with a view to conforming to requirements set by the interests or aspirations shared (or sharable) by members of 'his' community (however extensive that community is considered to be).[34] The thrust of the demand then appears to be to establish that he is an upholder of community interests and not an 'outlaw'—a matter to be settled in part, perhaps, by discovering something so minimal as that he is acting on maxims that *he* would be willing to see everyone act on, or even believes obligatory for everyone to act on. For the rest, the issue may, depending on the weight others are willing to attach to the above considerations, be settled by deciding that

33. A man might indeed think he is deferring to law and yet not be doing so; but it is important also to recognize throughout the present discussion that he cannot be deferring to law unless he thinks he is doing so.

34. Thus is exposed yet another (and perhaps the deepest yet) possible rationale for the "civil" of "civil disobedience."

these maxims are (or arguably should be) accepted by other members of 'his' community.

The impact of these considerations on the main thesis of the present paper is as follows: One can notice how the discussion turns (not exclusively, but at least) on various versions of the maxims of the civil disobedient's action, and, in this way, on various versions of what he is up to. The discussion is not unrelated to that in the earlier sections of this paper; indeed, if we return to the segments of the format offered in Section II under 2e, iii and 2e, iv, and to the amplifications of 2e, iii contained in Section III, we can begin to imagine how these imputations might possibly be thought supportive of some of the versions considered here of the maxim of the civil disobedient's action—though we can see also the magnitude of the investigations needed if such suggestions were to be taken seriously. But the discussion here exposes also a new dimension of concern for what civil disobedients are up to, viz., concern for how imputations about the principles or maxims on which a civil disobedient is acting influence descriptions (as in claim IV) of what he is doing. In sorting out some possible variations in these principles or maxims, the discussion has revealed in a new way the need to make discriminations keener than are common in thinking about what civil disobedients are up to. In beginning to make some of these discriminations, we have seen again how the prevalence of over-simple views has helped hide both the richness of the phenomena and the richness of the issues underlying debate about the nature and status of civil disobedience. It is not surprising that, in the face of the prevailing simplisms about these matters, our attention has often been misdirected and we have found ourselves perpetuating unrewarding controversies.

V

The discussion so far hardly exhausts the rewards of studying with more than common care what civil disobedients are up to. Not only should more be done with issues that *have* been raised (e.g., with ramifications of the problems about definiteness of intention just barely mentioned at the end of Section II), but investigations should be made of dimensions of the matter unmentioned so far.

For example, one frequently hears the claim that we give up our 'right' to civil disobedience only at the cost of ceasing to be moral beings.[35] This claim, together with slogans accompanying it—e.g., "Do not let the law become keeper of your conscience," "Do not permit the judgment of the law to be substituted for your own judgment"—appears to express a deep concern for the integrity of individual judgment and character. We should ask very care-

---

35. For versions and echoes of this claim, see Gandhi, *Non-Violent Resistance*, p. 174, and Harold J. Laski, *The State in Theory and Practice* (New York: Viking Press, 1938), p. 66.

fully just what social, political, or legal policies we are being advised to adopt in the light of this concern.[36] But we should also probe the concern itself and in particular ask, far more doggedly than has been common, precisely when a person who obeys a law (or disobeys it, for that matter) is *not* acting on his own judgment and in an integrity-damaging way. Surely, here is both another dimension of concern for what civil disobedients are up to and another place where popular assumptions threaten to have been too complacent and oversimple.

Nevertheless, enough has been said above to support the thesis of the paper. When speaking of civil disobedients generally, the range of plausible imputations concerning what they are or might be up to in engaging in civil disobedience has been shown to be significantly large. Furthermore, the steps between one imputation and another, though sometimes seemingly slight, have been seen to be worth noting. These steps bear importantly, as has been seen, upon certain claims concerning the nature and limits of civil disobedience—viz., those that find their rationales in connecting the presence or absence of certain features of cases of civil disobedience with the presumed aim or point of the act, as in the claim that civil disobedience is nonviolent; for the challenge of showing the requisite (empirical or conceptual) connections must, we now see, be met somehow—even if only by some reasonably convincing extension—with respect to *each* of the imputed aims and so on within the plausible range (e.g., each of those delineated in the subsections of e, iii and e, iv of the format offered in Section II). It is not enough to show the connections with respect to one, or with respect to each of some more restricted range. Similarly, the steps from one such imputation to another bear importantly upon efforts to assess the effectiveness and the justifiability of civil disobedience; for, if we leave unmarked even certain small and often unnoticed shifts in imputation (as, for example, the shift from imputing an aim of 'witnessing' something to oneself to imputing an aim of 'notifying' others of one's stand), we invite not only confusion about whether and what kind of disobedience will be productive in the achievement of the aims the disobedient has, confusion about what the tests of his success are to be (cf. the discussion of 'notifying' in Section III), and misunderstanding of the dilemmas he may face when his aims are multiple, but also confusion about what further program of aims his action might or might not fit into, and thus

36. Perhaps, for example, we are being advised to adopt some such policy as the following: When a person's convictions (or, merely, judgments) lead him to disapprove of (or even 'regret') (his) conformity to a law, let him violate the law—where "let him" means "don't try to stop him" and this in turn means "don't punish or threaten to punish (or, only, 'blame' or 'disrespect') him for doing this." (Cf. currently popular demands by students for amnesty in cases of 'protest' violations of university regulations.) As is made obvious by the looseness of this formulation, if by nothing else, there is room here for more discriminating approaches.

confusion about matters of importance in assessing the acceptability of what he is doing (Section III). Lastly, seemingly small shifts in imputations concerning the maxims or principles on which the civil disobedient is acting, and thus, by this route, concerning what he is up to, bear importantly upon our efforts to think clearly about what, in the end, our total response to civil disobedients should be. Our capacity to see shifts from one to another of these maxims or principles will not only put us in a position to see through some enormously misleading claims about why we should respect (or disrespect) civil disobedients, but will also make a difference in the correctness of our understanding of the forum in which various civil disobedients may be asking to be judged and in which, in all fairness, we ought at least to consider judging them.

It is true of course that the discriminations with which this paper has been concerned are ones that civil disobedients themselves have often not made or made clearly. That is an important fact about civil disobedience and about civil disobedients. We should not overlook it when we consider how to cope intelligently and helpfully with these phenomena.[37]

37. Earlier versions of parts of this paper were presented at philosophy department colloquia at the University of Minnesota and at Wichita State University. I am grateful for the benefits of the discussions that followed these presentations, as well as for the benefits of a discussion on this general topic several years ago with Robert Rowan.

7 Reform, Violence, and Personal Integrity
A Commentary on the Saying That One Ought to Fight for What He Believes Right

The popular slogan that one ought to fight for what he believes right appears to point a way for persons to witness the moral seriousness of their interest in reform. But exactly what way does it point, and, in particular, does it enjoin resort to violence for the sake of what one believes right? Pursuit of this question exposes some roots of our indecisive and often confused views about the acceptable means of revolution and reform and the eventual role of violence therein. Common understandings of 'violence' and 'fight for' do not carry us far. Further, there are doubtless differences in how the slogan's enjoinment of 'fighting' (and thus, if at all, of violence) is understood to be limited. These differences and the issues underlying them are exposed when we ask whether the slogan is to be understood to enjoin fighting or manners of fighting that might be called premature, gratuitous, or wasteful, and when we ask whether the 'ought' in the slogan is to be understood as, at best, a prima facie ought.

I

If a person believes certain reforms to be right, ought he to fight for them? He will doubtless think so if he accepts the popular view that one ought to fight for what he believes right. Perhaps that view commends itself to him because he believes that if people do not fight for what they *believe* right, then what *is* right will not prevail.[1] Perhaps, however, it commends itself to him on grounds dependent on this consideration but taking a different tack; he may see in it a way of witnessing to others, and also and not least of all to himself, his personal or moral integrity and seriousness of purpose. A person normally witnesses his beliefs most convincingly by matching them with actions appropriate to them (cf. 'put your money where your mouth is'), and

1. I do not here question this belief, but it obviously needs close examination.

thus witnesses his beliefs that certain things are morally right and that he is a morally adequate person most convincingly by matching these beliefs with actions appropriate to them. But what actions *are* appropriate to them? The slogan that one ought to fight for what he believes right seems to point a way.

But exactly what way does it point, and in particular does it enjoin resort to violence for the sake of what one believes right? Full pursuit of this question would expose some of the deepest roots of our indecisive and often confused views about the acceptable means of revolution and reform and the eventual role of violence therein. As sufficient time for that is not presently available, I shall pursue the matter only far enough to expose its bearing on our society's often inconstant views about uses and misuses of violence in witnessing one's moral integrity; for people have accepted or have been attracted by the slogan knowing that it ought to make *some* difference in the behavior that might legitimately be expected from a person presenting himself as morally adequate, but not being very clear about precisely *what* difference it ought to make—especially, perhaps, with respect to possible resorts to violence. If we could get clear on this point we could improve our understanding of the personal and moral stake persons who find the slogan attractive may or may not have in heeding calls for resort to violence on behalf of reform (or, for that matter, on behalf of anything else they believe right).[2]

Can we say right off that the slogan enjoins resort to violence? I think not, not at least if we depend only on common understandings of the key concepts involved. Fighting for things and resorting to violence do appear often to go together. But we cannot say that the former *must,* nor can we be quite sure that it need not, be accompanied by the latter precisely because our common understandings of the key notions are not firmly enough bounded or even firmly enough established to resolve or withstand serious controversy about the matter.

Common understanding, insofar as it is reasonably consistent, does not carry us much further than saying of violence that it is behavior or activity likely to injure, damage, or destroy persons or property, to do so suddenly and by means of externally imposed force. It does not carry us much further than saying of 'fighting for' that one fights for something by striving for it, striving to get it or on its behalf—e.g., striving to bring it about or defend it—and that in order to count as 'fighting,' the striving must perhaps reach at least a certain degree of vigor, firmness, and even aggressiveness, and perhaps also involve clashing with or struggling against 'opponents'—e.g., other men.

2. The idea that violence might contribute to reform raises no conceptual problems unless reform is thought to be not a result but a nonviolent process, and even here no problems occur if the process is sufficiently well-bounded for the violence to be clearly outside it though perhaps playing a role in bringing it about or furthering it.

Neither of these understandings is satisfactory for all purposes even in common parlance,[3] but they do proceed along the consistent lines most persons seem to have in mind when dealing with matters connected with our slogan. It is thus easy enough to see how people might remain unclear about whether fighting for something must involve violence. Suppose, for example, someone claimed that men could fight for preeminence in fields such as auto-racing or merchandizing without resorting to violence. The claim might be challenged on the grounds that the notion of 'fight' is in these cases simply being extended too far past its central applications to things like war and fisticuffs, and that it would be more appropriate to regard the men as simply struggling or striving for preeminence rather than 'fighting' for it. Alternatively, the claim might be challenged on the grounds that if one had appropriate, Gandhian-like sensitivity to human nature and the ways in which it can be injured, he would see that violence is unavoidable in any struggle among men who regard each other as 'opponents,' and thus is being resorted to in these struggles. I know of no knock-down arguments that would settle either way the controversies these challenges would engender, nor is it clear to me that, if one or more of the claims made were to crumble under reasoned probing (a possibility I leave open), some element of the common understandings of 'fight for' or of 'violence' might not crumble also.

II

But more than merely this conceptual looseness seems afoot in our continued lack of definiteness on the extent to which the slogan enjoins resort to violence. Undoubtedly, the popularity of the slogan hides wide differences in how its enjoinment of fighting (and thus, if at all, of violence) is understood to be limited. The effects of this will be explored below. But one might first seek to explain how the slogan can have gained popularity in circles where, again and again, the question of its precise connection with violence has somehow been evaded even though it seems such an important thing on which to get clear. Perhaps one or more of the following considerations has underlain these evasions—or at least this neglect. Each leads to an assumption that fighting for what one believes right could never reasonably involve resort to violence.

1. Suppose one understands the slogan to mean that one ought to fight for one's *beliefs* about what is right. This of course is a possible interpretation of 'fight for what he believes right,' and, if pushed in certain directions, could

3. Most notably, the characterization of violence omits the common but far from universal or consistently held view that violence is illegitimate force (a view that might lead to dismissal out of hand of our problem about the slogan), and the minority but increasingly popular view of the importance of what is called 'structural violence.'

lead to dismissal of the possibility that the slogan would on any occasion enjoin violence.

(a) Suppose, for example, that one distinguishes between (i) beliefs that people may or may not have, and (ii) states of affairs in which people have these beliefs. Perhaps the slogan enjoins fighting for the first, not the second. But of what, then, can the fighting consist? It must consist of somehow attempting to 'uphold' or 'establish' the truth or justifiability of the beliefs, not in a forum where the judges are some specific persons to be convinced or persuaded, but rather in some depersonalized forum (where, we might say, the judge is 'history' or 'truth'). It is easy enough for some persons, one imagines, to suppose that this endeavor could hardly be furthered by violence, and thus to conclude that our slogan, so interpreted, could hardly be enjoining violence.

Quite apart from whether such a conclusion could withstand serious examination, we might well object to interpreting the slogan in a way so [as to cut] it off from the general expectation that one man's conformity to the slogan's injunction will be likely to make at least some differences in the affairs and consciousness of other men. Because an undoubted source of the slogan's popularity is the idea that if men generally don't fight for what they believe right, what is right will not prevail, we might think more reasonable an interpretation of the slogan as at least enjoining a man's fighting to get or keep other people generally sharing various of his beliefs about what is right.

(b) But even on this 'more generous' interpretation of the slogan one might get the impression that resorts to violence would be ineffective or even ruled out. One might, for example, stressing certain accounts of the necessary unforcedness of genuine belief, think it obvious or at least correctly arguable that violence is unproductive or even counterproductive in attempting to get people to believe or keep them believing something.

This view is difficult to focus because one is not quite sure what temporal spans should be considered. But if the spans are not to be restricted to lengthy periods (a move that could leave us quite at sea about *what* experience shows), the view would simply underestimate the occasional productiveness of violence, and even relatively crude violence, in getting people to believe and in keeping them believing something. One can easily imagine how violence might in certain circumstances be enough to keep people believing something—as, for example, where the only threat at the moment is from a child about to cry that the Emperor has no clothes, and the child can be silenced by (hidden) violence.[4] One can also easily imagine how violence

4. Perhaps it will be said that such violence would not be right even if it were the only way of silencing the child in time, and that the slogan would not countenance it. But the slogan enjoins people to fight for what they believe right, and some people have thought it best for mankind, and even urgently necessary, that we all continue to believe that the Emperor has clothes.

could play a role in propagating beliefs. Perhaps, for example, people generally do not share one's beliefs in part because it has never occurred to them to think such things as he has thought—they are like persons to whom it has never occurred that the Emperor has no clothes. He wishes to give them the thought and, indeed, convince them of the fact; but he lacks a means of doing so or is being prevented from doing so. Resort to violence might help him seize a means—e.g., a radio station—or remove the obstacles—e.g., overcome his guards and escape. The violence would not be sufficient to get people to share his beliefs, but it might, in the ways just suggested, be helpful or even necessary and not at all necessarily counterproductive. Thus quite apart from considering claims about more subtle uses of violence in getting people to believe something, we hardly find, even on this interpretation of the slogan, sufficient grounds for dismissing the possibility that it might enjoin resort to violence.

2. Lastly, suppose someone, plausibly enough, sees the slogan as enjoining not merely fighting for one's beliefs on either or both the above interpretations, but also fighting for the preservation or attainment of those states of affairs generally that he believes right. Suppose further that the person in question believes right mostly or only states of affairs in which, among other things, people generally share certain attitudes or a certain spirit toward each other and toward the world and their situations in it, and suppose that the attitudes or the spirit are thought to be tautologically unforced and freely arrived at. There is no reason, of course, to imagine that they are thought sufficient in themselves to make everything right; they need merely be thought necessary. For, for example, the person may think it right to strive for justice on earth and may conceive this as involving at least in part the actualization of certain distributions of goods and remedies, and of certain procedures for determining the distributions. But he may also think that for true justice to be done, all this must be carried out with a generally shared spirit of fellow-feeling, a desire to be fair, and an attitude of kindliness. He may not think very clearly or seriously about the possible role of violence in bringing about this state of affairs, because he thinks principally of these latter elements of the description of what he believes right, and sees or thinks he sees that violence could never achieve or maintain these, or would even be counterproductive to their achievement or maintenance.

If so then, as in our earlier case, this man also may underestimate the possible role of violence in contributing to what he (presumably) wants. But even if this were not true, there would be a decisive argument against his view of (or perhaps only his lack of concern for) the extent to which our slogan does not does not enjoin violence. The slogan is hardly addressed exclusively to him or to people who think as he does about what is right; it is addressed to everybody. Many persons may not share his tender and righteous concern for the spirit in which things are done, or, though sharing it, may nevertheless think it right to settle for less if only less seems possible. They may think it right to have *at least* the actualization of certain distributions of goods and remedies and of certain procedures for determining the distributions. They may even think it right to have at least the former. Furthermore, they may think it right to have these distributions of at least some goods and remedies even though it is not possible to have them of all, and to have them for at least some communities and temporal periods even if it is not possible to have them everywhere and always. By the time one gets this far, violence may look to be not only necessary (and not counterproductive) in some circumstances for achieving what would be right, but *enough* to achieve it. The person who goes this far may or may not, when he moves to action, believe himself to be making dreadful and difficult decisions on the matter; but, as the slogan is addressed to him also, we cannot avoid considering whether it enjoins his resorting to violence.

In sum, this view, as well as the others, fails to provide sufficient grounds for dismissing the possibility that our slogan enjoins resort to violence on at least some occasions. And none of the views provides us with a sufficient excuse to avoid confronting the issue.

III

But how can we proceed further on the matter in the face of the conceptual looseness noticed earlier? If that discussion was correct, nothing is sufficiently clear about the concepts themselves for us to say with certainty sufficient to withstand reasonable attack either that the slogan does or that it does not enjoin resort to violence on at least some occasions.

Perhaps the most we can do is ask whether such enjoinment would be consistent with the spirit of the slogan—the spirit of the slogan being the common understanding of it figuring in its widespread popularity and acceptance.[5] This understanding doubtless operates principally with a modest notion of 'fight for,' and with what might be called a pre-Gandhian notion of violence—one depending on rather gross understandings of the nature of the injuries, damage, and destruction definitionally associated with violence. On the basis of these understandings, we might readily agree that one could at least sometimes 'fight' for what one believes right, do so in the spirit of the slogan, and yet not resort to violence. But it would not yet be clear that this would always be possible. That is, it would not yet be clear that refusal to resort to violence would always be consistent with the spirit of the slogan.

_____

5. Reserving judgment on whether acceptance of this understanding might not work to perpetuate error.

The common understanding of the slogan, as so far exposed, hardly seems to carry us this far.

Further exploration of the spirit of the slogan insofar as it bears upon this matter should start by confronting squarely the effects of widespread but unremarked and perhaps only dimly perceived differences in understandings of how the slogan's enjoinment of fighting and of various manners of fighting are (to be) limited. Though those differences are, not surprisingly, entangled with differing views on the extent to which 'fighting' per se and various manners of 'fighting' involve violence, the former are not to be explained solely by reference to the latter. Full exploration of this fact would expose some of the deepest roots of our indecisiveness about the slogan's enjoinment of violence. But time limitations make possible only brief mention of some of the considerations afoot.

These considerations appear when one asks: precisely what is the slogan generally understood to enjoin with respect to when and how one ought to fight?[6]

1. Clearly the slogan is not understood to, and does not, endorse or enjoin either *promiscuous* violence or *promiscuous* fighting—that is, for our present purposes, violence or fighting that, even in the view of the agent, would not contribute to success in preserving or attaining what he believes right.

2. But it is not clear whether the slogan is understood to endorse or enjoin fighting or manners of fighting that might be called *premature* or *gratuitous* or *wasteful* (or, *a fortiori,* violence that might be called premature or gratuitous or wasteful). Fighting or a particular manner of fighting might be called premature if it is engaged in before less objectionable methods with reasonable chance of success have been tried. It might be called gratuitous if its

---

6. As will soon be obvious, attempts to gloss the slogan on these issues can be difficult to focus. There are two main reasons for this: (i) It is difficult to distinguish attempts to render the slogan acceptable from attempts to take it for what it is. (ii) The slogan sets 'what one believes right' as indicating the end to which one's fighting is to be devoted, and one may be unclear about whether that indication is to be expanded into 'What one believes right, all things considered.' If the expansion is allowed, the comprehensiveness of the end will threaten to swallow any possible questions about the acceptability or unacceptability of various means of achieving it. What might be seen as possible disagreements about fitting means of achieving what one believes right may be seen instead as simply disagreements about what one believes right all things considered—as though the question of fitting means hadn't really yet arisen because, when everything, including the initial aim—e.g., obtaining justice for somebody—plus the use of the (possibly) unfitting means of achieving it, had been considered, one hadn't yet succeeded in identifying something he believed-right-all-things-considered and thus something he ought (according to the slogan) to fight for. The glosses that follow in the text will simply proceed in the face of these difficulties of focus, on the understanding that the difficulties remain in the background and may at any time muddy the significance of the results achieved.

contribution to success can be equalled by other, less objectionable, methods. It might be called wasteful if, though it is necessary for success, success cannot in any case be achieved because there is no chance of providing something else also necessary.[7] It would be easy to say that any intelligent understanding of the slogan would expand it to 'one ought to fight for what he believes right when doing so would not be premature, gratuitous, or wasteful, and one ought to resort to any particular manner of fighting only when use of that manner would not be premature, gratuitous, or wasteful.' But this expansion might simply be more of an attempt to render the slogan acceptable than to take it for what it is generally understood to be. Further, and much more interestingly, the view that the expansion is worth making seems to rest on an assumption that fighting itself is at least somewhat objectionable, and that some manners of fighting are more objectionable than others. Whether this assumption will or should find general acceptance depends in part on whether fighting or the manners of fighting are or should be understood necessarily to involve violence. But it depends only in part on this consideration—a point of considerable significance.

There is space at present only barely to suggest the nature of the (often) hidden disagreements and anxieties that become involved in the matter. They include such points of difficulty as: (a) the relative merits of encouraging cooperation and accommodation vs. encouraging competitiveness; (b) the relative merits of personal forbearance vs. 'spirit' or 'spunk' in 'fighting' for one's rights; (c) the nature and extent of one's personal responsibility to see to it that right prevails; (d) the viability and point of distinctions between fair means and foul in connection with the slogan—a matter having to do in part with whether and how the distinctions can be connected to the point of the slogan, e.g., to the view that if people generally do not fight for what they believe right, then what is right will not prevail.

We are not likely to reach agreement on the nature of the slogan's 'understood' limitations on methods until disagreements and anxieties about such matters as these have been resolved. But even if we were to accept the limitations suggested here to their full extent, and were also to designate resort to violence as generally understood to be the least desirable method of fighting for what one believes right, we still would not have eliminated the possibility that the slogan is understood to enjoin resort to violence on some occasions, viz., those on which violence would not be promiscuous, premature, gratuitous, or wasteful. If this possibility is to be eliminated, it must be by way of glossing common understanding of the slogan on one further issue.

3. The issue is this: Is the 'ought' in the slogan a 'prima facie' ought, so

7. If the agent thought, on such grounds, that the fighting or manner of fighting would not contribute to success, then it would count as promiscuous.

that, to the enjoinment of fighting would be understood the qualification: unless something more important would be lost thereby? This matter is especially difficult to focus because, as suggested earlier, if the indication of the end specified in the slogan is expanded to 'what one believes right, all things considered,' the 'prima facie' question threatens simply to get lost in the comprehensiveness of the end. Only if the end is somewhat less comprehensive (e.g., if it can refer merely to such relatively simple things as certain reforms one believes right), can the question above emerge as clearly interesting and important.

Suppose that we were to accept the 'prima facie' limitation, and treat common understanding of the slogan on the matter as follows: one ought to fight for what he believes right *unless* there are legitimate and over-balancing considerations to the contrary. The considerations one might cite more or less plausibly could encompass quite a range; but we are familiar with their types. They could amount to excuses, e.g., one is a paralytic and thus unable to engage in the activity called for. Or they could amount not to excuses but to justifications. Perhaps the justifications would apply especially to one person or a limited class of persons, e.g., the person(s) have a peculiar and especially useful social role or status (e.g., as mediators for or symbols of something) whose importance outweighs the value of the contribution they could make by personally engaging in the struggle and which would be destroyed by such engagement. Or perhaps the justification would not apply especially to any particular person(s), e.g., the value of what can be gained by anybody's fighting or resorting to violence (if that is involved) is outweighed in the instant case by the value of what will be lost.[8]

8. Naturally, the truth and acceptability of such claims may be expected to be sometimes controversial. Not the least of the difficulties this creates is the anxious worry it sometimes produces in persons subject to invitations or even demands that they engage in violence for the sake of reform, but who are inclined, on what they believe to be at least in part principled grounds, to abstain. If these persons cannot quite dismiss out of hand the idea that violence 'might' contribute to reform, and yet they continue to wish strongly to conform to the spirit of our slogan (even with all the limitations on the slogan's enjoinment of violence suggested above), they still may often enough find it difficult to rest easily in their opinion that violence would be premature or gratuitous or wasteful, or that the disvalue of what might be lost by violence outweighs the value of what might be gained. And even if they can rest easily with one or more of these opinions, they may still have reason to be anxious about the role the opinions in fact play in their abstinence from violence. They may worry, especially with respect to the argument about the disvalue of what might be lost by violence, how far down on their list of 'principled' priorities they can put their interest in reform and still claim to be seriously interested in it. And they may worry about the troubling availability, often enough, of less 'principled' reasons for abstaining from violence, e.g., fear for personal safety; is the 'principled' part of their abstinence so secure that they can remain untroubled in the face of this consideration about the true mainsprings of the abstinence? When caught in such anxieties, they may end by seeking engagement in violence precisely for the reassurance this will bring them about their courage and the seriousness of their

In their general forms, these excuses and justifications could be cited independently of the possible objectionableness per se either of fighting for things or of violence. But when that (possible) objectionableness is considered, the justifications may take forms of special interest to us.

What, in particular, if the objectionableness of violence in itself, without reference to more remote consequences, were to outweigh in importance the value of success? Acknowledgment of this in only some individually considered cases would be not in the least inconsistent with acceptance of the slogan as we are now supposing it to be understood. But what if the objectionableness of violence were to outweigh the value of any possible achievement to which it might ever contribute? Problems might arise about what serious and acceptable point our slogan could then have. If violence were always involved in fighting for what one believes right and never justifiable, then the slogan that we ought to fight for what we believe right would be either idle or unacceptable when interpreted as imposing only a prima facie obligation to fight, and it would simply be unacceptable without that interpretation. If, however, in agreement with common understanding, violence were not always involved in fighting for what one believes right, then, so far as violence is concerned, (i) the slogan would have point and be acceptable on the 'prima facie' interpretation even though violence were never justifiable, provided that the involvement of fighting with violence would always be sufficient grounds for rebutting the claim that one ought to fight, and (ii) the slogan would be acceptable without the 'prima facie' interpretation only if one could always fight for what one believed right without resorting to violence.

The maximal dissociation of violence from the slogan thus requires an assumption that resort to violence for the sake of what one believes right is never justified, and also requires either the 'prima facie' interpretation of the slogan or a clear possibility that people will always be able to fight for what they believe right without resorting to violence. I shall end by exploring this last idea.

IV

The notion of 'fight for' that figures in the general acceptance of our slogan may include only the idea of striving vigorously, firmly, and possibly aggressively to defend or promote something. If this understanding is accepted, then

interest in reform. Thus, even if people were to accept 'in principle' all the limitations suggested above and below on how the slogan is to be understood, their route to violence, in violation of those limitations but still in desperate pursuit of validation of their personal and moral integrity, would not be thereby assuredly blocked. This vital topic is decidedly worth another paper, but, if one were to begin at the beginning, it would have to be a paper much longer than could be offered here.

our central issue is now whether a person must ever engage in violence in order for his behavior to count as striving vigorously and firmly to defend or promote what he believes right. If we dispense at the start with cases where engaging in violence is tautologically connected to what is believed right (these cases being pretty clearly outside the boundaries of what is ordinarily contemplated by proponents of the slogan), we will see how slippery this issue is. The disagreements will really be about whether the striving has on some occasions been vigorous and firm *enough* to count as 'fighting,' even when falling short of resort to violence. Accusations and recriminations will occur when the strivings have not been successful. The idea behind this will be roughly that a man has not really fought for something if his, by hypothesis, unsuccessful efforts have fallen short of all he could have done to achieve success. On the assumption that the violence was possible and would not have been promiscuous, premature, gratuitous, or wasteful, his failure to resort to it would surely seem to be a case of his not having done all he could do.

But do we really require that a man have done all he could do, on pain of not regarding him as having fought at all, or, perhaps, not having fought in the spirit of our slogan? The attractiveness of such a requirement lies in the desirability of eliminating efforts that are just too faint-hearted or half-hearted for us to connect with the vigor and firmness suggested by 'fight for.' But we also recognize that a man can have fought and fought well even though he eventually admits defeat and quits or surrenders before exhausting his resources for continuing. Though we are perhaps rightly concerned that he have striven vigorously and firmly and exhibited no notable lack of courage or bravery, we surely want to allow him to decide at some point that the losses to be incurred by continuing will exceed the gains there is still any likelihood of getting.[9] We don't want to require that he have taken leave of his senses in order to count as a person who has fought for what he believes right. So why, we might ask, could not a man fight, and perhaps fight well, for what he believes right, though always stopping short of resort to violence?

The answer, I believe, is that he could. The difficulties in the way of accepting that answer, however, are two: (1) People too often do not see or see clearly enough what activities other than ones involving resort to violence *can* be pursued vigorously and firmly and yet at the same time not be promiscuous (because not in any way contributing to reform) or wasteful (because something else necessary for reform without violence cannot in any case be achieved); and (2) People too often do not see or see clearly how they can show themselves not lacking in courage or bravery on behalf of the interest in

9. He may come to believe that the continued fighting would be *wasteful*, in that success could not in any case be achieved; but he may also come to believe that, as the saying goes, "the game is no longer worth the candle."

reform except in military or para-military contexts. The challenge, and it is a stiff one, is to show that these two difficulties arise from failures in imagination or understanding. We should not be surprised if we do not meet that challenge to everyone's satisfaction.

In sum: The slogan that one ought to fight for what he believes right does not enjoin promiscuous violence. Perhaps, when we refer to the spirit in which it is generally understood, it does not enjoin premature, gratuitous, or wasteful violence, or violence the objectionableness of which would outweigh in importance the value of what could be achieved. We cannot, however, expect people to believe that the slogan *never* enjoins resort to violence unless we can convince them both that resort to violence would never be justifiable and also either that the 'ought' in the slogan is at best a prima facie 'ought,' or that one will *always* be able to fight in the spirit of the slogan without resorting to violence. We cannot expect the latter view to be accepted without convincing people that there are *always* nonviolent activities on behalf of reform that are neither promiscuous nor wasteful and that can be pursued with vigor and firmness, and also convince them that confining themselves to these activities in no way shows them to be lacking in bravery or courage. So long as the slogan has a grip on members of our society we must either accept the fact that it gives them a moral stake in resorting to violence on at least some occasions, or we must persuade them on the matters I have just mentioned.[10]

10. [This paper was] originally presented, along with ensuing comment, at the Conference on Rights and Political Action held by the Ripon College Philosophy Department and sponsored by the American Council of Learned Societies and the Council for Philosophical Studies, 10 October 1970. This paper is based in part on work supported by the American Council of Learned Societies and by the Graduate School of the University of Wisconsin–Madison. [The "ensuing comment" was by R. B. Brandt, "Comment on MacCallum," *Inquiry* 14 (1974): 314–17; see item 11 in the Bibliography, below. As published in *Inquiry* the subtitle of this paper was "A Commentary on the Saying that You Ought to Fight For What You Believe Right," and that is the way it is listed in the Bibliography. However, the subtitle on the paper MacCallum presented in Ripon, and, as subsequent notes show, the one he preferred (at least at the time he wrote those notes for revision), is as presented in this book: "A Commentary on the Saying that One Ought to Fight for What He Believes Right." We have followed this expressed preference even though it is probable that he would now, twenty-one years later, have gone back to the version as published in 1971, or perhaps phrased it still differently, so as to eliminate what has come to be regarded as the sexist use of "he." It might be added that there are still other changes, some of somewhat greater substance, between the paper as presented in 1970 and the paper as published in 1971. We naturally have followed the printed text except where MacCallum's later notes for revision required departure from it. Eds.]

8 Law, Conscience, and Integrity

Here are some questions about law and conscience, formulated roughly for the sake of conciseness:

1. Does the law's demand for compliance sometimes violate or threaten to violate individual consciences?
2. Is the law's demand for compliance a contributing condition to the formation or survival of conscience?
3. Have the demands of conscience played a role in the genesis of and in determining the content of the law?
4. Can law or legal systems survive consistent deferral to the demands of individual consciences?
5. Can they survive consistent failure to defer?

These questions all seem worthy of attention. I attend here only to the first, asking not only for an answer to it, but also for an account of our stake in an answer to it. I contend that, given the way the issues are generally seen, the law's demand for compliance can neither violate nor threaten to violate a person's conscience. It can, however, lead a person to violate his own conscience in a way revealing to him his failure to live up to his own aspirations for himself. When we ask what stake we could possibly have in protecting people from finding themselves in such situations, we uncover a model of personal integrity underwriting the importance generally attached to giving conscience (some) priority over law, a model whose acceptability is open to serious questioning. I end by suggesting some grounds for that questioning.

I

Here are some ways into the problem of 'conflicts' between law and conscience.[1] The first runs variations on a simple story.

1. I use double quotes around expressions that are being directly quoted or mentioned. Single quotes are used around expressions that are being used and not directly quoted but in need of

A little girl is playing on a railroad track, and a train is coming around the bend. A man walks by hurriedly, averting his face and quickening his pace; he is hastening to conclude a business deal of great importance to him. Though he remains ignorant of whether the girl was in fact slaughtered by the train, the incident lies heavily on his conscience for years after.

Another man is in the vicinity. He starts toward the girl to save her. But the embankment, made soggy by a recent rainstorm, gives way, plunging him helplessly into an icy river whose current sweeps him some distance downstream. The incident haunts him for years, but does it, *can* it, lie heavily on his conscience? If it does, he must regard his failure to reach the girl as resulting from some fault of his. Perhaps, contrary to fact, he feels that he could have kept himself from falling into the river if he had tried harder, or perhaps he comes to think that, being afraid of being himself slaughtered by the oncoming train, he may knowingly have chosen a route to the girl that reduced his chances of reaching her. We might regard this latter fanciful and try to talk him out of it.

A third man in the vicinity finds his way to the girl blocked by armed police. He too fails to reach the girl, and the incident haunts him for years after. Does it burden his conscience? We of course do not yet know; but how could it? The matter depends at least on whether he sees his failure as resulting from some fault of his. Naturally, the stories we can tell here are richer than in the previous case. Suppose he tried futilely to persuade the police to let him through or to save the girl themselves, and then tried furiously to break through the cordon. Suppose further that he senses no deficiencies whatever in his efforts in these regards—it was like trying to persuade a series of fence posts and like trying to fight his way through an impenetrable thicket; he simply could not do either. Could the incident, even so, lie on his conscience? The answer may depend on how he sees the police's being there and blocking the way so immovably and impenetrably, and whether he sees this as resulting in any way from any fault of his. Perhaps he feels in some way answerable for these features of the situation, feels both that he could have done something earlier to prevent them from being present and that, at that earlier time, he should have known and in some way really did know that something like this might occur—viz., that the operations of the legal system he supported, or at least did not subvert with all his strength, might someday make it impossible for him to do something he felt he must do.

These stories focus an understanding of "violate conscience" which allows that only something one does or fails to do can violate one's conscience, and that what violates one's conscience will, if it comes to pass, burden or trouble

---

having attention drawn to them because their use is, at least in the context, controversial or potentially at issue.

one's conscience. On this understanding, law could violate a person's conscience only if it were understood as something the person himself did, or, by extension, something resulting from what he did. This is one route into problems of law and conscience.

The major difficulty with this route is that it seems to miss what is on the minds of persons troubled about 'conflicts' between the two. These persons seem, at least in part, to treat law as though it were an alien and outside force impinging upon one in ways that may occasionally and seriously violate one's conscience. This view is most clearly expressed in the claim that it is wrong to force people to act in ways contrary to their consciences and that, in particular, it is wrong for the law to do this. A more marginal case of impingement of some sort is perhaps suggested when we are admonished, as we sometimes are, not to let the law become keeper of our consciences. Dealing adequately with the latter would make the present paper far too long, though the matter is touched on below. With respect to the former, however, I argue here that, insofar as such 'impingement' amounts or leads to violation of conscience, it does so by leading persons to violate their own consciences in ways revealing to them that they are indeed somewhat less admirable than they had hoped to be. The question we then face is that of what stake we have in protecting people from such confrontations with their own shortcomings.

II

Suppose that we start anew by attempting individually to view the law, as we are surely sometimes tempted to view it, as imposed upon us from 'outside' as implacably and unstoppably as the seasons of the year and, consequently, raise no questions whatever about the possibility that we have played some part in allowing this situation to occur or even in producing it. Seeing the law this way, we may also notice that its operation renders some activities utterly impossible (e.g., by bringing about death or incarceration or states of affairs such as that described above in the third of our cases about the girl on the track), but that its characteristic mode of prohibitory or compulsory operation is to render activities or omissions merely (though perhaps highly) dangerous or difficult or in some way unattractive or unrewarding. The borderline between these two main modes of operation is, of course, interesting, especially when one notices how nicely and conveniently it is obscured by the popular expression "out of the question," an expression likely to occur to us when the acts or omissions under consideration are likely to be followed shortly by our death, mutilation, or, even, incarceration. Postponing consideration of ramifications of that fact, suppose at present merely that the activities or omissions being (however) 'ruled out' are ones which would, absent the law, conform to the dictates of one's conscience.

The first thing to notice here is the importance of the expression "absent the law." There are two things to notice about it. It allows first for the fact that consideration of what the law directs enters into most people's understanding of what their consciences direct. Most of us think this reasonable enough, though the danger that it will be carried too far is precisely what leads some persons to admonish us not to let the law become keeper of our consciences. Obviously, however, not everyone carries it so far, and that is why we can have cases of conflict between law and conscience. This leads to a second reason for taking special note of the expression "absent the law," viz., the expression enables us, when considering whether the law *can* force anyone to act in a way contrary to his conscience, to take account of an important difference between the two main modes of prohibitory or compulsory operation of the law just sketched. I now turn to this matter.

Suppose, to repeat, that the activities or omissions being ruled out by the law in the one way or the other are ones which would, absent the law, conform to the dictates of one's conscience. Where the law has rendered them utterly impossible—e.g., where its operation has led to incarceration of a sort making impossible repayment of various debts, giving material help to the unfortunate, actively seeking to end or mitigate the effects of certain evils, or whatever else one might feel conscience-bound to do—has conscience *thereby* been violated? Well, in the first place, though the circumstances may be highly regrettable, the person's present failure to do these things, seen as attributable to *him,* does not in itself reveal a fault in him and thus cannot in itself reasonably be seen to violate his conscience, though it is, of course, true that the circumstances leading to his incarceration may reveal faults in him, or that faults may be revealed upon probing his role in creating the circumstances in which, the law aside, these acts of conscience from him would now have been called for, or upon probing whether he now believes these acts utterly impossible for him or whether he may not have a 'secret gladness' that they are now impossible. Such considerations aside, his failure to perform the acts when they have been rendered utterly impossible for him cannot reasonably be read by him or anyone else as violating his conscience since it provides no grounds whatever for reproaching him.

What, however, about the law whose operation made that failure certain? Can *it* be said to have violated his conscience? Given our present hypothesis about the way the law is being viewed, it could not have done so in a way that could burden his conscience, for he in no wise sees himself responsible for it. Furthermore, it could not have done so, at least within the confines of the present description of the case, by so 'forcing' him to act contrary to his conscience. This point, which might eventually need but will not here get extensive argument, emerges when one considers that the sphere of the actual operation of conscience is no wider than the sphere of what is thought by the agent to be possible. Conscience starts with what is thought possible. It can direct only what is thought possible and reproach only for what is thought to have been possible; feelings to the contrary do not stem from it. Hence, rendering something utterly impossible for a person may or may not, if he recognizes the impossibility, change the character of what his conscience directs him to do, but it cannot *per se* put him in a position where he acts contrary to, or even in a position where he is prevented from acting in accord with, his (present) conscience. It thus cannot, at least in these popularly conceived ways, amount to a violation of his conscience.

The law, in short, does not and cannot violate a person's conscience by 'forcing' that person to act contrary to his conscience by making it utterly impossible for him to do otherwise. It cannot violate a person's conscience in this way because it is impossible for there to be anything corresponding to the description of the way.

The situation is dramatically otherwise, however, when one considers the other main mode of the law's prohibitory or compulsory operation, viz., rendering various activities and omissions not utterly impossible but merely dangerous, difficult, unattractive, or unrewarding. Here, most importantly, insofar as we recognize that the law has *not* rendered the activities and omissions *utterly* impossible, we can imagine someone resisting the law's 'demands' and, in the end, engaging in the activities or adhering to the omissions when doing so is what his conscience directs. Because we can imagine this, our consciences do not let us off scot free when the law 'forces' us in these ways to act contrary to them. We recognize that it was not utterly impossible (though perhaps 'out of the question') to do otherwise, *and that is why we can recognize that what has happened has been contrary to our consciences.*

If the law 'violates' consciences by 'forcing' persons to act contrary to their consciences, then it must be in such a fashion as this. But if this is so, then the following understanding of the situation is surely appropriate: if law here 'violates' a person's conscience, it is by leading him, through the obtrusion of certain considerations upon his consciousness, to violate his own conscience by acting contrary to it.

This understanding raises in a highly interesting way the question of what is at stake in the resolution of such 'conflicts' between law and conscience. It suggests that a person whose conscience is violated by his being 'forced' to do something contrary to it is always a person to whom some fault or reason for disappointment in himself or failure to live up to his highest aspirations for himself is revealed because he has so acted while realizing that it was not utterly impossible for him to do otherwise.

(The point is not always easy to see clearly, but I think it is sustainable. Imagine some variations on the situation of a man about to be drafted to kill people whom he believes innocent of any wrongdoing and also not in any way dangerous or harmful to mankind. The cost of his refusal may or may not be visited upon him alone. Certain hardships may also be visited upon his parents, his wife, his children. To imagine various escalations in these hardships is to imagine cases where it may become less and less clear to him that allowing himself to be drafted would amount to failure to live up to his highest aspirations for himself; but these escalations and the considerations accompanying them would also be making it less and less clear to him that allowing himself to be drafted would, in the end, *be* contrary to his conscience.)

Where, then, we have cases of persons 'forced' by the law to act contrary to their consciences, we also have persons confronted by a failure to live up to their highest aspirations for themselves. My question now is this: why should we think that these persons *merit* or *have a right to* protection against such a state of affairs, or, more softly, why should we want to protect them from being put in such a situation? Do we, for example, think it best or right that one never be put in a position where he is called upon and yet may well fail to live up to his highest aspirations for himself with regard to acting in accord with his conscience? Or do we think that occasions for it such as those produced by law are somehow gratuitous and avoidable? Or do we, perhaps, think merely that occasions for it such as these are regrettable and that we should do our best to see that they are minimized?

III

Full discussion of the issues raised by these questions would require specification of just what protective policies are being proposed in the name of the wrongness of 'forcing' people to act contrary to their consciences. Specific policies are seldom proposed in the literature on the topic. We might imagine them to involve advice or directives to police officers (don't arrest people acting contrary to law in order to avoid acting contrary to their consciences), or to prosecuting attorneys (don't prosecute such people), or judges or juries (don't convict them), judges or legislatures (exempt them from punishment, lighten their punishment, or somehow exclude them from the class of offenders), or merely the general public (respect them, don't 'condemn' them). Getting clear on such things is important if one is to come to grips with the fears of persons in whom talk of 'protecting' conscience against the law raises visions of immense and dangerous social confusion. But I am interested here in the prior question of what stake we have in giving any 'protection' at all.

Consider that on the one side we have (or can imagine) persons who, when we are prepared to admire them at all, we may recognize as having extraordinary courage and strength of character and maybe even heroic virtue, and who, if we are not at all prepared to admire them, we may think of as dangerous or harmful fanatics or perhaps only kooky fanatics[2]—persons in any case,

---

2. I am here of course allowing for the possibility of 'erroneous' conscience.

who, no matter what the cost to them personally, resist the law's demands when the demands are contrary to their consciences and who, to make matters worse, may have unusually scrupulous consciences and thus be likely to confront the difficulty more often than ordinary men. On the other side we may have 'weaklings' who never, on such grounds at least, resist the law's demands when there is a conflict, though the extent to which the issue arises for them may be reduced if, as often seems supposed, their consciences are not so scrupulous. In between are more ordinary and perhaps also reasonably well-thought-of mortals. The first class will more than likely contain members whom we admire and might even wish, in our most inspired or fanatic moments, to emulate; but they are also persons whose consciences are most noticeably *not* being violated by the law's demands (unless we were to allow, and I think this would be too much, that a person's conscience can be violated even though he in the end acts in accord with it). Members of the second and third classes (most of us) are by comparison, at least on present grounds, less than fully admirable; they are persons who may very well be led, in view of the law and the impingement of its operations upon them, to act contrary to their consciences. Commentators who say that one should not be forced to act contrary to his conscience seem to have in mind the protection of these people, and my question is why these definitively somewhat less than fully admirable people merit or have a right to that protection. Precisely what ends or interests would this protection serve and which (e.g., such as development of character or integrity) might it subvert?

In an age with a more deeply theological orientation toward conscience than our own, one of the stakes might surely be thought to be salvation in the hereafter. Luther, for example, followed his best-remembered words at the Diet of Worms with yet other words suggesting just this point. He said: "Here I stand, I can do no other. It is not safe for a man to violate his conscience. God help me!" But even here, though salvation may be at stake should the law 'force' a man to act contrary to his conscience, we may still ask whether and under what conditions such a man would or should be eligible for salvation.

In a secular age, with a secularized view of conscience, other considerations must be brought to the fore. What are they?

As a way of finding them, return for a moment to the cases of 'strong' men who, no matter what the cost, resist the law's demands. Suppose we have such a person before us—a person who recognizes that compliance with his conscience is an option for him though difficult, dangerous, or in some other way unattractive to choose because of how the law may or will then deal with him. Suppose he resolves the issue in favor of conscience.

Shall we merely, or even at all, celebrate this as a triumph of the human spirit? Or will we find upon close examination that there has been much here to regret? Our answer will surely depend in part on our attitude toward the acts or omissions that constituted compliance with his conscience on this occasion. If we think them undesirable or evil, we will, though perhaps admiring something about the person's strength of character, not in the end regret the fact that compliance with his conscience had been rendered so difficult for him. We may, indeed, regret that it hadn't been rendered more difficult, though this may be mixed with regrets that his conscience hadn't directed him differently, and with the realization that if this person had failed to act in accord with his conscience on this occasion even this might not have been a totally happy circumstance (more on this below). If, on the other hand, we think the acts or omissions constituting compliance with his conscience had been right or good in themselves, or harmless, or at worst 'inconvenient,' then we might regret the fact that compliance had been so difficult or dangerous for him.

But why should we? Clearly, where we strongly approve of the acts or omissions as right or productive of good, we may simply regret anything diminishing the chances of their occurring. And both here and where we find the acts or omissions merely harmless or at worst inconvenient, we may see the threatened punitive measures of the law as noxious subversions of the happiness and tranquillity of the person in question and as noxious costs placed on his exercise of free choice. But it is common to believe that more than merely these are involved when the acts or omissions are matters of conscience. It is common to see the punitive measures of the law in such cases as endangering the development or preservation of one's personal integrity and indeed of his status as a moral agent and even as a man—for it is characteristic of modern views taking conscience seriously that they place it at or near the core of a man's identity and tend to see subversion of his conscience as doing violence in a fundamental way to his integrity as a person, as subverting his status as a moral being and as a man.

Of course, any such threats were, by hypothesis, weathered successfully in the cases we are presently considering. Should this change our attitude toward them? Perhaps it should. Perhaps the effects of the experience were beneficial with respect to these very things; his integrity may have been strengthened (analogues: with respect to his rectitude in the face of external threats and blandishments—fire tempering steel; with respect to the coherence and unity of his personality—the unifying effects of polarization produced by perceptions of external threats), and his status as a moral being and as a man may have been enhanced. We might, on the other hand, think that the whole episode served only to reinforce a harmful fanaticism or rigidity of character. Or, even if we did not think this, we might nevertheless think that it was somehow gratuitous, that life itself throws up enough 'testing' and 'weathering' and 'tempering' experiences, and that the law's introduction of further ones is in some ways at best an uncalled-for redundancy.

When we come to the cases of persons for whom there has been nothing even approximating a triumph of the human spirit in such an episode—persons who end by acting in ways contrary to their consciences and submitting to the law—we will find some of these issues raised even more sharply. Again, our attitude toward the event will depend in part on our attitude toward the acts or omissions directed by conscience and those directed by law, whether we see them as right or beneficial and thus to be encouraged, wrong or harmful and thus to be discouraged, or neither of these and thus perhaps to be tolerated. These attitudes in turn will influence in one way or another whether we see the persons as of failed and less-than-heroic virtue, as fanatics happily coerced or persuaded into conformity, or merely as people whose inclinations toward nonconformity turned out to be not quite so strong as they may have thought. But, unlike the persons who in the end act in accord with conscience, these will all have reason for disappointment in themselves with respect to the incident. The incident exhibited a failed aspiration and perhaps one of central importance to them. Have they, in this defeat, suffered a harm from which they have or should have a right to be protected? What empirical and what moral hypotheses would underlie such a claim? And what models of human life would sustain it?

IV

The leading candidates for such harm are doubtless loss of self-respect and certain supposed consequences thereof. About these the following points may be made:

1. Whether a person suffers such a loss and the degree to which he suffers it depend in part upon what expectations and aspirations he has had for himself. Depending upon whether we find these latter disappointingly low, proper, unrealistic and destructively high, or simply wrong-headed, we may adopt significantly different attitudes toward his loss of self-respect and its consequences. (As an example of finding his expectations or aspirations for himself simply wrong-headed, we might find his conscience annoyingly, irritatingly, or even improperly scrupulous, as when we find him painstakingly scrupulous about matters that we find of no importance or in a way that seems to us to interfere with the satisfaction of more important interests of his.)

2. Whether, and to what extent, a person suffers a loss of self-respect depend also on where he places the present episode with respect to the seriousness of the offense against conscience and the severity of the penalties incurred or threatened were he to have acted in accord with conscience (cf. the difference that a white, integrationist pacificist might plausibly find between being required to ride in the front of a segregated bus and being required to do combat service as a bombardier, and the difference between thirty days in the stockade and a death penalty).

3. The extent of *the harm constituted or done to him* by the loss of self-

respect depends on how he reads the magnitude of the loss. One can imagine readings on a scale sketched by the movement from "I am, alas, too human!" to "I am a cop-out, pure and simple," or "I am despicable!" It also depends on the longevity of the feeling (does it stick with him, persecute him, nag him, or does he 'adjust' to the situation by eventually, perhaps rather soon, turning a blind eye toward the episode?) and also on its consequences with respect to what sort of person it influences him to be and its influence on how he acts (does he pull down the flag of his aspirations, or does he, in the course of time, do quite the opposite? And what *are* his new aspirations?)

4. The *wrong,* if any, we feel done to him may depend on whether we think it fitting or unfitting that he have such an experience given what he really is like.

These considerations raise an impressive array of empirical, conceptual, and moral issues. I cannot see how anyone can approach many of them with confidence. But our attachment of importance to them suggests a certain vision of what it is to be a man (and I say "man" advisedly, as you will see), and, quite apart from what may be the empirical conditions necessary or benign in producing such a man, and quite apart from whatever 'righteous' considerations might lead us to be or not to be tough-minded about confronting whether we are or are not such men, we might ask what the vision is and whether there is anything to it.

Important constituents of the vision are found clearly enough in Chapter 3 of Mill's *Liberty,* where he identifies, as distinctive endowments of human beings, the faculties of perception, judgment, discriminative feeling, mental activity, and moral preference, and says of them that they can be exercised and thus developed only by making choices on grounds conclusive to one's own judgment and "consentaneous to his feeling and character." One needs only to add to this something about the centrality of conscience in this integral and importantly autonomous individual—perhaps along the lines of Bishop Butler:

> Appetites, passions, affections, and the principle of reflection, considered merely as the several parts of our inward nature, do not at all give us an idea of the system or constitution of this nature, because the constitution is formed by somewhat not yet taken into consideration, namely, by the relations which these several parts have to each other; the chief of which is the authority of reflection or conscience. It is from considering the relations which the several appetites and passions in the inward frame have to each other, and, above all, the supremacy of reflection or conscience, that we get the idea of the system or constitution of human nature.[3] . . . in reality the very constitution of our nature requires that we

3. In *Five Sermons* (New York: Liberal Arts, 1950), p. 8.

bring our whole conduct before this superior faculty, wait its determination, enforce upon ourselves its authority, and make it the business of our lives, as it is absolutely the whole business of a moral agent to conform ourselves to it.[4]

or of Arthur Garnett:

the conflict of conscience (moral approvals and disapprovals) with other desires (temptations) is not just an ordinary conflict of desires. It is a conflict in which the integrity of the personality is peculiarly involved. In an ordinary conflict of desires, in which there is no moral issue, the best solution is for one of the desires to be completely set aside and fade into oblivion without regrets. . . . But if the conflict be between "conscience" (the interests involved in moral approval and disapproval) and "temptation" (some opposed interest or desire) then it does matter which triumphs. The integrity of personality is involved. It tends to dissolve as a person slips into the habit of doing things he believes to be wrong. He loses his self-respect and his firmness of purpose.[5]

The constituents of the vision to which I wish to pay special attention are the autonomy requirement expressed so completely by Mill when he says that possession and development of those distinctive endowments of human beings depend on making choices on grounds conclusive to one's own judgment and consentaneous to one's own feeling and character, and the consonance-with-conscience requirement which both Butler and Garnett claim must be met if the parts of our inner natures are to be organized so as to satisfy our natures and, according to Garnett, preserve our self-respect and firmness of purpose.

One who accepts the vision with these constituents might indeed be anxious about cases where the law coerces people into acting contrary to their consciences. There is first the simple fact of action contrary to conscience—now to be seen as a threat to the benign organization of one's inner nature. There is second the seeming intrusion of considerations leading us to choose on grounds presumptively *not* consentaneous to our feeling and character.

But this last, of course, depends in the present context upon the first. It depends upon identifying something as dissonant with our feeling and character precisely on the grounds that that something is contrary to our conscience; the choice to comply with the law, made out of consideration of the baleful consequences of failing to do so, is to be thought dissonant with our feeling and character precisely because it is dissonant with our consciences.

One might give a quick and only slightly misplaced back of his hand to this

4. Ibid., p. 12.
5. In "Conscience and Conscientiousness," *Rice University Studies* 51.4 (1965): 76–77. Also in *Moral Concepts,* edited by Joel Feinberg (London: Oxford University Press, 1969).

suggestion by remarking that some people are cowards. Compliance with the law, contrary to conscience, is precisely in agreement with and suitable to the feeling and character of a coward. Etc.

If something has gone wrong in such a disposal of the problem, it has gone wrong because what is really a normative model of man has been taken for a descriptive model, though one of the strengths of the model is that if it is accepted widely and deeply enough as a *correct* normative account, it may more fittingly be treated as a descriptive account. That is to say, accepting it as a correct account of what ought to be the case will tend to give it a role as something to which one does in fact aspire or at least feels one ought to aspire, and a failure to measure up to it may then produce troubles of just the sort suggested by the model.

Should the model be accepted? It is the basis for common views on personal and moral integrity. It is highly individualistic and also, I believe, dominantly male-oriented. I end by suggesting how these are so and leave for some subsequent discussion whether they ought to be so.

It is highly individualistic in that the vision of personal integrity involved, a vision with inward-looking and outward-looking aspects, has as its rationale an interest in whether we have before us something sufficiently unified to count as a single person and sufficiently well-bounded to distinguish as one separable thing in an environment of other things.

As is made clear in the passages from Butler and Garnett, the person is viewed as a locus of various drives, impulses, needs, wants, thoughts, etc., but not as a mere assemblage of these. Rather, the person is seen as a locus of these so integrated with each other as to constitute a system of more or less harmoniously related 'parts.' In its inward-looking aspect, the person's integrity thus is seen to be a function of the extent to which his impulses, needs, wants, thoughts, etc. are harmoniously and 'coherently' integrated vis-a-vis one another. The rationale of this rests on an interest in whether the person is one "whole" or 'complete' thing rather than many things. The more harmoniously these 'inner' parts or aspects are related to one another, the more completely systematic the relations are seen to be and the easier it is for us to identify what we have here as a single thing rather than many things.

This side of the vision of the integrity of persons can of course be richly troubling. Consider how it is put by von Humboldt, quoted approvingly by Mill: "the end of man . . . is the highest and most harmonious development of his powers to a complete and consistent whole." Given the generally favorable attitude toward striving for and protecting the integrity of persons, this emphasis on completeness, consistency, and wholeness may be thought, for example, to enforce a disturbingly closed-off view of something so quick-silvery and open-ended as man sometimes seems to be. Plato might approve, but Walt Whitman would not. Consider Plato's criticism of certain actors in the *Republic* on the ground that "human nature is not two-fold or manifold, for one man plays one part only" (397e), and his criticism of the "democratic" man on the grounds that "his life is motley and manifold and an epitome of the lives of many" (561e); and contrast the following passage from George Kateb utilizing Whitman's view:

> Proteus could become the symbol of the tone of utopian life. The aim would be . . . to allow individuals to assume various "personae" without fear of social penalty . . . to strive to have each self be able to say, in the words of Walt Whitman's "Song of Myself": "I am large, I contain multitudes."[6]

And the matter has certainly disturbed Sartre and, less directly, John Dewey and other modern philosophers before and since. Sartre, for example, has been highly critical of people who long to be something "solid," something inescapable.

Of course, this so far neglects the central role given by Butler and Garnett to conscience in this inward-looking side of integrity, and the central position given that role may be all that preserves a plausible attractiveness for the view. It is true that we may have visions of being torn apart and thus destroyed by internal stresses produced by dissonances of desires and aspirations. But the valuing of *completeness, wholeness,* and *system* appears to go well beyond that consideration and to be attractive only if one sees them as in the service of "reflection or conscience" (to use Butler's nicely bridging phrase), i.e., as in the service of some model of rationality-*cum*-moral-stature.

Turning to the outward-looking side of the vision of integrity seeming to operate here, the side emerging when one presses on Mill's remarks about choosing on grounds conclusive to one's *own* judgment and consentaneous to one's *own* feeling and character, one can see this as underwriting the importance of the boundaries in the light of which we may determine what is a part of the 'system' of one's self and what is not. The self is seen as a bounded domain having an inertia or principle of organization and operation of its own and thus as one complete or whole and separable thing in an environment of other things. The upshot of attending to this side of the integrity of persons is that the integrity of a person or self is seen to be a function not only of the relations of his inner 'parts' or aspects to one another, but also a function of his relations to other things. Just as his integrity is seen to be increased with the harmony and coherence of the former, because he is thereby easier to see as one complete thing rather than many things, so his integrity is seen to be increased the more completely the state of his 'system' is determined by its

6. In *Utopias and Utopian Thought,* edited by Frank E. Manuel (Boston: Beacon, 1967), p. 256.

own inertia or principle of operation, because he is thereby easier to identify as one distinct thing in an environment of other things. His integrity is *damaged* or *destroyed* when things within this domain of his 'self' become disorganized, incoherent, or unsystematic. His integrity is *violated* when the domain is intruded upon and changes are produced within it that interfere with and counter or 'overcome' the effects of his own inertia or principle of operation. And, of course, the violation of his integrity (outward view) may damage or destroy his integrity (inward view).

If the inertia or principle of operation of the system is identified, as by Mill in the passage quoted, merely with the person's judgment and with consentaneity with his "feeling and character," then the fact that a man out of fear or other aversion does something that is contrary to his conscience would not in itself amount to a violation of his integrity by whatever induced the fear or aversion. But if the inertia or principle is identified with "reflection or conscience," as it clearly is by Butler, then the state of affairs just described *would* count as a violation of his integrity because it would constitute a case of externally induced interference 'overcoming' the law of the inner domain.

The emphasis given here to the self as a *bounded* domain and the emphasis on consentaneity with the 'law' of that domain confront us, when they one way or another receive the approbation and encouragement generally offered in praise of integrity, with important features of what has sometimes been called "atomistic individualism." One need hardly do more than mention this last expression to raise a picture of the argumentative thrusts and counter-thrusts that might be delivered here when the whole idea is carefully considered.

My claim, then, is that advocacies of the special rights of conscience against law are based in important part in such foundations as have been exposed here, foundations which surely merit further investigation.

Touching, in closing, on the dominantly male-oriented vision of man that emerges when the above concept of integrity is explored, the orientation is revealed by the fact that deference—I mean *real* deference—of the sort that may not be consentaneous with one's feeling and character and yet is often though perhaps subtly expected from women, is notably not a constituent of the vision of integrity exposed here; that is, it is not a constituent unless one is willing to say that women on this account do indeed have natures different from those of men. The ramifications of one view or the other here are potentially of some interest. I hope to explore them on another occasion.

9 The Extent to Which Legislators Should Serve Their Consciences or Their Constituents

Speaking for myself, the interest attaching to this topic emerges when we understand the word "or" in the above formulation as an exclusive "or," and we are on this understanding thus being asked to make a genuine and possibly a hard choice. On this understanding, we may put out of our minds any happy speculations about having it both ways. For example, we might otherwise have been attracted by the thought that many, if not most, legislators serve their consciences *by* serving their constituents. But having excluded this possibility from the cases we are considering, we must think very carefully about the conditions of conflict among the two options. We are viewing ourselves as being asked to consider situations in which a legislator cannot, on the same occasion and in every respect, both serve conscience and serve constituents. Either the legislator may serve each on each of these occasions, but less than completely, and that because the other is being served at least partially; or there is a series of situations on some of which conscience is being served to the exclusion of serving constituents, while on others the constituents are being served to the exclusion of serving conscience.

In the above formulation of the topic, the word "should" need not be understood as having only moral import. But it probably ought to be understood to have at least some moral import, and that is the understanding that most interests me. I shall consequently, after an initial discussion of the difficulty of coming up with good examples of what we are talking about, organize my discussion of the topic around two questions: Have legislators a moral obligation to serve their consciences? And have legislators a moral obligation to serve their constituents?

I. Finding Examples

One of my colleagues from whom I have learned a great deal stresses the value in philosophy of working through cases of what one is discussing as

153

substantial as one can find or imagine. I have tried to do that here. But I have not been able to find or imagine any substantial worthy, clear, and unequivocal cases. Perhaps that is mostly because I have set three limitations upon any possible worthy examples. I believe that these limitations are reasonable, and I am willing to defend them.

The first limitation is that the presence of a conflict between service to conscience and service to constituents is in the perception and judgment of the legislator. It is easy to imagine that *I* may perceive a conflict between *your* efforts to serve *your* conscience and service to *your* constituents. For example, I may perceive that your refusal to support legislation permitting abortion or contraception is an effort to serve your conscience at the cost of substantial service to your constituents. It may then be possible and significant for me to discuss where the priorities should be placed between our tolerance and support of your efforts to serve your conscience and your probable duty to serve your constituents. But this discussion may not touch you at all because it is a discussion of a matter that you do not yet find relevant. You do not find it relevant because you are unconvinced that any sacrifice of genuine and long-range service to your constituents is involved. The discussion that might touch you is a discussion of that issue.

I should like here to engage in a discussion that *legislators* find relevant, and the limitation above contributes to this end. The aim, therefore, will be to address legislators asking the question, "What shall I do?" rather than address persons examining the behavior of legislators and asking "What shall we do about them?"

When we look closely at the matter from this perspective, we may see that a great deal depends upon how the apparent conflict arises. The appearance of a conflict surely is a time for careful examination, but what seems clearest after examination? That a particular course of action is contrary to the legislator's conscience or that it will serve his or her constituents? If what seems clearest is that it will do one of these things, but not so clearly the other—a situation probably most common—then sharp questioning will and probably should be given by the legislator to whether it will do the other at all. (I do not, however, mean to suggest that what seems clearest does not need examination.) If what seems clearest is that the action is contrary to his or her conscience, then what the legislator will and should more sharply question than had been the case previously is whether the action will, in fact, serve the constituents, and contrariwise if the service of the action to constituents seems clearest. What is happening here is that a special burden of more careful questioning is being placed in one direction or the other because of the situation. There is nothing extraordinary or untoward about this. We do not like to make sacrifices and, when we have come to believe that they are imminent, we press especially hard on that portion of our conclusion that seems most dubious. The fact that an action is clearly contrary to their carefully formed consciences (see below) is taken by our legislators to be reason to doubt whether the action will genuinely, and in the long run, benefit their constituents. Contrariwise, legislators tend to take the fact that an action will clearly and genuinely serve their constituents to be reason to doubt whether that action *is* contrary to a carefully formed and informed conscience. In the end, I should think that as objective third parties we should not be offended if our legislators go with what seems clearest to them after all this questioning.

It is a matter of relative clarities. The clarities, however, may be equal. It is certainly not impossible that there actually be a conflict, and the legislators should take this possibility seriously. It is merely that I have been unable to come up with substantial actual or imagined cases where this is clearly so, where it is plausibly equally clear to legislators that a particular act will both serve constituents and be contrary to their own carefully formed consciences. Our discussion will probably provide some such cases.[1]

The second limitation is that the service to the constituents be "in the long run" and "on the whole." My intention is to exclude cases in which the service to constituents is admittedly only "in part" or "in some respect," and is also admittedly not "on the whole" or "in the long run." I wish to exclude these latter cases because they are resolvable simply in terms of what service to constituents amounts to and whether we should prefer long-run service and service on the whole to short-run and partial service that is neither of the former. It may be the case that there are conflicts between service to a legislator's conscience and partial service to constituents that is only short-run or "in some respect." But these cases raise no conflict irresolvable within terms solely of what services to constituents are preferable. If we want to reach the difficulties peculiar to our topic, we will therefore not pause to consider these cases. For example, we will not pause to consider a case where the public demands the dropping of an atomic bomb on some foreign territory, and where the legislator for one reason or another finds that support of this project is contrary to conscience, but is *also* quite willing to agree that dropping the bomb would be contrary to the long-range interests of the public. (Parenthetically, we should note that the long-range interests of the public do not include their interest in such things as salvation in the hereafter. Because of the separation of church and state in the American political tradition, such considera-

---

1. It did. The three cases brought forward shared the following characteristics: (a) there were victims of the immorality, (b) these victims were either foreign or non-citizen resident native populations, (c) they were helpless then and later to retaliate, and (d) they had no friends willing to retaliate then or later.

tions are, for at least American legislators, beyond the bounds of legitimate consideration.)

The third limitation is that the conscience to which service is being contemplated belongs to a person who admits, at least on this occasion, the relevance of concern for whether the conscience is correct and is being correctly understood. This limitation will be discussed more fully below where we consider whether legislators have a moral obligation to serve conscience. For the present, we should note that it does not mean that the legislator must *in fact* inquire into the correctness of his or her conscience, though it does demand that the relevance of such inquiries be admitted. One wonders how else in modern times service to "conscience" can be given any moral force at all. We do not have moral grounds for giving any consideration at all to a legislator allegedly trying to serve conscience who will give no consideration whatever to any challenges to whether the conscience is correctly informed. Note, it is not being claimed that the legislator must *defend* the conscience at all, let alone defend it to our or anybody else's satisfaction. The legislator may have feelings of the appropriate sort for which he or she cannot articulate reasons. The limitation is only that he or she should be willing to admit as relevant and, let us say, listen to at least some conceivable arguments or evidence to the effect that the conscience might be mistaken or misunderstood. He or she need not be willing to listen to any and every purported argument or piece of evidence that comes along, but he or she cannot refuse to listen to any conceivable argument or evidence. Substantial cases where this limitation is not observed are easy to imagine. For example, a legislator unwilling to consider any inquiry into the possible rightness or wrongness of his or her conscience and treating the conscience as something of which he or she is an unfortunate and helpless victim would be able to claim that support of desegregation would be contrary to that conscience while freely admitting that desegregation would be a service to the public because desegregation would be both just and politically astute. We should, however, note that it is precisely the treatment of conscience as something of which he or she is a helpless victim that frees the legislator to make the latter admission easily and clearly. If it were not for the "helpless victim" posture, I do not see that the latter admission could come either clearly or easily.

In sum, I have placed three limitations on examples, each with what I think to be good reason. First, the conflict between service to conscience and service to constituents must be in the view of the legislator because I am trying to address the legislator's problems. Second, the imagined service to constituents must be "on the whole" and "in the long run" because the conflict we seek must be clear and hard and thus not resolvable by appeal to the concept of genuine service to constituents alone. Third, the conscience appealed to must be one whose rightness or wrongness the conscience-holder believes to be relevant to the resolution of the conflict because without this limitation, the appeal to conscience can have no moral force.

II. Have Legislators a Moral Obligation to Serve Conscience?

Appeals to conscience, as just suggested, have often served as argument-stoppers. They have been used by persons who do not wish to defend their positions any further. We have tolerated such appeals in the past perhaps because they have found shelter under a tradition of religious toleration in a history of religious conflict. Religion itself is often a matter of conscience. Secularly, the leading idea is that, as we came ultimately to believe about religion, conscience is something private and highly personal. But toleration of argument-stopping appeals to conscience has been a mistake, and this can be shown if one reflects briefly on what conscience *is*.

Conscience has, in recent years, been denigrated with respect to its moral importance by being "psychologized." The psychologizing of conscience has underwritten attacks on the moral force of conscience by presenting conscience as merely a residue of one's personal psychological history. These attacks have been answered most persuasively, in my opinion, by viewing conscience as considered and responsible judgment of the moral qualities of one's acts, either retrospectively or prospectively. The persuasiveness of this view is supported by two considerations: First, attempts to sort out phenomenologically the promptings of conscience from internal twitches, whims, compulsions, prejudices, and hang-ups, and so forth, fix upon, rightly I believe, as one of the distinguishing marks of the promptings of conscience, a willingness not only to attach a certain importance to the views emerging from these promptings but also, connectedly, to recognize the relevance of inquiries into their rightness or wrongness. Second, when it comes to determining the *genuineness* of appeals to conscience (for they are often shelters for scoundrels or persons who are otherwise dissembling), a disinterest in what Hegel called "the test of truth" and a denial of its relevance are among the marks of non-genuineness.

If we adopt the understanding just offered, then our question becomes: Have legislators a moral obligation to act on their considered and responsible moral judgments, either retrospective or prospective? With this understanding of what we are inquiring into, we may avoid worries both about the moral force of conscience and about whether the authentic voice of conscience is being heard. But we will not avoid worries about erroneous or over-scrupulous consciences. The former have been sources of worry at least since the time of Aquinas, and we have worried about the latter at least since seventeenth-century England.

Something may seem to hang here on how one understands "serve conscience." If one understands this expression as mandating merely acting in accord with the dictates or "verdicts" of conscience (insofar as they point to the appropriateness of doing something in particular), there is still clearly a problem. If, however, one understands this expression as mandating action from some conception of what will benefit conscience, then the persistence of a problem may not seem so clear.

Have legislators a moral obligation to do as erroneous or over-scrupulous consciences may direct? In one respect, certainly not. Such consciences, though by hypothesis embodiments of considered and responsible efforts to determine the moral quality of actions either prospectively or retrospectively, are mistaken. The conclusions arrived at are wrong. Thus, if certain behavior is judged to be obligatory by such consciences, it may indeed be obligatory, but no thanks to the judgment that it is so. The judgment is *whether* the behavior is obligatory; it does not *make* the behavior obligatory.

In another respect, the situation is somewhat more complicated. Consider again what conscience is. We have considered it to be, whether erroneous or over-scrupulous or neither, a considered and responsible effort to determine something. In our tradition, we have achieved two rather nice things by giving such efforts some moral weight (note that I say *some* moral weight). First, we have given social support to such efforts. We have encouraged persons to take them seriously and to honor them. We do not thereby render them decisive, but we do not leave the judgment-makers dangling either. The efforts are not regarded as irrelevant in such a way that they can make no difference whatever if the judgment-maker gets the matter wrong. Second, we have relieved ourselves of the sticky problem of determining who are to be the authoritative second-guessers to the judgment-makers. Our hypotheses are that the judgments have been considered and responsible. If they are nevertheless wrong, then this will normally mean that the issue is somewhat complicated, and an issue on which persons will differ. This does not mean that no one will be right or wrong on the issue, but it does mean that its resolution may very well pose significant political problems, and that the moral autonomy of each of us will be somewhat endangered by the setting up of public authorities whose decisions on such matters will be final and authoritative. We thus, to preserve what moral and political autonomy we can, give moral as well as political weight to conscience. We show this by the way we treat people who, in our opinion, get it wrong. We let them off the hook both politically and morally where we feel we can, and we mitigate whatever penalties normally attach to what they did when the behavior is not conscience-directed.

Our first realization throughout should be that the persons whose consciences these are are not convinced that the consciences are mistaken. A question often raised in this connection is whether the persons have taken sufficient precautions to assure that the consciences are correct. Concerning this question, it would be popular and easy to say that many persons who have such consciences have not cared. As we have already noticed, it seems that they regard their consciences as private and personal things, and do not suppose that, so long as other people are not held to them, it matters. But this position is deficient on grounds already suggested as well as on one further ground in the instant case. Remembering that the persons being considered here are legislators presumably engaged in recognizably public business, the allegation that what is being considered is a purely private and personal affair is implausible. It thus is clear that these persons should, if they do not already, care about whether their consciences may be erroneous or over-scrupulous.

But it is also clear that their caring will not guarantee success, and we are then still left with the question of what we are to say and do. It depends upon what *they* are led to do. In terms of the overall problem posed by our topic, if they find that the directives of their consciences outweigh what are, in our view, their other moral obligations—for example, their obligations to constituents (see below)—they are to be congratulated for the effort they have taken, and the moral strength they may have shown in pursuing the dictates of their consciences, but they are not thereby to be allowed unhindered progress toward the achievement of their intended goals. As with civil disobedience, these are awkward positions for one to maintain simultaneously. The issue of whether they *can* be maintained simultaneously may require extended discussion. I believe they can.

An important question here is: What hindrances may be placed in the legislator's way? For it is a matter of no small importance to think what preventive or obstructive behavior here would be permissible. May we indulge in punishing the legislators, or merely in voting them out of office when we next have the opportunity to do so in cases where their conduct has been offensive to us in this way? The latter measure, that is, voting them out of office when we next have an opportunity to do so, may be understood occasionally as a form of punishment, but it is clearly to be distinguished from genuinely punishing them—putting the legislators in prison, for example, or fining them. No impartial person would object merely to voting them out of office. But, as already remarked, the question of punishing them raises issues similar to those raised by civil disobedience, and we may expect substantial disagreements to arise in these cases. As with civil disobedience, questions of motivation and intention bear some weight but do not settle the problem.

Concerning consciences that are neither erroneous nor over-scrupulous, I take it that there is no great problem. If such consciences determine that something is morally obligatory, then it *is* morally obligatory. But it is not morally obligatory because the conscience has determined it to be so. Rather, the conscience has determined it to be morally obligatory because it *is* morally obligatory. Note that we are not here talking about whether the moral obligation in question does or does not outweigh any possible obligation to serve constituents. We are talking only about the effects of conscience upon moral obligation.

III. Have Legislators a Moral Obligation
to Serve Constituents?

The first thing to notice in examining whether legislators have a moral obligation to serve their constituents is that if legislators *believe* that they have such an obligation, then the conflict we are exploring will very likely be *within* conscience, rather than between conscience and something else. Such conflicts are, or should be (especially as conscience is characterized here), meat and potatoes to moral philosophers. They are nevertheless important here, and we shall touch on them. They give us, for one thing, an occasion to re-characterize the conflict in question. If it is to be treated as a conflict within conscience, then it might be best regarded as a conflict between some vision of moral obligations to constituents, and some vision of whatever moral obligation(s) one has that cannot be filled simultaneously with meeting the obligations to constituents. It is a matter of weighing the obligations on either side, something that must be done on a case-by-case basis.

Our overall topic, in the present formulation, has embedded in it certain presumptions concerning political arrangements. It is important to bring these to view so that we are certain to be aware of them and of their effects upon the way we treat the topic. The first appears in the use of the word "constituent." The relationships of legislators to the people subject to their legislation are various. When the people subject to this legislation are called "constituents," something rather special is being suggested. An open tyrant would not call citizens "constituents," except perhaps ironically. Constituents are thought of not only as persons subject to the legislation, but as persons for whose sake the legislation is made, and even more than this. The relationship being suggested is one in which the persons subject to the legislation are being in some way served by the legislators, and even *represented* by them. The concept of representation thus comes into play, and, as is commonly known, this is a complex matter. It is not so well understood as it might be, and there is room for much elasticity in our notions of what it involves. For the present, we need merely note that we can all imagine the relationships of legislators to subjects or citizens being different from this, and the fact that the relationship is to be one of representation is politically, socially, and morally significant, especially when one comes to consider the obligations of legislators.

Other things are embedded in our likely understanding of the problem. Because of our own political environment, we are perhaps quick to assume that the problem is formulated in a context involving more than one legislator. But it is quite possible, of course, to imagine a single legislator doing all the legislative work that is required or demanded. For example, consider Moses or Solon. The presence of more than one legislator raises the possibility that a legislator is assigned responsibility for representing fewer than the total number of persons for whom the legislation is being created—in short, that the legislator has as constituents a proper subclass of the total body of citizens subject to the legislation. Suppose that we have a collegiate legislature rather than a single legislator; the choice then is between supposing that each legislator represents each and every citizen of the whole community for which legislation is being created, and supposing that each legislator represents a proper subclass of the total body of the citizens. In the past we have not thought our way through this choice too well. If there are persons subject to the legislation who are not being represented by the legislator, then we have a moral problem (and a political problem) of somewhat different character than we would otherwise have. The question is whether the legislator legislates "over" persons whom he or she does not represent.

This is one aspect of larger problems about unborn generations of citizens and about non-citizens who may be affected by the legislation in question. The central trouble-making feature of these problems is whether a legislator serving his or her constituents will be a legislator serving fewer than all those persons for whom he or she legislates or who will feel the effects of that legislation. The legislator would not clearly be doing service to the latter though he or she may contingently achieve it in the sense of creating legislation that may benefit those other people though not intended for their sakes. No one expects legislators to legislate for the whole world or for all time. But we are discomfited by such matters from time to time.

The initial problem is obfuscated by the fact that legislators are, in our political environment, collegiate. Somehow, the confused and ill-thought-out idea prevails that if each person subject to the legislation is represented by someone among the legislators, then the resulting legislation can be, in every sense that we desire, for the sake of all persons subject to it. But there is no good reason to suppose that if each legislator faithfully executes the responsibility to serve his or her constituents, all the constituents individually or collectively will thereby have been served. This particular lack of clarity in our political tradition will emerge again as potentially important when we come to consider below the possibility that service to one's constituents will require behavior recognizably immoral.

Turn now to another presumption that may be operating undetectedly in our minds. Imagining our own political setting, we may suppose that the legislative work is being carried on in an environment also populated by a judiciary and an executive. These things, however, might be otherwise. It is conceivable either that the legislator performs also the functions we assign to executives and judiciaries, or that, as in some politically primitive societies, there are no distinct offices of these latter sorts. What we presume here will make a difference in our assignment of a range of legitimate tasks to the legislator, and will make a difference thus in the responsibilities that we assign to him or her. There may be limits on the way *legislators* may serve constituents. A legislator is perhaps not mandated to serve constituents in every way possible, but only in certain ways, presumed to follow from the status of being a legislator. Thus, for example, if one takes John Stuart Mill's view of the job of representatives, a view corresponding less well to the practices of American legislatures than to the practices of the British Parliament (but not thereby unnecessary to consider in connection with American institutions), then the way in which a legislator will seek to serve constituents is limited to controlling—that is to discussing, evaluating, and limiting—the making and executing of laws of the community with a view to the ways in which these laws do or do not express the interests of constituents. Such a person would not accurately be called a "legislator," but might nevertheless, in the profusion of theories of representation, come to be called so. Furthermore, in Mill's view the legislator is fit for this role primarily by virtue of his or her representative character, which in Mill's view means his or her status as a specimen or sample of what the constituents are like.

This view of the job of legislators has a profound effect upon our capacity to find the conflict we are seeking to understand. If legislators are to be representative of their constituents by virtue of being specimens or samples of those constituents, then the best way they can behave is by just "behaving naturally." That is to say it would be part of their appropriate behavior as representatives of their constituents to act on their consciences when their consciences directed them to do this or that. Presumably, as specimens or samples of constituents, they are to be considered together with their consciences as "representative." This means that their consciences and what these consciences may direct them to do are together part of what makes them samples or specimens. Thus they would be serving their constituents appropriately by giving expression to their consciences and the dictates of those consciences. Their special service to constituents would arise out of their status as specimens or samples of these constituents, and that status includes their having the consciences they have, with whatever directives those consciences provide. This is an illustration of the complications introduced to our topic by the varieties of theories of representation afloat in our political heritage. Obviously, our overall topic would have had little interest if Mill's were the only view of representation we take.

One further remark on "constituent." A constituent is a member, but not generally the only member, of a constituency. This fact, as Hanna Pitkin has pointed out, is of the utmost importance in understanding the concept of political representation. It means that political representation—unlike private representation, in which there is a relationship between a representative and a principal—cannot be understood as generating a responsibility discharged merely by the representative's doing what the person represented desires. In the case of public representation, the representative cannot even discharge his or her duty by doing what the majority of his or her constituents desires. The legislator must understand that even the members of any particular minority among the constituents must still be represented in the sense that their desires must be understood to be relevant and taken into consideration. What more is required is not easy to specify. Perhaps these people still have a hold on the representatives in the sense that they must somehow still be served. I can merely point to this problem, not resolve it.

Calling attention to the problem, however, usefully introduces the importance of close understanding of what it is to serve constituents. If serving one's constituents meant simply doing what they direct one to do, then the legislator probably would be called upon to do what he or she otherwise had a moral obligation not to do. But it seems more likely that serving one's constituents does not amount merely to following directives from them, but rather also, and sometimes conflictingly, to doing what will benefit them or further their interests, at least in the judgment of the legislator. In discussions of the matter, a dichotomy has often been posed between one of these construals and the other.

The latter construal is presented as dangerous because it threatens to disenfranchise the voter. It invites the legislator to ignore the voter's vote as indicating *directly* what should be done and to regard only some other conception, differently arrived at, of which actions would benefit or be to the interests of the voter. But the dichotomy providing a framework for the posing of this threat is an illusion. Consider Tussman's caution that voters' directives to legislators cannot be so unequivocal and so clear that the legislators are called upon merely to follow the directives. Even where the voters speak loudly and clearly, which must be a rare thing indeed, they do not speak only once. That is, they want more than merely one thing and they tell the legislators about their wants for other things as well as for that on which they have spoken loudly and clearly. And the significance of their votes with respect to issues is most often highly indefinite. Thus, whatever directives they may be thought to deliver are at most, as Tussman says, like the sketches of a prospective house handed by the client of an architect to the architect. They merely suggest what is wanted, a suggestion that normally, even at its clearest, needs to be solidified and embodied by essentially creative work on the part of the architect. A legislator is given so many and such indefinite directions—possibly conflicting with each other—from the electorate (even considering only majorities), that substantial creative work remains to embody the accumulated directives in specific legislation. Of course, the legislation itself consists of a not purely unequivocal set of directions to administrators and administrative agencies. The latter also most often need to engage in considerable creative embodiment of directions given to them by legislatures. This problem surfaced abundantly in World War II, as well as in certain other crisis periods both before and after, where legislators sought to create, by means of broad legislative acts, merely some broad directions to administrators that were then supposed to be executed in a discretionary way by the latter. The question before the U.S. Supreme Court in this type of case is whether these directives are too broad to be valid pieces of legislation. This question has been raised in connection with legislation in diverse fields of law, for example, in criminal legislation. A common question there has been whether the legislatures have not tried to create something—for example, in vagrancy statutes—too broad to protect the constitutional rights of citizens.

So, it seems that with both legislators and administrators the sharp dichotomy between merely following the directions of those whose expressed wishes are supposed to be authoritative and doing something more creative that will serve the latter's interests and intentions is a false dichotomy. In receiving directives, legislators and administrators cannot normally avoid engaging in some considerable creative judgments concerning where the interests and intentions of voters and legislators (respectively) lie and how to further them. At the same time, they must be cautioned against forestalling the possibility that the "authorities" (voters or legislators) *can* make errors and should be permitted in accordance with our political ideology to make them. They must, in short, allow the "authorities" the right to risk making errors, and not forestall the exercise of this right by second-guessing.

It would be a mistake, I believe, to treat this overall problem on an issue-by-issue basis. Our legislators are said to be our representatives, and it is true that they bear the primary burden of representing us. But as Hanna Pitkin points out, they are acting in a governmental context of some complexity, and it must not be forgotten that the whole government is said to be a representative government. One implication of this fact is that other agencies of the government than the legislature bear some responsibility for the representativeness of representative government.

Also, legislators cannot deal with issues on an issue-by-issue basis, nor should we suppose that we can render a faithful account of their problems and challenges if we overlook that important fact about what they do. One result of considerations such as these just mentioned is to loosen the tightness of our fixed grasp upon the idea that legislators should always act in accordance with the wishes of their constituents when their constituents have specifiable wishes in connection with any particular matter. We should, as Pitkin suggests, ask only that the legislators be generally responsive to the wishes of their constituents in two senses: we should not normally expect them to act contrary to the wishes of the masses of their constituents when these wishes are easily knowable, and we may legitimately expect from them an account of their decisions when these decisions do appear to have been contrary to those easily knowable wishes, an account that explains how these decisions were arguably in the interests of the mass of their constituents.

The above view of what "service to constituents" amounts to, a view that currently prevails, offers many escape hatches from threatened conflict between service to constituents and service to conscience. To indicate the effects of the availability of those escape hatches, we need merely ask whether *you* believe that genuinely serving constituents' *long-range* interests or benefiting them "on the whole" can ever amount to carrying out, in their name, something that you believe to be immoral or unjust.

Plato would have answered a similar question with a resounding "no," but we need not. There are numerous conceptions of benefit and interests that are independent of moral considerations and thus may conceivably conflict with the latter. Thus, it is conceivable that attempts to serve one's constituents' interests, on this common view of what that must mean, may conflict with attempts to serve one's conscience. And this is even on the assumption that one's conscience is *not* outrageously erroneous or over-scrupulous. Still, you can doubtless sense the enormous strength of the tendency to suppose otherwise.

The likelihood of a clear conflict arising depends, as suggested earlier in this discussion, in part upon whom we identify as the legislator's constituents. If the legislator is, for example, serving an exclusive and wealthy suburb, and *only* the persons in that suburb are his or her constituents, then we may expect that serving them *may* amount to forwarding their interests by behavior that would be knowingly unfair to other persons in the general community for which the legislation is being adopted. You might test the situation by imagining yourself to be a constituent-resident of this legislator's district and telling this person to follow the dictates of his or her conscience whenever a conflict between those dictates and serving your interests appears to arise. It might be easy for you to imagine such a conflict if you are considering only your short-range and partial interests. But what about your long-range interests and your interests "on the whole"? Will you readily admit that a conflict between both serving the latter interests and serving your legislator's considered and responsible conscience can occur? An unequivocal answer to this question is essential to understanding the nature of the problem we are trying to confront.

In thinking about one further aspect of the question heading this section we might consider whether the status of a legislator-with-constituents carries with it a moral obligation to serve constituents at all. One could imagine such an obligation absent on grounds other than the ground that the service was immoral. Except possibly for the immorality of the service, however, the assumption that legislators have such an obligation is commonly made without question and, I believe, rightly so. One may, however, have assumed the status of legislator unwillingly, involuntarily, or inadvertently, and in that case the addition of moral obligations onto one's agenda may be unclear or nonexistent. This would be highly unusual and would require supposing rather bizarre circumstances to make it plausible. Nevertheless, the existence of the obligation we are discussing may still seem somewhat less than perfectly clear because, for example, apart from one's involuntary or inadvertent assumption of the status of legislator, the *regime* of law and government under which the legislator is working may not be totally acceptable. Indeed, it may be unacceptable in any of several ways. Legislators are normally only *part* of systems of law and government. The question of whether to cooperate with *that* regime of law or government, or *that* political system or scheme, may have no particularly clear answer. The regime may be or have become terribly unjust or disturbingly so. The formulation of the overall question given us may invite the bypassing of issues such as these, or seem to do so. For the question is not whether to serve the regime but whether to serve one's constituents. The problem then becomes whether serving one's constituents *simpliciter* can lead to immoral behavior, as certainly one imagines that serving a political system, scheme, government, or law or serving constituents *within* and in terms of such a system, and so forth could do.

IV. Conclusion

Supposing that constituent interests could, in the considered opinion of a legislator, be benefited in the "long run" and "on the whole" by behavior sharply and clearly contrary to the considered and responsible conscience of the legislator, I think we should say that the legislator has no moral obligation to serve the constituents by trying to benefit them in this way. Legislators are responsible for doing many things besides considering and voting on legislation. Thus, the appropriate course of action for a legislator to take in this circumstance is not immediately clear. That course cannot be determined without considering the alternatives and those will vary with the activities in question. Sometimes a simple abstinence will be enough. Sometimes resignation will seem called for. Various alternatives may take personal strength and sacrifice, as well as sacrifice of opportunities to do further good. There may be a need to balance considerations of some delicacy here, and there is nothing automatic about it, nothing that can be settled by clear and helpful rules beforehand. What seems to be clear on these occasions is that we would not want our legislators to continue serving their constituents only at the price of their personal integrity. That is why we certainly must continue to offer outlets at least as drastic as protest and resignation. We should not demand of persons who are legislators that they continue to serve the public no matter what.

We must, of course, be perceptive concerning the stakes, and ingenious concerning the availability and costs of various alternatives. In evaluating the stakes, I suggest the following scales of evaluation: first, the relative weight of reasons on behalf of saying that either conscience or constituents are being served; second, the relative importance to conscience of the service to it, and to constituents of the service to them; third, the relative weights of the obligations to serve, respectively, conscience and constituents. I have not said anything helpful here about the last two scales or about interscale weighings, but the discussion is already too long. How one engages in these weighings is undeniably important, but is merely among the important matters that remain to be treated in connection with this topic.[2]

2. I should like to thank Susan Feagin, my wife, for considerable substantive as well as logistic help with this paper.

10 Dworkin on Judicial Discretion*

Mr. Dworkin's most interesting thesis is that judges do not 'have discretion' even in so-called 'hard cases' of the sorts discussed at one time or another in the cited works by Salmond, Pound, and Hart.[1] His exposition of this thesis contains two sources of serious confusion. I shall address all my remarks to showing what these are and to speculating on what lies behind them.

A. He tangles two questions: (1) Are judges *authorized* ever to decide by means other than the application of standards?[2] and (2) Must dutiful judges ever *do* this, whether or not authorized to do so?[3] The tangle produces an

---

1. See Ronald Dworkin, "Judicial Discretion," *Journal of Philosophy* 60 (1963): 624–38 at p. 625 (first two paras.) and note 1 on pp. 624–25.

2. See Dworkin, "Judicial Discretion," p. 631 (first para.).

3. See Dworkin, "Judicial Discretion," note 6 on p. 634 and Section 4 and p. 631 (para. 2, last sentence).

*This paper has not previously been published. It was presented in a Symposium on Philosophy of Law as a commentary on a paper by Ronald Dworkin on the topic of "Judicial Discretion," at a meeting of the Eastern Division of the American Philosophical Association, 28 December 1963. The proceedings were published in *The Journal of Philosophy* 60.21 (October 10, 1963), Dworkin's paper on pp. 624–38, an abstract of MacCallum's on pp. 638–41. The present version, somewhat revised from the form in which it was written and presented in 1963, was at one time slated to be published in an anthology, along with Dworkin's paper. Although (judging from correspondence MacCallum had with the editor planning the work) a publisher had been obtained, the volume was never published. MacCallum consented to having his paper used on condition that Dworkin's paper appeared in the volume and also had not been so revised as to make MacCallum's piece inapplicable. His consent, then, was explicitly conditional. Dworkin's paper has not been revised (at least no revision of it has appeared) though some of Dworkin's views were later modified, presumably in the light of MacCallum's comments. Apart from its intrinsic interest, then, it is important for its relation to Dworkin's views on discretion and the role of rules in judicial decision, as presented in Dworkin's later "The Model of Rules," *University of Chicago Law Review* 14 (1967): 14ff. and his *Taking Rights Seriously* (Cambridge: Harvard University Press, 1977), of which "The Model of Rules" constitutes Chapter 2.

After the symposium MacCallum set down a set of Afterthoughts, for which see the Addendum below, pp. 175–77. Eds.

168

ambiguity in the discussion of whether judges 'have discretion.' The discussion sometimes seems concerned with answering the first of the questions, i.e., treating 'discretion' as a power or privilege to use a way of deciding, and sometimes the second, i.e., treating 'discretion' as the way of deciding. Perhaps the difference is not kept clear because Dworkin assumes that officials are authorized to do whatever, and no more than, they must do in order to carry out their duties. But the truth of this assumption is not obvious, and at least the threat of a hiatus may appear. For example, Dworkin relies heavily upon references to what people generally expect of judges, and this information may possibly be important in determining what judges are *authorized* to do; but it would rightly be thought of little value by anyone interested in what judges must in fact do. Such a person would recognize that the problems actually faced by judges may not be generally well understood, and that common expectations might therefore be quite misleading. We consequently must get clearer which of these two questions Dworkin is asking, and if he is asking both, we must know this also, and guide our remarks accordingly. I will return to this point at the end of my paper.

B. Suppose we ask: are judges *authorized* ever to decide by means other than the application of standards? Dworkin invites serious confusion again by being, on the face of his essay, inconsistent concerning what would follow from such an authorization. He is most often content to conclude that a judge so authorized would be *expected* to decide on the basis of nothing more than his private preferences.[4] This, however, is prima facie inconsistent with his admission that persons may be granted such authority even though "under an obligation to make every decision so as to further a specific policy" and, thus, *not* expected to decide on the basis of their private preferences.[5] It furthermore threatens, subject to the ambiguity already noted, to render his discussion of discretion irrelevant to the thesis he is attacking, because he has already declared that the characterization of judicial decision making under his attack is *not* a claim that judges should decide whimsically.[6]

I shall explore later what might lie behind this inconsistency, but for the present note that if a person may have the relevant authorization even though still "under an obligation" to make every decision further a specific policy, then the interesting and important contrast for Dworkin to make in establishing his thesis is *not* that between judges and officials such as the scorers in Scorer's or Limited Scorer's Discretion whose decision wholly or in part cannot legitimately be criticized on *any* grounds, but rather that between judges and officials such as generals making military decisions in wartime, or base-

4. See Dworkin, "Judicial Discretion," Section 9 and p. 638 (final para.) and p. 631 (para. 1, last sentence).
5. See Dworkin, "Judicial Discretion," p. 633 (first three paras. of Section 7).
6. See Dworkin, "Judicial Discretion," note 2 on p. 625.

ball managers choosing relief pitchers. The latter officials are not authorized to decide whimsically, but they are acknowledged by Dworkin to have been granted discretionary authority. His major task is therefore to show *their* situation to be relevantly unlike that of judges.

Focussing *only* on how Dworkin seeks to do this, one sees his basic argument against ascribing discretion to judges to be this: If persons subject to an official's decision are entitled as of right to some particular decision, viz., the 'correct' decision, then the official has no discretion. There are such entitlements in all relevant judicial cases. Therefore, judges have no discretion in these cases.

The real difficulty with this argument is not in its first premise. No matter how we resolve the ambiguity and the apparent inconsistency already noted in Dworkin's use of the expression "has discretion," the premise remains plausible if one attends to what Dworkin intends, in his characterizations of 'discretion,' by the word "standards"—viz., a reference to bases of entitlements, rather than merely bases of evaluations. I would agree, therefore, that the premise sets out sufficient although not necessary grounds for saying that an official has not been authorized to use, and *need* not use decision-making of the sort discussed in Salmond, Pound, and Hart. Hence, so far as Dworkin's argument here is concerned, I cannot see the need for any further discussion of the adequacy of his account of 'discretion.'

The second premise of the argument, however, raises immense problems. I shall discuss some of these problems, and shall also find opportunity to reconsider the difficulties I mentioned at the start of this paper, by considering the following two questions: (1) To what might we reasonably be entitled in the way of judicial decisions, given the conditions under which judges do their work? and (2) What is the connection between this and what we *are* entitled to as of right?

1. We can reasonably be entitled to 'the correct decision' in every case only when (a) there *is* one and only one correct decision in every case, and (b) *either* that decision is not difficult to discover even in haste, *or* there are always sufficient opportunities for correcting mistakes. *Both* these conditions, (a) and (b), must be fulfilled; and while I state them as necessary grounds for reasonable claims to the entitlement in question, I would not be surprised if Dworkin thought of them as both necessary and sufficient. I suspect, further, that we have here an opportunity for insight into Dworkin's inconsistency on the point mentioned earlier. To remind you: Dworkin argues that if judges had discretion, they would be entitled to decide whimsically and there would be no legitimate basis for criticizing (or justifying) their decisions; but he also admits that generals making military decisions in wartime are *not* expected to decide whimsically, that their decisions *can* be criticized and justified, and yet that they *have* discretion. How is it that these three things can, according to Dworkin, go together in the case of generals, but not in the case of judges? The answer may be this: it would not be reasonable to expect the correct

decision from generals in all cases because, even though the first of the above conditions (a) is or may be fulfilled (that is, there is or may be a single correct decision in each case), the second, disjunctive condition (b) is notoriously *not* fulfilled. For generals in wartime often must make difficult decisions in haste, and they are sometimes without sufficient opportunity for correcting mistakes. Even so, because condition (a) is fulfilled, generals cannot decide on whimsy, they are not free to decide as they wish; and we do have grounds for criticism or justification of their decisions.*

With judges, on the other hand, this second condition *does* seem fulfilled; while judicial decisions are admittedly often difficult, it does seem that they need never be hasty, and that there are always sufficient opportunities available within the judicial system for correcting mistakes. If so, then only the failure of the first condition to get filled (if the conditions *were* both necessary and jointly sufficient) would justify our failure to demand always the correct decisions from them.

But (I believe Dworkin would say), if the first condition were not filled (that is, if there were not in each case a single correct decision), then there would be no grounds for criticizing or justifying judicial decisions where this was so, and judges might legitimately decide whimsically in those cases. As there *are* always grounds for criticism and justification, and whimsical decisions *would* never be legitimate, there *is* always one and only one correct decision in each case, and we are entitled to it.

I offer this to Dworkin, although he may not take it, as a plausible account of the considerations behind his divergent treatment of military discretion and judicial discretion.

But, consider the connection of the last stage of this account with the first of the conditions mentioned above. It is true that if there is no legitimate basis for criticizing or justifying a decision, then we can hardly talk about that decision as either correct or incorrect. But, *is* it true that wherever we have grounds for criticism and justification, we can reasonably talk about *the* correct decision? I think not, and yet I think that Dworkin's arguments toward the end of his paper, if they are to make his point, require him to affirm this.

Talk about the 'correctness' of judicial decisions makes clear sense only where there is a fairly well-established accumulation of policies, principles, rules, etc., which judges are expected to apply and which guide judges in making decisions. Decisions can be called 'correct,' as opposed to simply 'good' or 'praiseworthy,' only if they can be justified by appeal to what is *recognizably within* this accumulation of policies, etc. Further, a decision can

---

*The sense of this paragraph is unchanged from MacCallum's manuscript, but the editors have simplified the grammar somewhat and made some changes in the wording. This and the next two paragraphs were part of a single long paragraph in the original text. Eds.

be called '*the* correct decision' only if it and no other decision can be so justified. That is to say, for example, that if each of two or more different decisions in a given case could be justified by appeal to some portion of the recognizably established accumulation of policies, etc., then none of these can be declared *the* correct decision unless there is within that accumulation some further policy or principle offering guidance in circumstances of such conflict and guiding us to the choice of that decision over the others.

Consequently, someone might challenge the reasonableness of claiming entitlement to *the* correct decision from judges in every case by arguing that there are at least some instances where judges cannot find, *within the recognizably established accumulation of policies, etc.,* guidance sufficient to lead them to one and only one decision in an instant case, either because the accumulation offers insufficient guidance as to the relative weights to be attached to realizing various policies or acting in accord with various principles and rules found antagonistic to each other, or because clearly applicable policies, etc., do not unequivocally guide them to one and only one specific decision. This need not be because of deficiencies in judicial understanding; there may sometimes be, for example, simply no clear basis for claiming that a policy *as applied* in a particular case, or a principle *as glossed* (with respect to a commonly accepted or authoritative formulation) was, at the time of the application or gloss, a part of the recognizably established accumulation of policies and principles of the legal system. Debates about such a matter may be endless; for, what is a policy or a principle after all? Each is something which may be useful as a guide and as a basis for criticisms and justifications; but is either something apart from our understanding of it, such that we can *always* continue to find out things about it as time goes on? Such a view has its hazards. And if the view has its hazards with respect to *one* policy or principle, then it has its hazards with respect to *collections* thereof, and as well with 'priorities and balances' among them.

Although challenges to such claims can certainly be made, nothing Dworkin says shows that they must always be false or even suspicious. And, I believe, he misunderstands their importance. Their importance is not that they suggest a difficulty in *discovering* correct decisions, but rather that they suggest a breakdown in the reasonableness of maintaining that there *is* one and only one 'correct' decision to be discovered.

The situation, furthermore, may be one in which some decisions might surely be 'incorrect,' even though not every possible decision *but* one. Thus, the implication need not be that judges in these cases are *released* from normally binding policies, etc., but rather that the latter, although they may have guided the judges some distance, have not guided far enough. Hence, it is misleading for Dworkin to speak of these as cases where, *ex hypothesi,* judges must be supposed not bound to apply standards at all and where no grounds for justification or criticism could reasonably be put forward.

Dworkin might argue here that the relevant judicial decisions are on the pattern of simple affirmations or denials and that to say of *these* decisions that the policies, etc., haven't guided the judge far enough is to suggest that they haven't guided him at all, because they seem not to have excluded any alternatives whatever. But this would ignore interim decisions to which the judge may have been guided; the policies, etc., may at least have guided the judge to where he could recognize that the final decision, however it went, could not go on *this* ground or *that* ground, etc.

This, I take it, sums up the most important issue on which Dworkin and I might disagree. But notice also a point concerning the *second* condition for regarding as reasonable entitlement to *the* correct decision in *every* case. It is true that judges do not make decisions in such pressure-filled circumstances as do generals in wartime, and I surely agree that there is enough difference in circumstances to make such entitlement immensely more reasonable in the former case than in the latter—at least so long as one considers only this condition of the reasonableness of such entitlements. But, if I understand Dworkin, he requires that the entitlements be better than simply immensely *more* reasonable; he requires that they be *utterly* reasonable; for he is arguing that judges do not have discretion even in very, very hard cases. It is worth asking even here, therefore, whether we should give him that much, knowing what we know about the pressures under which judges must work and the practical problems connected with scheduling and paying for timely appeals.

This point has a further importance because it is precisely here that one might be tempted to suggest, as Dworkin seems to approach suggesting at the very end of his paper, the *heuristic* value of demanding *the* correct decision in every case. It will keep courts and citizens on their toes, help ensure the orderly development of the legal system, etc. Always ask for a little more than it is reasonable to expect. Come to think of it, the less-forgiving of us do this with respect to generals anyway.

But, while this may seem attractive when the challenge seems to be something which could be met if we only exerted more *effort,* it is less attractive if the exertion of more effort doesn't seem relevant to the challenge. In particular, it may be only self-deceptive when the challenge is to the *significance* and *truth* of the claim that there is always a single correct decision to which persons *could* be entitled.

2. This brings me to my last point—consideration of the question: what is the connection between what we might reasonably be entitled to in the way of judicial decisions, given the conditions under which judges do their work, and what we *are* entitled to as of right?

This question reintroduces consideration of the ambiguity noted at the beginning of this paper. If entitlement to *the* correct decision in every case would be unreasonable because there isn't any such decision in some cases, then there are grounds for saying that, despite common beliefs and expectations about the judicial system, there is no such entitlement. The argument would not be decisive, but its strength would lie in the claim that a system which fails to provide adequate arrangements for achieving x does not, despite general beliefs about the matter, provide *for* entitlement to x, and hence cannot provide entitlement *to* x. If some established conventions and expectations continue to support claims to such entitlement, then an external observer of them may declare either that they involve self-deception and put judges sometimes into dreadful positions—positions where the alternatives are either futile agonizing or artful dissembling—or that the conventions and expectations embody a heuristic policy of the sort just sketched above. But, what would be the value of that policy now? By hypothesis, greater expenditure of effort on the part of judges would not meet the challenge. Perhaps, however, something incidental but dangerous could be avoided? What would this be? I have already shown, I believe, that rejection of the claim that there *is* one and only one correct decision in every case does not amount to rejecting the relevance of appeals to public grounds for criticism and justification of decisions. Hard cases don't come labelled "hard cases," and cases which are hard in some respect need not be hard in every respect. A good many publicly debatable issues would have to be discussed before we would even be in a position to *suspect* that we had before us a case in which either of two or more decisions would be equally in accord with the recognizably established accumulation of policies, principles, rules, etc. constituting our legal system, and in which, therefore, the judge was in some sense free to choose from among those decisions. And, even if we did get this far, this would not tie our hands in criticizing the choice he eventually made as influencing (for the worse, perhaps) the *development* of the legal system.

In sum, the second premise of what I take to be Dworkin's key argument is perhaps false, and the determination of its truth or falsity depends upon the resolution of at least the issues I have raised. Perhaps his thesis could be established by other arguments, but not by *this* argument until at least the issues raised are resolved favorably for it. These issues include, most importantly, the following: (a) Can we rely *solely* on the common expectations of persons living within the ambit of a legal system in determining to what the operation of the system entitles these persons, or must we also look closely at the actual operation of the system in order to discover what the system *could* actually provide? Upon our resolution of this issue hinges our understanding of the relevance of studies of what judges can reasonably be expected to do, to studies of what they are authorized to do. (b) Can we reasonably expect judges to provide *the* correct decision in each and every case before them? Our resolution of this issue depends not only upon our estimate of the *effort* we could reasonably require of judges, but also upon our estimate of what it is *logically* possible for them to provide, given the materials with which they are obliged to work.

Addendum: Afterthoughts*

I think that the most interesting and (potentially) rewarding part of the discussion was as follows: We were talking about judicial discretion in fixing sentences. It was agreed on all sides that judges might abuse this discretion. (We didn't get to it, but it does seem to me that whenever we can talk about the *abuse* of discretion, we can also talk about the *absence* of discretion—at least if we are to be faithful to Dworkin's notion of 'discretion' as amounting to more than merely 'power of judgement.') It was also agreed that the possible abuses clearly went further than merely departures from the way in which judges ought to go about making up their minds; they went also to the *content* of the decisions—e.g., as fixing sentences too close to upper or lower statutory limits (given the actual offence and its circumstances).

These agreements seem to me of immense importance, although I didn't focus on the matter very well during the discussion. From the agreements, one may draw either of two conclusions:

1. Suppose we hold that the area of discretionary authority is precisely what it seems to be on the face of a statute fixing upper and lower limits of penalties for some offense. It would follow from the above admissions that (a) judges have discretion to fix sentences anywhere within this range, and that (b) we may legitimately criticize a sentence a judge sets, even though within this range, if it is too severe or too light—as it may very well be. Dworkin cannot accept this, because he cannot accept the conjunction of (a) and (b); he holds that if an official has discretion, we cannot legitimately criticize what the judge decides. He must hold, therefore, that the sense of "discretion" used in (a) has shifted to where it means nothing more than 'power of judgement'; it is no longer the sense of "discretion" in which he is interested. It is therefore an error for him to hold that we have here a case of judicial discretion of the sort he is discussing.

2. Alternatively, one might hold that the area of discretion is actually much smaller than that set on the face of the statute. The story here is a well-worn one. Its implication might be that within the limits of the *actual* discretionary authority of the judge (as determined not only by the statute, but also by a heritage of accepted dispositions of cases under this and analogous statutes) the judge may be as free as the scorers in Scorer's Discretion; within *these* limits, no decision would be clearly incorrect, nor would any be clearly more correct than the others. Further, within these limits we would have, except insofar as we were concerned with the development of the legal system (in

---

*These "Afterthoughts," written out in longhand, were found among MacCallum's papers, attached to a typed copy of the paper they refer to. They were, evidently, set down shortly after the symposium in which "Dworkin on Judicial Discretion" was presented, either with a view to later revision or just with a view to clearing his own mind. They provide a good example of the care and conscientiousness with which MacCallum approached the consideration and discussion of the topics with which he dealt—and, indeed, philosophical questions in general. Eds.

which case, talk about the "correctness" of decisions would either drop out
or shift in significance), no grounds for wishing the judge to go about making
up his mind in one way rather than another (e.g., why *not,* as far as '*correctness*' is concerned, simply let him toss the dice in order to settle, within *these*
limits, what the sentence will be?).

On this view, indeed, judicial discretion would have precisely those characteristics Dworkin supposes that it must have; but now we must challenge a
statement of fact on which Dworkin bases his claim that judges don't ever (in
the range of cases he is interested in) have this kind of discretionary authority.
He says that we never, outside the cases mentioned in his note 6, regard a
judge as free to decide as he wishes. When thinking about a very broad area
of possible decisions in each case, this appears correct. But, if we think of
discretionary areas in the manner of (2) above, is his claim any longer clearly
correct? Once we reach that *very small* area of judicial discretion, is it really
the case that *within that area* we believe that there is a single decision to
which we are entitled? Clearly, the answer now is no. It is true, and this
became even clearer during our discussion at the meetings, that Dworkin does
not believe that a person granted discretionary authority is necessarily freed
thereby from *all* legitimate criticism of his decisions. This is precisely why
his comparisons of judges to the scorers in Scorer's Discretion and Limited
Scorer's Discretion were so misleading. In all the *other* cases of persons having discretionary authority cited by Dworkin (generals making military decisions in wartime, etc., through to judges sentencing offenders), he agrees that
this authority would be 'abused' if decisions were to be made on a throw of
the dice or by some equally arbitrary means. But this already concedes a great
deal, and in the light of it, one must re-examine those of Dworkin's inferences
based on noticing that we never, in any case, believe that judicial decisions
may legitimately be arbitrary. The short answer to Dworkin here is this: of
course we never believe that judicial decisions may legitimately be arbitrary;
but we don't believe that those military decisions Dworkin mentions may be
arbitrary either, etc. But the reasons *both* judges and generals may nevertheless have to exercise discretion are different, and Dworkin seems not to see
this. Military decisions sometimes have to be made in a hurry, and irretriev-
ably; that is why we don't feel we always observe correct decisions from
generals. Judicial decisions don't, at least, have to be made in *such* a hurry.
What, then, would be in the way of feeling that we always deserve correct
decisions from judges?—i.e., *the* correct decision in each case? Suppose I
say, as I have: because there sometimes isn't any single 'correct' decision.
Dworkin is bound to reply (it seems to me) that if I were correct, then there
would be no legitimate grounds for criticizing the way judges go about deciding; but there always are such grounds; therefore, there must always be a
single correct decision.

My reply, in turn, is simply that the presence always of legitimate grounds for criticizing the way judges go about deciding is perfectly consistent with the occasional absence of single 'correct' decisions—viz., when, despite the absence of such decisions, there are nevertheless many decisions which would clearly be *in*correct. Insistence upon limiting the way in which judges go about deciding could, in such cases, be simply an attempt to insure that these clearly incorrect decisions will not be reached.

Of course, it would follow from what I have said that we could not only sometimes criticize the *way* a judge went about deciding, but we could also criticize his decision as *in*correct, even to the extent of saying that we were *entitled* to a better decision than his was. Nevertheless, it would not follow from this that there was a single correct decision.

11 Violence and Appeals to Conscience*

Appeals to conscience and to violence can be seen as alternative ways of trying to get something done or not done when someone is standing in your way. But discussion of that worthy topic is foreign to my intention here. Rather, my intention is to discuss appeals to conscience offered in defense of violence by persons who engage in or support the violence. Furthermore, I want to focus on defenders of violence who are appealing to their *own* consciences, rather than to the consciences of the persons they may be addressing. The former appeals strike me as at once more interesting and more troubling than the latter.

It is not clear how available such appeals have been in human history. The notion of conscience does not seem present in all human communities, and may be found in a clear way only in relatively few. Some commentators argue that it is much more widespread than that and even universally present, but, though the issues raised in their arguments are interesting, we have insufficient time here to pursue them. We had better settle for the fact that in many

*This unpublished paper was dated April 1974 and listed by MacCallum as "Working paper for the Buffalo Conference on the Justification of Violence," a conference held April 11–13, 1974, at SUNY Buffalo coordinated by Newton Garver. It is central to a project MacCallum was working on for some time, prior to and also after his disabling stroke, on the nature and interrelations of violence, conscience, peace, war, nationalism, and international relations. His reading on these topics was characteristically thorough and well-annotated. He several times gave a course entitled "Nonviolence" and seminars on "Conscience and Violence." A paper entitled "What Is Wrong with Violence?"—included here as Chapter 14—is referred to in this paper (see note on p. 186) as an "unpublishable paper." Apart from whether it is "unpublishable"—it certainly has its problems, and by itself it might very well be "unpublishable"—it is clearly unfinished, and not a paper MacCallum was able to get back to and revise. It is included in this volume because it takes on a different aspect in this context, and it has a central relation to this major theme of MacCallum's later work. (See editorial note to p. 188.) As MacCallum says in the third paragraph of the present chapter, "This paper is a preliminary study of a large topic." Eds.

of the communities of which we here are in one way or another members, the notion of conscience has figured importantly in connection with issues surrounding violence, and seems not yet dormant.

This paper is a preliminary study of a large topic. It prepares the way for, but does not engage in, full-scale discussion of the social importance of appeals to conscience in defense of violence, the ways in which such appeals come to gain social recognition and limited social acceptance, and their validity. It deals with how to recognize when such appeals are being made, where they are placed on the spectrum of appeals we are likely to make, the boundaries and limits of their use, and the interlacing of pragmatic and doctrinal considerations controlling what can count as straightforward and nonskeptical challenges to them. These are all matters one must understand before getting on to rewarding discussion of the larger questions.

More specifically, the objectives of the paper, after two introductory sections devoted to the problem of recognizing appeals to conscience, are two: (1) to exhibit the boundaries and limits of appeals to conscience in defense of violence, and to show thereby that such appeals will normally encompass only a portion of the range of our views about the rightness and wrongness of violence, and (2) to trace the interaction between various doctrines concerning the moral significance of appeals to conscience, on the one hand, and to suggest thereby some of the diverse routes that straightforward challenges to these appeals may have to take. The over-all objective of the paper is to provide an introductory charting of these complicated waters.

The general tone of the paper on many matters is too conservative to express my feelings. I have, however, concentrated on trying to capture a certain level of understanding of some basic phenomena. My motto might be: understanding first; rational reconstruction later.

I. The Apparent Rareness of Appeals to Conscience in Defense of Violence

Invocation of conscience in defense of violence may seem a less familiar phenomenon than invocation of conscience in defense of abstinence from violence. If this is so, however, it is merely because the word "violence" appears more often, though not invariably even there, in the latter cases. One hears things like "It would be against my conscience to engage in or contribute to violence in any way" (offered in, e.g., a defense before a draft board), and "It would weigh on my conscience if I resorted to violence" (explaining, e.g., why one isn't taking karate lessons as a personal response to the problem of crime in the streets), though one also hears "It would be against my conscience to take part" (in, e.g., a bombing raid), and "It would weigh on my conscience if I supported that kind of stuff" (e.g., the death penalty).

In contrast, the word "conscience" rarely appears in defense of engagement in or support of violence. One doesn't hear such things as "My conscience dictates that I resort to violence in such a situation" (where, e.g., the summary suppression of criminality seems needful), and "It would weigh on my conscience if I were not to resort to violence in such a case" (e.g., to 'teach' someone a needed 'lesson'). Rather, one hears things like "It would weigh on my conscience if I didn't help those people" (e.g., to fight off the invaders), "It would weigh on my conscience if I didn't stay" (and, e.g., fight, given a chance to escape), "It would weigh on my conscience if I didn't try to make those people pay for what they did," "It would go against my conscience not to join up" (enlist, report for induction and 'go through with it'), "It would go against my conscience to ignore those people in distress," etc.

This asymmetry between defenses of abstinence from violence and defenses of engagement in violence is hardly surprising. Reference to something *as* violence, though it suggests decisive grounds for abstinence only to rare persons, does suggest grounds for abstinence to most all persons. Numerous discussions of violence explore this fact, and I won't pause to explore it here. One may be clear, in any case, that if what he is abstaining from involves violence, he may give or suggest grounds for abstinence merely by mentioning that fact.

In contrast, reference to something as involving violence fails to reveal anything at all about why any normal person should engage in or support it. Mention of the violence thus does not forward the defender's case. Rather, in the interests of strength and economy of defense, one is likely to choose characterizations of the case such as those offered above, characterizations revealing or suggesting, directly or indirectly, grounds for engaging in or supporting the violence. Something constituting or involving violence is characterized as "helping those people," "making those people pay for what they did," etc.

The asymmetry noted does not, therefore, indicate that conscience plays a lesser role in underwriting violence than it does in underwriting abstinence from violence. Indeed, remembering that conscience has often been regarded as the voice of God, one need only think of *both* sides of what is done in God's name to see the improbability of such an inference.

II. The Difficulty of Distinguishing Between Appeals to Conscience and Mere Citations of the Causal Role of Conscience

When one digs past the common idioms, how prevalent will defenses of violence by appeals to conscience be found to be? One may start on this question a few steps back. It needs a sizable context.

Is there *any* violence that the perpetrator believes wrongful? People do, of course, change their minds about what they are doing or have done. In consequence, they stop what they are doing or regret what they have done. But I am trying to focus on the moment when they 'go ahead,' or afterward when they are still in much the same mood about the violence they engaged in or brought about. Here, it seems clear that even at the moment of 'going ahead,' the perpetrator may sometimes think the violence wrongful, or at least think or be disposed to think that no explanation, excuse or justification will show it not wrongful. For one thing, he may be in an 'I don't care' mood, either because of rage, or, more clearly to the point, because he desires to enjoy or indulge himself and therefore is shutting his mind or trying to shut his mind to any serious consideration of what he is doing. We may suspect, also, rare cases of persons who in effect say "evil, be thou my good!" More prosaically and more clearly, there are persons who, being offended or resentful, act in a way we would call perverse, a way knowingly counterproductive to their own conscious aims, or perhaps intended to sustain someone's bad opinion of them (even their own—cf. Sartre's *Saint Genet*).

Persons aren't, however, always decisive or decided about what attitude to take toward what they do. This fact may sometimes trouble us in dealing with cases like those above, as well as in other cases to be considered below. Borderlines between attitudes may quite often be unclear, and matters of the slightest nuance may lead us to conclude that one attitude more than another is the dominant one. Attributions of 'thoughts' or attitudes here will often give rough justice at best.

But what of persons who seem on the whole prepared to defend the violence or to defend their part in the violence—the latter sometimes being only a matter of defending themselves against the idea that their behavior was blameworthy? Casting the net so wide, we may distinguish between explaining, excusing, and justifying one's behavior, and also, perhaps, between explaining one's behavior and explaining oneself. (I use these words in ways that seem to me natural in the United States while recognizing that different uses might be found elsewhere.)

"Explain" is being used broadly in the last instance, but not, of course, in a way intended to suggest distinterestedness. One who is trying to 'explain himself,' whether to himself or to others, is seldom giving a disinterested account, even though he may aim to give a true and valid account. He hopes, rather, to explore and exploit the sources of the facts to show him blameless (i.e., not blameworthy), or, perhaps, less to be blamed than might otherwise have been supposed. His explanation may work to justify or excuse his behavior, or merely to explain it.

Thus, a person may *explain* his behavior: He says "I can't stop" (I get these fits. They are involuntary), or "I didn't notice" (It was inadvertent). He may seek to *excuse* it (i.e., offer an excuse): He says "I was on the ragged edge"; "I was overcome with emotion"; "I've had an unfortunate life" (underprivileged, etc.); "I burned with resentment." What is 'explained' is presented as not wrongful though perhaps regrettable. What is 'excused' (i.e., that for which an excuse is offered) is perhaps presented as wrongful, but not so wrongful as you might have thought.

Behavior which is justified (i.e., for which a justification is offered) is never presented as wrongful. But it may be presented as merely alright,* instead of right: "He struck the first blow," etc. And, when it is presented as right, it may be presented as productive of good—"I needed it more than he did, and this was the only way I could get it"—or as preventive of or resistant to evil—"He was holding them hostage and about to kill them," or as duti-ful—"It was my responsibility to clear the demonstrators off the streets."

Can appeals to conscience enter equally into all of these? Apparently not. But there are difficult cases. One must in particular distinguish between ap-pealing to or invoking conscience as a touchstone of the rightness, alrightness or wrongness of what one does, and citing conscience for the causal role it may play in what one does. In several of the above cases, conscience may be cited, but only as having (had) some causal role in the behavior; it would not, in these cases, be *appealed* to as a touchstone of the rightness, alrightness or wrongness of the behavior.

Imagine a person referring in the past tense to the workings of his con-science in bringing it about that he engaged in or supported violence. He now, let us suppose, believes that conscience to have been erroneous, and what he did to have been wrong, though he may still believe that he was right to do what he did because his conscience directed it. He refers to that conscience to excuse or explain what he did, and, perhaps, to justify his doing what he did, but not justify what he did. He thinks what he did was wrong. He is citing the causal role of his conscience in bringing about that he did what he did, not appealing to or invoking his conscience in defense of a claim that what he did was right or alright.

The description of this case is controversial. One difficulty is that it requires us to be ready to distinguish between the rightness or wrongness of what the person did, and the rightness or wrongness of his doing it, and to agree that our reactions to each may diverge in this and other cases. We are to agree, for example, that we may think what the person did was wrong but that his doing it was right, i.e., that he was right to do it, or that what he did was right but that his doing it was wrong. But there may be cases where what he did cannot be clearly distinguished from his doing it (though the hint of paradox in the formulation of this supposition emerges if we ask "clearly distinguished from his doing *what?*"). Or one may be inclined to doubt that the wrongness of what he did can always be distinguished from the wrongness of his doing it. (One might say that sometimes they clearly *can* be distinguished, as when the

---

*MacCallum used the spelling "alright" and "alrightness" for the expressions "all right" and "all rightness," which appear on this page and later. After some hesitation the editors decided to leave the author's spelling as it was. Eds.

person had no proper authority to do what someone with proper authority would have been right to do; but another commentator might argue here that what the person did cannot be correctly described if mention of his lack of authority is omitted, in which case, when what he did is correctly described, it will be seen as wrongful.) The distinction, in short, raises difficult issues in the philosophy of action. Those issues can hardly be resolved here, and I can only hope that you will extend me some rope in operating with the distinction.

Another difficulty, and one with which we certainly will have to grapple, is that first-person citations of the causal role of one's conscience are not clearly confined to cases of one's past behavior. Sometimes, at least, it seems that one is citing his conscience for its causal role in his present or even his (prospective) future behavior, and not for its role as a touchstone for him of what is right, alright, or wrong about that behavior. (Third-person citations of the former sort would be less interesting and not really *apropos* here; people often explain the present and (prospectively) the future behavior of *others* by citing the causal role of the workings of the others' consciences.) It is sometimes *extremely* difficult to tell which of these two accounts is being offered, and, when both are or seem to be in the wind, which predominates.

Roots of this difficulty are to be found in several places. While all persons treat the conscience as a constituent of the psyche, and at least in that sense something psychological, some persons treat it as having moral significance in some primary way, while other persons treat it as purely psychological and having moral significance at best in a remote and derivative way—e.g., in a way that inculcated habits might have moral significance by being linked, through the process of inculcation, to what is accepted in the community and thus to what conduces to fulfilling communal expectations, creating communal feeling, and, if communal judgments have been reasonably correct, promoting the survival of the community. These different views of the essentialness or contingency of the moral significance of conscience, and the consequent differences in viewing it as something basically moral or basically and purely psychological, are now well-embedded in our cultural heritage. It is not surprising, therefore, that we should not always be certain of which of the two views of his conscience a person is taking, and that he too should have at least moments of unclarity about the matter, as well as times when he takes now one and now the other view of his conscience.

But even before the 'psychologizing' of conscience, considerations were present capable of producing our difficulty in its general form. There has been a recurring tension in the history of conscience between a view of conscience as something of which one is a helpless, or largely helpless, victim, and a contrary view of conscience as a guide leading one in a direction in which it is often *very* difficult to go. The distance between these views of a person's relation to his conscience is roughly indicated by the apparent gap between Luther's "I can do no other!" (probably an apocryphal remark, but one that has taken root in our cultural history) and the modern idea that one 'ought to try to live up to' one's conscience, however difficult this may be to do. The divergence goes to the heart of the social and personal functions of citations of conscience, and I shall have things to say about this aspect of the matter later. For the present, we may note that there are traces of each view throughout virtually the entire history of the concept, though the first view seems somewhat more prominent in the theological stages and the second somewhat more prominent in the secularized stages. Their concomitance has been a source of confusions about conscience central to our concerns here.

Consider: A person who tends to think himself powerless to resist the dictates of his conscience, much as he might think himself powerless to resist the dictates of an all-powerful dictator (and for much the same reason if conscience is the voice of God and God is, for example, as He is depicted by Hobbes in "Of The Kingdom of God By Nature," Chapter 31 of *Leviathan*), may tend also to think of his conscience as bringing it about that he does some of the things he does. His citations of his conscience in connection with his behavior may therefore be more like explanations than justifications of his behavior, albeit explanations hopefully getting him wholly or partially off the hook of blameworthiness (surely Luther's case). When violence is involved, he is, for example, on the whole more likely to be explaining his engagement in violence than justifying the violence in which he is engaged.

On the other hand, a person who sees his conscience as a guide leading him toward a perhaps distant and certainly hard to reach target of aspiration will tend to see his progress toward that target as far from inevitable or forced. His citations of his conscience in connection with his behavior will hardly seem to him to explain the behavior independently of the idea that the behavior is thereby justified (i.e., that a justification of what he did is thereby afforded). For, he knows that he would not have followed his conscience if he had not the aspiration to do so, i.e., to 'live up to' the demands of his conscience, and that this aspiration is inseparable from his view of his conscience as a touchstone of what is right.

These divergent views, being entangled in our cultural history, are often enough entangled in our heads. Furthermore, now one and now the other of the views finds support from what might be called the 'pragmatics' of the situations in which we find ourselves. It is sometimes best, when pleading conscience, to present ourselves as in the grip of something in whose grip we are powerless; at other times, we want when pleading conscience to think of ourselves and present ourselves as willingly and dedicatedly doing the 'high-minded' thing. Thus, the pragmatics of conscience pleading, a topic to be discussed more fully below, are likely to keep both views on tap, with now one and now the other emerging from the cellar of our psyche.

This whole affair often leaves us not knowing how to read persons who plead conscience in 'explaining' (in our larger sense) what they do. We are often unsure of when they are defending what they do, and when they are only defending themselves in doing it. (And this unsureness in turn creates confusion in our thinking about the connection of conscience and reason, and about the alleged inaccessibility of conscience to reason—a matter to be dealt with below from a somewhat different vantage point.)

We are here, I take it, more interested in when they are defending what they do than in when they are defending themselves in doing it. But the latter has become so entangled with the former, and its features seem always lurking so close by even when not dominant, that we will find our subsequent discussion occasionally broadening so as to include matters arising from it as well.

III. Some Boundaries of and Limits on Appeals to Conscience in Defense of Violence

So much for recognizing the appeals, I now want to argue that appeals to conscience encompass only a portion of our moral lives, and, consequently, that appeals to conscience in defense of violence encompass only a portion of the range of our views about the rightness, alrightness, and wrongness of violence.

Start with a wide context. When violence is justified (i.e., when justification is offered) are appeals to conscience always present or in the offing? Surely not. For example, because of common human attitudes toward the non-human, violence toward the latter will not often be thought to require such a 'high' ground of defense. (There is here another interesting asymmetry between justifications of violence and justifications of abstinence from violence. Appeals to conscience in support of *forswearing* violence on the non-human—on God's creatures, etc.—are surely more common than appeals to conscience in support of engagement in or approval of violence on the non-human.) Appeals to considerations of personal safety and perhaps even personal convenience will be thought strong enough.

There may be some difference in sensitivity toward the inanimate and the non-human animate, though in some places, e.g., Spain, there seems not even much difference at times with respect to that. Aside from questions about property rights, the overcoming by violence of non-human obstacles or threats to one's aims or the aims of others is generally thought (or at least has been generally thought prior to our age of ecological awareness) to raise no questions whatever with respect to the inanimate objects of that violence except considerations of prudence and perhaps of decorum and waste. Violence toward the non-human animate may be thought to raise at least the additional question of *pain,* though such violence is of course not always accompanied by pain, as when, e.g., it is instantly lethal.

With the exception of those perhaps few places in the modern world where the violence may be thought even so to raise no need for stronger justification, the infliction of pain or death will be thought to require more justification than merely consideration of one's personal convenience. Yet it will not commonly be thought to require anything so strong as considerations of conscience. Appeal to one's personal safety or survival (without any background notion that one has an obligation to continue living or to remain unmutilated) is generally thought both sufficient (considerations of property rights aside, such considerations sometimes complicating things though not defeating the claim just made) and uncontroversial.

Sometimes, it is true, violence toward humans is also thought sufficiently and uncontroversially justified by consideration of one's safety or survival. But we will be led to think that there is no difference in this respect between animals and humans only if we confine our thinking to one class of cases— viz., cases of a person's being *attacked by* animals or humans. Another class of cases reveals a dramatic difference, and thereby reinforces the common idea that, so far as violence is concerned, violence against humans must be the primary site of appeals to conscience. The latter class includes cases of what the law would call "necessity" as distinguished from "self-defense." Imagine, for example, two 'lifeboat' cases, in one of which one's companions are humans and in the other of which they are animals. In each case one's safety or survival depends either upon throwing the companions overboard— so that the lifeboat will stay afloat—or upon eating at least some of one's companions so as to prevent starvation before rescue. To put the matter mildly, there will be more controversy about such usage of one's companions when they are humans than when they are animals. (Whether this should be so is another thing.)*

---

*The paragraph following this one appeared originally in brackets. We include it here as a footnote. In MacCallum's typescript this paragraph was lined out, was probably not read when the paper was delivered at the Buffalo conference. But it seems likely that he would have included the gist of it in a published version if his research program had not been interrupted the way it was. MacCallum's paragraph reads as follows:

> Several years ago I began exploring some of the conceptual substructure of such facts as these in an unpublishable paper called "What is Wrong with Violence?" which some of you have read. It seems to me inappropriate to rehearse that incomplete and not yet completely thought out story here, though some of it will perhaps emerge in the discussion. I think, at least, that the approach is congenial to that in Newton Garver's early paper "What Violence Is" and Michael Pritchard's "Violence and Human Dignity," and it is given a good context in Terry Nardin's fine paper "Conflicting Conceptions of Political Violence."

Garver's paper appeared in *The Nation*, 24 June 1968, pp. 817–22, and was reprinted with some revisions by the author in *Philosophy for a New Generation*, edited by Arthur K. Bierman and James A. Gould (New York: The Macmillan Co., 1970), pp. 353–64. Pritchard's paper was published locally by his department at Western Michigan University (in *Proceedings of the Heraclitean Society* 1.2 [1973]: 69–82); revised portions of it are included in Pritchard's book *On*

But even in the case of 'justified' violence toward humans, appeals to conscience need not clearly always be present or in the offing. To start with, the issue may depend upon the degree of the violence, and also upon its type. Depending, of course, on what one is willing to count as violence, the violence or its consequence *may* be too slight to require the big guns of conscience. I underline "may" because some persons get uptight about the slightest deliberate or foreseeable and unavoided damage of, or violation of the integrity of, another person. On the whole, however, injuries that are foreseeably slight are taken more lightly and may possibly be justified by lesser appeals. Similarly, and doubtless connectedly, the same thing may be true of some types of violence. If one allows a distinction between physical violence and various forms of psychic violence, for example, some persons may be inclined to take some of these less seriously than others and thus think lesser justification needed for perpetrating or supporting them.

The full story of the boundaries and limits of appeals to conscience in defending violence toward humans surely, however, depends on more than differences in the degree and kind of violence. What further about the context determines whether an appeal to conscience is made or even thought of?

Conscience is often said to be inherently and essentially opposed to desire. This remark suggests something about the contexts in which appeals to conscience are made; it suggests that the contexts are ones in which conscience *is* opposed to desire. The suggestion is worth following a bit, though, as we shall see, its purview is too limited.

The opposition of conscience to desire could be understood merely as distinctness from or independence of desire, the idea being that the dictates or urges of conscience are thought to run (be formed) independently of desire. Surely, the opposition of conscience to desire means at least this, though it is often taken to mean more. Often it is taken to mean that conscience is in conflict with, and contrary to, desire.

Conscience does often play a role when one's thoughts, feelings, and desires are not unified so to speak, and when one's thoughts or feelings about what is right or wrong are not totally integrated with other thoughts, feelings or desires one has. We are familiar with the idea that one hears from conscience when inclined to do something contrary to it; its voice signals the presence of countervailing tendencies within one. This is a highly interesting

Becoming Responsible (Lawrence: University Press of Kansas, 1991), ch. 5. Nardin's paper was published in the *Political Science Annual,* vol. 4, edited by Cornelius P. Cotter (Indianapolis: Bobbs-Merrill, 1974), pp. 75–126. We are grateful to Professor Pritchard for supplying some of the information provided here and in the preceding editorial note and confirming the rest. In Pritchard's own words: "Nardin's article actually has an extended (and sympathetic) discussion of Gerry's unpublished 'What Is Wrong with Violence?' "—included in this volume as Chapter 14—and Pritchard suggested this as "an additional reason for including" "What Is Wrong with Violence?" in this volume. Eds.

fact about the settings of at least some appeals to conscience in defense of violence (and of abstinence from violence, for that matter). It is worth pausing over for a moment.

There are varying views of the ramifications of the presence of counter-vailing tendencies within a person. In particular, when one of these counter-vailing tendencies is conscience, the person's integrity is often said to be at stake. (And when conscience directs violence against other persons, their in-tegrity may also be at stake and the situation may thus present an interesting problem in balancing the values of integrities and of various injuries thereto.) But even when conscience is not involved, the presence of countervailing tendencies within a person is generally thought to present a problem to the person; the person is imagined unable to yield to the tendencies countervailing each other—for to say that they are countervailing is to claim that yielding to them would take one in contrary directions—and the situation thus looks to be one in which something must be given up if not sacrificed, though follow-ers of Dewey, for example, would deny that this needs to be the case.

The suggestion of this account of appeals to conscience is then that appeals to conscience in defense of violence (and of abstinence from violence) often occur in a setting in which the person's feelings, thoughts and desires on the matter are not fully integrated, [one] is inclined in contrary directions, and may first of all have a problem about 'getting himself together.' The back-ground assumptions and models of human nature operating to sustain a view of this 'problem' *as* a problem, and operating to influence what will be rec-ognized as a resolution to it, need to be examined with, eventually, special attention paid to the role of confrontation with choices about violence in cre-ating such states of affairs in persons.*

But clearly the opposition of conscience to desire is not the only setting of cases of appeals to conscience. There are strikingly different, though mutually compatible, settings. Conscience is also heard from, for example, in settings of *external* opposition to one's doing what one believes right. Quite indepen-dently of whether one is the seat of contrary tendencies respecting whether to engage in or abstain from certain behavior, consultation of and appeals to conscience may be occasioned by the fact that our thoughts or feelings about the rightness or wrongness of the behavior in question are not generally ac-cepted and unchallenged in our communities (the communities of which we are, relative to the matter in question, considering ourselves a part or at least

---

* The following two sentences appear in the original text in brackets: "I started such examination in the paper mentioned above, and in another paper called "Law, Conscience and Integrity" which is in a book edited by Care and Trelogan called *Issues in Law and Morality*. Perhaps the matter can be pursued further in the discussion." The "paper mentioned above" is "What is Wrong with Violence?" (1970), Chapter 14 of this volume. "Law, Conscience, and Integrity" (1973) is Chapter 8 of this volume. Eds.

somehow subject to). This may be either because the generally accepted and unchallenged views are contrary to ours, or because there are no generally accepted and unchallenged views in the community on whether the behavior is right or wrong.

Further, appeals to conscience may occur in yet different settings, ones in which there is neither internal nor external opposition to one's doing what [one] believes right, but rather where there is, externally, indifference. These are cases where one's views on the rightness or wrongness of the behavior in question are not generally shared in the community but neither are they challenged. While people generally may be bemused, amazed or irritated at the views, no one cares enough to challenge them. The person whose views they are is regarded merely as having an over-scrupulous or quirky conscience because he cares (in this way) about things other people don't find worth caring about or caring that much about.

These last two settings, as interesting as the first, suggest together that appeals to conscience in justifying violence (or abstinence from violence) may signal exercises, possibly important exercises (depending upon the community and the views prevalent there) of personal discretion or judgment, i.e., of socially undirected choice. The choice would be socially undirected either in not being required (e.g., there is no prospect of a penalty if one fails to choose as one chooses) or not being unilinearly supported—both, of course, being compatible with the choice's being prohibited or condemned.

The three settings together exhaust, I believe, the settings along this dimension of appeals to conscience. This fact, if it is a fact, is of some importance because exploration of it can reveal something of why appeals to conscience encompass only a portion of our moral lives, and, consequently, why appeals to conscience in defense of violence (and abstinence from violence) may encompass only a portion of the range of our views about the rightness and wrongness of violence (and abstinence from violence).

Consider, for example, what the claim about the three settings amounts to. If it is correct, then appeals to conscience signal either a lack of integration of one's own tendencies on an issue, a lack of integration of one's own views with the predominant views of one's relevant communities on the rightness or wrongness of the behavior in question, or a lack of univocal social direction on the issue in those communities. The rough contrapositive of this claim is as follows: when our views and feelings on right and wrong are, in a case at hand, not in any way discordant with other feelings, views and desires of ours, and are generally accepted and unchallenged in the relevant communities, then there is no occasion to be aware of or to consider conscience. The truth of this contrapositive explains why most of us do not, in the ordinary course of our lives, regard our abstinence from murder as a matter of conscience.

This is ground on which we must tread carefully. Some persons, for example, have leaped from the observation that our abstinence from murder is not ordinarily thought a matter of conscience to the mistaken inference that matters of conscience are concerned with relatively trivial things. To say "It's a matter of conscience" seems to them the same as saying "No one cares very much." Thus, whether to tell a white lie or steal a small sum of money may be matters of conscience, but not whether to murder or rape.

Given the ringing affirmations of conscience down through at least the more recent portions of human history, there is something obviously wrong with this position. But there is some truth in it too. The truth lies in *precisely* the considerations adduced above, neither more nor less.

A rough taxonomy of cases based on those considerations could be used to spell this out and thus make clearer the portion of our moral life carved out by appeals to conscience and so-called "matters of conscience." What follows is such a taxonomy, with special attention paid, in illustrating its stages, to cases involving violence, even though other cases might sometimes seem more natural illustrations of the stage at hand. Each stage will be illustrated by at least one case in which the person whose conscience is engaged thinks the violence wrong, and one in which he thinks the violence right, though only the latter cases are strictly of concern to us here.* The first four stages are ordered in a range from community approval to community disapproval. The fifth stage concerns only the countervalence of tendencies within a person.

1. An activity is encouraged, endorsed or even demanded in the relevant community, but one thinks it wrong and acts accordingly as a matter of conscience.
   (a) anti-violence illustrations.
      (i) One refuses to engage in or approve of bullfighting in Spain though bullfighting is encouraged there.
      (ii) One refuses to be connected with the slaughter of animals for food though such slaughter is endorsed in countless ways in the relevant community.
      (iii) One refuses to engage in military service though this service is demanded of persons such as him in the community.
   (b) pro-violence illustration (a rough and perhaps unfair, though serviceable, label).
      — One refuses in Norway, let us say, to abstain from the

---

* The editors have deleted the following sentence which appears in MacCallum's original dittoed typescript at this point. It is appropriate only for oral delivery in a conference setting: "I should be pleased if you were to think of other and perhaps better illustrations." Eds.

uses of torture in pursuit of urgent national or military goals though torture is prohibited (i.e., abstinence from such practices is demanded).

2. An activity is a matter of indifference in a community, but one thinks it wrong and acts accordingly as a matter of conscience.
    (a) anti-violence illustrations.
        — One forswears the killing of insects or hunting or fishing or the eating of meat or fish though whether one does so is a matter of indifference in his community.
    (b) pro-violence illustration.
        — One refuses to forswear *all* forms of corporal punishment of his children though whether parents use or abstain from using mild forms of corporal punishment of their children is a matter of indifference in the community.

3. An activity is tolerated in the sense that, though it is an occasion for disappointment, it is thought 'understandable' and not to be punished or condemned, and one thinks the activity quite wrong and acts accordingly as a matter of conscience.
    (a) anti-violence illustration
        — One abstains from verbal abuse of another even when very angry at him, and has community backing in this, though people would be 'understanding' if he did otherwise. (For this to be a case involving violence, one must see it as Gandhi and some psychologists would see it.)
        (b) pro-violence illustration.
        — Thinking conscientious objection to military service to be quite wrong, one refuses to endorse it and gains much sympathy for his position though people would not harass him if he took the contrary position.

4. An activity is tolerated in the sense that, though it is grounds for criticism, blame and even condemnation, it is not punished, and one thinks the activity wrong and acts accordingly as a matter of conscience.
    (a) anti-violence illustration.
        — One refuses to engage in even mild maltreatment of his pets, and he would be criticized though not punished if he did mildly maltreat his pets.
    (b) pro-violence illustration.
        — One 'stands up to' a bully in defense of another person, and would have been condemned as a coward but not punished had he failed to do so.

5. An activity is prompted by various feelings, desires, or beliefs
   a person has, but he believes the act to be wrong and acts
   accordingly as a matter of conscience.
   (a) anti-violence illustration.
       — One abstains from eating meat though he had previously
         developed a taste and appetite for meat.
   (b) pro-violence illustration.
       — One carries through his part as a member of a firing
         squad though he is sickened at the thought of killing
         someone.

This rough taxonomy and its illustrations exhibit both why people may
sometimes be inclined to regard matters of conscience as dealing with minor,
or at least not major, moral issues, and why this inclination is untrustworthy.
The characterizations of each of the first four stages support the inclination so
long as one thinks of the minority who make such affairs a matter of conscience as merely aberrant, an attitude in turn supported by many of the cases
that would come most naturally to mind to persons who are in the comfortable
majority. The bulk of members of our society might very well, for example,
regard all our illustrations in the anti-violence categories except for the one
involving military service, as cases of mere (relatively inconsequential) ab-
errance or quirkiness; but some of the illustrations in the pro-violence categories might convince them that matters of conscience are not always about
small potatoes.

Still, we must remember that some highly significant moral matters concerned with violence do not ordinarily fall within the limits of our taxonomy
because questions of conscience do not ordinarily arise in connection with
them. Consider our common abstinence from murder, and perhaps also the
conditions of a great deal of military and para-military (e.g., police) service. For most people in most communities at most times, the first never
arises as a matter of conscience, and for substantially fewer but still significant numbers of people the second may perhaps also never arise as a matter
of conscience.

Military service and abstinence from murder can, however, *become* matters
of conscience when, for example, one is seriously tempted or inclined to do
otherwise. And matters of conscience can become derivatively associated
with each. For example, a person who has *committed* a murder may find that
the murder weighs on his conscience and that, consequently, he is confronted
with derivative matters of conscience, e.g., whether to confess the murder
and whether and how to make amends for it.

There are no limits, so far as I can see, on the sorts of wrongs that, because
they weigh on a person's conscience, can raise matters of conscience in this

derivative way. As I will argue below, all these derivative cases will fall within the limits of the taxonomy offered earlier. But, because of the reaction of the person who believes himself a wrongdoer and the reaction of his community, some wrongs will not weigh on his conscience and thus will not give rise to such derivative matters of conscience. Two conditions controlling this, in particular, are worth looking at for the further information they yield on the limits of the purview of conscience in our moral life. They are:

(a) the person's sense of the wrongfulness of his act must not be so overwhelming that 'weighing on his conscience' is too little to say about its effect on him, and

(b) the act must not be something for which others are successfully seeking what the perpetrator regards as full retribution.

Consider the second condition first. Does the fact that someone is held criminally liable for an act diminish the likelihood that the act will weigh on his conscience? Yes, because undergoing the punishment attendant upon being held criminally liable is often regarded by the person as 'paying his dues' and, in effect, making 'right' again with himself and with the world. Many criminals are, indeed, exceedingly disturbed when this view of punishment is challenged, and it is easy to see why. They regard it as essential if there is to be any hope of putting them right again with the world and with themselves. In this respect, they are pleased to adopt a retributive view of punishment; they want to treat their punishment as putting them right again. How, after all, can a person who has done something he believes to have been wrong come to good terms again with his conscience and with the world? Can he never do so?

This plea is supported at several points by our society generally. We do not generally believe that, except with respect to extraordinary cases, a wrongful act must forever weigh on the perpetrator's conscience no matter what penalties are paid and 'other' amends made. That would be too much like eternal damnation for every sin. We thus generally allow that the weight of wrongdoing can somehow be removed. A person is regarded as able to 'make things right,' 'make amends,' 'erase the stain,' for all but the most extraordinary cases. Punishment, good works, restitution, are ways of having this done or doing it. Further, we enforce and try to teach the idea that a person who still feels a weight on his conscience after a certain amount of such recompense and amends making is morbid or obsessed unless, again, the case is extraordinary (and more on that below). Thus, it is common, at least *after* the commission of the (believed) wrong, to hold the hopeful doctrine that the slate can (and should) be wiped clean.

In the light of this account, consider where questions of conscience normally arise in connection with acts that are criminal or actionable at law, such acts being the central cases of fulfillment of condition (b) above. (We are not, of course, considering here cases of conscience-driven *resistance* to law.) They arise either where the actor has not been held liable or where he has not felt the penalty he paid to be sufficient. Except for such cases as these, e.g., the undetected thief who returns the money years later, and the released convict who plunges into good works to make amends, questions of conscience don't normally arise in cases the law covers.

These considerations suggest that conscience 'takes up the slack' with respect to the adequacy of communal reactions (as, e.g., found in the law) in meeting the standards one applies to oneself concerning appropriate responses to the wrongness of one's behavior. Conscience does not operate where, in the view of the wrongdoer, there is no slack.

But even where there is such slack conscience does not always operate, and condition (a) above shows why. It is designed to cover, by excluding, cases in which persons are so overcome by remorse for what they have done that it would misrepresent their situation to say that what they did weighed on their consciences. Remorse can be too strong, too overwhelming, or so it seems to me, to be described by reference to conscience. There is a rationale for this position. It echoes the earlier idea that conscience operates when one's feelings, beliefs and desires are somehow not fully integrated. We have seen already that that view is too limited to account for all cases of the operation of conscience, but the exceptions noted earlier had to do with the particulars of the relations of the person's ideas of the rightness and wrongness of his actual or prospective behavior to the ideas prevailing in his community. But, consider now the case of a convicted criminal who hangs himself in his cell out of remorse for what he did. In his case, no considerations about communal reactions need be present, and furthermore his psyche is so overwhelmed by remorse for what he did that it seems false to say that there are countervailing tendencies of any sort in him relevant to the deed or to making amends for the deed.

Condition (a) thus suggests that, at least from the perspective of the believed wrongness of behavior, conscience operates only up to a certain level of intensity of feeling. This does not mean that conscience deals only with minor pecadilloes, a view already rejected, but only that some wrongs are too overwhelming for consciousness of conscience to come into play.

What would we think after all, of someone who declared, as his reason for abstaining from some truly monstrous violence, that such behavior was contrary to his conscience? We would expect or at least hope for something quite different, viz., an expression of total revulsion at the thought of engaging in such behavior, a revulsion not peculiarly moral but, rather, coming from every facet of the thought and feeling of the person expressing it. (Suppose someone were seriously entertaining the thought of engaging in such behavior. Would even our "Have you no conscience!" quite cover the case?) Likewise, we may anticipate finding cases in which *refusal* to engage in activities involving violence is believed to constitute a betrayal of friendship or fellow-feeling so gross that one would be misdescribing the depth and comprehensiveness of his massive psychic rejection of the thought of such betrayal if he were to declare, however ringingly, that the betrayal would violate his conscience.

Where both conditions (a) and (b) apply and consequently there is a slack to be taken up between societal reactions and those of the wrongdoer concerning appropriate responses to his wrongdoing, and yet where his sense of wrongdoing is not too overwhelming for conscience to operate, questions of conscience may arise for him in connection with whether and how to make (complete) amends. All these questions will fall comfortably within the limits of the rough taxonomy offered above, for, to put the matter briefly, even if the person is not himself a site of countervailing tendencies on whether and how to make amends (stage 5), the society in general will either believe that amends have been or are being fully made, or won't care nearly so much about failures to make full amends as about the acts for which full amends have not been forthcoming. Thus, depending upon just how strongly they do feel about failures to make full amends, the various cases will fall into one or the other of the previous stages of the taxonomy (stages 1–4).

What, in sum, can we now say about the limits of the purview of conscience in our moral life and consequently about the extent to which appeals to conscience in defense of violence may cover our morally relevant reactions in defense of violence? When honest, the appeals will figure only when (1) there is a lack of integration in the pleader's own tendencies on whether to engage in or support the violence (he is not totally in favor of it and totally inclined toward it), (2) there is opposition between his views and the predominant views of a (for him) relevant community on the rightness, in context, of the violence in question, (3) there is a lack in the community of univocal social direction or even of much interest in the issue, or (4) the violence plays a role in his efforts to 'make right,' in a way the community has not required of him, some wrong he has committed. Furthermore, such appeals will generally though not exclusively arise only when the direct or indirect subjects of the violence are human. (Note that the illustrations in our taxonomy dealing with pets and with hunting, etc. were illustrations of conscience-directed abstinence from violence, not of conscience-directed engagement in or support of it.) And the appeals will not arise when the violence plays a role in the expression of an overwhelming and massive psychic reaction by the perpetrator or supporter, no matter what the moral origin of this reaction.

This summary of the limits of the purview of conscience in our moral life is, unfortunately, a bit complex to absorb at a single sitting. But, if I have it right, it suggests interesting leads for further thinking about the role of appeals to conscience in defense of violence, and it exhibits the achievement of the aim of this section of the paper, viz., to show that such appeals will normally cover only a portion of our morally relevant reactions in defense of violence. The latter, I take it, is something that we want to know so that we will know both what has been done and what remains undone when this style of justification of violence has been examined.

IV. The Pragmatics of Appeals to Conscience

Even if the above limits on appeals to conscience have been correctly set, it does not follow that appeals to conscience will always occur within those limits. Further features of the situation will influence whether such appeals are actually made. Some of them will now be considered. The objective is to trace the interaction between various doctrines concerning the moral significance of appeals to conscience in defense of violence, on the one hand, and the pragmatics of the appeals, on the other hand. What is wanted is a charting of some of the diverse routes that straightforward challenges to the appeals may have to take. The charting would be a beginning to rational coping with the appeals when the appeals are taken more or less at their face value. Some people may wish, of course, not ever to take the appeals at their face value. I should be inclined to argue with them on the grounds that appeals to conscience are an important part of our cultural heritage, and that we would be well-advised to take them seriously when they are offered in defense of violence. But that argument can hardly be launched here.

Start with some of the pragmatics. Why should anyone justify violence by appeal to conscience? Obviously, the situation shares something with any attempt at justification. Normally, one is attempting to meet or anticipate an inquiry, challenge or reproach. Two remarkable things about appeals to conscience, however, emerge readily to distinguish them. The first is that it seems at first look a very *personal* approach to the problem, and the second is that it seems intended to be a very high-minded approach.

First, concerning the personalization, we noted at the beginning of the paper that we are focusing on a person's appealing to his *own* conscience in justification of violence he engages in or supports. Appeals to the consciences of others are, after all, hardly more than shots in the dark—a claim that superficially may seem false but then seems true as one thinks more about it. And this remark about 'shots in the dark' suggests the special interest that attaches to a person's appealing to his own conscience in an attempt to meet or anticipate inquiries, challenges and reproaches from others. His conscience is not only something perhaps personal to him, but is also not directly accessible to others.

Because a person can appeal to his conscience in a private as well as in a public way—i.e., he can do it in (exploring the) justification to himself of something—accessibility is not equally a problem with every appeal to conscience. But it may be thought a special problem with public appeals. It may seem to present difficulties about possible dishonesty or error on the part of the conscience-pleader that cannot be directly checked by third parties. But the significance of such considerations depends on, among other things, what the alternatives are, and how attractive other features of appeals to conscience may be.

The extent to which appeals to conscience are personal is variable. It can range, for example, from the emphasis suggested by "*my* conscience tells me" to the emphasis suggested by "my *conscience* tells me," or even merely "conscience tells me." The first emphasis contrasts my conscience with yours and confines the claim notoriously to mine. The second contrasts my conscience with other internal promptings, desires and tendencies of mine, and sets my claim conspicuously on this high ground. The first may be communicating something like "for my part . . . , but of course I don't know about you," though it may also be communicating something like "*my* conscience tells me . . . , *and so why doesn't yours also?*" or "doesn't yours also, at least on reflection?" These last understandings come closer to the second of the above contrasts, which, quite different from the first, may be communicating something like "my conscience, the universal voice in all of us, tells me. . . ."

Only, perhaps, if we contrast this last understanding with radically different alternative defenses of violence will we see what could be left of the *personal* side of appeals to conscience in such an understanding.

Consider some alternatives. Assuming that we wanted a high-minded appeal—and we might not always want it, because we might imagine that a lower-minded one would sometimes prove more effective in getting agreement or cooperation, e.g., an appeal to straightforwardly prudential considerations—we could appeal simply to a contribution of the violence toward the promotion or production of a good, the avoidance or resistance of an evil, or the fulfillment of a duty. Often, these alternatives *are* chosen, and it seems that they are often thought available and in the offing when appeals to conscience are honestly made. Why are they not always chosen, when available, directly in preference to appeals to conscience? A number of considerations may be involved.

Because theories backing the attribution of special weight to conscience vary, one who appeals to conscience may be presenting himself in particular as anything from a dutiful soldier or child of God, to a person who, by following his personal star, is seeking only to develop or maintain his personal and moral integrity. Consider only the first way at present. If he presents himself in the first way, then, in appealing to conscience, he is in particular invoking the authority of God in support of the claim that the violence in question is right or alright. Invocation of God's authority would be at best in the offing, however, if he were to justify the violence merely by appeal to the good it would do or the evil it would resist or avoid, or to the duty (other than a direct duty to God) that it would (perhaps only in part) fulfill.

This difference in the focus of the first of these appeals could of course influence the range of relevant challenge and counterchallenge in any attempt to continue exploration of the justifiability of the violence. Unless respondents were to reject as irrelevant the invocation of God's authority to justify the violence (the respondents being atheists, perhaps), or were to regard that authority as overweighed by some other more important consideration, further discussion must proceed not by focusing directly or perhaps occasionally even at all on the role of the violence in producing good, preventing evil or fulfilling duty, but upon these things at best only as they shed light on what God really directs. Equally and more directly important would be examination of the conscience-pleader's claim to have gotten straight the position that God, through his conscience, was directing him to take. And respondents could surely probe this region. Is it really his conscience the person is hearing? (Or is it false conscience? This is sometimes though not always a way of asking again whether it is really his *conscience* he is hearing.) Is it erroneous (or uninstructed or unenlightened) or true conscience? Has he got straight what it is telling him? Is he applying it correctly to the situation at hand? These will be the important questions.

These questions seem to pull us quite far from any consideration of the violence at issue. This result, however, may be only apparent. For, the principal mode of preparing the ground for these questions would likely be to shed doubt on the likelihood that God would authorize or command that violence, and the principal way of shedding the doubt may be precisely to focus the discussion heavily on the violence and the role it plays or doesn't play in producing good, etc., though the relevance of this role will lie only in the light it throws on what God directs *via* an assumption that God is good.

But now consider another, now obvious, alternative to such appeals to conscience. Consider why a person who takes the position that conscience is God's voice in him doesn't simply justify his engagement in or support of the violence by saying right off that God directs it. Why does he, instead, say that his conscience directs it?

Clearly, one answer is that the latter is more informative than the former. It tells how he knows that God directs his engagement in or support of the violence. In telling this, the appeal warns off what might be wasteful challenges based on scripture or natural theology, though the latter may of course possibly be thought to shed light on the likelihood that God would direct the person as is claimed and thus become indirectly relevant to assessment of the correctness of the person's identification and application of the claims of his conscience, just as with the earlier consideration of the good the violence would produce, etc.

Nevertheless, in effect if not in intention, the appeal to conscience understood as we are presently understanding it is more personal and more difficult to challenge than the alternative appeals just considered because the rhetoric of western theology has sometimes seemed to attach such overwhelming authority to that still, small, unshakable voice within us. Though much church doctrine is concerned with conditions under which the claims of conscience are overborne by other considerations and may, anyway, be erroneous, the high importance of the claims has been supported at various points by strains of individualism elevating the idea that we as individuals each have an individual relationship to God and that consequently He speaks to us individually in ways that are clearer and less mistakable than other evidence of his intent. This is an anarchic strain in theology vis-a-vis any organized or cooperative efforts among humans to seek salvation, but it nonetheless surfaces from time to time, and is worth mentioning here because it represents at its most extreme the theological backing for the weight of appeals to conscience.

This perspective doubtless supports the widespread idea that appeals to conscience are undiscussable. By eliminating the idea that there might be *more reliable* indices of God's intent, the perspective certainly does diminish the practical possibility of discussions of whether conscience is erroneous. But, even so, if *appeals to* conscience are not confused with *claims of* conscience (in the sense of the claims that conscience makes upon us), and are instead correctly identified as merely our attempts to pick out and apply the claims that conscience makes upon us, attempts not guaranteed success even by the theological perspective just sketched, then that perspective will be seen not to support the idea that appeals to conscience are undiscussable in every way. What we have instead is backing for an hypothetical, viz., if our appeals to conscience in defense of violence correctly pick out and apply what conscience in fact directs or authorizes, then no further discussion of the justifiability of violence has point if God's wishes are taken as final and there is no better index of His wishes. But the fact remains that our appeals to conscience may not have correctly identified or correctly applied the claims of conscience, and this possibility remains discussable, as before. When, let us say, the upshot of my appeal to my conscience in defense of violence disagrees with the upshot of your appeal to your conscience, we have a problem on this latest account but not an insoluble problem, for one or both of us may have incorrectly identified or applied the claims of our consciences.

But what if we exhaust this possibility and appear to be confronted with a genuine confrontation of corrected consciences? Assuming the above extreme view of the priority of the claims of conscience, one might expect to find tendencies to deny that genuine confrontations of the sort just supposed could ever exist. God does not say one thing to one person and another to another, etc. But some fall-back positions are available if one intensifies the individualism of the theology. If we as individuals each have not only an individual but a personal relationship to God, then God, for whom we are not merely his creatures but his children, may have special plans for each of us, and may, *via* our consciences, enlighten us in different ways.

Given that salvation depends upon attending to God's word, this last suggestion works to make conscience even more sacrosanct and impregnable to attack than before. But it also changes drastically what is justified by appeals to conscience. We can no longer say that the *violence* is straightforwardly being justified; rather, it is the conscience-pleader's engagement in or support of the violence that is being justified—justified as in pursuit of a laudable aim, viz., fidelity to conscience and thus to God's plan for him. The most that can be said about the violence is that engagement in it or support of it has been argued right or alright *for this particular conscience-pleader.*

The effect of this extremely individualistic theology on the pragmatics of appeals to conscience, then, is that at the same time that it renders appeals to conscience in defense of violence less 'discussable,' it shifts attention from the status of the violence vis-a-vis God's wishes to the status of the conscience-pleader vis-a-vis God's wishes. This may be all the conscience-pleader wants. He may want above all to present himself as (and of course may also want to be) a virtuous person laboring for personal salvation according to the light God has shown him. Such a defense of himself will be difficult to distinguish from a defense of the violence only when he is engaging in and not merely supporting the violence, and when we find it difficult on theoretical or practical grounds of the sorts mentioned much earlier in this paper, to distinguish the violence he is engaging in from his engaging in it.

In any case, this extremely individualistic theology leaves us in a tangle. Though we can still challenge the correctness of each person's identification and application of the claims of his conscience, we seem to have lost our grasp of an important goal, viz., the goal of offering and scrutinizing justifications of violence in order to arrive at a unified approach to the violence in question. For we now open the possibility that my corrected conscience will tell me to engage in the violence and your corrected conscience will tell you that I should be stopped. This prospect does not show the whole idea to be absurd, for each stand may be God's plan for us. But it does throw a new issue into the hopper at the same time that it removes the viability of the old goal. If we are all God's children, then we must respect God's plans for our brothers and sisters as well as His plans for us. The new issue is: How do we show respect for both?

This question may be thought to make a terrible mess of things. We are imagining violence most probably committed directly or indirectly *on* humans, and some people appealing to their consciences in support of the violence, and other people appealing to their consciences in opposition to it. We are then asking: what does our respect for God's plans for each of the latter two groups (each of whom may, of course, have members who are also members of the first group, but then again may not) require of us? On the whole, we may be confident that we will seldom if ever be confronted with such a situation (assuming the consciences to be corrected consciences). Yet the logic of this extreme view of the nature of appeals to conscience invites us to consider it.

Furthermore, the view must not be so fantastic, because at its most anarchic it is echoed by an extremely popular modern secular view of the nature of conscience. We have already mentioned the beginnings of this view. Instead of declaring contingent whether God, through conscience, tells us all the same thing, the view tells us that it is contingent whether conscience, as the voice of our highest vision of moral and personal integrity, tells us the same thing. And, instead of the moral authority of God backing conscience, the view tells us that conscience is backed by, because it is the voice of, fidelity to our highest aims for ourselves.

Just as we would wish to respect God's plans for others as well as his plans for us, so we have been taught to wish to respect each person's search for the highest moral and personal integrity of which that person is capable. Thus, both accounts abandon, at least prima facie, the goal of a unified approach to violence *via* the route of appeals to conscience. We have reached the apogee of the *personal* thrust of appeals to conscience in defense of violence, and it wears both a theological and a secular face.

We can climb down from that apogee on the secular as well as on the theological side. Having climbed up already on the theological side, we can see how to climb down. On the secular side, the descent is equally easy. Conscience merely becomes more and more the acquired or inherent embodiment of the moral sense or moral awareness or moral perceptiveness of the community of mankind. The descent thus brings again to life the goal of a unified approach to violence through appeals to conscience. And again, the descent gradually broadens the grounds on which the identification and application and possible erroneousness of the claims of conscience can be indirectly as well as directly probed and challenged, e.g., by asking after the good the violence promotes, the evil it resists, the duty it fulfills.

Further, at the bottom as well as at the top of the personalization of the secular conscience, one can ever so easily see conscience as having a theological as well as a secular face. Where conscience, as here, is treated as the acquired or inherent embodiment of a unitary moral sense or moral awareness or moral perceptiveness of mankind, natural theology, explaining this as founded in the nature of humans as fashioned and implanted by God, can snap the secular account into a theological framework which gives justificatory weight to appeals to conscience precisely because conscience, being founded on a human nature implanted by God, indicates much about God's wishes for humans.

In sum, the character, weight, and focus of appeals to conscience vary as noted. The pragmatics of appeals to conscience vary accordingly. If we were always clear-headed on where we stood in the spectrum of views sketched, a precisely charted pragmatics of appeals might be possible. But most of us are not so clear-headed on where we stand as that would require. Furthermore, we each of us know that this is most likely true of others. In consequence, a faint air of opportunism or disreputability may attend appeals to conscience in defense of violence. Appeals to conscience are admittedly high-minded, but is this person, in troubling to defend violence in that way, purporting to rest everything on God's wishes for mankind or only on God's wishes for himself, or on the moral sense of mankind or on only the requirements of his own personal and moral integrity? Does he claim special and perhaps even authoritative insight into any of these, or is he simply putting forward his understanding of them and saying that, for his part, this is where he will stand? Will he regard his defense as in any way discussable with a view to possible modification, or does he expect the defense to forestall any challenge of his stand? The suspicion that the conscience-pleader may, even if only unconsciously, tack and haul among these positions as benefits his case is difficult to eliminate when we find ourselves in opposition to him and know that variance is so easy in our own heads from time to time.

Perhaps the best that can be said in a catch-all way is that a person who appeals to conscience in defense of violence is trying to put the discussion immediately on a plane where it is clear that moral or religious or highly personal feelings or beliefs about his or our moral integrity or his or our cosmic fate are being invoked, and where further discussion, if it is to proceed at all, must do so either by turning aside from confrontation with these feelings or beliefs or by challenging their genuineness or their appropriateness.

Anything more specific will have to start with the varied specifics. Hopefully, the discussion here has offered some leads on what these may be and how they may be sorted out. Chasing them down and sorting them out may require ingenuity as an interviewer and considerable sensitivity to the nuances of what is said to one or what one reads. It seems to me a task worth trying to do really well before one launches too heavily into the task of rational reconstruction, i.e., the task of spelling-out what can survive our critical scrutiny of the acceptability of appeals to conscience in defense of violence.

12 Competition and Moral Philosophy*

This paper is intended to lend plausibility to the claim that moral philosophy has not taken competition and competitive situations seriously enough and that this fact goes far to explain the seeming unhelpfulness of much modern moral philosophy in dealing with some of the more prominent social and moral issues of the day. A full-scale exploration and defense of the claim

*Unpublished paper. An earlier version was presented as the lead paper in a symposium at the Western (now Central) Division meeting of the American Philosophical Association in April 1975, so we have attached that date to it. But, as indicated in author's note 33, the paper has undergone several revisions since. One of the editors (RM) had the advantage of considerable discussion of it with MacCallum after MacCallum's stroke, in the period from about 1979 to 1981, and was therefore able to determine which of several versions was the last that MacCallum left and to make some final revisions of the text in accordance with MacCallum's inferred intentions. Thus we are confident that the version published here is as definitive of the author's final intentions as it is possible to get, and that this contains MacCallum's last thoughts on the matter, though it is certain that if he had been enabled to rethink and perhaps rewrite it, in accordance with his usual practice, it would have been revised still further.

It is probable, in fact, that he had hoped and planned to do so. In his book *Political Philosophy* (1987), MacCallum referred to the present paper in such a manner as to indicate that he planned to work on it further and to publish it in the foreseeable future (which unfortunately never arrived). The relevant passage (in the second note on p. 86 of *Political Philosophy*) reads as follows:

> The reader will be aware that heavy use has been made in this book of Hohfeld's format. Persons who think that every right must have a correlative duty will not like this. In my opinion, they are wrong, and I have argued a relevant type of case in my "Competition and Moral Philosophy." . . .

"Competition and Moral Philosophy" is also listed in the bibliography to ch. 12 (p. 197) as an "unpublished paper," which would be very strange indeed if MacCallum had intended it to remain unpublished. The only other work of his own MacCallum lists or refers to is "Negative and Positive Freedom" (pp. ix and 193). The Hohfeld reference is to Wesley N. Hohfeld, *Fundamental Legal Conceptions as Applied in Judicial Reasoning* (New Haven: Yale University Press, 1919), a work MacCallum greatly admired and almost invariably used and taught in his course in Philosophy of Law. Eds.

203

would require a *much* lengthier performance than is possible here, and so my aim is more modest. This paper is confined to adducing some considerations that will, hopefully, lead one to think that there is something to the claim and that the claim is worth exploring further.

The considerations adduced support in two different ways the following more specific ideas, viz., (a) that moral philosophy hasn't developed adequately the conceptual apparatus needed for precise and accurate description and discussion of the moral relationships of persons whose competition with each other is approved of or deemed permissible (e.g., where the competition is relied on either as an unavoidable or, given the alternatives, desirable means of settling or determining something, or of entertainment),[1] and (b) that consequently moral philosophy is far from having attended to issues which will emerge as significant once such competition *is* looked at closely. In developing these ideas, I proceed by (1) showing some deficiencies in present treatments of competition, and (2) making the *beginnings* of moves to remedy these deficiencies. More remains to be done. Hopefully, these beginnings will stimulate interest in the matter.

I

The inadequacy of present treatments of competition is manifested principally in neglect of certain moral issues that would be seen as critically important if competition were taken seriously. These issues arise from our need to cope with situations in which striving to achieve something is deemed desirable or proper, but success per se may not be.[2] More specifically, where competition is relied upon or tolerated, it is deemed desirable or proper for persons to compete, i.e., for them to *strive* to succeed in the competition, but also desirable or entirely proper that not all who compete (can) succeed, and perhaps even that none who competes always succeeds.

The presence of competition entails the presence of a competitive situation. It is impossible at present to characterize competitive situations precisely without begging issues to be raised (and not all resolved) below. But one may offer a provisional and rough characterization. Competitive situations are situations in which:

> (i) two or more creatures or groups of creatures (or selves?) seek to get or attain something that not all who seek it can get or attain, or that the seekers believe not all can get or attain; there is or is believed to be less of that thing, whether by

---

1. These are not the only circumstances in which the issues addressed here arise. But they will do for starters.

2. The expression "desirable or proper" covers only part of what would have to be considered in a full-scale treatment of the topic. For "proper" one could here equally well substitute "suitable" or "fitting."

accident (e.g., so-called 'natural' scarcities of food or arable land), design (e.g., the apportionment of prizes in a contest), or necessity (e.g., the status 'fastest runner') than would be needed if each seeker were to get what is sought;

(ii) the question of which will get it or attain it is not yet settled—i.e.,

   (a) none has already gotten or attained it in an undisputed way (undisputed either with respect to title to it or with respect to continued use, possession or title); and

   (b) there is no general agreement (in decision though perhaps there is agreement in prediction) among those seeking it or planning to seek it as to which, in particular, will get or attain it; and

(iii) there is a way of recognizing which does eventually get or attain it—viz.,

   (a) there is a way of determining which eventually gets undisputed title, use, or possession; or

   (b) there is a way of determining which has (the best) claim to title at various times; or

   (c) there is a way of determining which has beneficial (although not undisputed) use or possession at some stages.

[The] disassociation of the desirability or propriety of striving from the desirability or propriety of success in the striving is what is puzzling about competition from the standpoint of common moral theory. It is common enough, of course, to believe that morally significant benefits can result from strivings which do not succeed (e.g., benefits in the development of the skills or character of the strivers), and also to believe that the aims of strivings (e.g., private benefit) may not reveal the principal reasons for thinking them desirable (e.g., that they further the public good—cf. Bentham). But it is not common to believe or at least clearly to hold that from a moral point of view it is alright or even desirable that things be *arranged* so that not all who strive succeed, or that, though things are not arranged that way, it is perfectly alright and perhaps even beneficial that they are that way. These latter beliefs appear to encroach upon either the moral rationality or the moral autonomy of the strivers, for they suggest, with respect to any arbitrarily chosen striver, a moral interest in his or her striving, but, in some way, a lack of moral interest in the success of his or her striving. The striver's having the aim to succeed is being encouraged or supported, but the aim itself is somehow not being taken seriously because there is no interest in whether this striver in particular achieves that aim.*

---

*The material in the preceding two paragraphs has been moved by the editors from the notes into the body of the text, and a slight change has been made in each of these two paragraphs to fit this change in location. Eds.

This is a rough account. One can get clearer by getting more specific. One leading feature of relevant competitive situations is that in these situations it is deemed desirable or proper for someone to try to do something that it is also desirable or proper for someone else to try in one way or another to prevent.[3] What should we say of persons so situated? What, precisely, are the moral relations of persons who are, from a moral point of view, 'exposed' to each other in this way?

The word "exposed" is used here advisedly. Part of what is meant is found in the use of the term by the economist John Commons, who substituted the term "exposure" for the Hohfeldian notion of 'no-right.'[4] Given a system of rules or principles, a person has a 'no-right' vis-a-vis another person when, with respect to some activity in which the latter person may engage, the first person has no claim against the second that the second not engage in the activity. (This also applies, with appropriate changes, to omissions.) Precisely this relationship—though not it only—exists between persons engaging in competition with respect to those of their activities regarded as legitimately competitive.

But Commons's notion of exposure falls short of delineating the respects in which such competitors are exposed to each other.

1. A may be exposed, in Commons's sense, to B in that B has no duty *to* A to refrain from some activity. But B may nevertheless have a duty to C to refrain from the activity. For example, A, B's neighbor, may be exposed in Commons's way to B's chopping down all the trees on B's property tomorrow. But B may have a duty to C not to do this because C, in reliance on the trees being there, has contracted with B to rent B's property as a picnic ground next week. With respect to activities regarded as legitimately competitive, in contrast, it is not only the case that one competitor is exposed in Commons's sense

---

3. Economists may not find it obvious that this is a leading feature of competitive situations. They may see competitors as persons or organizations who are possibly so related that nothing any *one* competitor does either (i) interferes with the capacity of others to sell all they produce, or (ii) affects the cost of selling all that is produced. (I owe this point to Ingrid Rothe.) Insofar as competitors are related to each other in this way they are indeed not thereby common participants in what I call a competitive situation. Clearly, however, calling persons or organizations so related *competitors* involves some departure from what lay persons understand by "competition," a departure underwritten by awareness of attentuated similarities between persons/organizations related in this way and persons/organizations related as common participants in what I call a competitive situation. To see this, consider carefully what would support and what would subvert a claim that a particular producer of shoe laces and a particular producer of cheese were competitors.

4. John R. Commons, *Legal Foundations of Capitalism* (Madison: University of Wisconsin Press, 1956, first published New York: Macmillan, 1924), pp. 97ff., 6. Both Commons and Hohfeld were talking about legal relations. Their schemes, however, are serviceable in the broader application of them made here if sufficient caution is used.

to another competitor's engaging in these activities, but also that the other competitor is typically under no duty whatever or to anyone to refrain from engaging in those activities. Thus it is typically a feature of activities thought legitimately competitive that the exposure of a competitor to such activities by fellow competitors amounts to more than merely the fact that they are thought to have no duty *to her or him* to refrain from engaging in the activities. It amounts in part to the fact that they are thought to have no duty *whatever* to refrain from engaging in the activities.

2. A may be exposed to certain activities of B in this new and stronger sense in situations where we would say that these activities of B are of no legitimate concern to A. For example, B, a sane adult with no dependents and with financial means sufficient to forestall the likelihood that she will become a public charge, caters to her alcohol addiction, but only while remaining quietly in her house. A is merely someone who lives down the street. This is plausibly a case where we would say both that A is exposed in our new and stronger sense to B's drinking, and that B's drinking is of no legitimate concern to A, at least in any way that would license A to interfere with or attempt to block B's drinking. (This would be J. S. Mill's cup of Madeira.) This case shows that our new and stronger sense of 'exposure' isn't sufficient to reveal the moral relationship of competitors to each other vis-a-vis legitimate competitive activities. For, when A and B are competitors, the exposure of each to such activities by the other is an exposure to something for which each has a legitimate concern, or in which each has a legitimate interest—a concern or interest sufficiently strong to (provide a basis for) license to interfere with or attempt to block at least some of the activities in question. Thus, A's exposure to B's legitimate competitive activities is not of the sort where we would normally say that B has a *protected* right against A to engage in all those activities—a right such that A has a correlative duty either not to make B's activities impossible, or, even, to make them possible.[5] Some care is needed in dealing with this feature of the situation; for, B may have protected rights of some sorts against A to compete, and this doubtless will involve protected rights to engage in *some* legitimate competitive activities—e.g., swinging the bat, under certain conditions, in baseball—but not others,—e.g., scoring. For the present, enough has perhaps been said to show that, at least roughly speaking, the exposure of competitors to each other's legitimate competitive activities occurs in a setting distinctively different from the settings of the talk about moral autonomy (and the consequent absence of duty) occupying moral philosophy—the latter settings being ones in which a freedom or liberty to act is accompanied by, and cashed-in by, the presence of duties on the part of

5. For this distinction, see K. E. Tranøy, "An Important Aspect of Humanism," *Theoria* 1 (1957): 37–52, esp. p. 45.

other persons at least not to interfere. Such duties are, in cases of competition deemed acceptable, at least notoriously not comprehensive, and it is this lack of comprehensiveness that makes possible identification of the cases as cases of acceptable *competition*. Thus, the 'exposure' characteristic of this competition has people in a situation in which, morally speaking, no offence is being committed against them when something is done by another person that they are acknowledged nevertheless to have a legitimate interest in preventing, an interest strong enough to license at least some attempts by them directly or indirectly to interfere with and block what is being done.

More must be said about the moral relationships of persons in such competition.[6] But enough has been said to indicate that something critically true of the relationships of such competitors is simply undealt with in moral philosophy—viz., that here are persons who may, without offense, interfere with and try to block at least some of each other's activities even when the latter activities themselves are in no way offenses against the persons trying to block them or against anyone else.

When one thinks of the various areas in which this mutual exposure characteristic of competitive situations is or may be importantly present, one gets an idea of the range of moral problems which, though they may have been touched in moral philosophy, have not been touched at their core because the largely ignored relationship of exposure is *at* their core. To no one's surprise, I am sure, they include:

(a) various issues of war and peace, and of the justifiable limits of warfare and of pacificism.

(b) various issues raised in the political sphere by competition for votes, especially in mass and technologically oriented and equipped societies.

(c) various continuing issues raised by competitive activities in economic, general social, and even, more specifically, intellectual life.

Roughly speaking, when involvement in such situations is or is thought by participants to be either unavoidable or desirable (and participants are aware of this), the relationship of exposure delineated above is importantly present.

It has been underemphasized in moral philosophy no doubt in part because of the emphasis in moral philosophy on the notions of responsibility and duty (and, too, the frequent though not universal facile assumption that claims

6. For example, what are the positive obligations of competitors? A useful exercise would be to try giving a really careful description of, for example, the positive obligations of a football player relative to (a) blocking an opposing lineman out of a play, and (b) picking up a fumbled ball and running with it for a touchdown. One could then ask whether there are comparable complexities in the positive obligations of, e.g., attorneys acting for clients in civil suits, auto dealers competing for shares of the market, persons taking the Law School Admissions Test.

about rights can always be translated into claims about duties—but this is ground that must be gone over carefully). Mutual exposure, though it may be *surrounded* by duties, occurs precisely where, and in the respect that duties are absent; where duty is absent, responsibility is generally, though perhaps not universally, thought also to be absent. Thus, the attention of moral philosophy has not been directed to such relationships except perhaps tangentially and, as it were, by default—as a matter touching on limiting cases. The relationship is commonly regarded as pre-moral, as is suggested for example by the frequency with which it is, when writ large, assimilated to a Hobbesian state of nature which is in turn, perhaps wrongly, treated as a pre-moral condition of humanity. Its pre-moral status even when writ smaller is suggested too, for example, by treatments such as W. D. Lamont's of such 'pure spheres of moral autonomy' as anterior to the notion of right which he believes fundamental to morality.[7]

Alternatively, and perhaps supplementarily, the exposure characteristic of competitive situations is perhaps sometimes seen as essentially contractual in origin.[8] This would be to see it as coming about as it commonly does in games and athletic contests. The exposure would be part of a status one had assumed or adopted voluntarily, and thus would be legitimated by one's consent. No further consideration of it would be needed apart from consideration of the issues normally raised in connection with the nature and limits of consent.

Yet another reason for lack of attention to exposure in moral philosophy, a reason probably related closely to the first one offered above, is the tendency of moral philosophers not to take seriously enough the importance of considering the relations of persons when, as Aristotle put it, conditions are not so favorable as they might be. Some remarks by Abraham Edel suggest what I have in mind:

> If relative scarcity shows itself within a field of abundance . . . general orientation should be toward recovery of abundance by increased productivity. In this sense the ethics of abundance urges men to get together for the increase of the common good rather than regard as their central moral task the development of principles by which a limited good may be partitioned. Thus predatory habits are avoided by establishing the goal of abundance even in a period of scarcity. . . . The situations of tragedy are not removed but the ethics that gives a central role to abundance aims to make them the exception *rather than the type in terms of which moral principles are to be framed.*[9]

7. *Principles of Moral Judgement* (Oxford: Clarendon, 1946), pp. 72–75.
8. A point made to me by Thomas Kearns.
9. "Scarcity and Abundance in Ethical Theory." In S. W. Baron, Ernest Nagel, and K. S. Pinson, eds., *Freedom and Reason* (Glencoe, Illinois: The Free Press, 1951), p. 116 (italics added).

And:

> The ethics of abundance is to the ethics of scarcity as the abolition of the
> causes of war is to the Hague regulation of war practices.[10]

These remarks report a tendency to model the moral relations of persons
on a hopeful ethics of abundance that treats scarcity as either aberrational or
eliminable or at least mitigable but in no case as an unshakeable and modelling fact of moral life. (Marcus Singer has suggested to me that the tendency
may be founded on the idea that there is no scarcity of *moral* goods.) Naturally, persons with this tendency shrink from the idea that mutual exposure
might be a fundamental and modelling feature of any portion of moral life.

One might further, or supplementarily, consider the parts possibly played
in this neglect by the socialization of philosophers and their social roles,
especially in capitalist market economies.[11] And, though this is perhaps excessively speculative, one might consider the psychological impact of recognition of the presence of exposure on persons of the sort who become philosophers. When exposure is present, morally significant matters are, as yet,
unsettled; their resolution awaits the outcomes of the contentions, or whatever, between the parties mutually exposed. The resolutions are thus, in an
important respect, uncontrolled and undetermined. But philosophers generally, and moral philosophers in particular, seem no lovers of vertigo. Their
affection for reason may manifest this psychological fact about them. Reason
may easily be identified with (a kind of) control, the antithesis of vertigo. If
this were so, then one should not be surprised that such persons shrink from
recognition of the importance of mutual exposure in the moral relations of
persons.

The fact remains that our lives are suffused with competitive situations in
which natural or artificial scarcity and mutual exposure are elements. Somehow, in the name of a hopeful ethic of abundance or whatever, we manage to
turn a blind eye toward the full ramifications of this fact and thus remain
unequipped to deal with it. We perhaps think of it as something that will
disappear if we just hang in there long enough. But in the meantime? We
compete or we are at least treated as though we are competing, and we don't
really know how to behave toward each other in many of the contexts in which
this is so. And moral philosophy, it seems to me, continues to be too hopeful
to help.[12]

---

10. Ibid., p. 116, note 10.

11. In commenting on an earlier version of this paper, Bernard Gendron rightly pointed out
that I had ignored such considerations.

12. Compare Santayana: "the abolition of all competitive existence has been set up as the aim
of virtue. Such virtue, however, draws the ladder up after it as it climbs; and the earth remains

II

So much for what can pique an interest in the moral relations of competitors. If one is going to make a careful approach to these issues, even to the point of talk about when competition is unavoidable or, given the alternatives, desirable (a point on which the importance of the enterprise is sure to be challenged by partisans of ethics of abundance), one must have at hand a careful characterization of competition or of situations that are competitive. This, if adequacy requires at least fidelity to the bulk of what is commonly said or implied in description of competition or competitive situations, is surprisingly difficult to provide.

Consider where one is likely to find serious discussions offering or implying characterizations of competition or of competitive situations.

Economists tend to contrast competition with control or regulation.[13] In the light of this contrast, they discuss (i) whether competition is a useful way, and under what conditions it is a desirable way, of organizing the economic life of a community (with the notions of 'optimum price,' 'fair or just price,' and 'optimum production' thought tautologically connected to a definition of competition or of pure competition),[14] or (ii) the extent to which the economic life of a given community is or is not competitive.

Anthropologists and *sociologists* tend to contrast competition not with control or regulation, but with cooperation. In the light of this contrast, they discuss the predominance or interaction of these 'contrasting' forms of interaction in various areas of the social life of communities. Do they identify competition with conflict, and conflict in turn with dysfunctionality? They are divided on both issues.

---

altogether abandoned to the less sensitive sort of virtue that begins with the will to live." *Dominations and Powers* (New York: Scribners, 1951), p. 228.

13. They also contrast competition with monopoly and with concentrated oligopoly. Perhaps, however, they do this only by virtue of seeing these as specific relevant forms of control or regulation. Such an understanding is suggested, for example, by the discussion between economists reported in *Planning, Regulation and Competition*, Hearing before Subcommittees of the Select Committee on Small Business, U.S. Senate, 90th Congress, 1st Session, June 29, 1967 (Washington, 1967). In their discussion, all the above contrasts, as well as others, surface. (See pp. 5, 16, 17, 24, 26, 47.) But the discussants appear satisfied with the way the contrast implied by the question to which they are formally addressing themselves—viz., Are planning and regulation replacing competition in the new industrial state?—provides a framework for their discussion. Generally speaking, though the greater specificity of some of the other contrasts may be what makes them relevant for certain important questions, our present concerns do not seem to require that specificity. The reluctance of some economists to allow contrasts without such specificity may have its source in the thought that some regulation is required for competition and thus regulation in general cannot be contrasted with competition. This issue will be discussed below.

14. Whether this connection *should* be thought tautological is another matter. I owe this point to Ingrid Rothe.

Social scientists in other disciplines exhibit, so far as I can see, even less in the way of unified perspectives. But one finds them discussing situations they treat as competitive in connection with their interests in such things as social contract and other individualist theories of the state, political and military struggles or contentions for power, the international and domestic political functions of war, various mechanisms for the achievement of distributive justice, limitations on the effectiveness of law and of political power, and the nature of adversary proceedings such as judicial trials. Game theorists and theorists of games, athletic contests, and play also discuss situations they treat as competitive, and, often enough, venture to offer characterizations of competition.

Thus, though moral philosophy has not taken competition seriously enough to attempt careful characterization of it, various characterizations have been offered or clearly implied by economists, sociologists, anthropologists, and others to whom competition has long seemed of great importance.

Unfortunately, these characterizations have seemingly diverged in spectacular ways. For example, competition has been said to be a form of conflict (Beals and Siegel[15]), but it has also been said to be something of which conflict is a form (Boulding[16]); it has been contrasted with rivalry (Folsom, Mead, Knight[17]), but also has been treated as a form of rivalry (Hamilton[18]) or even as rivalry *simpliciter* (*O.E.D.*, Lyon, Watkins, Abramson[19]); it has been contrasted with cooperation (H. Martineau, Keating, Russell[20]), but co-

15. A. R. Beals and B. J. Siegel, *Divisiveness and Social Conflict* (Palo Alto: Stanford University Press, 1966), pp. 20–21.

16. Keneth E. Boulding, *Conflict and Defense* (New York: Harper, 1962), pp. 4–5.

17. For Folsom and Mead, see *Cooperation and Competition Among Primitive Peoples*, rev. ed., edited by Margaret Mead (Boston: Beacon, 1961), p. 17. For Knight, see Frank H. Knight, *On the History and Method of Economics* (Chicago: University of Chicago Press, 1956), p. 92.

18. Walton Hamilton in the *Encyclopedia of the Social Sciences*, vol. 4 (New York: Macmillan, 1930), p. 142.

19. L. S. Lyon, M. W. Watkins, Victor Abramson, *Government and Economic Life* (Washington, D.C.: The Brookings Institution, 1939), p. 249, n. 1.

20. Harriet Martineau, *Each and All* (Boston: 1832), iii, p. 39 [This is MacCallum's reference. But the closest we can come to locating anything like this reference, and it is hardly a direct hit, is: Harriet Martineau, *Illustrations of Political Economy*, no. 11, *For Each and For All: A Tale* (Boston: Leonard C. Bowles, 1833). The whole work consists of seventeen volumes, and this volume seems to come closest to MacCallum's intent, considering both its title and its contents. However, page 39 does not in any way fit MacCallum's reference, and also is not in Chapter "iii," but in Chapter 2. The whole of Chapter 3 would fit, approximately, so we shall leave it at that, without trying to pin the allusion down to any specific page. Perhaps some more meticulous reader would let us know at some later time if some more exact reference can be given. No special prize will be awarded for providing this information, except the gratitude of the editors. Eds.]; James W. Keating, "Sportsmanship as a Moral Category," *Ethics* 75 (1964), 30; Bertrand Russell, *New Hopes for a Changing World* (New York: Simon and Schuster, 1951), p. 130, but see also p. 78.

operation has also been said to be an essential element of it (Cooley[21]) or of at least some forms of it (Rappoport, Orwant, Caillois[22]); likewise, it has been contrasted with regulation (see note 13 above), but regulation has also been said to be required for it (Commons, Adams, Mueller[23]). Similar divergences are to be found in treatments of the relationship of competition to awareness (Cooley v. Beals and Siegel[24]), to strife or agôn (Simmel v. Kolnai[25]), to chance (Caillois v. Caillois[26]) and to ill-feeling (Cooley v. Shirk[27]).

One may reasonably suppose that some of this divergence is only apparent and that, for example, it arises in differing understandings of the notions of conflict, rivalry, etc. But more is afoot than merely this. What is here being manifested is in large part a difference between what I shall call (provisionally) the 'title' and the 'possession' views of competition.

These views are plausibly related to instances of what the sociologist Max Weber would call "ideal types." The following string of quotes from an essay by Weber gives an account of his notion of 'ideal type' sufficient for our purposes here:

> [An ideal type] is not a *description* of reality but it aims to give unambiguous means of expression to such a description. (90)

> [Its function is the comparison with empirical reality in order to establish its divergences or similarities, to describe them with the most unambiguously intelligible concepts and to understand and explain them . . .] (43)

> [It] is formed by the one-sided *accentuation* of one or more points of view and by the synthesis of a great many diffuse, discrete, more or less present and occasionally absent . . . phenomena, which are arranged according to those one-sidedly emphasized viewpoints into a unified *ana-*

21. C. H. Cooley, "Personal Competition," *American Economic Association Studies* 4.2 (1899): 79, 95–96.

22. A. Rappoport and C. Orwant, "Experimental Games: A Review." In *Game Theory and Related Approaches to Social Behavior,* edited by Martin Shubik (New York: Wiley, 1964), pp. 283, 296; Roger Caillois, *Man, Play and Games* (Glencoe, Illinois: The Free Press, 1961), p. 39.

23. John R. Commons, *Institutional Economics* (New York: Macmillan, 1934), p. 713; Walter Adams in *Planning, Regulation and Competition* (cited above), p. 16; Willard F. Mueller, same volume, p. 24.

24. Cooley, "Personal Competition," p. 79; Beals and Siegel, *Divisiveness and Social Conflict,* p. 18.

25. Georg Simmel, *Conflict* (Glencoe, Illinois: The Free Press, 1955), pp. 57 ff.; Aurel Kolnai, "Games and Aims," *Aristotelian Society Proceedings* 66 (1965–66): 106, 108, 109.

26. Caillois, *Man, Play and Games,* pp. 72–74, 157–158.

27. Cooley, "Personal Competition," p. 148; Evelyn Shirk, *The Ethical Dimension* (New York: Appleton-Century-Crofts, 1965), p. 303.

> *lytical* construct (*Gedankenbild*). In its conceptual purity, this . . . construct cannot be found empirically anywhere in reality. . . .[28]

> It has the significance of a purely ideal *limiting* concept with which the real situation or action is *compared* and surveyed for the explication of certain of its significant components.[29]

On this account, ideal types may be expected to have an artificial simplicity. They have nothing to do with averages, nor do they have anything to do with what is thought desirable. They are to be judged, one should expect, as helpful or unhelpful rather than adequate or inadequate. In the present case, their helpfulness would consist in the extent to which they provide us with two things: (a) reference points for unambiguous descriptions of the enormous variety of situations commonly regarded as competitive, and (b) a basis for a plausible account of divergences in characterizations of competition and of the essential features of competitive situations. (Cf.: "It is a matter . . . of constructing relationships which our imagination accepts as plausibly motivated and hence as 'objectively possible' . . .")

This last point is of especial importance here. For, appreciations and depreciations of competition and of the moral status of competitors appear heavily influenced by the adoption of something very much like one or the other of two ideal types that I shall sketch below as [parts of] a *model* setting out the essential features of all competitive situations and thus revealing how these situations are correctly to be viewed. This use is obviously not that contemplated by Weber in the passages cited above, but is hardly surprising, however ill-advised. We shall, for the next several pages, be tracing its ramifications, and then shall return to a more Weberian understanding of the matter.

The title model attaches to competition the notions of entitlement or merit, and award. It emphasizes connections between competition and rules, and it encourages us to see competitions as tests or trials of superiority in some respect or other. Suggestive of this, perhaps, Ely states that not every struggle of conflicting interests or struggle for wealth is competitive; that competition is a struggle "which has its metes and bounds."[30] And Commons says "Competition is not Nature's 'struggle for existence' but is an artificial arrangement supported by the moral, economic, and physical sanctions of collective action."[31] And Caillois says that without rules there are no competitions.[32]

28. Max Weber, "Objectivity in Social Sciences and Social Policy." In his *The Methodology of the Social Sciences,* translated and edited by Edward A. Shils and Henry A. Finch (Glencoe, Illinois: The Free Press, 1949), pp. 90, 93. The second passage is from "The Meaning of 'Ethical Neutrality' in Sociology and Economics," same volume, p. 43 (italics omitted).

29. Weber, *Methodology,* p. 93.

30. Robert T. Ely, *Competition: Its Nature, Its Permanency, and Its Beneficence* (Publications of the American Economic Association, Third Series), 2.1 (1901), pp. 58–59.

31. John R. Commons, see note 23, above.

32. Caillois, *Man, Play and Games,* p. 75.

The ramifications of this understanding are great. Suppose, for example, there is something both you and I want; we have a fight over it or for it. Are we *competing* for it? Not on this understanding, unless we see the fight as a test of which of us excels the other in some way—e.g., in toughness or pugilistic skill—and see the thing over which or for which we are fighting as something to be awarded to the victor or something to which the victor will be entitled. This perspective can, and most usually does, provide a special basis for distinguishing between what is fair and unfair or what is to count and what is not to count as a legitimate move in the fight; for, if the fight is to be a test of something, the occasion ought to be so limited as to isolate that something so that, as much as can be, it and only it determines the outcome. Even in a 'no-holds-barred' fight between you and me, one may regard it unfair or grounds for nullification of my claims to have won if I receive help from a confederate who, perhaps, trips you, bashes you on the head, or passes me a handgun. Thus, the rules of which Caillois speaks (or at least semblances thereof) are intrinsic to the point or function of the competition.

Similarly, if two persons see something each wants, and race toward it, they are not, on this understanding, competing for it unless they see reaching it first as a mark of a superiority providing a basis for award of or entitlement to the thing in question. And likewise, depending upon the superiority to be affirmed in reaching the thing first, there will be 'metes and bounds' determining the acceptability of the outcome or upshot as a basis for entitlement or award.

But fights and 'footraces' for things need not be understood in this way at all. The emphasis in the struggle or striving may be so heavily on attainment of what is fought for or raced toward that no thought is given to the fight or race as a test of superiority, and attainment may be thought to have little to do with award or entitlement. The fighters or runners may be driven simply by need or desire to possess the thing in question (where 'possessing' it is to be distinguished from 'owning' it and is thus neutral with respect to questions of entitlement, as in the case of a person who is said to possess stolen goods). When this is so, are the fighters and runners (therefore) not competing with each other, and the fights and races not instances of competition? What, for example, of the so-called competitive struggle for survival in nature? And what of so-called mercantile competition?

The tendency to see struggles for survival and strivings for goods and markets as competitive exposes what I call the 'possession' model of competition. On this understanding, competition results from scarcities in what is needed or desired, and consists in the (at least roughly) concomitant strivings of two or more creatures for all or some portion of what is scarce—i.e., all or some portion of something the (equally accessible) supply of which is insufficient to satisfy all who need or desire it. Scarcity by itself does not produce such striving (because, e.g., one creature may defer to another), but commonly produces it where there is equality of hope of success (as Hobbes would say) arising from each considering that he or she has at least some chance for success though others may also need or desire and thus 'compete' for the thing in question. Alternatively, it arises where the creatures in question are unaware that other creatures also need or desire the thing. The striving is there regarded as competitive because, as there is not (equally accessible) enough to go around, each achievement by one creature disadvantages another creature in at least some respect by rendering something the other creature wants or needs either inaccessible or more difficult of access. Because the scarcity can be either natural or artificial, and because the desired good can be preeminence or glory, games and contests of skill can be understood as competitive on the possession model if one focuses more on the *attainment* of preeminence or glory than on *entitlement* to it, and more on the role of competitive behavior as a means to this attainment than on its role as a test of the skills or qualities mainly useful in the attainment. The view of competition as a test, while allowably present, thus becomes adjunctory at best. Resultingly, the identification of certain behavior as unfair or as invalidating the results, though allowably present, is no longer seen principally as helping to isolate the skills or qualities being tested as the principal or only operative factor in success, but rather as a control preventing the competition from becoming so sharp and vicious as to be contrary to the public interest in the welfare of third parties or possibly even the welfare of the contending parties.

The following grid affords a perspicuous account of the two models with respect to a number of different grounds on which they can be compared.*

These remarks [as summarized in the grid] apply to struggles for survival and for goods and markets [in the following way]. It is true that struggles for survival are sometimes talked about as proceeding according to a rule of 'survival of the fittest,' a slogan encouraging us to see the struggles as tests of something—e.g., relative capacities to survive—but many 'participants' do not, because they could not (being grasshoppers and saber-toothed tigers), see it that way. Furthermore, participants who do or would like to see the struggle that way may find it difficult to see survival (thought of as the goal of the struggle) as something *awarded* (unless by God) in recognition of merit or superiority in relative capacities to survive, or as something to which one claims entitlement based on superiority in capacity to survive. The notions of award and entitlement seem idle in a situation such as this, where, by hypothesis, nothing is enjoined in the behavior of other creatures toward one who has, for the moment at least, succeeded in surviving. One might argue

---

*This paragraph and the ensuing grid have been moved by the editors from the notes into the body of the text. A slight change has also been made in the paragraph immediately following the grid. Eds.

	'Title' Model	'Possession' Model
1. Function or point	To test, 'try' (cf. trial) or 'prove' superiority or relative merit with respect to skill(s) or attribute(s) *Emphasizes:* display and 'proof' of skill, merit, etc. *Deemphasizes:* want or need satisfaction	To obtain or attain needed or desired things or states *Emphasizes:* want- or need-satisfaction (incl. self-protection) *Deemphasizes:* connection of results with possession, or lack, of merit or excellence
2. Criterion of success	Entitlement to a special status such as 'winner,' 'best,' 'champion'	Attainment, possession, or protection of the needed or desired things
3. Temporal span	Characteristically, though not universally, definite and limited	Often and sometimes notoriously unclear
4. Range of competitive activities	Characteristically well-defined and limited	Often unclear
5. Roles of rules and standards regarding range and character of competitive activity	*Primary:* to isolate and give play to the skills or attributes being tested, and to render other factors (relatively) inoperative *Secondary:* (where necessary) to protect competitors and others from harms thought too severe to be tolerable in the context	*Primary:* (a) protection of community and third party interests from victimization by competitive activity that is too 'uncontrolled' or vicious; (b) protection of competitors from injury thought too severe to be tolerable (because, e.g., it may make them public charges); (c) prevention of competitive behavior that might make competitors or partisans 'irreconcilable' with respect to the possibility of future tolerant or cooperative relations with each other *Secondary:* to encourage development, through competitive activities and preparation for them, of skills, attributes, and activities thought socially beneficial or admirable
6. Role of chance	(a) when needed, to settle initial order or position of play (b) to heighten interest (even at cost of reducing conclusiveness of the competition as a test of skill, etc.)	Open
7. Roles of subsidies or 'handicapping'	Dysfunctional unless what is being tested is relative 'achievement' from different starting places with respect to degree of skill, etc.	To (a) equalize opportunity for success (for any of a wide range of plausible reasons), or (b) make it reasonable for persons (etc.) to become or remain 'competitors'

that the survivor is 'entitled' to survive at least in the sense that it is committing no offense by surviving; but this suggests something dubious, viz., that
'losers' in the 'competition' to survive would somehow be committing an
offence if, contra conceivability, they managed to survive, as if they had taken
or knowingly received something not rightfully theirs.

In the case of mercantile 'competition,' arguments for the 'possession' as
distinct from the 'title' view are less clear. Participants are all capable of
seeing success in this sphere as a mark of superiority of some sort or other,
and hence of seeing their striving as testing the presence or degree of some
merit or other. Furthermore, the striving consists of promoting and engaging
in transactions involving goods to which participants are or hope to become
entitled; indeed, the transactions have most specifically to do with the convey-
ance of title or of some beneficial aspect of title to these goods. Lastly, the
rule-surroundings of the activity are prominent; e.g., some distinctions between fair and unfair 'competition' are firmly marked by law where there is a
legal system, and are often present, though perhaps less firmly marked, where
law is absent. But close examination of the *ways* these important features of
the 'title' model of competition are present, will show something amiss.

Consider the rule-marked distinction between fair and unfair competition.
Its main rationale in the title model is that it helps isolate, from extraneous
factors, the skill or characteristic whose presence or degree is being tested by
the competition. Is that its main rationale in the case of mercantile 'competition'? Clearly not. For, the main aim of such 'competition' is surely not to
test the presence or degree of certain skills or characteristics on the part of the
'competitors,' though participants may on occasion be happy to read the results that way, and though the community at large may think these skills or
characteristics socially beneficial and thus approve of struggles encouraging
their development. The main aim of participants, rather, is thought more fundamentally to be attainment of the wealth or market-share possession of which
marks success in the endeavor—and in large part because these are goods
thought worth having quite apart from how one gets them and thus quite apart
from the fact that possession of them marks success in a competitive endeavor. The focus is thus on the attainment of these goods rather than on how
one attains them; consider how little interested many people profess to be in
'competing' for such goods if they could attain them in an 'easier' or 'less
objectionable' way. The distinction between fair and unfair competition, and
its enforcement, serve here instead two quite different principal aims: (1) to
protect non-participants (or, more precisely, persons who are not themselves
competitors in the competition regulated by the distinctions in question) directly from victimization in the struggle of the competitors for the goods or
the market; (2) to protect competitors directly and non-competitors indirectly
from the effects of competitive behavior passing normal boundaries of mo-

rality or decency. Naturally, the distinction between fair and unfair competition doesn't bear the burden of all the social protection offered under this second heading. If a person bombs his competitor's place of business, he is unlikely to be prosecuted under the heading of unfair competition. The criminal law has other resources for dealing with the case. And even if these resources were seen as regulating some over-all competitive struggle for existence and prosperity, they deal characteristically with conduct either too outrageous to be called merely unfair, or conduct thought too dangerous to be tolerated though not unfair.

In any case, it seems to me clear that the standard view of participants in commercial competition is that their activities are principally for the sake of obtaining goods and market shares, and at best secondarily for the sake of testing the presence or absence of participant's skills or merits. And the rules of fair and unfair competition are firstly for the sake of protecting public and participants rather than for the sake of isolating, as the operative factors in success, any particular skills or attributes possessed by participants. Furthermore, though success may be judged by consideration of the extent of the goods to which one has come to have title, titles to these goods are *counters* of success; they are not awards or prizes one receives as a result of success, nor does the status 'holder of these titles' constitute a status to which one becomes entitled in consequence of success.

What we have in the end, then, is this: Our predominant views of athletic games and contests, and board games such as chess, constitute near approximations to adoptions of what I call the 'title' view of competition, and our predominant views of mercantile competition and 'struggles for survival' constitute near approximations to adoptions of what I call the 'possession' view of competition. But we waver in each case, and we sometimes see things quite differently. We sometimes see as 'the point' of athletic contests and games the acquisition of the prizes, awards, glory, deference, and other goodies that, often enough, follow from entitlement to the status of 'the best,' etc. When we do this, we veer away from the 'title' view and toward the 'possession' view of the competition. To see cases where the tension between these two views appears, consider cases of innovation in sports such as the introduction of the forward pass in football and the introduction of the fiber-glass pole in polevaulting. Or, consider Bobby Fischer's behavior before and during his more important chess matches. On the other side, we sometimes see the outcomes of struggles for survival and commercial competition as indexes of fitness, skill, or merit, or at least as *tests* of something.

The 'title' and 'possession' models of competition thus do not have firm instantiations among the situations we recognize as competitive. But, if we can resist the temptation to regard them as models setting out versions, no more than one of which can be correct, of what is essential to competition, they can provide us with firm reference points for feeling out and describing the nuances of our attitudes toward and intellectual ingestions of these situations. In particular, they can provide an opportunity, I believe, to think clear-headedly about the *exact respects in which* various competitive situations may be either unavoidable, or, given the alternatives, desirable, and the exact respects in which we might wish to re-form these situations so that they will either conform to or diverge yet further from either of the types.

For example, on the 'possession' model of competition, the anthropologists' *contrast* between competition and cooperation makes some sense. Where competition is seen as driven by need or desire for scarce goods, cooperation can be seen as an alternative style of dealing with the supply and distribution of these goods. Similarly with the economists' contrast of competition with regulation or control.* But, if one has the 'title' model of competition in mind, competition is not to be seen as a contrasting style of dealing with the supply and distribution of goods, because it is not to be seen as a style of dealing with the supply and distribution of goods at all. It may be *linked* with a style, but it is not itself a style. It may be linked with a cooperative style, or with a style of regulation or control, or whatever. The questions to be asked in connection with the 'title' model of competition are whether there are alternative ways of determining superiority or relative merit with respect to the possession of various skills or attributes, and whether we have a legitimate or at least unobjectionable interest in doing this. The other interests providing a context for this latter interest might be quite various— e.g., an interest within a system of control and regulation or of cooperation in having important tasks done as well as can be, or a relatively idle but diverting interest simply in who can do some particular thing best. The ways in which success in the competition is linked up with the satisfaction of the needs or desires of the successful competitors (or even of the unsuccessful ones), with the supplies of goods and goodies (including honor and glory), may be unplanned and spontaneous or highly organized. The linking may be unavoidable or avoidable only at too great a cost, or it may be avoidable at a tolerable cost. It may meet with one's sense of justice or not; it may promote the development of things one wants developed, or it may not. But, in any case, these links with the satisfaction of needs and desires, with goods and goodies, are not, on the 'title' view of competition, intrinsic to the competition. The competition is not, per se, a way of organizing the distribution of these things. The *desirability* of the competition may depend heavily on the extent to which we can break some of these links and fashion others. But it need not depend solely on this. It may depend also on whether we have or can

---

*The remainder of this long paragraph has been moved by the editors from the notes into the body of the text. Eds.

ever find a legitimate or unobjectionable interest in determining superiority or relative merit with respect to the possession of any particular skills or attributes, and whether we can find other ways of making these determinations.

We are now in a position to deal with the claim that cooperation, on the one hand, or regulation and control, on the other hand, cannot be *contrasted* with competition because they are essential to it, and thus (perhaps) components of it. On the possession model, cooperation or regulation and control may be 'essential' in that they are depended on to establish and maintain the use of competition as a mode of goods-distribution. Cooperation, for example, may be depended on to secure acceptance of the mode; or a sometimes complex, coercion-backed regulatory scheme may be relied upon to produce or secure continuance of use of the mode (on the latter, cf. the *Senate Hearing Report* cited in note 13 above, pp. 16, 24, 28, 48). On the title model, in contrast, cooperation and/or regulation and control may be needed to assure that the competition *when* used will test what it is supposed to test. Cooperation, for example, may be needed to produce the efforts, and may be depended upon to secure the restrictions of efforts, that will isolate and reveal the comparative extents of the capacities or characteristics being tested. Likewise, coercion-backed regulation and control may be relied on for the same purposes. In either case, it is clear that though these measures may in these different ways be 'essential,' the competition occurs where and in respects that matters are not covered by these 'essentials.' In the possession model, for example, the 'essentials' function to create or sustain conditions under which competition can and will be used; they do not thereby play a constitutive role in making what is used competition. In the title model, they play a role more nearly intrinsic to what competition is, but still they serve only to isolate and focus competitive efforts so that outcomes will test what they are supposed to test. In each case, no matter how much cooperation or regulation and control may be needed, the outcomes of competitive efforts must in some important respects remain undetermined thereby. If this were not so, we would have no grounds for regarding the situation as competitive. Precisely because of this consideration, the contrasts in question can, so far as the 'essentialness' question is concerned, continue to be crucial to our understanding of what competition is.

III

When we come to considering again the moral relations of competitors in competitions regarded as unavoidable or desirable, all these things will be relevant. In helping us fix the vision of competition with which we must or wish to work, and *then* seeing what is intrinsic and what is extrinsic on that view, and *then* seeing which of the things extrinsic can be avoided at reasonable cost or less and which cannot, we can discuss, more clearheadedly I believe, what the legitimate ranges of competitive activity ought or must be considered to be. We can then talk sensibly about what the ranges of mutual exposures of the kind mentioned earlier ought to be or must be, get a firmer sense of what other moral relations might be found among competitors vis-a-vis their competitive activity (e.g., do they have obligations or duties to compete, 'play the game,' 'give it a good try'?). What could emerge from this is an improved understanding of what all of us are up to in an astonishingly and (perhaps) dismayingly large portion of our lives.

There is no claim here, of course, that the upshots will be clean, crisp, and easily manageable. And it might be well, in closing, to develop briefly some reasons why, reasons that have not been much attended to in the discussion above.

When we see a situation as competitive, and see (some) persons involved in the situation as competitors, we see the persons' actions as having certain motivations, and the persons as having certain goals, or we see the actions *as though* they had these motivations and the persons *as though* they had these goals, realizing that this may not be true or strictly true, but believing this interpretation to reveal something important about the situation of the persons. Doing either can, of course, if communication is possible, encourage the persons themselves to see themselves and their actions in these ways if they don't already do so. There are several respects, however, in which such a perspective may distort our or their view of what is the case, or significantly alter what becomes the case.

First, a person may find herself or we may find her in nests or networks of situations each of which could be seen or should be seen as competitive. It may be difficult or even impossible to sort this out so as to provide a fitting or helpful account of what the person's goals and the motivations of her actions are or ought to be given such nests or networks of situations plausibly seen as competitive and in each of which her actions may be seen as 'moves' of some sort or other. An action that might count as a score or win in one competition may count as or lead to a loss or disadvantage in another competition in which the person may plausibly also be seen to be engaged. When this is foreseen, what ought the person to do or be advised to do? Can we or she rank the importance of the competitions to her (as she is, or as she ought to be)? Sometimes doubtless yes, sometimes doubtless no.

Secondly, no matter how many competitive situations she may plausibly be seen involved in, she or we may resist, or maybe ought to resist, seeing her merely or even at all as a competitor in some or all of those situations. This is merely to deny that a person's goals and the motivations of her actions ought always to be seen as those appropriate to a competitor, even when she may plausibly be seen as embroiled in a competitive situation and, hence, as a competitor. She may or perhaps should reject, or at least try to disassociate herself from, the status in some, or even (why not?) in all of those situations. Or, she may reasonably merely protest having her goals and motivations *reduced* to those readable from status as a competitor in this or that or any competitive situation. She may not or perhaps should not be seen merely as one who competes. Her (legitimate) goals and motivations can perhaps simply not be captured in this way.

Thirdly, a person's goals and motivations may change *en route,* as it were. They may slip, sometimes insensibly, into or out of those readable from her status as a competitor, and one may think none the worse, or even all the better of the person for this. An auto-racing driver who stops her car during the race to help another driver in distress, and thus sacrifices all chances of winning or even placing in the race, would provide a case in point. And sometimes 'competitors' come to believe that the game is not worth the candle. The story is told of the powerful leader of an Indian sect who, when a student at an American university and running a race at a track meet, stopped running before reaching the finish line though he was at the time in the lead. When asked why, he replied that he had gotten tired. Whether one finds this reply (and event) absurd or the height of good sense may vary with one's views on a number of matters. But persons sometimes cease competing in mercantile competition or in parlor games for similar reasons. Reverse shifts are also possible, viz., that persons come to take on the goals and motivations of competitors, or even expand those goals and intensify those motivations, when finding themselves in situations where these seem plausibly appropriate responses.

The general lesson is this: Seeing situations as competitive, and persons as competitors, has its dangers if we, whether as mere observers or as participants, allow this perspective to lead us to see the motives and goals of participants as *solely* those which could be read off from their status as competitors, and to freeze this view of their goals and motivations for the duration of the competition(s) in question. This truth will, of course, complicate our efforts to get clear about the moral relations of competitors to each other.[33]

33. Earlier versions of this paper were read to the philosophy departments at the University of Wisconsin–Madison and the University of Massachusetts–Amherst, and at a symposium at the Western Division meetings of the American Philosophical Association in Chicago in 1975 (where the commentators were Robert Binkley and Bernard Gendron). The present version benefits from the discussions on and surrounding those occasions as well as from discussions on the topic with Ingrid Rothe, Susan Feagin, the late Paulette MacCallum, Gilbert Chambers, Loy Littlefield, and Judith Andre [and Rex Martin].

13 Justice and Adversary Proceedings*

My intention in this short paper is to provide sufficient background for us to discuss an important issue in legal theory having ramifications also for moral theory. Overall, the issue is whether legal theory, and moral theory as well, have not in recent times been infected more than has been realized by a damaging supposition—viz., that the principal job of moral and le-

---

*Unpublished, and one of the last papers MacCallum was able to work on, even though the date he listed at the end is February 1977. MacCallum's notes of April 1975 list it as a "completed" paper, and tell us that it was "delivered as a principal paper at the University of Western Ontario Colloquium on Philosophy of Law" (1974) and also that "it will, when a finished paper is produced, be published in a volume devoted to the proceedings." Obviously a "finished paper" was never produced—open heart surgery in May of 1975 intervened—but different versions of the paper were read at various places, including Illinois Institute of Technology and the Department of Philosophy of the University of Wisconsin Center System, meeting in Madison 5 March 1977. Luckily Professor Kenneth Cooley of the University of Wisconsin Center at Waukesha, the commentator at the Madison session on MacCallum's paper, was able to supply us with a copy of the paper MacCallum read on that occasion. Careful comparison with other versions seems unquestionably to bear out the conjecture that the version published here was the last version MacCallum worked on before his stroke in the autumn of 1977. After that event he was not able to work on it further, but it was his intention to return to this and related topics after he had finished his book on *Political Philosophy* and some other work he was committed to pursue. Professor Cooley also informed us that MacCallum had said that the following items would be useful background material for understanding and discussing this paper on "Justice and Adversary Proceedings": Jerome Frank, "The 'Fight' Theory Versus the 'Truth' Theory," in his *Courts on Trial* (Princeton: University Press, 1949), pp. 80–102; Ronald Dworkin, "Judicial Discretion," *The Journal of Philosophy* 60.21 (October 10, 1963): 624–38; G. C. MacCallum, "Dworkin on Judicial Discretion," ibid., pp. 638–41 (the original and longer version of which is Chapter 10 in this volume); Roscoe Pound, "The Causes of Popular Dissatisfaction with the Administration of Justice," part I, *A.B.A. Reports* 29 (1906): 395–417, reprinted in Ray D. Henson, ed., *Landmarks of Law* (Boston: Beacon Press, 1960). Eds.

gal judgments is to settle questions of entitlement in a certain way and that, when questions of entitlement are settled in this way, conflicts can be resolved accordingly, and truly competitive relations among persons on those matters will be rendered unnecessary. This severely limiting supposition creates all sorts of problems for the attempts of legal and moral theory to be helpful in the day-to-day affairs of persons. It amounts to refusal to consider that competition may be a modelling fact of portions of our legal and moral lives. This paper initiates a discussion of these large issues as they surface in the confined setting of treatments by legal theorists of Anglo-American legal trials viewed in the standard way as adversary proceedings.

I

The use of so-called adversary proceedings in legal systems deriving from that of the English has waxed and waned from time to time, with variations also in the purity of the adversarial nature of the proceedings. But the idea that the use of adversary proceedings is characteristic and distinctive of these systems has flourished uninterruptedly. Further, because of the former importance of trial practice in the work of lawyers in these systems, the ideology of legal practice has been much influenced by the thought that lawyers participate in adversary proceedings. Thus such proceedings have long been thought a central part of Anglo-American legal experience.

There are interesting problems about what is to count as an adversary proceeding, and about how we are to tell what is to count. In my concern to get to other issues, I may perhaps short-change these problems here. If so, our subsequent discussion may provide a remedy. For the present, we may say that adversary proceedings are formally, as well as in many essentials, normally zero-sum situations centrally involving, with respect to their zero-sum aspects, exactly two persons or groups of persons. The involvement is bilateral in that both parties are present, participating, and reciprocally affected by what goes on. They have, furthermore, sole responsibility for initiating and carrying forward the proceedings. The issues over which they contend are limited in scope. The natural outcome of their contention is not determined solely at the option of one of the parties, though it depends at least in part on what each party does in the proceedings. For example, each party must, during the course of the proceedings, submit to an ordeal of opposition from the other party. In 'pure' adversary proceedings, this is the only ordeal to which the parties must submit.

Some but not all adversary proceedings are also judicial proceedings, though the ones with which we are principally concerned will be. Likewise, not all judicial proceedings are adversary in nature, not even in Anglo-American systems. Indeed, not even all judicial trials in Anglo-American systems are adversary proceedings, the principal countercases being inquisitorial in their form and substance.

Further characterization of adversary proceedings would explore these contrasts and differences, and also explore some difficulties past which this sketch has glided. But for the present, we may accept Anglo-American legal trials, with a complainant, plaintiff, prosecutor, or appellant on one side, a defendant or respondent on the other, and a judge, as reasonably adequate examples for our purposes of adversary proceedings.

To some commentators, the prominence of adversary proceedings in the ideology (and, as thought, in the practice) of legal systems deriving from that of the English is to the credit of the systems (cf. Lon Fuller, "The Adversary System"*); to other commentators, it is to the discredit of the systems.** In debates about this, attention has only occasionally been paid to the way in which the form of adversary proceedings promotes a confrontational rather than a reconciliatory posture on the part of parties to social conflict. There is much worth exploring here. For example, what does it show about the strength and nature of our attachment of questions of justice to questions of entitlement? And what does it show about the relative priorities we attach to justice on the one hand, and to amity on the other, in the resolution of various kinds of conflict? And what does it suggest about contrasts and possible connections between justice on the one hand and amity on the other? But this paper travels, at least for a while, down a more traveled path.

Here, the leading question has been: what are the merits and defects of adversary proceedings as contributions to the administration of justice?

In recent times, that question has been turned into: what are the merits and defects of these proceedings as a method of truth discovery?—the assumption being that adversary proceedings contribute to the administration of justice by

---

*This is the only reference MacCallum gives, which suggests that he expected his audience to be familiar with Fuller's paper and also indicates further that he did not regard his paper as in shape for publication yet; in a version prepared for publication the reference would have been more complete and very likely in a note. The reference is to Lon L. Fuller, "The Adversary System," in *Talks on American Law: A Series of Broadcasts to Foreign Audiences by Members of the Harvard Law School Faculty,* edited by Harold J. Berman (New York: Vintage Books, 1961), pp. 30–43. The talks were broadcast in 1960. Eds.

**Here MacCallum's text has the following, in parentheses: "(cf. Roscoe Pound, "The Causes of Popular Dissatisfaction with the Administration of Justice," *American Bar Association Report* 29, part 1: 395–417 (1906), reprinted in *Landmarks of Law,* edited by Ray D. Henson (Beacon Press, Boston, 1960), see esp. pp. 186ff.)." This parenthetical aside has been moved to this note by the editors. Eds.

being a method of truth discovery.[1] It is not clear, however, that adversary proceedings ought to be viewed in this way as primarily and determinatively a method of truth discovery. The belief that they ought to be surely predominates among legal theorists in modern times. But there is reason to think that such a belief rests uneasily at best in the heads of practitioners. Practitioners, especially those who haven't yet quieted the dissonance between what theorists insist on and what their own experience shows them, who would like to see their profession as an elevated one, and who would like to take canons of legal ethics seriously in both their letter and their spirit, often *want* to see adversary proceedings and [to] judge them only as a method of truth discovery. But they find that, on the whole, they cannot. It doesn't jibe well enough with what is expected of them and what they come to believe they had better expect of themselves.

What has gone amiss? I shall not attempt to suggest the whole story, but shall here only explore the idea that there are other legitimate (or at least legitimated) understandings of the nature and functioning of adversary proceedings, that several of these are plausibly afloat among legal practitioners, and that the failure of influential theorists to take this fact seriously and probe it adequately has tended to leave practitioners in quandaries and the public generally confused if not mistrustful.

Each of the plausible understandings legitimates differently the interests of and demands made on adversaries and their representatives, and each has indigenous to it a somewhat different version of what the administration of justice in such a proceeding would amount to.[2] Taking each seriously involves seeing that each finds sufficient support in the history, theory, or economics of legal practice to be sometimes in the offing and sometimes in the foreground in the minds of practitioners. Probing each, in revealing that each

---

1. One's grasp of this view may be improved by noticing that it asks us to see adversary proceedings generally as Rawls sees trials, viz., as cases of imperfect procedural justice. These are cases in which there is a criterion for the just outcome that is defined separately from and prior to the procedure which is to be followed, and the point of the procedure is to reach that outcome though it cannot be relied upon always to do so. The idea roughly is that there are prior rules, principles, or standards defining a just outcome depending upon the facts of the situation, and, as Rawls puts it, the "procedure is framed to search for and to establish the truth in this regard." In contrast, the alternative understandings of adversary proceedings introduced below are captured reasonably well when thought of as seeing the proceedings as cases of what Rawls would call 'pure procedural justice.' These are cases where there is no independent criterion for a just result, but where instead there is a correct or fair procedure such that the outcome is likewise correct or fair, whatever it is, provided that the procedure has been properly followed. The ramifications of the difference are substantial. [The reference to Rawls is to John Rawls, *A Theory of Justice* (Cambridge: Harvard University Press, 1971), section 14, pp. 85–86. Eds.]

2. Cf. note 1 above.

validates different attitudes, practices, and notions of what the administration of justice amounts to, will, for example, show that no code of legal ethics can succeed wholly that does not base itself upon the revisions needed to reconcile the conflicts (in what is validated) that are generated by the differing understandings. The revisions may be in legal theory, or they may be in legal practice. In either case, the stake of the practitioner in them will lie, in important part, in his or her need for a realistic and coherent account of his or her professional obligations in adversary proceedings.

Our interest in the whole matter lies in the prospect it offers of exposing the mechanism of the profound mismanagement by prevailing modern legal theories of a confined but important legal setting in which the relations of persons are truly competitive. The mismanagement consists in the suppression, in the name of the truth-discovery model of adversary proceedings, of the full extent to which these proceedings are competitive. The result is obscuration of, if not blindness to, the extent to which we need to think anew what the connections are between justice and adversary proceedings.

II

What are the alternative understandings that open up the prospect of such exposure? Apart from being seen as a method of truth discovery, adversary proceedings are also sometimes described as (1) regulated fights, battles, or (judicial) duels, (2) legalized gambles, and (3) sporting games or contests.[3] These three distinguishable understandings have, however, most often been jumbled together under the heading of the first, and I shall consider principally the first in the following remarks.

Though all three understandings are afloat in the literature, modern legal theorists move readily and quickly to discount their importance as modelling understandings of adversary proceedings.[4] The discounting has taken three

3. Adversary proceedings are also seen as at least sometimes none of these things but, instead, as window-dressing for negotiation, bargaining, and even highly symbiotic mutual back-scratching by the professionals involved. (Cf. Abraham S. Blumberg, "The Practice of Law as Confidence Games" in abridged form in Vilhelm Aubert, ed., *Sociology of Law* (Baltimore: Penguin, 1969), pp. 321–31, from *Law & Society Review* [1967]: 15–39.) This view should be distinguished from a claim that adversary proceedings and prospects thereof serve to trigger negotiations and bargaining, and are often depended upon to do so. That claim is not itself an understanding of what adversary proceedings are and is in no way in conflict with the understandings being considered here. The window-dressing view, which may in a complicated way be in conflict with the other understandings, is not taken up here, though it would eventually have to be in any full treatment of the subject. Consideration of it here would be premature because we must first consider, as we are presently doing, the coherence and power of the ideology giving the proceedings their value as window-dressing.

4. A modelling understanding is one serving as a frame of reference for organizing accounts of the phenomena.

forms. I shall close this presentation of background material by sketching each, showing its inadequacy, and supporting thereby the idea that we must take these alternative understandings seriously and explore their ramifications for our main topic.

1. First, it is said that the idea that adversary proceedings are regulated fights, etc., is at best a caricature of the facts and thus cannot be taken seriously. The short reply is that the counter-idea that these proceedings can be seen as a method for discovery of the truth is hardly more faithful to the facts and, were we not so fond of it, would be seen also as a caricature or anyway no better than a hopelessly unrealistic representation of the facts. Too much is legitimated in these proceedings in the way of efforts to obscure, distort, misrepresent, and even hide the truth.

A longer reply would explore and expose the extent to which the undeniable presence of devices intended to serve and often serving the discovery of truth is compatible with a modelling understanding of the proceedings as, for example, regulated fights. Compatibility would be shown when it is shown that the presence of the devices can be explained plausibly as a feature or as occasioned by a feature of some particular fight model, for example, that the devices are present because of the kind of fight it is, a matter affected by social policy considerations limiting or dictating the weapons used, the kinds of offense and defense permitted, etc. The extent of our capacity to offer such an account is surely substantial. There is no need for it to be complete and completely satisfactory. All we are seeking are grounds for blocking the ready dismissal of the fight model and allied models in favor of the truth-discovery model. As has already been suggested, the latter model is itself not free from serious difficulties in accounting for facts running counter to it. We have yet to be shown that the difficulties with the fight model are so grave, and the difficulties with the truth-discovery model so small, that the first may readily be dismissed in favor of the second.

2. The next form of discounting holds that the fight model is not independent and competing with the truth-discovery model, but is in fact subordinate to it. This position concedes that adversary proceedings consist in regulated fights, but asserts that the holding of these fights *constitutes* a method of truth-discovery, and a very good method too. The difficulty is with whether it is a good enough method to make the subordination thesis plausible.

Notice first that the outcome of the use of the method is identical to the outcome of the fight, viz., a judgment for one litigant or the other. Insofar as it is an outcome of the use of the method, the judgment is supposedly based on the truth revealed by the method, and held to be acceptable because the method is a very good although not perfect one for revealing the truth, a method balancing our interest in truth-discovery with our respect for individual rights, etc. But insofar as it is an outcome of the fight, the judgment declares a winner of the fight, and it is widely recognized that the fight is sometimes won through the success of efforts to keep the truth hidden and the like. I have already remarked on the legitimacy of such efforts in adversary proceedings. They are not only common but strategically important. Outcomes due to them are as legitimated by the proceedings as any other outcomes.

In consequence, the subordination thesis requires us to believe both that the outcomes of adversary proceedings (*qua* method of truth discovery) are based upon truth revealed by a very good though not perfect method of truth-discovery, and that the outcomes (*qua* outcomes of regulated fights) may legitimately result from the success of efforts to keep the truth concealed. We perhaps are not thereby being required to hold two inconsistent beliefs, but the claim that they are *not* inconsistent may take some explaining. The question is just how convincing that explaining will be. Until we get it and are convinced by it, we may, I think, be excused for continuing to entertain the hypothesis that the subordination thesis is false and that the two models are independent and competing models. Not since we abandoned the idea that victory in these regulated fights reveals the truth because God arms the victor has the subordination thesis been acceptable without elaborate explanation. It is certainly not sufficient without elaborate defense to support the dismissal of the fight model as a viable modelling understanding of adversary proceedings.[5]

3. The third way of discounting the seriousness of the alternative models accepts as sound the criticisms just offered of the first and second ways. It is to argue that no one could seriously want to adopt any of the alternative understandings because adoption of any of them would be inconsistent with a

---

5. One common view, though certainly not the only possible view, of some central difficulties with which the subordination thesis would have to cope is found in the following passage written by Karl Llewellyn commenting on legal practice in the U.S. He says: "The tradition was in many ways self-contradictory. Organized legal ethics never in this country worked out solutions for the conflict of duty to the court and to the client. Duty to client reads in terms of taking advantage of each technicality the law may show, however senseless. It reads in terms of the distortion of evidence and argument of the utter bounds of the permissible. Duty to court reads in terms of shaping every piece of the machinery that can be made to give, toward better functioning. It reads in terms of trying issues of fact to reach the probable truth. Duty to self resolved the conflict, as canons of ethics did not. The resolution was in favor of the client. The other tradition remains strong enough on paper to make the canons of legal ethics still a jumble of cross-purposed words. The picture is not pretty. The lack of beauty is, as is obvious, caused partly by cartooning. But as with a cartoon that bites, the overdrawing leaves the picture true: the sequence of best brains drained off into a single channel." [From] K. N. Llewellyn, "The Bar Specializes—With What Results?" In *The Administration of Justice*, ed. by Raymond Moley and Schuyler C. Wallace, for the *Annals of the American Academy of Political & Social Science* (Philadelphia, 1933), p. 181.

desire to give primacy to the discovery of truth. There are two replies to this suggestion.

(a) The first is that the issue of which models should be taken seriously cannot be settled solely by considering which one *wants* to adopt. One must ask the somewhat broader question: which is it *rational* to adopt? Here one needs merely to notice that the economics of trial practice have traditionally supported the regulated fight model more fully than the truth-discovery model. Notice, for example, how unrealistic the following attempt of the Supreme Judicial Court of Massachusetts to ignore this sounds:

> Manifestly, the practice of the law is not a craft, nor trade, nor commerce. It is a profession whose main purpose is to aid in the doing of justice according to law between the state and the individual and between man and man. Its members are not and ought not to be hired servants of their clients. They are independent officers of the court, owing a duty as well to the public as to private interests. (*In Re Bergeron,* 220 Mass 472)[6]

Surely, to say that these professionals are not and ought not to be the hired servants of clients, and are independent officers of the court, is to ignore the economic base of the profession. This is not merely to ignore the question of where lawyers' *interests* lie, but also to ignore the question of where their *obligations* lie. If we want lawyers to be 'independent' officers of the court and not the hired servants of clients, then perhaps we had better see to it that they are paid by the court and not by the 'clients.' So long as we fail to do this or something having roughly the same effect, the 'regulated fight' model will seem at least as reasonable if not more reasonable to the practitioner than the model of truth discovery. Court-appointed attorneys, legal aid and public defender offices are perhaps moves in the direction of change, but the old traditions of client-retaining and financing are still too strong for these developments to have had yet more than a slight impact on the ideology of legal practice.

(b) The second reply (to the suggestion that no one could seriously want to adopt any of the models alternative to the truth-discovery model because adoption of any of them would be inconsistent with a desire to give primacy to the discovery of truth) could usefully occupy the center of our attention in the upcoming discussion. In outline, the reply is that our vision of the contribution that adversary proceedings can make to the administration of justice has been so dominated by the idea that adversary proceedings must be seen

---

6. Quoted with approval in Maurice Wormser, "Legal Ethics in Theory and in Practice." In Raymond Moley and Schuyler C. Wallace, *The Administration of Justice,* p. 194.

as a method of truth discovery, that every other model has been rejected by having applied to it the standards of evaluation appropriate only to this one. Commentators have persistently and uniformly evaluated the other understandings as though these understandings were in fact being offered and used as methods of truth discovery. No one has looked at them independently of this supposition and pursued the following question of each: if this were the correct and accepted account of the nature and functioning of adversary proceedings, what conceptions of justice would be indigenous to these proceedings and what, consequently, would the contribution of the proceedings to the administration of justice look to be? This question offers at least the possibility of shaking us loose from our fixation on the idea that adversary proceedings can contribute to the administration of justice only by contributing to the discovery of truth. Being shaken loose from this fixation will not be a cure-all, but can lead to exposure of some of the roots of the moral tensions and cross-purposes of legal practice and, consequently, of our legal experience.

Take, for example, the regulated fight model. Though some appreciable latitude of interpretation seems ineliminable, on that model entitlement is not something about which conclusions are reached by means of the proceedings, but perhaps rather something determined by the outcome of the proceedings. Thus, the point of the proceedings is not to discover and enforce the truth about who, prior to the proceedings, was entitled to what, but rather to result in an award of entitlement on the basis of performance in the fight. Justice in the first case would centrally involve reaching correct conclusions about matters the truth about which could have been known prior to the proceedings. Justice in the second case depends centrally upon what happens in the proceedings, just as justice in declaration of the winner of a boxing match depends centrally upon what happens in the match. The central questions for morality and social policy would then revolve around why we would ever want to distribute entitlements on such a basis. That is an interesting question about which I have a number of ideas. None of them are very startling. But they do seem to expose features of our legal and moral experience slighted by legal and moral theorists.

A reminder might be useful, in closing, to the effect that none of the models seems fully to fit the phenomena. In particular, the regulated fight model may seem highly implausible in the light of the paragraph just above. Could it be correct that garden-variety Anglo-American judicial trials are not centrally efforts to find out who is entitled to what on a basis of events occurring prior to the trial, and making awards in the light of what is learned? Any other account would seem bizarre to many people. Furthermore, considerations of social policy would seem massively to support the idea that this is what the proceedings *should* be. Nevertheless, we can note:

1. that there are important facts about the proceedings that disturbingly fail to fit this view;
2. that at least many of the facts supporting it may be compatible, on our previous understanding of what this compatibility amounts to, with contrary models; and
3. the situation is thus disturbing enough to warrant serious exploration of what considerations of social policy could underwrite some of the other modelling understandings of the proceedings.

Perhaps, as none of the modelling understandings now in the field seem to fit the facts completely, we ought to chuck them and start anew. One reason I am not prepared at present to do that is that continued exploration of these (already existing) modelling understandings seems to me to hold such promise for exposure of the social policies fundamental to our legal and moral experience.

Appendix

In civil trials, it is appropriate for the lawyers on either side to:

1. Examine witnesses they know to be telling the truth in such a way as to try to make these witnesses disbelieved by the judge or jurors.
2. Not call a witness because they know that if the witness were put on the stand, a truth damaging to their client would be revealed.
3. Fail to submit in evidence items establishing truths damaging to their clients.
4. Avoid asking questions of witnesses when truthful answers to those questions would be damaging to their clients.

These are legitimate ways in which the truth may be distorted, obscured, or hidden by counsel for either side in civil cases, and by defense attorneys in criminal trials. Which, if any, are legitimated for prosecuting attorneys in criminal trials? So far as I presently know, only 3 is clearly excluded. Number 1 might be thought nasty, but not beyond the bounds of the permitted. Numbers 2 and 4 are clearly permitted (though not required—and here is a difference [from] attorneys in the other roles mentioned; it is arguable, at least, that they have an obligation to their clients to act in accord with numbers 2 and 4, and possibly also number 3. For them not to [do so] would be thought monstrous by most professionals). The permissibility of numbers 2 and 4 for prosecuting attorneys is founded on the idea that it is the responsibility of the defense to do what needs to be done in these areas. Some commentators, though not many I suspect, would think it also permissible for the prosecuting attorney to violate numbers 2 and 4; but most commentators would think it improper or in some way inappropriate, though not monstrous, for the prose-cuting attorney to do so. Doing so transgresses against the tradition of self-help at the heart of the adversary system so far as the actual course of the proceedings is concerned.

14 What Is Wrong with Violence?*

This paper does not consider possible accounts of why we should *never* countenance or bring about violence, but only accounts of why we should never do so without some special justification or excuse. The problem of when, if ever, violence would be excusable or justifiable is surely important to discuss

*This paper was discovered among MacCallum's papers when work on this collection was already considerably advanced. Although it is not possible to date it with precision, it appears to have been worked on in the period 1968–70, especially in 1969–70 when MacCallum was in Europe on an ACLS fellowship, to have been put aside to be continued at some later date, and then to have been worked on only intermittently. MacCallum's curriculum vitae of 1971 and 1972 indicates that "What Is Wrong with Violence?" was given as a public lecture at Aarhüs University in April 1970 and as a seminar to the Philosophy Institute at the University of Bergen in May 1970, though we cannot tell whether the paper here published for the first time is the paper so identified. In April 1970, MacCallum also lectured on "Reform and Violence" at Aarhüs University and gave a seminar "On Violence" to the Filosofiska Institutionen at Stockholm University; in May 1970 he gave a lecture entitled "Violence and Morality" at the Philosophy Institute of Oslo University, and in June 1970 a talk on "Violence" to the Philosophy Faculties of the University of London. His fellowship year was clearly occupied with this topic. But we have not found among his papers anything to determine the exact content of the talks, papers, lectures, and seminars MacCallum gave in these places in spring 1970. MacCallum became chair of the Department of Philosophy at the University of Wisconsin in the fall of 1970, serving for two years. This was a particularly busy and stressful period, which included among other things planning for and supervising a move of the department from Bascom Hall and several other buildings to its present home in Helen C. White Hall, and this could partially explain the paper's being put aside at that time. He could have had little time then for *any* philosophical work. However, in May 1971 MacCallum found the time to give a talk on "Reform and Violence" at the Waukesha Campus of the University of Wisconsin and on "Philosophical Work on Violence" to the Philosophy Faculty at Temple University. The present paper is referred to above, in Chapter 11, "Violence and Appeals to Conscience," at p. 178. Largely for these reasons it was decided to include the paper in this volume—it can be thought of as a sort of appendix to the collection. Though it is in somewhat rough and unfinished form, and undoubtedly would have taken on quite a different aspect if MacCallum had been able to work on it further himself, it is

235

eventually, but one can hardly do so in a sound way until he understands precisely why excuses or justifications are called for, and it is quite enough for the moment to consider that. So far as I can see, violence has not been discussed in this fundamental way. The focus of attention has been on when violence is justifiable or excusable—or, as it is often put, on when and whether violence is ever a 'necessary evil.' Few if any persons seem to have considered seriously why it is an evil at all. Thus, there is work here that needs doing.

I

When asked what is wrong with violence, our readiest answer seems to lie in citation of the connection of violence with injury, damage, and destruction, and, via these, on at least some occasions with pain and discomfort. But the connection is not a simple one.

It is not simple in part because the notion of violence is itself complex. Violence appears sometimes to be treated as an impulse or force or stock of psychic or physical energy (as in "Violence raged within him"), sometimes as a form or kind of action or activity (as the activity of wind or waves suggested in "The violence of the storm was shattering"), sometimes as a tool or instrument for the achievement of a purpose (as in "He didn't use violence"), and sometimes as a result of a certain sort, perhaps one brought about in a certain way (as in "Look at the violence that was done here").

These appearances of difference can of course be rationalized by reference to one central notion. But a great deal depends on the central notion one chooses, and there may be no one unmistakably 'correct' choice. One could, for example, treat violence as most basically a form or kind of action or activity, and consequently regard such an expression as "Look at the violence

---

not, in our judgment, "unpublishable," as MacCallum called it. There are a number of passages, amounting in some instances to whole paragraphs or even whole groups of pages, that were marked off in brackets, perhaps signifying places where MacCallum felt a serious problem lurked, perhaps portions he planned to revise, perhaps sections he omitted when reading the paper to some group or other. We have found no way of telling, though we do know, on the testimony of Professor Michael Pritchard, that the paper was circulated to and read by some participants in the Buffalo Conference on Violence of 1974, where MacCallum presented his paper on "Violence and Appeals to Conscience," and that these two papers supplement each other well. After some consideration it was decided not to mar the text by incorporating these brackets. Other changes, such as corrections of obvious typing errors, have been silently made. Words in brackets were inserted by the editors as emendations obviously needed. The author's notes were taken out of the text proper and incorporated into footnotes, with the various references filled in by the editors, as with some previous papers in this volume.

Following the paper itself there is a set of "Notes for 'What Is Wrong with Violence?',", MacCallum's own title (which MacCallum had attached to his working copy of the paper), which provide the author's own abstract of the paper and an account of at least some of its deficiencies. See p. 255 and pp. xxxi–xxxii. Eds.

that was done here" to be an elliptical way of saying "Look at the results of the violence (i.e., the violent action or activity) that took place here."

Proceeding in this fashion, one might see the connection between violence, on the one hand, and injury, damage, and destruction, on the other hand, as this: violence has only a *tendency* to bring about injury, damage, destruction, or, better, violence has a tendency to do this with respect to certain possible objects or objects within certain ranges. The restriction is better because, to take an example, the violence of a storm on top of Mount Everest may have been shattering though nothing up there was in the slightest danger of injury, damage or destruction, there being no people up there, etc., though if there had been people up there, they and their tents would have been in considerable danger. Taking this approach, one would have the burden of somehow characterizing the ranges of objects or things that violence, perhaps definitionally, has a tendency to injure, etc. One would need to allow for the possible importance of shifts of context (e.g., the lower threshold of activity qualifying as violence in a nursery *might* (I am not saying "would") be lower than the lower threshold on the high seas). And, since one's concern would be principally with characterizing this lower threshold, one would not wish to include within the range either things that are too tough (e.g., Mount Everest itself) or things that are too tender (e.g., orchids, which may be damaged or destroyed when subjected to rough handling that falls short of violence). Furthermore, in rationalizing the relationship of this central notion of violence to the others suggested, one would have, for example, the related but embarrassing problem of explaining why, if such an expression as "Look at the violence that was done here" is an elliptical way of saying "Look at the results of the violence (i.e., the violent action or activity) that took place here," one could not always point to the results and say "Look at the violence that was done"; for example, one could not do this in the case of our storm on top of Mount Everest (sans people and tents) because, when the storm is over, there is nothing appropriate to which one can point.

Confronted with this latter problem, we might consider starting out in a different way. One could treat as most fundamental the view of violence established in "Look at the violence that was done here," and understand a person who utters "The violence of the storm was shattering," to be saying that the activities of wind or wave constituting the storm were shattering, these activities being called "the violence of the storm" because they were such as likely to wreak violence on certain kinds of things that were or might have been in their path. (Our basic task would then be to characterize what it is for violence to be done to something. Violence as a kind of activity would then be characterized as activity of a sort that would be likely to do violence to things within a roughly delineated range of things if any such things were in its path, etc.)

I favor this latter approach. As providing a central notion by reference to which the other idioms may be rationalized, it presents no specially difficult problems. More importantly, it seems to me to provide the firmest and least troubling basis for characterizing the whole family of notions and for a coherent and intuitively fitting account of why people commonly think there is something wrong with violence. Rather than arguing these points, however, I shall simply lay out some of what can be done once this choice is made.

II

One can sometimes be taken to see 'the violence that was done' though this is not always clearly so. One might find it strange to be told that he was being taken to see the violence a speaker had done to language, or the violence a commentator had done to another man's thought. But being taken to see the violence that was done is clearly sometimes possible, and cases where it is possible are, I believe, central to our understanding of what it is for violence to be done. One cannot base a sharply delineated metaphysic of violence on these cases, but analysis of them can provide a reasonably secure basis for comprehending the network of not-very-sharply-bounded concepts in this area. It can at least provide us with a reference point from which we may reasonably see other cases as extensions and elaborations of these cases.

When we are taken to see 'the violence that was done' we expect to see manifestations of injury, damage, or destruction. If we do not find them, we are likely to ask, "Where is the violence that was done?" Perhaps it has been cleaned up or repaired, or perhaps it is not readily observable (the damage was deep; the injury was not what we had been looking for), or perhaps it is not what we are prepared to call injury, damage, or destruction, though the person taking us to it and so-calling it believed it to be so. But some such explanation of the defeat of our expectations must be forthcoming for the claim that violence was done to remain intelligible.

This is the clearest and tightest connection I have found between violence, on the one hand, and injury, etc., on the other. When one moves to other cases of 'violence done,' cases where we cannot clearly 'be taken to see' the violence that was done, either one will need to expand one's notions of what is to count as injury, etc., well past the 'brute' notions of these with which we ordinarily operate—expand them in ways that make their application more debatable, more 'metaphysical,' and all the same highly interesting and possibly important—or one will need to shift to a notion of 'harm' that doesn't clearly involve them. Furthermore, when one moves from our 'basic' idiom ("the violence that was done") to a discussion of some of the other idioms—e.g., "the violence of the storm was shattering" and "Violence raged within him"—one will find that, though the threads of connection with injury, damage, and destruction, or at least with 'harm,' are still there, they

will not be so thick, and he will find that he can pick them up in variously
different ways.

Showing all this is too big a job for the present paper, though some of it
will emerge in what follows. For the present, we might pause and ask
whether, given the restricted but clear connection just exposed, we can yet
say much about the wrongness of violence even in that restricted setting.
When violence has been done, and is of a sort that we can be taken to see,
then something has thereby been injured, damaged, or destroyed. Our further
views on this fact, however, will depend on what we think about the disvalue
of injury, damage, and destruction per se.

One way of putting the matter is to say that we must show violence connected with those cases of injury, damage, and destruction that are disvaluable. But there is a deeper point here. Suppose that we judged injuries, etc.,
harmless in certain cases because we thought that what was injured, etc., was
of no account or even positively noxious. Should we conclude from this that
countenancing or bringing about violence, insofar as it amounts to countenancing or bringing about injury, etc., is not always but only sometimes in
need of special justification or excuse? One may find two significantly different reactions to the suggestion, each exposing a highly general world-view.
One [reaction] is to think, "Yes, that's right. The countenancing or bringing
about of violence, and thus of injury, etc., is surely not in need of any special
justification or excuse; for this, in itself, is not wrong. It is only wrong when
what is thereby injured, etc., is of some account. As many things are inconsequential and many other things are clearly noxious, it is silly to think of
needing generally a special excuse or justification; the question does not become important until we have some special reason to think that the things in
question are of account." The other reaction is to think, "No, that's wrong.
The general presumption must be in favor of supposing everything to be of
some account, and a showing that something is inconsequential or noxious
will simply constitute a form of the excuse or justification one needs for countenancing violence and thus, injury, etc., to it."

Which of these reactions is right? Or, if neither is unquestionably right,
which is most reasonable? The answer one gives will make a significant difference in his account of the wrongness of violence. I find both these reactions
in myself, and perhaps you do also. There seem to be historical, economic,
and sociologic—or quasi-sociologic—explanations of this. For example, the
view that much in the world is inconsequential and that, while many things
may show on their faces that they are consequential (e.g., humans, or at least
members of one's own community), one must generally have some special
reason to believe that various other things are consequential before becoming
concerned about their injury, etc.: this view may have established itself because of its congeniality to ambitious, hardy, and (very beneficially) none-

too-reflective inhabitants of a frontier such as John Locke thought the New World to be, viz., a place where, no matter how much a man 'took' there was as much and more left for others. It would be less congenial, however, to persons who think of the planet as a place where essential resources are rapidly disappearing, and who are full of doubts stemming from realization of the faultiness of past judgments concerning what on that planet was important and what was not. It might also be less congenial to persons who thought, as Locke also thought, that the world and its contents are God's property and that we are but stewards set to watch over it in God's interests.

Such 'explanations' as these may be thought to expose reasons, or at least the beginnings of reasons, for holding one or the other of the two views in question. Doubtless this is so. But I am not at all certain what the outcome should be, and cannot explore the matter further here. I seek merely to expose it to view so that one may see precisely how it lies in waiting for one who wishes to explore the wrongness of violence.

III

In pushing more broadly into the discussion of what is wrong with violence, we must sooner or later consider what is supposed or presupposed about the way injuries, etc., are produced when we consider them to be 'the violence done.' For, from the fact that something has been injured, damaged or destroyed, it does not follow that violence was done. One's leg may be injured when he slips and falls on an icy path. The finish on a valuable table may be damaged when rain is blown on it through an open window. One's liver may be destroyed over a period of years by a slow-acting disease. None of these is clearly a case where violence has been done. If we are to grasp what is or may be wrong with violence and, in the instant case, with 'violence done' (where we can be 'taken to see it'), we must, therefore, consider not only what is or may be wrong with injury, etc., per se, but also whether there may be something wrong with them produced in the way characteristic of 'violence done' in addition to what, if anything, is wrong with them per se.

What is the way in question? There seems no clearly marked boundary between that way and other ways. But the following considerations figure in our willingness to view injuries, etc., as cases of violence done.

1. *External imposition.* To the extent that the change whose outcome is injury, damage, or destruction has been recognizably effected by forces external to the thing injured, damaged, or destroyed, we are willing, if certain other conditions listed below are also met or approximated, to regard the outcome as violence done. If, for example, a tornado uproots a tree which then strikes a man, breaking his leg, his broken leg, as well as the uprooted tree, would easily count as part of the violence done by the tornado. But if the man's leg has been broken in a fall on an icy path on a calm and sunny

day while he was proceeding unhurriedly to the postoffice, the injury would not so clearly count as a case of violence done, the reason being that we have in this latter case no clearly acceptable candidate for the external force or forces effecting the change whose outcome was this injury.

In order to forestall some criticisms of this conclusion, a few caveats seem necessary. (a) The icy condition of the path certainly played a role in bringing about the fall resulting in a broken leg. Indeed, we might in some circumstances say that the man slipped and fell because the path was icy (though we might not say this if the path had been icy all winter and the man had been walking it daily without accident; in such circumstances we might think it more appropriate to say that the man slipped and fell because he got careless). But even where we are inclined to say that he slipped and fell because the path was icy, here, unlike the case of the uprooted tree, the man's own behavior has so obviously played a role in bringing about this injury that we might justifiably object, unless the circumstances were extraordinary, to saying that the injury had been effected by the icy path. (b) One might find momentarily attractive the idea that the forces effecting the fall were located in the man and perhaps in nature but not in the leg that was injured, and hence that they were external to the leg. But the necessary argument to an embarrassing conclusion here can hardly be very strong. When a man's leg has been broken, for example, we can equally well say that the injury was to him and that it was to his leg, that he is now injured and that his leg is now injured, that we now have an injured man and that he now has an injured leg, etc. Apart from concerns we may have when on the scene of the actual event and trying to cope with it, in the light of which we may, e.g., want to locate who was injured or locate where he was injured, there is no clear reason for choosing only one of these lines of description of the outcome. (c) One might be brought up short by the idiom "violence to oneself." If one can indeed do violence to oneself, then perhaps the forces effecting the change resulting in violence done need not be external to what is thereby injured, damaged or destroyed. The difficulty with this hypothesis, however, is that the notion of self-inflicted violence is one of a set of notions—including those of self-mastery, self-indulgence and self-deception—all of which are widely recognized to be problematic for the same reason, viz., they seem to require for their intelligibility the dichotomizing of the self into two elements or aspects—the master and the mastered, the indulger and the indulged, the deceiver and the deceived, and, in our case, the perpetrator and the victim. It is true that heroic attempts have been made to avoid this result. But none of those I know have succeeded. In the last paragraph of Sartre's famous chapter on self-deception in *Being and Nothingness,* for example, I, at least, do not find the dichotomizing avoided in his summing-up of the matter. (Consider the way he there hypostatizes self-deception itself as a thinking, willing agent.) I conclude that, rather than being a countercase to my claim about externality, the problematic character of 'violence to oneself' would, if anything, confirm the point.

2. *Suddenness of change.* Suppose a change whose outcome has been injury, damage, or destruction to have been recognizably effected by forces external to the thing so changed. If so, then, to the extent that the change has been a sudden one, we are, subject perhaps to one further condition mentioned below, willing to regard the outcome as violence done. Roughly stated, the point of this consideration is merely that some changes occur too slowly for their outcomes to count easily as violence done, even though the outcomes clearly involve injury, etc. The outcome of a gradual or corrosive change such as would be brought about by 'painting' a steel door daily with a weak acid solution until the door is destroyed or at least obviously damaged is difficult to see as violence done because the process of change toward the critical outcome (patent damage or destruction) lacks the characteristic abruptness of cases of violence done.

3. *Radicalness of change.* Given that a change whose outcome is injury or damage is fairly rapid and recognizably effected by forces external to the thing changed, the more radical the change is, the more willing we are to count the result as violence done. If, for example, the only recognizable change is an injury that is very slight (e.g., a slightly cut finger), we are relatively unwilling, but if it is relatively severe we *are* willing, to recognize the result as violence done. *A fortiori,* when the result is destruction we are willing.

In sum, when injuries, etc., count as 'the violence done,' we know, suppose, or presuppose that they have been effected by forces external to the thing so affected, that they were brought about fairly suddenly, and that the resulting changes in the thing are more or less marked or notable. The first of these conditions seems to me strong enough to qualify as a necessary condition. The other two do not, unless one interprets them as requiring that the change be not too slow and not too slight; but interpreting them in this way gives them a spurious definiteness.

One can begin providing a rationale for the operation of these three conditions, and also carry on directly the exploration of what is wrong with violence, by noting the following remarkable fact: Quite apart from any initial identification of the outcome of a change as injury, damage, or destruction, we are in some of our moods inclined to suppose that change preeminently satisfying the three conditions just mentioned is wrong, and wrong simply by virtue of its having satisfied these conditions. We think it wrong because, if it satisfies these conditions, it damages, destroys, or violates the integrity of the things so changed.

I say that we think this in 'some of our moods' because (1) we are not always prepared to see the subjects of change preeminently satisfying our three conditions as having integrities that could be damaged, etc., and (2) even when we do so see them, we are not always prepared to regard the damage, etc. [as] disvaluable. We are most strongly inclined to think both of these when the subject of the change in question is a human being; but embedded in our cultural (e.g., theological) history are considerations supporting us strongly in extending these views to things that are not human beings, and even to 'the whole of our environment' or 'all of creation.' Some of the considerations supporting and subverting these extensions have already been suggested. The matter is difficult to discuss because the concepts involved are not sufficiently well-bounded to lend themselves to precise treatment. But it is important to venture on the discussion because the common undifferentiated view that violence is wrong draws considerable support (and perhaps rightly) from these extensions, as well as from the central cases of violence done to human beings.

IV

Even in the case of human beings, however, there are difficulties. One must familiarize himself with these difficulties in order to develop a sense of proportion about the later difficulties with the extensions, and also in order to expose portions of the conceptual networks to which appeal must be made in working out the difficulties in both cases.

Suppose, for example, I give permission to a surgeon to amputate my leg in a high-speed but also presumably highly-skilled operation, and suppose that the operation goes as planned. The change has been sudden, radical, and apparently effected by an external force. Has my integrity been damaged, destroyed or violated, or only the integrity of my body, or not even that?

If the integrity of my body were merely its wholeness or completeness as a normal human body, this integrity would seem to have been damaged, destroyed, or violated by the operation. But suppose that quite a few years earlier my arm had been amputated. My body would not, at the time leading up to this latest operation, have had any wholeness or completeness as a normal human body. Nevertheless, supposing that no more surprising facts are to be revealed, the integrity of my body was damaged, destroyed, or violated by this latest operation; or so, at least, we might be inclined to say. What supports this inclination is a view of the integrity of my body as consisting of its wholeness or completeness as *my* body, and pursuit of this point will reveal why the amputation *violated* as well as damaged or destroyed the integrity of my body.

The human body is normally viewed as not merely an assemblage of parts but a system of more or less harmoniously integrated parts. When speaking of its integrity we can thus be speaking of its completeness or wholeness as such a system. When so viewed, the integrity of the body will have both inward-looking and outward-looking aspects. The inward-looking aspect will emphasize the integration of the body's parts that supports our view of them as parts of a system. The more harmoniously the parts are related to each other, the more completely systematic the body is seen to be, and the easier it is to identify as one complete thing rather than many things. The outward-looking aspect will emphasize the importance of the boundaries in the light of which we may determine what is a part of this system and what is not. The system is seen as a bounded domain having inertia or principle(s) of organization and operation of its own, and thus as one complete or whole thing in an environment of other things. The upshot is that the integrity of the body is seen to be a function both of the relations of its parts to each other and of its relations to other things. The more harmoniously the parts are related to each other, the greater the integrity of the system because the easier it is to identify as one complete thing rather than many things; likewise, the more completely the state of the system is determined by its own inertia or principle(s) of operation, the greater its integrity because the easier it is to identify as one distinct thing among other things.

When the situation is so conceived, one can see that the integrity of my body was probably violated as well as damaged by this latest amputation, just as it probably also was by the earlier amputation many years ago. Each amputation removed a part from the bodily system, thus, expectably, throwing the remainder of the system into a state of at least temporary disequilibrium from which it must have recovered in order for me to survive. I obviously did recover in the earlier case, and the remainder of my body, in establishing new equilibriums, reconstituted—or, better, constituted—itself as a system; the integrity of this system was, in turn, violated by the second amputation. The part removed in each case was an important one, and thus the system-change needed for recovery was expectably great. The removal was furthermore very sudden, and thus the disequilibrium produced in the remainder of the system was presumptively significant; there was no question of a series of adjustments to small disequilibriums produced by gradual removal or atrophying of a part. Lastly, the removal was effected by an external force and thus was an effect of an intrusion upon the system. Thus, with regard to its inward-looking aspect, the integrity of the body-system was significantly damaged if not destroyed, both by simply the removal of a significantly integral part of the system (thus destroying its wholeness or completeness as *that* system), and by the consequent disequilibriums making difficult the identification of the remainder as (at least yet) a (complete) system. With regard to its outward-looking aspect, the integrity of the body-system was violated by the intrusion of external force in effecting a significant change within the domain of the system—an intrusion interfering with the determination of the state of the system simply by its own inertia or principle(s) of operation. (We could assimilate this either to cases of violating someone's privacy—viz., intruding upon it—or if we see the system's inertia or principle(s) of operation as constituting the 'law' of the system, to cases of violating a law.)

The notions suggested here by such terms as "system," "equilibrium," and "harmonious integration" are certainly not well-bounded and are potentially treacherous. They cannot here be given the examination they deserve, but they are surely not nonsensical and, I will simply claim, have not been used here unreasonably. What seems to have been shown by using them is what can be meant by saying that the integrity of my body has been damaged and violated, how it was both damaged and violated by the amputations in question, and how this was so because those admittedly very radical changes in my body were produced very suddenly and were effected by an external force.

I say that these things 'seem to have been shown' because, if we contemplate the possible *occasions* of the amputations (e.g., if we ask why I gave the surgeon my permission for the last one), we may begin to have doubts about the analysis. In what state was the leg when I gave permission? Was it badly mangled, or gangrenous? Or was it a perfectly healthy leg that I wanted removed for cosmetic affect* (e.g., to complete my planned pose as a war hero)? The analysis works most smoothly in the latter case, but that of course is also the least likely case. The difficulties with the other cases are roughly of two sorts: (1) They suggest that, from the inward-looking point of view of integrity, the leg or at least part of it was already not integrated very well into the rest of the system or that there were already serious disequilibriums traceable to the condition of the leg. This makes the amputation itself seem less a disruption of the system. (2) They also suggest that in one way or another the amputation was necessary to *save* the system or at least what would be left of it. These considerations are forceful, though if one were to press on them they might not in the end appear decisive (consider that the amputation of the whole leg removes a source of disruption and a threat, but it also removes more than that). But they are directed at best to whether the integrity of my body was *damaged* by the amputation. Their focus is thus on the inward-looking aspect of integrity. Even if they were decisive, we would need to consider still whether the integrity of my body had been *violated* by the amputation—a matter resting principally on consideration of the outward-looking aspect. If either of the two difficulties is thought to disturb my claim about that, it must, I fear, [be] only because violating integrities is generally thought to be bad, and it is difficult to see the amputation as a bad thing if it were necessary to save the system (or what would be left of it). But surely,

---

*It is not clear to the editors whether MacCallum wanted this word to be "affect," in the sense, say, of *affectation,* or "effect." Eds.

beneficial or not, the amputation does constitute an intrusion into the domain of the body-system—an intrusion interfering with the determination of the state of the system by its own inertia or principle(s) of operation. It thus violates the integrity of that system. Though I agree that if it were introduced precisely in order to remedy the effects of previous and perhaps catastrophic intrusions (e.g., the mangling of my leg in an accident) it might look more like an interference with the self-determination of the states of the system, nevertheless it still itself constitutes an interference—as witness what would happen if the operation were not performed; the results might not be happy ones, but they would constitute the playing out of the effects of the operation of the system's own inertias and principles of operation. That we would think it best for the integrity of the system to be violated in this way merely shows that we do not always think such a thing to be bad, given certain circumstances. But citation of those circumstances constitutes here precisely the justification for something that would, in their absence, surely be counted bad in the present range of cases. (One must of course discuss why it would be counted bad, 'and something will be said of this later.)

Turning now to the more interesting and complicated question of whether *my* integrity, and not merely that of my body, has been damaged or violated by the amputation, we might start by asking whether the former doesn't follow from the latter.

In a new sense of "integrity" that now appears on the scene, it clearly does not. The integrity of persons is often considered to be their rectitude—their uprightness and honesty. Surely, on this understanding, damage to and violation of the integrity of my body need not involve similar effects on my integrity. The amputation in itself surely did not damage or violate my integrity so conceived, and indeed it is difficult to see how this integrity could be violated or even straightforwardly damaged at all, though it could be lost or compromised or just never developed.

But this vision of integrity is connected to, or is perhaps but an aspect of another—one having, as with the notion of the integrity of the body, both inward- and outward-looking aspects. And when this further vision of integrity is operating, damage to and violation of the integrity of persons may indeed by connected with similar effects on the integrity of their bodies.

The inward-looking aspect of this vision focuses on the person as a locus of various drives, impulses, needs, wants, thoughts, etc. These are not by any means clearly seen as *parts* of the person, and neither is it at all clear that their relationships to each other are systematic enough to support a view of them as clearly constituting a system; further, and even more crucially for the question just asked, it is not clear precisely how they are related to the body, though some relationships are surely often supposed (one need mention only the so-called 'mind-body problem' to conjure up visions of the issues that must be met here). Nevertheless, in the face of all these unclarities, it is clear enough that the inward-looking aspect of a person's integrity is thought to be a function of the extent to which his impulses, needs, wants, thoughts, etc. are harmoniously and 'coherently' integrated vis-a-vis each other. And the rationale for this is strikingly similar to that found in the inward-looking view of the integrity of the body. The question is whether we are being presented with one thing or with many things, one person or—so to speak—many persons.

This vision of the integrity of persons has of course been richly troubling. Given the generally favorable attitude toward striving for and protecting the integrity of persons, the emphasis on completeness and wholeness may be thought, for example, to enforce a disturbingly closed-off view of something so quicksilvery and open-ended as men sometimes seem to be. Plato might approve, but Walt Whitman would not; consider Plato's criticism of actors in the *Republic* on the grounds that one should be one person and not many; and consider the following quote from George Kateb utilizing Whitman's view:

> Proteus could become the symbol of the tone of utopian life. The aim would be . . . to allow individuals to assume various "personae" without fear of social penalty, . . . to strive to have each self be able to say, in the words of Walt Whitman's "Song of Myself": "I am large, I contain multitudes." [1]

And the matter has certainly disturbed Sartre and, less directly, John Dewey, as well as other modern philosophers before and since. Sartre, for example, was critical of people who long to be something 'solid,' something inescapable, though it is not clear how far he would be able to avoid the view of integrity used above. In his famous lecture "Existentialism is a Humanism," he sums things up by saying, "What we mean to say is that a man is no other than a series of undertakings, that he is the sum, the organization, the set of relations that constitute these undertakings." [2] This does not seem to me to escape the view of integrity just used.

The connection of this inward-looking view of integrity with integrity-as-rectitude is via the notion of honesty, and is especially clear in the interesting and paradoxical cases of honesty to oneself. I spoke earlier of the difficulty

1. George Kateb, "Utopia and the Good Life." In *Utopias and Utopian Thought,* edited by Frank E. Manuel (Boston: Houghton Mifflin, 1966), p. 256.
2. Jean-Paul Sartre, "Existentialism is a Humanism," translated by Philip Mairet. In *Existentialism from Dostoevsky to Sartre,* edited by Walter Kaufman (Cleveland & New York: Meridian Books, 1956), p. 301.

with the notion of self-deception and of Sartre's attempt to cope with the dichotomizing of the self that the intelligibility of the notion seems to require. The difficulty is precisely that self-deception seems to involve the disintegration of the self. Listen to Sartre attempting to sum-up the results of the discussion in his famous chapter:

> the first act of self-deception is to flee what it cannot flee, to flee what it is. The very project of flight reveals to self-deception an inner disintegration in the heart of being, and it is this disintegration which it wishes to be.[3]

Much can be made of these two sentences, and I don't wish to suggest that I accept them entirely (insofar as I understand them), but they certainly show the way to connecting integrity-as-rectitude with integrity as the internal coherence and integration of the self.

Concerning whether damage to or violation of the integrity of the body, such as the amputation we have been considering, will amount also to a damaging or destruction of this inner integrity of the person, the issue seems in the first place to depend on how we resolve problems of the mind-body type mentioned earlier. Apart from that, the upshot seems at best a contingent matter. Will the amputation in itself, for example, amount to a disruption or lessening of the harmony and coherence of my impulses, needs, wants, drives, thoughts, etc.? Perhaps not. But it may lead to such a disruption or lessening so clearly and immediately that we would be tempted to count that, along with absence of the leg, as unqualifiedly one of the outcomes of the surgery. This would be especially tempting if the person had or was preparing for a career in which the leg was essential.

The claim that the integrity of something (in this case a person) has been *violated* will, as before, be hinged principally to the outward-looking aspect of the integrity of the thing. And, as before, this aspect will emphasize the importance of the boundaries in the light of which we determine where the thing ends and other things begin. The thing is again seen as a bounded domain having an inertia or principle of operation of its own, and thus as one complete or whole thing in an environment of other things. The thing's integrity is violated when this domain is intruded upon and changes are produced within the domain that interfere with and counter or 'overcome' the effects of the thing's own inertia or principles of operation. The less this happens and the more completely the state of the thing is determined by the operation of its own inertia, etc., the greater will be its integrity.

The integrity of a person is thus, on the outward-looking view, a function

---

3. Sartre, "Self-deception," in Kaufman, ed., *Existentialism from Dostoevsky to Sartre*, p. 270.

of what is commonly called the autonomy of the person. A thing's autonomy, or the extent to which it has autonomy or is autonomous, is in part a function of the extent to which it is in need or want of nothing not already contained in itself. It is also a function of the extent to which what happens to the thing is self-determined. (These two aspects of autonomy are connected in ways that could be explored if one had the time and space.) Not surprisingly, the concept of autonomy is not a very clear one because we are not clear on whether we want to understand it so that it has realistic applications to things of this world, or rather so that it is a limit which the situations of such things might approach but never reach. The difficulty here of course lurks close-by even in the outward-looking view of the integrities of bodies. But its connection with the integrities of persons has always been more prominent and has always most excited philosophers.

The connection of the integrities of persons with their autonomy raises a host of metaphysical, moral, social and psychological issues. Compare the Kantian and post-Kantian discussions up through Sartre of the autonomy and, not incidentally, the freedom of persons. And, to mention matters even more widely associated with social philosophy, consider the way recent social thinkers have been made uncomfortable by the view of men as somewhat autonomous, and thus viable, domains. When they most dislike it, they call it "atomistic individualism," and there have been numerous recent attempts, whether in the name of overcoming loneliness or alienation or whatever, or merely in the name of a more nearly correct account of the metaphysics of the situation of men, to break down these boundaries (or, as they are sometimes called, "barriers") between self and other. In some social movements, this appears in attempts to establish 'gemeinschaft' or tribal styles of communal life. But one also finds hesitation about the rigidity of the boundaries supposed to exist between persons and their non-human environments; the newer views of some speculative biologists (cf. Waddington) on the profound effects on men of their immediate physical and biological environments may suggest to some that far too much importance has been attached to the distinction between what is inside and what is outside these boundaries. In both cases, the internal-external distinction in the light of which we see persons as well-bounded entities is under attack. The attacks will surely have enormous ramifications for our thinking about men and the world if we take them seriously. We should not be surprised to find these issues lying in wait for us when we discuss the possible wrongness of violence.

It is difficult to proceed in the face of them, but perhaps we could push on for the moment with a somewhat modest notion of autonomy. The aspect of autonomy generally most at issue in discussions of the integrity of persons is that concerned with the self-determination of what happens to one. It connects easily with integrity-as-rectitude, as is evidenced in the usefulness of "uprightness" in characterizing rectitude; 'uprightness' suggests a certain strength underwriting independence from external pressures and blandishments in determining what one shall do and what shall become of one. It seems safe to say that we can operate with a fairly crude notion of this side of autonomy in view of the particular and rather special problem with which we are concerned at this stage of the discussion. We are interested in whether the amputation of my leg, to which I by hypothesis gave permission, constitutes a violation of my integrity. We are interested in this because the amputation constitutes a preeminently sudden and radical externally effected change at least in my body and perhaps also in me, and I have argued that such change has occurred whenever violence has been done, that we are in some of our moods inclined to believe such changes wrong because they damage, destroy or violate the integrities of what is so changed, and that this reaction is at least part of what underlies the common opinion that violence is wrong. I am now exploring what supports and what subverts the reasonableness of this substructure of the common view. We have so far seen that the amputation in question—an instance of such change though not *thereby* a case of violence done—did indeed damage and violate the integrity of my body. The question is now whether it damaged or violated my integrity, though we have already seen that there are reasons to worry about the full relevance of this because, since it is not clear just how I am connected to my body, we must be at least slightly unclear about whether the amputation brought about a change in me as well as a change in my body. The effect of all this on the concept of integrity that we may reasonably use here is that the range of changes we are considering (preeminently sudden, radical, and externally effected) consists of such relatively dramatic changes that we may not need a very subtle or far-reaching notion of autonomy-as-self-determination to deal with them.

Turning to the amputation and its connection with my autonomy, if it did indeed produce a change in me as well as in my body (and when confronted with this issue I feel like a person confronted with an optical illusion that looks now concave, now convex), and if the change counted as a radical change in me as well as in my body (and, indeed, this might be dubious though the rest be clear), then the case is worth exploring further. The problem now is whether the radical change in me was simply that I no longer had my leg. If so, then, because I gave permission to the surgeon, the amputation did not violate my integrity as an autonomous decider of what is to happen to me—at least on common understandings of what this means, and on the presumption that I was not coerced, tricked, or beguiled into giving permission. But precisely in this case the status of the amputation as effected by an external force (and thus also its status as a case of violence done to me) may muddy because I seem to have played a bit too much of a role in its occurrence. Compare here the case of the man whose leg was broken in a fall on an icy

path, and the man whose leg was broken when he was struck by a tree uprooted by a tornado.

If the radical change produced in me by the amputation was not, or was not
solely, the loss of my leg, then my permission to amputate my leg may not
have been so clearly permission to produce that further change in me, and the
question of whether the amputation violated my integrity as decider of what
would happen to me would have to be re-raised. (And in either case, if I had
been coerced, tricked, or beguiled into giving permission, we might rightly
be uncomfortable in various ways about whether my integrity-as-decider had
been violated. If pursued further, this uncomfortableness would reveal an underlying network of mixed and controversial views on what men are and what
they ought to be—e.g., views, some of which have already been mentioned,
about the interplay of intellect, will, and environment.) Further, if I had not
given permission at all to the surgeon, then no conclusion would be immediately obvious. For, it would depend on whether the amputation occurred
against my expressed wishes, or took place without my being asked because
I was unconscious or delirious, or took place without my being asked simply
because, though I was in condition to respond, nobody asked me—either
through an oversight or as a part of somebody's scheme. Only in the first case
would it be perfectly clear that my integrity-as-decider had been violated.
(And, again, the other cases would, if we pursued them and tried to rational-
ize our reactions to them, lead us to an underlying network of highly debatable views on the nature and state of men.)

Through all these difficulties, the important thing to notice for our present
purposes is the central role played by the view that persons are well-bounded
entities in the common and still developing sentiment that there is something
wrong with violence to persons. If it is going to be necessary to re-think the
former, then it is going to be necessary to re-think at least part of the latter.
The view of persons as bounded and at least somewhat autonomous entities
contributes to our sense of a *person* (as distinct from merely a person's body)
as something violable, and thus something on which change may be externally imposed. It thus supports our increasing tendency to think that violence
may be done to persons in ways distinct from merely doing violence to the
bodies of persons.

V

Do things other than persons and the bodies of persons have integrities that
could be damaged, destroyed, or violated? We are in some of our moods
inclined to think so, though we are inconstant and unclear about how far the
idea should be extended. Whether everything which has been subjected to
sudden, radical, and externally effected change has an integrity that could be
violated is an issue that could take us far afield. Such questions cannot be

discussed now, though they must eventually be discussed, and we might expect to find when we do so the reappearance of at least some portions of the networks of concepts and problems just exposed.

And of course new concepts and problems will appear. For example, matters are often unclear with the extensions just suggested because (i) we are not accustomed to thinking of what has been changed as a thing and thus do not readily think in terms of 'its' autonomy or integrity (as with an area devastated by a storm cutting across political boundaries and across boundaries between town and country and between tilled and untilled, tended and untended, land), or (ii) we see the thing in question as so clearly noxious or of no account that we find it idle to have an interest in its autonomy or integrity.

Extensions of the notion of integrity to things other than persons and their bodies draw support at many points, as is well known, from analogies with persons and persons' bodies—analogies strongest in the case of higher animals, weaker in the case of lower animals, plants, etc.

But the extension from the human to the non-human is also often guided by consideration of human interests and fundamentally based on connections between the things in question and human autonomy. This is most obvious with things in which we, as Locke would say, 'have a property,' or contemplate having a property, things which we have built, things on which we have lavished or contemplate lavishing attention and labor. The extension can be complex in such cases—sometimes involving a view of the things as having integrities of their own, and sometimes instead or as well a view of them as somehow a part of oneself or as somehow tied in their fate, actually or potentially, to one's own integrity.

We also find extensions underwritten by considerations connected to but more remote from notions of personal property. The non-human contents of the world are sometimes thought of, collectively or individually, as a 'heritage' 'left' to us by preceding generations or by God, or a heritage simply presented to us by 'Nature,' to be husbanded and held in trust for the use and benefit of present and future generations. This view is currently popular in the U.S., which rightly feels itself confronted with critical ecological issues, preeminently including so-called environmental 'pollution.' The view leads us to think of the state in which we 'received' the world as having special importance (as though the world were an estate for whose management we might eventually be praised or reproached or damned, the judgement being based on the condition of the world when we 'turn it over to others' as compared with its condition when we 'received' it). Or cf. de Jouvenal: "While any farmer or industrialist knows that he must provide for the upkeep of his plant, the basic 'plant' we have received, the Earth, seems to us to call for no stewardship."[4] We ourselves are then, at least for purposes of this judgment,

4. Bertrand de Jouvenal, "Utopia for Practical Purposes." In Manuel, *Utopias*, p. 231.

seen as external to this world, and our own behavior toward it counts, at least when we are active toward it, as an impingement of external forces upon it, and thus, if our action is precipitous and dramatic, as violating its integrity vis-a-vis its initial state. (Cf., "When anything becomes extinct, there is an uncanny feeling that somewhere a hole has been made in the fabric of creation."[5])

And one might find extensions underwritten by more abstract considerations such as those brought forward in the following argument: Imagining change is imagining a subject or subjects of change, and is thus to operate with at least some (however indefinite) notion of the boundaries of what has been changed. To imagine further that the change has been effected by a force or forces clearly (by hypothesis in the statement of the issue) external to what has been changed, is to give those boundaries sufficient firmness to support at least the beginnings of thinking in terms of our further requirement. For, in order to imagine the forces clearly external, one must grasp, more or less, the contrasts giving the case its sense. One must have at least a primitive grasp of the difference between forces that are external and forces that are not, and thus must have some notion of what it would have been like if no external forces had operated and, to put the matter crudely, what had been changed had been 'left undisturbed' or 'left alone.' And the latter, which is consistent both with change and with absence of change just so long as neither is effected by external forces, solidifies a notion of the boundaries of what has been changed as enclosing a domain within which events could proceed more or less autonomously and thus a domain the integrity of which could be violated.

These are examples of lines of thought we would have to examine if we were to pursue further the aspects of the common views that extend to non-humans the idea that things have integrities that might be damaged, destroyed, or violated when subject to the sort of change we've had in mind.

VI

If all this discussion is to play a role in a general account of the disvalue of violence done and the at least *prima facie* wrongness of countenancing or bringing about such violence, one must sooner or later carry further the two lines of investigation suggested by this paper—viz., the connection of violence done with injury, damage, and destruction straightforwardly conceived in their more or less 'brute' forms, and its connection with a broader notion of harm to things stemming from consideration of damage to, destruction of, or violations of their integrities. One must push further into claims about the wrongness of these. Whether or not one is inclined to find the matter problematic, one might agree that it would be nice to be able to *show* these things,

5. A quote from *Time* magazine, "Letters Column," European edition, 16 February 1970, p. 2.

and at least that understanding them thoroughly is essential for sound reasoning about when, if ever, violence is excusable or justifiable.

This paper has, of course, been concerned with only some aspects of the possible wrongness of violence. The discussion has been confined to the possible wrongness of violence having been done to something in cases where we can be taken to see the violence done, and to what problems are met in attempts to give perfectly general accounts of this. We did not reach other cases of violence, for example, cases where violence has been done to language or to a man's thought. And since, to take only some obvious examples, violence even of the sort we can be taken to see is often done to things by wind and waves as well as by people, we did not reach, except in a most casual way, matters concerned with the possible wrongness of *engaging-in* or *using* violence. Nothing, for example, was said about the possibly* deleterious effects of engaging-in violence or** made here between whether their engagement was deliberate or inadvertent or even unconscious, and whether if deliberate it was aimless or purposeful. Nor was anything said about the possibly* deleterious effects of such violence on persons or societies or segments of societies which, even though not the perpetrators and perhaps not even the subjects of the violence in question, are affected by their witnessing or hearing of it and are led thereby, according to some hypotheses, either to indulge in their own tendencies toward violence or to engage in 'prudential' or morally righteous counter-violence or abandonment of social techniques abstaining from the use of violence.

Such things are on the minds of many people concerned about the possible wrongness of violence. My justification for not reaching them is that I have been fully occupied elsewhere, and occupied with matters I think more basic to an account of the wrongness of violence.

---

*At both these places "possible" appears in the original. The editors have changed this to "possibly." Eds.

**This "or" was "on" in the original. A line or two may have been omitted in the typescript available to us. Eds.

Notes for "What Is Wrong with Violence?" *

The Problem: Why is countenancing or bringing about violence in need of any special justification or excuse?

Two Preliminary Claims:

1. The notion of violence is complex (and therefore correct accounts of its wrongness may be expected also to be complex). Some views of violence:
   (a) violence as an impulse or force or stock of psychic or physical energy
   (b) violence as a form or kind of action or activity
   (c) violence as a tool or instrument for the achievement of a purpose
   (d) violence as a result of a certain sort (achieved, perhaps, in a certain way)
      (i) sometimes a result that we cannot clearly 'be taken to see' (e.g., violence done to language or to a man's thought)
      (ii) sometimes a result that we can clearly 'be taken to see' (e.g., violence done to a park or to a forest).
2. Though none of these may be inescapably the fundamental notion, choice of the last (dii) as central provides a foundation for the most coherent and least troubling account of why violence is generally considered wrong.

Some Central Claims About (dii):

1. If violence (dii) has occurred, then something has been injured, damaged or destroyed.
   Comment: But is there anything wrong per se with injury or damage to or destruction of things? I touch on this issue, but hardly pursue it.
2. If violence (dii) has occurred, then something has been changed, and the change has been
   (i) effected by external force(s)
   (ii) fairly sudden [and]
   (iii) fairly radical.

---

*These notes were appended to MacCallum's working copy of "What Is Wrong with Violence?" They are included here as providing both an abstract of the paper provided by the author and also an account by the author of some of the defects of the paper. Whether this addendum was provided for some audience, for people to whom MacCallum circulated the paper for comments, or simply for MacCallum's own use—perhaps in some never pursued revision—does not appear from the information available to the editors.

3. If change preeminently satisfying these three conditions has occurred, then we are in some moods inclined to think that the integrity of what has been so changed has thereby been damaged, destroyed, or violated.

Comments: (a) Therefore, if violence (dii) has occurred, then we are in some moods inclined to think that the integrity of something has been damaged, destroyed, or violated.

(b) But are we right when we think this way about the connection between violence and integrity? I try to explore rationales for thinking this way—to find reasons that could be offered for it (focusing on the connection suggested in claim 3, and providing a fairly extensive explication of 'integrity').

(c) But, even if, or insofar as, we are right in thinking this way, would this be enough to show something wrong with violence (dii)? Is there anything wrong per se with damage to or destruction or violation of the integrities of things? I touch on this issue (with special reference to the notions of autonomy and, incidentally, freedom), but hardly pursue it.

Bare-Bones Results: We can show that countenancing or bring[ing] about violence (dii) is in need of special justification or excuse if we can show (a) that there is something wrong per se with injury and damage to and destruction of things, or (b) that there is something wrong per se with damage to and destruction and violation of the integrities of things, *and* that change satisfying the three conditions mentioned above (2i, ii, iii) always damages, destroys, or violates the integrity of what is so changed.

Matters not touched upon in the paper:

1. Is there anything else that might, non-derivatively, be wrong with violence (dii)?
2. Precisely what might, derivatively or not, be wrong with violence of other sorts (e.g., violence to language or to a man's thought) or with violence when differently conceived (e.g., as a form or kind of activity)?

**Bibliography of the
Writings of Gerald C. MacCallum, Jr.**

Index

Bibliography of the Writings of Gerald C. MacCallum, Jr.

1. Review of Richard Wasserstrom, *The Judicial Decision. The Philosophical Review* 72 (April 1963): 253–55.
2. "Dworkin on Judicial Discretion." *The Journal of Philosophy* 60. 21 (1963): 638–41. An Abstract. Unpublished longer version included in this volume as Chapter 10 (cf. item 16 below).
*3. "Censorship in the Arts." *Arts in Society* 2.4 (1964): 3–23.
4. Review of Harold R. Smart, *Philosophy and Its History. The Philosophical Review* 74 (1965): 546–47.
*5. "On Applying Rules." *Theoria* 32.3 (1966): 196–210.
*6. "Legislative Intent." *Yale Law Journal* 75 (1966): 754–87. Reprinted in (1) R. S. Summers, ed., *Essays in Legal Philosophy* (Oxford: Basil Blackwell, 1968), pp. 237–73 (with author's corrections); (2) Philip Shuchman, ed., 2d ed. of Cohen and Cohen's *Readings in Jurisprudence and Legal Philosophy* (Boston: Little, Brown and Company, 1979), pp. 371–96 (somewhat abridged, and without author's corrections). An extract is reprinted in J. P. Evans, *Statutory Interpretation: Problems of Communication* (Oxford: University Press, 1988).
*7. "Berlin on the Compatibility of Values, Ideals, and 'Ends'." *Ethics* 77.2 (1967): 139–45.
*8. "Negative and Positive Freedom." *The Philosophical Review* 76.3 (1967): 312–34. Reprinted in (1) Bobbs-Merrill Reprint Series, 1968–69; (2) *Contemporary Political Philosophy,* ed. by Anthony de Crespigny and Alan Wertheimer (Chicago/New York: Aldine-Atherton, 1970), pp. 107–26; (3) *Philosophy, Politics and Society* (4th Series), ed. by Peter Laslett, W. G. Runciman, and Quentin Skinner (Oxford: Basil Blackwell, 1972), pp. 174–93; (4) *Concepts in Social and Political Philosophy,* ed. by Richard Flathman (New York: Macmillan, 1973), pp. 294–308.
9. "On Feeling Obligated to Do What a Constitution Requires." In *Political and Legal Obligation: NOMOS XII,* ed. by J. Roland Pennock and John W. Chapman (New York: Atherton Press, 1970), pp. 214–18. This essay comments on Gray L. Dorsey, "Constitutional Obligation," *ibid.,* pp. 179–213.
*10. "Some Truths and Untruths About Civil Disobedience." In *Political and Legal Obligation: NOMOS XII,* ed. by J. Roland Pennock and John W. Chapman (New York: Atherton Press, 1970), pp. 370–400.

*Signifies published in this volume. Notes to Bibliography come at the end, pp. 261–62.

*11. "Reform, Violence, and Personal Integrity: A Commentary on the Saying that You Ought to Fight for What You Believe Right." *Inquiry* 14 (1971): 301–12. This is followed by "Comment on MacCallum," by Richard B. Brandt, pp. 314–17.

12. "Comments" on Ronald W. Dworkin, "Philosophy and the Critique of Law." *Society: Revolution and Reform,* Proceedings of the 1969 Oberlin Colloquium in Philosophy, ed. by Robert H. Grimm and Alfred F. MacKay (Cleveland: Case-Western Reserve Press, 1971), pp. 82–91. Dworkin's paper is on pp. 59–81.[1]

*13. "Law, Conscience, and Integrity." In *Issues in Law and Morality,* Proceedings of the 1971 Oberlin Colloquium in Philosophy, ed. by Norman S. Care and Thomas K. Trelogan (Cleveland/London: The Press of Case Western Reserve University, 1973), pp. 141–59. This is followed by "Comments: My Conscience and Your Conduct," by Hugo Adam Bedau, ibid., pp. 161–66.

14. "Reply" [to Bedau], in *Issues in Law and Morality,* pp. 167–68.

*15. "The Extent to Which Legislators Should Serve Their Consciences or Their Constituents." In *Ethical Issues in Government,* ed. by Norman E. Bowie (Philadelphia: Temple University Press, 1981), pp. 23–40.

*16. "Dworkin on Judicial Discretion" (1963). Published for first time in this volume. Expanded version of paper commenting on Ronald Dworkin's "Judicial Discretion" and presented along with Dworkin's at the American Philosophical Association Eastern Division meeting in New York, December 1963. (See item 2, above.)

*17. "What is Wrong with Violence?" (1970). Not previously published. Presented, in varying versions, at Aarhus University (Denmark), University of Bergen (Norway), and perhaps elsewhere, in Spring 1970.

*18. "Violence and Appeals to Conscience" (1974). Not previously published. Prepared for and presented at the Conference on the Justification of Violence at SUNY Buffalo, April 11–13, 1974.

*19. "Competition and Moral Philosophy" (1975). Not previously published. Presented as lead symposium paper at the meeting of the American Philosophical Association, Western (now Central) Division in Chicago, April 1975, and in varying versions at other places since. The commentators at the Chicago meeting were Bernard Gendron and Robert Binkley. There is an audio tape in the MacCallum files on which MacCallum recorded his responses to questions and objections raised and improvements suggested a number of years later (at some time in the period 1979–81, after MacCallum's first stroke) by one of the editors (RM), which warrants our confidence that the version published here is definitive of MacCallum's final intentions with regard to this paper.

20. "Democratization and the Military." In *Democracy and the Military: A Public Assessment,* subtitled "'A Series of Discussions' Sept. 14, 16, 21, 24, 28, 30" (Madison, WI: Center for Conflict Resolution, September 1976, 42 unnumbered pages), 6 single-spaced mimeographed typed pages. It is doubtful that this can count as previously published; on the other hand, it is not clearly "unpublished." The appropriate term may be "quasi-published." The booklet in question was a collection of working papers for a conference held in September 1976 and contains nine contributions by eight contributors from different occupations and different parts of the world. (The address of the Center for Conflict Resolution is 731 State Street, Madison, Wisconsin 53715.)

*21. "Justice and Adversary Proceedings" (1977). Not previously published. A later version (1977) of a paper originally presented at a University of Western Ontario Colloquium on Philosophy of Law, November 1974, and presented in a number of places in varying versions afterward.

22. *Political Philosophy* (Englewood Cliffs: Prentice-Hall, 1987). A volume in the Prentice-Hall Foundations of Philosophy Series. Part One: Political Community—One: The Idea of Political Community; Two: Human Nature, Mutual Reliance, and Ideals; Three: The State; Four: Nations and Nationalism: Ideological Foundations. Part Two: Government—Five: Government in Political Philosophy; Six: Authority; Seven: Legitimacy and Consent; Eight: Constitutionalism, the Rule of Law, and Limited Government; Nine: Sovereignty; Ten: Representation. Part Three: People—Eleven: Subjects, Citizens, and Aliens; Twelve: Obedience to Law and Political Obligations; Thirteen: Civil Disobedience and Revolution; Fourteen: Political Life and Human Life.

23. [One other item worth listing, though it is not strictly speaking "published," is a 20-minute talk MacCallum gave on WIBA Radio, Madison, June 1967, on "The Morality of the War in Vietnam." No doubt tapes exist of this broadcast, though none is in our possession.[2] "Patriotism" was the title of a "discussion on WIBA Radio," 1 February 1968, but it is not apparent from our records whether this was an address MacCallum gave or a discussion in which he participated.]

Notes to Bibliography

1. "These comments . . . were made on a penultimate version of Professor Dworkin's paper," according to a note appended to the foot of the first page by the editors of the volume, who were, apparently, beset by more than the usual number of problems that beset editors of conference volumes. In a letter to the editors of 23 April 1969, MacCallum said:

> I am not certain where my responsibility is respecting my contribution to the volume. My remarks at the meeting addressed themselves to the version of Dworkin's paper that he had sent me earlier. I tacked a bit to take account of differences between the paper and his oral presentation. . . . As he stepped to the podium, he handed me another written version that I have now had time to read. . . . It is different in matters of substance from both his earlier written version and his oral presentation. It is also, in my opinion, better than either. Is this the version, so far as you know, that will be printed in the volume? If so, then my remarks will have to be revised, and I am not sure how soon I will find time to do this. . . . (These difficulties were rather surprising to me as Dworkin had predicted that alterations of his first version would be stylistic only.)

In a letter of 30 November 1969 written from Hotel Limonar, Malaga, Spain (MacCallum was then on the first leg of his ACLS fellowship travels, when his main subject of attention was to be "Conscience and Violence"), MacCallum said:

> Have at last received Dworkin's paper, and . . . I now must tell you that . . . the paper is so radically and astonishingly different from what he delivered at the Conference that virtually none of my initial commentary can survive.

> Counting his oral delivery at the Conference, I have now been subject to four versions of this paper, each significantly different from the others. . . . my initial commentary fits the first version, but is utterly inadequate for the second and third. . . . I should now emphasize that even the second version as it stands would require very nearly a totally new commentary from me.

> I don't believe that our initial agreement required me to write commentaries on each of two quite different papers. I should like to be as cooperative as possible, but I simply cannot afford at present to throw away my initial commentary and . . . work out something quite new to fit one of these last two versions of his paper. I am too pressed for time on other projects.

> I trust you to find a resolution that will be fair to all concerned and that will wind up the affair before too much longer.

This is about as testy as MacCallum ever allowed himself to become, and at this distance, over twenty years later, it has its amusing aspects, though at the time it is not likely to have been found amusing by any of the principals. The editors responded that having read MacCallum's commentary in conjunction with Dworkin's last written version, it appeared to them that MacCallum had made a sufficient number of substantial points to justify its inclusion in the volume, and that they would publish the paper along with a note of explanation.

MacCallum's final letter on this matter, sent from Madison on 7 December 1970, requested that the explanatory "footnote be put at the beginning of the article rather than at the end—simply because my comment's relationship to Dworkin's present paper is sufficiently tenuous to make the footnote unusually important to read *before* my comment is read." This is what was done, though its effect on the typical reader of the volume is not readily ascertained.

2. What we do have is an outline so clear and fully worked out that it is easy to construct from it what MacCallum said on the matter. MacCallum's thesis was that "The war is immoral." The argument—and MacCallum, as was typical of him, presented *arguments*—is presented dialectically, with thesis, "administration" replies, and counter-replies, in a way reminiscent of Acquinas. It should be added, however, that one of the editors (MGS), in further discussion with MacCallum, learned that he had other arguments that told the other way, which there was no time to present within the limits of a twenty-minute broadcast and which made for a more complicated story than that provided by the broadcast alone. Nonetheless, the nature of his commitment was clear.

Supplement to the Bibliography

There are a few but only a few other items that seem worth mentioning, not because they have been published, since they have not—and it seems clear that MacCallum would not have wanted them to be published—but because they are relatively finished, and this notice will serve to inform interested scholars that they can be consulted in the MacCallum Archives in the Weinberg Memorial Library of the Department of Philosophy of the University of Wisconsin–Madison.

1. "Why Should Anyone *Want* a Voice in Decisions Affecting His Life?" This was presented as a symposium paper at a meeting of the Western Division of the American Philosophical Association in April 1971; the lead speaker was Carl Cohen.

2. "Comments on Benjamin's Paper." This was presented at a conference held in Kalamazoo, Michigan, in October 1976, as comments on a paper read by Martin Benjamin.

3. "Constitutional Sources of Roosevelt's Three 'Rights.'" This is the most puzzling of the apparently finished but unpublished papers, both because it does not have the author's name on it and because the one extant copy is a carbon copy on onionskin paper. We are not even convinced that the piece is by MacCallum. However, internal evidence—such as an interpolation in MacCallum's handwriting—indicates that it may be, and that it is most likely, if it is by MacCallum, an early paper, written some time though not long after 1950, prepared for some unspecified occasion, and then not used or referred to again. Nonetheless, MacCallum did keep this particular paper in his files and there is evidence that he disposed of a number of others. The "three 'rights'" referred to are (1) "the right to security of the home—a decent home to live in, including: (a) adequate recreation, (b) better housing, (c) sounder health"; (2) "the right to a livelihood—to make a comfortable living out of life, including: (a) homes located where the residents can engage in productive work, (b) decent wages, (c) reasonable hours, (d) reasonable profit, (e) fair price protection against monopoly and unfair competition"; and (3) "the right to social insurance: including: (a) old age pensions, (b) security of savings and honest[y] of investments, (c) security against unexpected or seasonal unemployment." The paper begins:

> From 1929 through 1935, FDR occasionally mentioned and sometimes discussed three asserted rights of American citizens.

And the problem is generated because:

> These purported "rights of each individual" are not mentioned in our constitutional text, nor has the Supreme Court asserted that we have them. . . .

We represent it here with this bare mention because it may provide some indication of the way MacCallum's thinking developed on matters of legal and constitutional interpretation, on the relations between rights and duties, on the development of rights and liberties, and on the matter of legislative intent.

Is the paper by MacCallum? MacCallum's Curriculum Vitae and Scholarly Activities Report dated 27 September 1972 lists a number of lectures and papers that do not obviously correspond to anything published or said to be in progress. Thus: "Federalism and Judicial Review," Oxford 1958; "Rules and Judges," Cornell 1959; "Tenure, Legitimacy, and the Problem of Political Obligation," Cornell 1960; "On the Language of Justice," comments at a Western Division meeting of the APA in 1965; "Political Philosophy and Changing Democratic Ideals," University of Washington 1965; "On Deference to Experts," Green Bay 1967; "Loyalty and Dissent in a Democratic Society," Green Bay 1967 and elsewhere in 1968; "On Constitutional Interpretation, Philosophy, and Social Reform," Oberlin Colloquium 1969; and "The Study of Philosophy and the Study of Law," Aarhüs 1970. Most of these are referred to as papers, and MacCallum tended to talk from prepared texts. Yet no vestige of any of these remain. The paper on "Roosevelt's Three 'Rights'" was not listed, yet it does remain. Furthermore, it contains some pre-echoes of MacCallum's reliance on Hohfeld's analysis of rights and duties and the concomitant denial of the correlativity of rights and duties, which MacCallum made much use of later. Some other themes that play a role in the later papers can also be found in this paper. Let the interested reader decide.

Index

Abramson, Victor, cited 212*n*

"Absent the law": things to notice about the expression, 141–42

Abundance: ethics of, 209–10. *See also* Scarcity

Accumulation of policies, principles, rules: judges' relation to, 172; constitutes our legal system, 174

Adams, James Luther, cited, 104*n*, 113*n*

Adams, Walter, cited, 213*n*

Administration of justice. *See* Justice

Administrators: relation to legislation, 163–64. *See also* Legislation

Adults and children: differences in status, 49

Adversary proceedings: normally zero-sum situations, 225; not all are judicial proceedings, 225; use of has waxed and waned, 225; characterized, 225–26; model of, 226; considered as method of truth discovery, 226–27, 231–33; alternative models of, discounted by legal theorists, 228–31; alternative understandings of, 228 and *n;* defects of truth-discovery model of, 228; modelling understandings of, 228 and *n*, 232–33; fight model of, 229–30, 232; subordination thesis with respect to, 229–30; economics of trial practice supports fight model of, 231; key question re, 232. *See also* Damaging supposition; Inquisitorial trials; Truth

Adversary system: tradition of self-help at heart of, 234

Aesthetic creativity: conditions of, 57

Agency: problems concerning, 31–32

Agency model: of legislative intent, 29–33

Agents: freedom of, 87–88

Amputation example: in relation to violence, 245–46

Anglo-American: legal systems and experience, 225, 226; judicial trials perhaps

should be governed by truth-discovery model, 232–33

Anthropologists: on competition, 211

Anti-social behavior: relevance of, to censorship issues, 43–46; ways in which certain materials can lead to, 52–53; censorship not only way of reducing, 55

Appeals to conscience: often shelters for conscience, 157; sorting out genuineness of, 157; a mistake to allow as argument-stoppers, 157–60; how can be seen, 178; offered in defense of violence, 178; apparent rareness of, in defense of violence, 179–80; common idea of primary site of, 180, 186; difference between, and citations of its causal role, 180–85; in defense of violence, limits on, 185–90; contexts in which made, 187; setting of, in defense of violence, 188–89; taxonomy of cases in relation to violence, 190–92; pragmatics of, 196–202; interaction between doctrines of moral significance of, and pragmatics of such appeals, 196; not to be confused with claims of, 199; apogee of personal thrust of in defense of violence, 201

Appeals to violence: how can be seen, 178

Applying a rule: sufficient condition for, 72–73

Applying rules: different claims about distinguished, 66; distinct from appealing to rules, 66; reflecting on rules not necessary for, 67; unlike applying yardstick to wall, 71; in legal contexts, very like applying coercion, 71–72; practice of, 72. *See also* Cases; Deciding cases; Judges; Litigation on appeal; Rules

Aquinas, Thomas, 157

Aristotle: important distinction suggested by, 46*n;* mentioned, 209

Aschenbrenner, Karl, cited, 80*n*